ADVENTURES
IN WONDERLAND

ADVENTURES IN WONDERLAND

A Decade of Club Culture

Sheryl Garratt

HEADLINE

First published in 1998
by HEADLINE BOOK PUBLISHING

First published in paperback in 1999
by HEADLINE BOOK PUBLISHING

10 9 8 7 6 5 4 3 2

ISBN 0 7472 5846 5

Typeset by
Letterpart Limited, Reigate, Surrey

Printed and bound in Great Britain by
Mackays of Chatham PLC, Chatham, Kent

HEADLINE BOOK PUBLISHING
A division of Hodder Headline PLC
338 Euston Road
London NW1 3BH

For Mark, Liam and everyone who lived through this.
And for Gavin – who didn't live long enough

CONTENTS

ACKNOWLEDGEMENTS

What makes clubbing fun in the end is not the music, the clothes, the decor, the drugs or anything else – it's the people you do it with. So big shout to all those who have driven me round the country, blagged me in at the door, queued for the loo with me, talked crap in the corner with me, had me back to their place, or piled back to mine. All those who have bought drinks and plane tickets, shared cubicles and hotel rooms, and offered lifts of all kinds.

Mark McGuire has helped me research this book on dancefloors around the world for over fifteen years, but there were other partners in crime along the way: David Corio, John Godfrey, David Swindells, Nicky Holloway, Camilla Deakin, Lee Harpin, Portia Bishop, the Tower Bridge Necking Crew, the FPK Posse, Charlie Chester, Youth and Weasel, Gavin Hills, Frasier Hills and Lewis Pennington have all driven me around, out, or over the top at various times. Thanks also to Dave, Jimmy, James, Steve, Paul, Robert and all the rest for taking me higher, to Charles Gant at *The Face* for covering whenever I got kidnapped, and to all those who have proved more than just good hosts, but especially Lincoln Cheng in Singapore and Ibiza, Toni Palmer in Majorca, Andrew Bull in Hong Kong, Joe Coneely in Sydney and Bill Coleman in New York.

Many people gave up their time to talk to me for this book, and although not quoted directly, their comments informed it. Some were clubbers sharing memories, some were police officers talking off the record, some were dodgy geezers with records. My thanks to them, and also to everyone who helped with information, cuttings, contacts and setting up interviews: Damian Mould and all at Slice PR, Laurence Verfaille and all at Electric PR, Katherine McKenzie, Merchandising Matters, Richard Benson, Jeremy Langmead and his team at the *Sunday Times*, Dom Phillips and his team at *Mixmag*, Ben Turner at *Muzik*, Q magazine, Sam Wollaston at the *Guardian*, Jane Taylor at the *New Statesman*, Alan Haughton and Mark Gilman at Lifeline, John Freeman, Jayne Casey, Lee Ellen Newman, Eugene Manzi, Zzonked, Groove Connection, Andy Spinoza, Judy at Network, Dr Katie Milestone, Eddie Deighton, Bill Brewster.

My parents June and Frank, Jessica Leix and Lia Taylor offered support at home during the writing of this, especially by helping look after my son. Dave Little, who helped brand acid house with his logos for Boy's Own and Spectrum, designed the cover with Juan Cortés. All of the photographers who allowed their pictures to be used here did so for little financial reward. In books it's also customary to thank your editor for their patience, and Lindsay Symons has shown me why.

There are a few books which have been invaluable to me. *Altered State* by Matthew Collin with contributions from John Godfrey is the definitive history of Ecstasy culture, and is well worth seeking out. *State of Bass* by Martin James is the best book so far on the evolution of drum'n'bass, and Jonathan Fleming's *What Kind Of House Party Is This?* was the first to collect interviews from all of the scene's founders. On the subject of dance music, any work by Andrew Smith, Simon Reynolds or Jon Savage is also always worth checking.

Finally, extra special thanks to Pete Tong for suggesting I write this book in the first place, to all the DJs and promoters who read the manuscript and offered comments/corrections, but most of all to my friends John McCready and Chris Heath for their support throughout, whether it be cuttings, books, tapes and helpful comments on sections of the manuscript, or long phone chats and late-night drinking sessions when needed.

All interviews by Sheryl Garratt, unless credited. Some parts of this book are based on features originally published in *The Face* and the *Sunday Times*.

1997 FOUR SCENES FROM THE GLOBAL DANCE

I – Paris, mid-March

It's past midnight in Dior's awesome atelier, the night before John Galliano's first ready-to-wear show for the French fashion house. The designer has fallen on the floor by the tape machine in a melodramatic fake swoon. 'I'm having a moment!' he screams, as he listens to the tape his friend Jeremy Healy has made for tomorrow's show. 'It's a fashion moment!' The collection is inspired by Chinese paintings and glamour pin-ups from the forties and fifties, and just as he does for every Galliano show, Healy has created a soundtrack to match: banging techno mixed with sampled snatches of interviews with Hollywood glamour girl Jayne Mansfield ('I have very expensive tastes,' she purrs) and a cut-up from the soundtrack to *The Last Emperor*. 'Oh, the girls will love it!' Galliano exclaims.

The two met when Healy's girlfriend modelled in Galliano's graduate show from St Martin's College in London. Healy was already working as a DJ at a nomadic London club called the Circus, and had also enjoyed fifteen minutes of fame in 1982 with a group called Haysi Fantayzee. (They had one big hit, a song called 'John Wayne Is Big Leggy'. 'It was a brief thing,' he explains. 'More of a hairstyle than a musical act.') Galliano asked if they could work together, and the DJ has created music for every one of his catwalk shows since. His friends thought he was wasting his time: 'There was no money then, no glamour, no supermodels.'

Now, this twenty-minute Dior show will cost around £2 million. The venue – an abandoned museum – has been completely transformed for the occasion, crowds outside clamour to get in or just get a glimpse of those with invitations, the world's top models will sway their hips to Healy's mix, and the DJ presides over it all from a booth by the catwalk, whiling away the time before the show by shouting out veiled insults to the élite fashion crowd through a megaphone.

Ten years ago, all of this would have been unimaginable. A young Londoner in charge of a French couture house. Supermodels strutting down the catwalk to the sound of banging club tunes. But things have changed. Two years previously, when John Galliano was appointed to the house of Givenchy prior to moving to Dior, Healy recalls standing with his friend in the bay windows of the spectacular atelier, looking out over Paris and marvelling at how things had turned out. 'I can't believe this is us,' they said. 'Two little boys from Peckham.'

The DJ laughs. 'It's a trip.'

II – Hong Kong, late June

Britain is about to leave a small island seized during the nineteenth-century opium wars, when our nation fought for the right to peddle drugs to the Chinese. The Royal Yacht *Britannia* is moored in the harbour, ready to sail away. The Red Army is massed on the border, ready to march in. And in Kowloon Bay, the youth of Hong Kong are doing what the young all over the globe now do if there's an occasion to be marked: they are dancing all night at a rave. Ten thousand people – far more than the organisers of the twelve-hour Unity event initially anticipated – have paid HK$850 (£50) each to crowd into the vast exhibition centre and dance to PAs by Grace Jones and local bands, plus DJs including Britain's electro-dub master Adrian Sherwood, Paul Oakenfold, Pete Tong and Boy George.

They are not the only British DJs to be flown in for the festivities. Brandon Block, Lawrence Nelson, Graeme Park, Allister Whitehead and Seb Fontaine are all playing at smaller parties during the changeover week. Peter Upton, the ambitious expat Brit behind an event called One Nation, says that club culture has helped ease tensions in the run-up to reunification: 'It's nothing new, just a repeat of what happened in Britain ten years ago. But although it sounds corny, it *has* helped bring people together.'

The euphoric scenes at Unity seem to confirm this view. Western girls in Union Jack mini-dresses dance alongside Asians in rubber fetish outfits, and there's a sense that Hong Kong's growing club culture is moving up a level. 'They've got a taste for it now,' one of the Unity team says backstage. 'There'll be no turning back.' Pete Tong, who is recording the highlights for transmission on Radio One the following week, agrees. 'It's nice to think that we might have left a time-bomb ticking on the edge of Communist China.'

Tong has been here before, a decade ago, making a stop-off *en route* to Australia where he and Nicky Holloway, another DJ from the suburban soul scene in the south of England, were to play a few club dates. Then, it seemed impossibly glamorous to fly all that way to play records. Now it is commonplace, and as we enjoy a drunken tour of the local clubs and bars the night after the rave, the DJs discuss recent gigs everywhere from Australia to Uruguay, Japan to South Africa. Oakenfold has just played in Thailand, and next week he'll be jetting off to play a private party for the daughter of an oil millionaire in Texas before settling down in Ibiza for the summer. Boy George talks of a similar offer he's just had to perform at a private party in the Middle East. Years after his band Culture Club hit their peak, he's still selling records: the mix CDs he makes with Pete Tong for release by the Ministry of Sound's label take only a few days to record, and sell over half a million copies each.

Unity promoter Andrew Bull, meanwhile, doesn't expect Hong Kong's new masters to object to further parties. He has just organised a second club tour of China with London's Ministry of Sound, and says that discos are a part of urban life there. There are more than fifty in Beijing alone, and most towns have a few big, chrome-plated, seventies-style clubs. So far, they've seemed quite receptive to the Ministry's more modern dance package. The prominent displays of British mix CDs in the Hong Kong branch of HMV Records show what is at stake here. Like Russia, which is also showing a keen interest in events organised by British promoters, China could soon be a massive new market for such music and merchandise.

III – Ibiza, August

Mike McKay and his girlfriend Claire Davies have just finished having sex, or at least simulating it, with help from a couple of female strippers. They do this at dawn every Tuesday morning during the summer season, on a stage suspended over a swimming pool in the Ku club, where Mike and his brother Andy attract a crowd of about 8,000 to their weekly Manumission night. Hardly the shy, retiring types, they've even allowed it to be filmed for *Ibiza Uncovered*, a documentary series on the island's excesses that is running on Sky TV and making stars of some of the young Brits who came here looking for seasonal work and fun.

Manumission are the biggest but by no means the only British promoters invading the Balearic clubs this season. Cream, Ministry of Sound, Clockwork Orange and Renaissance are all running successful nights on the island, unfurling their banners in clubs like Pacha, Amnesia and Es Paradis, the logos of their corporate sponsors prominently displayed. Companies that would once have gazed with horror and incomprehension at the transvestites, freaks and bald, topless girls covered in silver body paint dancing on the podiums now pay handsomely to be associated with it all.

In Ibiza Town after midnight, a more effective kind of advertising takes place. Strange parades wind through the narrow streets of the lively Sa Penya barrio, walking past the crowded restaurants and pre-club bars in outlandish costumes to draw attention to that night's club events. A procession of Roman centurions, Egyptians in gold loincloths and a near-naked Cleopatra hand out flyers for Ku. Beautiful girls in leopardskin outfits are advertising a jungle-themed party at Pacha. But tonight's clear winner goes to the PVC-clad man walking along on stilts, driving a team of topless female 'ponies' in leather harnesses to promote the weekly parties organised by British club Miss Moneypenny's in the millionaires' yacht club El Divino. The stilt-walker is Sebastian Blockley, a Londoner who has been a regular visitor to Ibiza since discovering it on the hippie trail in 1967. His wife Caroline is one of the ponies, and at Moneypenny's later she strips off to dangle a crystal pendant from her genital piercings and performs little pieces of S&M theatre for the dancefloor. 'It's great fun,' she tells me. 'Half work, half holiday.'

On El Divino's opulent balcony overlooking the marina, I sit and watch dawn break with Jim Ryan and Lee Garrick, old friends from my home city of Birmingham and half of the team behind Miss Moneypenny's. In the late eighties, Ryan set up a small clothes stall with help from the Enterprise Allowance Scheme, and Garrick came to work there on another government-sponsored work scheme. Prime Minister Thatcher wanted a nation of entrepreneurs, and now here we all are: DJing, writing, clubbing, dancing, stripping, dealing, blagging, all of us exporting a culture her government unwittingly helped us create.

IV – New York, late September

John Digweed is nervous. The first few times, he admits, he came close to throwing up before going on. A DJ with more than ten years of experience, he has played to huge crowds across Britain since making his name at Renaissance in Mansfield, and even bigger crowds around the world. But this is different. This is New York, the cradle of club culture. When it was first suggested that he and his regular DJ partner Sasha play at Manhattan's Twilo club in August 1996, Digweed wasn't sure: 'I was worried it was going to be demoralising.'

His fears proved unfounded. In fact, the date went down so well that they started a monthly residency there after touring commitments in Australia and South Africa were out of the way. But still he gets nervous. This is Twilo, after all. The venue once known as the Sound Factory. The most revered club in New York's underground since the closing of the Paradise Garage, with one of the finest sound systems in the world. The club where Junior Vasquez plays every Saturday to an adoring crowd. The club where the early British house promoters and DJs all came to pay homage, to listen, lose it and learn. The club where Mike Pickering and Paul Oakenfold once played at the peak of the acid house boom, only to find the atmosphere distinctly unwelcoming. The third turntable was bolted shut. Signs in the DJ booth announced, 'This is Junior's house'. It's the kind of reception British DJs learned to expect in Manhattan, a city where outsiders rarely make an impact unless they choose to move there.

But Sasha and Digweed's monthly residency at Twilo is yet another sign that times have changed. Some of the old Sound Factory crowd are still in evidence – like the glamour queen dancing topless on the speaker to show off expensively sculpted breasts, only those outsized high-heeled shoes betraying the fact that she is a he. But mainly this is a new generation, more interested in the club culture they've read about in imported British magazines. While British dance acts like the Prodigy, the Chemical Brothers and Orbital are making an impact in the charts, British DJs like Sasha and Digweed are pulling a new crowd into the clubs.

'New York is dead,' one of the city's big-name DJs tells me glumly the next day. Juice bars are being turned into licensed premises, venues are being renamed and refurbished, mixed crowds are being replaced with white, straight clubbers with more money to spend. Meanwhile, many of the old stars are squabbling amongst themselves, or trying too hard to relive past glories. There are still clubs that are kicking it, but few that look likely to spawn new musical forms, create new movements as they did all the time in the eighties. An icon still revered for his contributions to dance culture, he says he's using the time to travel, to DJ around the world, to earn some money from remixes and productions and wait for things to settle before playing a regular night in New York again.

The torch has been passed on, he says. For now.

PART I
BEFORE

PUT THE NEEDLE
ON THE RECORD

Let's start with a dirty word: disco. The music John Travolta danced to in *Saturday Night Fever*. The music described in the 1989 edition of the *Penguin Encyclopaedia of Popular Music* as a 'dance fad of the Seventies with a profound and unfortunate influence on popular music'. Disco sucked. Disco was punk's greatest enemy. Disco was about naff chrome and mirrorball clubs with girls dancing round their handbags and lads watching at the bar, gulping down the courage to ask one of them to dance when the music slowed for the nightly erection section.

But disco was originally something far more subversive. And buried in its history is the roots of house music, of much of the music we dance to now. The club culture we enjoy today was conceived under a mirrorball, born to the sound of Donna Summer, and grew up in the confusion that came about when the music went mainstream, stagnated and died. So if we are to understand the great acid house explosion of 1988, the raves of 1989, and the superclubs that came after; if we are to understand where garage, house and techno actually come from, we have to go back way before Travolta ever donned that white suit and danced to the Bee Gees.

We have to understand that this is a music that came into existence because it *could*, a way of life that has always stood at the very forefront of change. Designer drugs, drum machines, synthesisers, samplers, speakers, lights, lasers, motorways, mobile phones – dance culture has always taken the very latest technology has to offer and twisted it to its own hedonistic ends. But it has also been at the forefront of *social* change. Clubs have always been places hidden from the everyday world, where we can experiment with new identities and lifestyles, where people forced out on to the margins could find space to escape, dance and feel free. Where they could *transcend*.

Because of this, club culture has always been distrusted by the authorities. It has often been illegal, underground, subversive. The fight for the right to party has often been part of a greater fight: in fact, some of the first people to dance in discothèques did so because they refused to have their fun spoiled by the racism of the Nazis.

The word *discothèque* is derived from the French word for library, *bibliothèque,* and it originally meant a collection of recordings – usually classical. According to Albert Goldman's 1978 book *Disco*[1], the first place of public entertainment to use the word was a bar in the rue Huchette in Paris before the Second World War. At La Discothèque, you could request a spin of your favourite jazz record as you ordered your drink. But dancing in Paris was generally to live jazz and American-style swing bands until the Germans marched in to occupy the city and banned the music, literally driving it underground. Crude PA systems were rigged up in the cellars of the Left Bank, and those who wished to defy their new rulers could dance to the jazz they loved on vinyl instead, the labels often covered over with those of less risky records in case of a raid. Illicit and probably quite thrilling as a result, the first discothèques were created by Europe's enduring passion for the music of black America, and a spirit of defiance.

After the war, Paul Pacine continued the trend of dancing to records rather than live music with his Whiskey à Go-Go clubs, the first of which opened in Paris in 1947. Jazz records formed the soundtrack, and the drink of choice was the newly fashionable Scotch whisky, which also inspired the themed décor: endless tartan and at least one wall covered with the lids of whisky cases. Johnny Walker, Ballantine's, Dewar's, Cutty Sark, Haig & Haig: in the post-War years, these brand names had a heady glamour in mainland Europe. The formula worked. Soon Pacine had a chain of discothèques across the continent, and the idea of creating clubs specifically for the playing of records caught on.

Pacine's response to the increasing competition was Chez Régine, opened in 1960 and managed by the vivacious Régine Zylberberg, who started out as the toilet attendant at the first Whiskey à Go-Go and became one of the club's biggest attractions. She launched her club on the idea of élitism, making it seem like the place to be. For the first few weeks, Régine kept her new club empty. She put a sign out in the street straight after opening time saying the disco was full, letting the word get around until she had people clamouring to get in. When she finally did open up, the place was instantly packed. Hype didn't start with the superclubs.

She also got a lucky break. Soon after, the American cast of the musical *West Side Story* came in and showed her a new dance that didn't need a partner and that was easy for even the rhythmically challenged: the twist. Régine's quickly became *the* place to twist the night away, and society folk who once danced in couples to bands in ballrooms were now twisting alone to records, in discotheques.

Discothèques came to Britain at the start of the sixties as French imports, appealing to the young and fashionable. Unlike the church hall dances and rock'n'roll record hops that had preceded them in Britain, they weren't just about playing records. They were a complete custom-made environment, where the décor and the ambience were as important as the music. La Discothèque in Wardour Street tuned into the new sexual freedoms with double beds on and around the dancefloor. In 1962, the Place opened up in Hanley near Stoke-on-Trent with red lighting and all-black décor except for a gold-painted entrance hall, mock leopardskin wallpaper in the toilets, and a small sitting room called the Fridge that was all-white with blue lighting – the first chill-out room, perhaps.

Improvements in sound systems made it possible for the first time for records to be as loud as live bands, and the Musicians' Union in Britain fought the spread of this new fad fiercely.[2] But dancing to records was still considered inferior to live music, and most clubs kept DJs for the early part of the week, reverting to bands at weekends. At first clubbers were unwilling to pay to get into a club to hear records – after all, they could hear them on radio for free. But as discothèques developed, the *atmosphere*, the feeling the crowd generated in a place, was what made the admission price seem worthwhile. The artists making the music were no longer the focus in such clubs: the people on the dancefloor were the stars.

A break from the dance palaces of the past, these clubs were seen as fashionably classless, a symbol of the new values of swinging London where status was not dependent on your title or your wealth. 'Success in a given field is the criterion and, in the case of girls, physical beauty,' wrote George Melly, describing the new door policies in *Revolt Into Style*.

It was New York which turned the discothèque into the disco, but the first establishment to open in New York was modelled on the French clubs and intended exclusively for the rich and the famous, the jet set. Opened by Olivier Coquelin in 1960, Le Club had wooden panelling, vast tapestries, open fires, a swish dining room, a board of governors and annual membership fees. Henry Ford and the Duke of Bedford were amongst the initial backers. Asked to find a DJ for the club, society bandleader Peter Duchin recommended Slim Hyatt, a polite, well-dressed African-American with no experience whatsoever. Until Duchin had been unable to afford to pay his wages, America's first disco DJ had been working as his butler.

The next big discothèque came five years later, after actor Richard Burton left his wife Sybil for Elizabeth Taylor. Rebuilding her life, Sybil decided to bring the more democratic club culture of Swinging London to Manhattan in the shape of Arthur's. Modelled on the Ad Lib, a Soho club where the Beatles and the new aristocracy of Swinging London held court but where admission was open to anyone who looked cool enough, the club was an instant hit in New York.

The DJ at Arthur's was an accomplished twist dancer called Terry Noel. He kept a picture of Elvis in his booth but played an eclectic mixture of Motown and rock, anything from Frank Sinatra to Bob Dylan. He experimented with lights and mirrors in the club, and saw himself as doing more than just playing records: his selections were *responding* to the crowd, controlling the atmosphere on the floor. 'There's a feeling the crowd emanates,' he told Albert Goldman. 'It's like an unconscious grapevine. They send you a signal and then you talk back to them through the records.'

The original moody DJ, he refused requests because of this. When

Hollywood tough guy John Wayne came up to demand a record one night, Terry Noel picked it out of the rack, checked with the actor that it was the tune he wanted to hear, and then snapped it in half and said that he couldn't play it because it was broken.

But still, the music at Arthur's and its many imitators was always secondary, a backdrop. Like Studio 54 later, these New York clubs were watering holes for the Beautiful People, featured in the gossip columns and interesting places to preen and be seen. Surfing the disco boom in the late seventies, Studio 54 was where the rich and the famous came to lose it on the dancefloor and the secret basements below, to consume the cocaine that was often discreetly slipped into their pockets for free, and to mingle with characters from Manhattan clubland. Bianca Jagger once rode in on a white horse, Grace Jones performed her most outrageous cabarets there, and the action was overseen by a giant man in the moon effigy, spooning glittery snow into its ample nose. But although it may have been one of the most famous clubs ever, with as many people outside clamouring to get past its notoriously picky doorman as were inside some nights, it is telling that few people then or now could name the DJ.

The clubs where people danced with such abandon that they forgot who they were, the discos where new musical forms began to grow from the chemistry between DJ and crowd, were not clubs for the in-crowd. They were clubs for outsiders, for those who were made to feel they didn't belong in society at large: black, Latin, and mainly gay, they grew out of a night in Manhattan when a small group of drag queens were pushed just once too often.

Before the Stonewall riots, gay bars in America were seedy, furtive places where a light bulb flashed over the door if someone unfamiliar came in, warning the patrons to separate on the dancefloor. Homosexuality was seen as an aberration, a medical condition, something hidden and shameful. By the sixties, gay activism was growing in cities like New York, and the more liberated, open approach to sexuality advocated by the hippies had begun to break down barriers. But the love that dared not speak its name didn't begin to shout it in the streets until the summer of 1969.

Gays in the bohemian Greenwich Village area were running out of places to go that summer. The Tele-Star and the Checkerboard had closed down. Recent raids had shut two more apparently aptly named after-hours clubs, the Sewer and the Snake Pit. Then, on 22 June, the actress Judy Garland was found dead of a drug overdose in her home in London. Her tragic life and stoic endurance had made her an icon for many gay men, and after her funeral on the afternoon of Friday 27th, the mood in the remaining bars was sombre.

It wasn't the best time for the New York police to carry out a routine harassment raid, but at 3 a.m., eight plainclothes officers crashed into the Stonewall Inn at 53 Christopher Street and arrested the employees for selling liquor without a licence. The customers were allowed out one by one and gathered outside on the pavement waiting for friends, but when the police van arrived to take away the staff, including three struggling drag queens, their anger exploded. In the ensuing riot, the police ran back and locked themselves inside the club while the crowd outside tried to set the place alight. The battle continued on the following nights, with shouts of 'Gay power!' heard on the streets for the first time. Police attempting to chase down the rioters were shocked when, realising their strength in numbers, the gays turned and forced the officers to flee instead.

'There was a strong sense of gay community and a strong fighting spirit, an intoxicating sense of release,' remembers writer Robert Amsell. 'Crowds were growing, as if from the pavement. There was kissing, hugging, fondling.'[3]

Still celebrated across the world with Gay Pride parades, this show of defiance is now seen as a turning point, after which gay people finally began to expect and demand the same space and freedom as anyone else. The resulting euphoria is hard to imagine in these more tolerant times. There was a sense of release, a rush of energy and a mood of defiant hedonism that was reflected in the clubs, where repression was replaced with excess. With names like the Haven and Salvation, the new gay clubs offered an escapist world of sex, drugs, music and dancing, a place where people could be themselves, lose themselves, feel accepted and part of a community, if only for a night.

From these clubs rose the first DJ superstar. In the space of a few years in Manhattan, DJs had moved from being mechanics who were there to operate the turntable to curators who took pride in their choice of records. Now Francis Grasso turned DJs into artists able to use their turntables and records to create new music live, in front of their crowd.

Grasso took over from Terry Noel at the Haven, but became a celebrity at the Sanctuary. Housed in an old church in the Hell's Kitchen area of Manhattan, when the club opened in 1970 it was called the Church: the decks were on the altar, church pews served as seats, and a huge painted devil's head leered from the wall surrounded by naked angels indulging in just about every sexual act imaginable.

Objections from the Roman Catholic Church resulted in a name change and the angels' genitalia being covered with plastic grapes, but this did nothing to curb the wild abandon of the crowd. Drug-dealing was open, and although sex was confined to the toilets, the boys on the dancefloor simulated it by grinding against each other, sometimes forming long humping daisy chains across the club. (In a sanitised form, this dance later became known as the bump, and was popularised in the UK by a pop group called Kenny, who made a chaste hip-to-hip nudging a real favourite in school discos at the end of 1974.)

Grasso played a progressive mix of soul, rock and African percussion tracks, but it was his mixing skills that caused the sensation. As Albert Goldman wrote:

> He invented the technique of 'slip-cueing'. Holding the disc with his thumb while the turntable whirled beneath insulated by a felt pad, he would locate with an earphone the best spot to make the splice, then release the next side precisely on the beat . . . His *tour de force* was playing two records simultaneously for as long as two minutes at a stretch. He would super the drum break of Chicago's 'I'm A Man' over the orgasmic moans of Led Zeppelin's 'Whole Lotta Love' to make a powerfully erotic mix.

No longer confined to simply playing record after record, the DJ could mould the music to fit the mood of the crowd, their responses in turn spurring him on to greater feats of virtuosity on the decks. 'Francis was like an energy mirror,' wrote Goldman, 'catching the vibes off the floor and shooting them back again.' At peak moments in the night, he would flick off the house lights, plunging the club into darkness before illuminating the stained glass windows.

By the time the Sanctuary was finally closed in April 1972 after a combined raid by the police and fire departments, similar discos were spreading all over Manhattan and beyond. The growing power of the DJs in these clubs to break new records was reflected in the charts a year later. 'Soul Makossa' was an obscure record by African artist Manu Dibango that had been rediscovered by DJs in New York and had become a dancefloor favourite. The attention led to its release as a single, and it shot into the US Top 40. 'Love's Theme' went to number one soon after, a lush instrumental originally written by Barry White as an overture to an album by female vocal trio the Unlimited Orchestra.

In the vast New York club Infinity, gay men would rip off their shirts when the music got intense and dance tracing patterns in the air with fans. Increasing numbers of straight clubbers made their way on to the dancefloor there too, attracted by the atmosphere, the intoxicating music and flashing lights, by the sheer *spectacle* of it all. The music was moving out of the shadows and into the mainstream. Disco had arrived.

THE ROAD
TO PARADISE

Club culture is restless, fluid, constantly changing and feeding off itself. It is a culture created by the people on the dancefloor, reflecting both what they bring with them to a club *and* what they are trying to escape from in the world outside. It is a culture that happens in many different places at the same time, and so if different people claim to be the first or if they tell stories that contradict each other, they can all be telling their own truths.

This is a selective history, focusing on the events that led up to 1988, on the people who set the fuses for the explosion in Britain that year. It tells only a few stories, because it is impossible to tell them all. But some clubs act as flash points, a focus for the energy in the culture as a whole. The Paradise Garage is one of those clubs, a venue still talked about with reverence by DJs who were living on the other side of the world and hardly out of nappies when it hit its peak. So since we have to pick one moment as a starting point, one or two people as the focus, our story starts in the South Bronx one summer at the end of the sixties, when Larry met Frankie.

Lawrence Philpot was born in Brooklyn on 20 July, 1954. His mother Minnie Levan, a dressmaker, had relatives in Frankie Knuckles' neighbourhood in the Bronx, and so they'd often go there to visit. Larry was a year older, but when they met the two adolescents hit it off straight away. They had a lot in common. At first they saw each other mainly in the school holidays, but as they grew older they became virtually inseparable. So much so that if someone saw one of them alone in Manhattan, they'd often call him by the other's name – not because they looked at all alike, but because it was hard to see one of them without thinking of the other.

Both of them were to become DJs. Later, Frankie Knuckles was to move to Chicago and became the godfather of house music. Larry Levan – he dropped his father's name – was to rule the decks at the Paradise Garage in New York. At his best, some say that he was the greatest DJ who ever lived. Frankie Knuckles isn't about to argue. 'If it wasn't for him, we wouldn't have the culture that we have now. I wouldn't say that one person single-handedly did it all, but he is definitely at the centre of it.'

Growing up, Knuckles used to think that he had two strikes against him. Like his best friend, he was black, and he was gay. He doesn't think that way now, of course, but times have changed. The clubs he and Levan went to in their teens helped forge that change, giving people who lived on the margins of their own communities, let alone society as a whole, a place where – for a night at least – they could transcend everything, where they could be themselves, lose themselves.

Levan was the first to go to Manhattan and explore the delights the Greenwich Village area had to offer in those heady days after Stonewall, but he soon persuaded his friend to come too. 'It was the first time I'd ever seen a drag queen,' recalls Knuckles. 'It was the first time I had ever heard any kind of music played at that kind of level, at that kind of *intensity*. And that was it. That started it.'

The first club they went to regularly was the Planetarium, a subterranean gay bar with dark blue walls, a steel floor and the constellations painted all over the ceiling. It was a tiny room, but to them it was the universe, and Frankie Knuckles can still recall every last detail of it. Sitting by the grand piano in the impressive New York studio complex where he and his friend David Morales now work on their productions and mixes, he smiles as he describes the club to me.

'When I think about being that young, and all the risks I took, like most teenagers do, playing around with this drug and that drug and smoking a ton of reefer and all the rest of it, you think you're not going to have much brain, let alone brain *cells* left if you should live to be my age. But it's amazing that I can pretty much still remember everything. And at the weirdest times, I will see or hear something that will spark a memory.'

After that summer in the Planetarium, the two youths started seeing each other almost every day. When Knuckles was sixteen, Levan took him to the Loft for the first time. In the Village on Lower Broadway by Bleeker Street, the club was a house party in the most literal sense: every Friday and Saturday from 14 February 1970, David Mancuso covered his ceiling with balloons, laid out a buffet and ran an all-night party in the industrial loft where he lived and worked as a designer.

'The Loft wasn't a very big place,' recalls Knuckles. 'You walked in there and it was dark, it was crowded, but there was one solid rhythm in the room and everyone was latched on to it. There were whistles, people beating tambourines, sound effects of sky-rockets going off. It was just the most amazing thing.

'Larry kept saying, "I am so in love with this man! He looks like Jesus Christ. Just wait till you see him!" He took me from the main dancefloor into the back where the kitchen was, and just as we approached this little hallway, there's an opening in the wall and you could see right into the DJ booth. David Mancuso was standing in there, and he *did* look like Jesus Christ. He looked like Jesus Christ with a flashlight between his legs. Because he had no lights in the booth – I guess he didn't want any light to disturb the dancefloor. He had on a kaftan shirt, the long curly dark hair with the beard, and the most piercing eyes.'

To many of his regulars, David Mancuso was a god-like figure, revered and respected. Over a brilliant sound system, he played Motown, rock, African, Latin, and later Philly soul along with hard-edged Euro funk bands, and many who were later to become major players in the New York club scene had their first taste of under-ground clubbing at the Loft. 'He didn't play records unless they were very serious,' recalled Larry Levan years later. 'I used to watch people cry in the Loft for a slow song because it was so pretty.'[1]

This wasn't clubbing as a pastime, it was clubbing as a religion, a release, a way of life. For many, these parties were the only places where they truly felt they *belonged*. An orphan, perhaps Mancuso was trying to create the family he never had. Certainly, he wasn't in it for the money. He saw the nights as part of a long tradition in America of rent parties, where people threw open their house for the night and charged admission to help with the bills. 'I was very much into the underground thing,' he said, explaining why he has never advertised or promoted his events. 'Maybe it was my hippie background.'[2]

Entrance was by invitation only (each invite specifying the number of guests you were allowed to bring), and no alcohol was served, keeping it just about within the law. In fact, the crowd was said to be so close-knit that when one party had to be cancelled because of trouble with the authorities, it took just twenty phone calls to spread the word.

In language that shows the prejudice of his time, Albert Goldman describes his impressions of the early Loft:

> Though all kinds of people showed up, 60 per cent of the regulars were black and Puerto Rican ... When Saturday night would roll around and all the public clubs would shut down, hundreds of boys, all steamed up and ready to romp, would converge on the Loft. The moment you hit the room, your nostrils were distended by the stench of black sweat. The dancers were mostly men stripped down to the skimpiest work clothes and wringing wet ... On a hot summer night in the un-air-conditioned loft, a visible cloud of steam, of human effluvia, hung over the floor and misted the lights.[3]

A year after their initiation as Loft babies, Knuckles and Levan were approached by Nicky Siano, a youth in his early teens who was planning to open his own space when the Loft closed for David Mancuso's annual holiday. By then, everyone knew the two teenagers, because at just about any party that went on, they were at the centre of the dancefloor. 'We'd get shit going, pretty much,' says Knuckles. 'We were like ring-leaders. We weren't bad influences, but we would get the party started.'

The club was called the Gallery, and Siano offered them a job: handing out flyers, decorating the space, setting up the buffet and the fruit displays, making the punch. They had another job, too. They were each given a blotter with 300 hits of LSD 25 to hand out as people were coming in, to get them in the mood. They were to put each one straight into the mouth, and make sure the recipient swallowed it straight away – partly to ensure there was no evidence in the event of a raid, but mainly to make sure that no one was pocketing theirs, that everyone was on the same trip at the same time.

'Halfway through the night, all of a sudden I just got this rush, and everything just completely turned around,' recalls Knuckles. 'The music amplified, the *feeling* of the music amplified, and just visually everything had intensified. I didn't understand what this was about. Larry said, "You've been handling this shit all night, that's why!" '

Levan told his friend that guitarist Jimi Hendrix used to take three hits of LSD 25 in blotter form, put them on his forehead and tie his bandanna round his head so that while he was sweating on stage, he would absorb the acid into his bloodstream through his skin. Knuckles thought this was just an interesting story until he noticed that Larry was wearing a bandanna too: sure enough, there were three tiny squares of acid stuck to his sweating forehead underneath.

Still, he didn't lose his head for business. That first night Knuckles gave his acid away as instructed; Levan sold his, gleefully showing his friend all the money he'd made. When their boss found out, they came to an arrangement. They would pay him $100 for the blotters each week, and they could pocket any proceeds. He also gave them their apprenticeships as DJs. 'He would show us how to work the equipment and teach us an appreciation of the music, how to put it together and what a song is supposed to do. Which is what a lot of DJs now don't know. A song is supposed to inspire. It's supposed to evoke emotions in people and *take them there*.'

Frankie Knuckles was the first to get a proper job as a DJ, working for six months in 1971 at Better Days, a gay bar on 49th Street which has remained influential in New York, with DJs such as Tee Scott and later Bruce Forest. Levan finally blagged his way behind the decks at the Continental Baths a month later, working as a warm-up for the main DJ twice a week and operating the lights for him every other night. The bathhouses had sprung up in those heady days after Stonewall, when the old repression and shame vanished and for many gay men liberation meant having as much sex as possible with as many other men as possible. The bathhouses facilitated this, with orgy rooms and clean, private spaces for anonymous sex with strangers.

But they were also social centres. Under the Ansonia Hotel in the West Seventies, the Continental Baths was one of the more sophisticated establishments. The public areas were open at weekends to straight couples, who came to enjoy the floor-show and get a vicarious thrill from imagining what those clean-cut young men walking round wrapped only in towels were doing in the secret back-rooms.[4] Jazzman Cab Calloway played there, and singer Bette Midler made her name performing live at the Baths in 1972, with a young Barry Manilow accompanying her on piano. Still, Frankie Knuckles resisted going to see his friend there: 'Bathhouses just had a certain stigma about them that I didn't want to be attached to.'

Finally, after he'd lost his job at Better Days, he went to the Baths on the holiday weekend of 4 July. It was *three weeks* before he was to see daylight again. 'It was like a world within itself. Everything was in there.' As well as the dancefloor and an Olympic-sized swimming pool, there was a restaurant, bars, shops, a cinema, a gym, even a beauty salon. Larry Levan lived in an apartment inside the complex, and Knuckles found himself spending more and more time there.

When Levan took over as the main DJ in 1973, Knuckles took his friend's old job, moving into another apartment inside the Baths. It was a time of change in dance music. Songwriters Kenny Gamble and Leon Huff had just launched their Philadelphia International label, and their lush, orchestrated but unmistakably R&B-based records began to take over from Motown on the dancefloor. America was in recession. Nixon was hanging on in the White House despite the whiff of Watergate corruption. The end of the Vietnam War had left the country demoralised and confused. The silky, sophisticated Philly sound offered a welcome escape. The O'Jays, the Three Degrees, the Intruders, Harold Melvin and the Blue Notes, and later the likes of Teddy Pendergrass, Jean Carne and Lou Rawls soothed and uplifted, while later anthems like the Philadelphia All-Stars' 'Let's Clean Up The Ghetto' and McFadden and Whitehead's 'Ain't No Stopping Us Now' offered an upbeat optimism that was welcome in hard times.

The name of the studio orchestra encapsulated the family feel the label tried to foster: some of the best session musicians in the country,

Mother Father Sister Brother (or MFSB for short) underpinned most of the Philly hits as well as recording a few of their own. The lush strings of MFSB's 1973 epic instrumental dance track 'Love Is The Message' became a staple in New York discos, an anthem that could still be heard on the dancefloors a decade later.

In 1974, Levan moved on from the Baths and Knuckles took over, playing all night, every night of the week until the place closed two years later. This kind of relentless playing to a discerning audience gave them an apprenticeship few DJs now will ever enjoy, a familiarity with the music that enabled them to communicate through the records, building a narrative, relaying messages to the crowd with the records they chose. 'Playing there every night, listening to music over and over,' Knuckles recalls. 'That's how I got most of my education.'

By then Levan was dating Richard Long, a talented sound designer who had once worked on the door at the Planetarium. He was working on the bass speakers that were to be used for the 1974 movie *Earthquake,* which were designed to make the audience feel that the quake was rumbling underneath them. Together, the DJ and designer turned his showroom at 252 Broadway just above Canal Street into a club on Fridays and Saturdays, which became known as the SoHo Place. Levan, still just nineteen, built the club up until it got so full it was impossible to move. When this forced them to close, they were approached by psychiatrist Michael Brody, a dedicated clubber who was about to start a weekly party inside an old meat locker in his loft at 143 Reade Street.

'What was really incredible about it was that Larry had control over the cooling in the room,' remembers Knuckles. 'It would be almost pitch black at some points. He'd let it get like almost oven hot in there, and then just when you thought you couldn't take the heat any more, he would dial the temperature down.'

Levan had a *Four Seasons* sound-effects record by Walter Carlos (later to become Wendy Carlos), and he would fade the music out and put on 'Spring', which started off with a wind noise and then went into a thunderstorm recorded in complete stereo. 'It was the most incredible thing, to hear the bass rumbling through there from the thunder. Whatever song he was playing would just fade out and this thunderstorm would creep up. Then you'd hear a song like "Date With The Rain" by Eddie Kendricks in the background. There'd be all this thunder and lightning going on, you're standing there dripping with sweat, and then all of a sudden it just got so *cool* in there.'

By the end, Reade Street was so overcrowded that Levan would open the windows to let the music out to the people waiting on the street. Michael Brody decided it was time to expand, the DJ promised not to play elsewhere until bigger premises could be found.

In 1975, David Mancuso moved into a new loft at 99 Prince Street and helped set up the first record pool, giving record companies a means of distributing their product free to the increasingly influential DJs. It was already common for DJs to create extended live mixes in the clubs by cutting between two copies of the same record, or to record mixes at home and play them in the clubs on reel-to-reel. DJ Tom Moulton used to create them on his simple home recording equipment, using the vocal and the instrumental side of the same song and making tape edits with a razor blade, then selling the finished mixes to other DJs on tape. When record pools became established in 1975, he had the idea of putting such mixes on vinyl for promotional use. They went out in the form of twelve-inch records stamped 'for disco DJs only' to stir up interest in the release of the shorter, seven-inch version a few weeks later.

The first new record format in thirty years, the twelve-inch allowed the mix to play longer, but also louder: the extra space between the grooves gave a far higher sound quality than crackly seven-inch singles. It's not clear which was the first tune to come out this way, although Calhoun's 'Dance Dance Dance' is remembered as one of the earliest. Inevitably bootlegs followed, and in 1976, the disco label Salsoul released the first commercially-available twelve-inch, a version of Double Exposure's 'Ten Percent' extended from its original three minutes to something closer to eleven by DJ Walter Gibbons. Aimed directly at New York's underground club scene, its success meant it was soon followed by more.

The resident DJ at the gay, black Brooklyn disco Galaxy 21, Gibbons already had an enviable reputation as a live mixer, a man who could make even the impossibly slow intros to tracks like MFSB's 'Love Is

The Message' or Diana Ross's 'Love Hangover' work on the dancefloor with his skilful edits. He also anticipated the break-style mixing that would form the basis of hip hop by cutting between two copies of the same record, extending a short drum break into something that would keep the dancefloor moving for minutes on end. He even hired a young Frenchman, François Kevorkian, to play percussion in his club, marooned out in the middle of the dancefloor and drumming along to his mixes.

As an experiment, it wasn't too successful: Kevorkian had never been to an underground club before, and was unfamiliar with the music. However, it soon became common for DJs to have synth players working alongside them in the booth, and Kevorkian's experience served him well: he became an influential DJ, remixer and producer in his own right, and one of the first to openly acknowledge the influence of reggae dub techniques on his disco mixes.

'I thought I was the best DJ in the world until I heard Walter Gibbons play,' DJ/producer John 'Jellybean' Benitez said years later. 'Everything he was doing back then, people are doing now. He was phasing records – playing two records at the same time to give a flange effect – and doubling up records so there would be a little repeat. He would do tremendous quick cuts on record sort of like the B-boys do. He would slam it in so quick that you couldn't hear the turntable slowing down or catching up. He would do little edits on tape and people would freak out.'[5]

As he grew in confidence in the studio, Walter's Salsoul remixes became more radical and inventive, stripping off the heavy orchestration and exposing the bare bones of the rhythm. When he became a born-again Christian, however, he felt unable to play songs that weren't spiritually uplifting, and the sexual content of disco made it increasingly difficult for him to work. He died in 1994.

As disco continued to develop, Michael Brody had acquired the lease on an old cast-concrete parking garage on the docks at 84 King Street, and with financial backing from his lover Mel Cheren, a record company boss who was in the process of setting up the independent disco label West End, he began building the Paradise Garage. Brody designed the layout, Richard Long worked on the sound system, Larry

Levan badgered them both for what he wanted and even lived in the club for a while as it was being built to save money.

Like most underground clubs in New York, it was to be a juice bar, which avoided the kind of restrictions and snooping then associated with the licensing board. 'Having it just as a private club without alcohol was much better,' explains Mel Cheren. 'The idea was to create an atmosphere like the Loft, where black, white, straight and gay could party together under one roof without any kind of hostility. That's the best way of bringing people together. If people can dance together, they can live together. It was the best sound system. Everything that went in there was the best.'

It proved to be an expensive enterprise, and in January 1977 they decided to open for business in the completed entrance room to raise more funds. The launch was not a great success. The sound system got stuck in a blizzard at an airport in Kentucky, and people were left outside in the cold for hours. 'The people who came that night never came back, and it took years to build it up again,' recalls Cheren, who says that the Garage as it is now remembered didn't really kick off until the start of the eighties.

The construction parties continued, however, and slowly the club began to expand and take shape. By the time it opened fully in the autumn of 1978, disco had been taken into the mainstream with *Saturday Night Fever*. Nik Cohn, a British writer living in New York, had seen the phenomenon as a product of the recession: kids could no longer run away from home, drop acid and drop out. Instead they worked hard to help support their families, escaping into the fantasy world of the disco on Saturday nights. He wrote a story based around the characters he'd observed in a Brooklyn disco called 2001 Odyessy that was published in *New York* magazine in June 1976. (Subsequently, he was to claim that he hadn't spent a great deal of time in the disco, modelling his characters instead on some soul-obsessed Mods he'd met in West London a few years before.)

The film version came out in the US in December 1977. It made a star of John Travolta and revived the career of the Bee Gees, who dominated a soundtrack album that was to sell so massively that the film and music industries would from then on be inextricably linked. By 1978 it was estimated that there were over 1,500 discos in New

York City alone, a boom so big that it was inevitably followed by a crash.

Codified, commercialised, disco began to stagnate. Middle-of-the-road crooner Andy Williams made a disco record. Middle-aged middle America hummed along to a tune like the Salsoul Orchestra's 'You're Just The Right Size' without dreaming what it implied, and the US Navy almost adopted the Village People's 'In The Navy' for a recruitment campaign until its camp subtext was explained. Reduced to a formula and severed from its black soul roots, the music was considered production-line fodder, mechanical and soulless. As the Garage struggled to establish itself, Larry Levan began to do remixes for West End. The first perhaps shows the state the music was in by then: it was a disco novelty record by *Sesame Street*'s Cookie Monster called 'C Is For Cookie'.

By 1980, Travolta had hung up the white suit and pulled on cowboy boots instead, launching a whole new fashion for country with *Urban Cowboy*. Bored of the formula, mainstream America had retreated from the dancefloor too. Disco was considered over, a finished fad, and many of the major labels closed down their disco departments or modified them into more generalised dance departments.

But in the underground, the music didn't die, it just mutated. No longer able to afford big studios and full orchestras of session musicians, producers instead began to explore the possibilities of synthesised sound more fully, creating a pulsing new electro-disco. Gay men still wanted a place to dance, to feel free, and the black and Hispanic crowd which formed the core of the Garage's clientele were still doubly marginalised. As the club began to take off in a big way in 1981, Larry Levan's dense, druggy remix of Taana Gardner's hypnotically slow disco workout 'Heartbeat' sold 100,000 copies in New York in just one week.

Like all good clubs, the Garage felt like a secret society. 'A typical night at the Paradise Garage began *after* 4 a.m.,' wrote Frank Owen, an Englishman who went to the club, met his future wife there, and quickly made his home in New York.

At a time when most club-goers were finally heading home, Garage devotees were trekking through the near-deserted SoHo streets ... They came for the atmosphere, the electricity, the 'religious experience'. But mostly, they came for the music, the 'garage sound' – that classic combination of booming bass, honky-tonk piano and soaring gospel-derived vocals. Once inside, they walked up the ramp of the old parking garage, took a right at the Crystal Room – a rest area lined with glass blocks – and headed into the main space to the dancefloor. There they were met with an image both frightening and thrilling – 2,000 nearly-naked figures oiled with their own sweat cavorting shamelessly with one another like a scene from a pagan ritual. Six, eight, ten hours later, these same people would emerge into the morning sunshine, their dilated eyes protected by sunglasses, exhausted, dishevelled, but happy. The dreary everyday world seemed transformed. If only for a moment.[6]

Membership of the club was not easy to obtain. Every so often, hopefuls would wait in a line outside on a weekday to see Michael Brody, who would quiz them about their sexuality, and why they wanted to come to the club. Besides the VIP cards that allowed celebrities like Mick Jagger, Diana Ross, Grace Jones, Eddie Murphy, Mike Tyson and Stevie Wonder to party in the DJ booth, there were two kinds of card: one admitted the holder to the mainly straight Friday nights, the other allowed entrance to Saturday too. People would often swear they were gay in order to try and get the coveted Saturday membership, but few succeeded. As a result, the club kept an intimate, party atmosphere despite its size.

Coffee and soft drinks in the club were free, as were the ice lollies and fruit in the summer, brownies and doughnuts in the winter. At Christmas and Thanksgiving, clubbers were even served turkey with all the trimmings. As for the drugs, the punch was said to have been spiked with acid for the first three years until the crowds got so big it felt dangerous. After that, a mixture of cocaine and Ecstasy fuelled the floor.

First synthesised by the German pharmaceutical company Merck in 1912 and patented by them two years later, MDMA – or, to give Ecstasy its full name, 3, 4-methylenedioxymethamphetamine – was not developed as a slimming aid as is often now claimed, but was probably intended for use as an intermediate chemical in the preparation of other drugs. In any case, it was soon forgotten as war broke out, and it wasn't researched in any depth until the late sixties, when Californian chemist Alexander 'Sasha' Shulgin rediscovered it in the course of his methodical explorations of consciousness-changing compounds.

Shulgin had a federal licence to experiment with any psychedelic drug he wished in his home lab, thanks to his usefulness as a consultant to the Drug Enforcement Agency, but his primary interest was in their effect on the human mind. Each substance he synthesised was tried on himself, his wife Ann and a select group of friends, and they carefully recorded their experiences. After trying MDMA, he came to see it as a 'penicillin for the soul'. A drug which didn't induce psychedelic hallucinations but which simply opened a window allowing the user to see into him or herself, it therefore 'could be all things to all people'.

The comments of his testers will be familiar to most people who have tried the drug: 'I feel absolutely clean inside, and there is nothing but pure euphoria. I have never felt so great, or believed this to be possible. I am overcome by the profundity of the experience.' 'Everyone must get to experience a profound state like this. I feel totally peaceful. I have lived all my life to get here, and I feel I have come home. I am complete.'[7]

In 1977 he gave it to Leo Zoff, an elderly psychologist who saw its therapeutic potential and abandoned his plans for retirement to travel across the States introducing it to other doctors and therapists. It is estimated that around half a million doses were administered to patients in the following decade, with MDMA – or Adam, as the therapists often called it – proving useful in helping a wide range of disorders from post-traumatic stress and phobias to marital problems.

Despite the efforts of these explorers to keep the drug secret, in 1983 a group of cocaine dealers in Texas began marketing MDMA as Ecstasy in bars and clubs – the more accurate brand name of 'Empathy' was briefly considered, but proved less seductive. Students and young professionals took it up with great enthusiasm, buying it legally over the counter in bars, where it came with a 'flight manual' of instructions for safer use and could even be charged to a credit card. It quickly spread into gay clubs across the States, but it was the spectacle of respectable white youths in Texas losing it with such abandon that attracted the media, and then the attention of the Government. Despite the protests of therapists – MDMA was the first drug ever to have a team of lawyers briefed to defend it – it was made illegal in the US in July 1985. By then, however, it had become an integral part of gay dance culture, and the ban did little to control its consumption.

But the euphoria on the dancefloor of the Garage was about more than just drugs. 'The reason it was so important is because everyone and their mothers were there every weekend checking it out,' recalls François Kevorkian. 'It was so obviously and blatantly superior to anything else going on. You had the best sound system around, the most talented DJ you can imagine with amazing records that no one else could get: things he'd made himself and things others had made exclusively for him.

'He built sets with stories that went into one another. I'm not saying that he only played vocals, but there was a concept there that he studied and became an amazing practitioner of. He was able to truly *use* songs . . . And he used those lyrics to talk to people. It was very, very common for people on the dancefloor to feel like he was talking to them directly through the record. And it was a two-way thing. There was an unspoken mental energy flowing back and forth. I think, more than anyone else I've known, he was the one that could pick up on this.'[8]

Asked for his most memorable nights in the club, Mel Cheren pauses. 'I don't think that there was a night that *wasn't* memorable. I would say I was going for an hour and leave five or six hours later. It was mesmerising. Everyone has certain talents, natural abilities. Some people are born with the talent to paint, some people are born with the talent to write. Larry had the talent for music and he could take 2,000 people and make them feel like they were at a house party. That was his magic. He wanted to educate people through lyrics.'

Levan himself explained his technique as follows: 'Out of all the records you have, maybe five or six of them make sense together.

There is actually a message in the dance, the way you feel, the muscles you use, but only certain records have that. Say I was playing songs about music – "I Love Music" by the O'Jays, "Music" by Al Hudson – and the next record is [Phreek's] "Weekend". That's about getting laid, a whole other thing. If I was dancing and truly into the words and the feeling and it came on, it might be a good record, but it makes no sense because it doesn't have anything to do with the others. So a slight pause, a sound effect, something else to let you know it's a new paragraph rather than one continuous sentence.'[9]

Mel Cheren had first-hand experience of this kind of communication. 'Larry and I had our ups and downs. He did a lot of mixing for me for my record label, West End, and we'd have a disagreement or whatever and we wouldn't talk. If he was angry with me, he played songs that said "*Fuck you, excuse me*." He actually had a record that said that. I would be dancing right under the booth, I'd look up at him and be like, "Give me a break!" and I would just walk off the dancefloor with him watching me.

'One night, we hadn't been talking for a while, and I was dancing, and he was playing "Gotta Get You Back Into My Life" and songs like "*I love you*". And all of a sudden I turned around and there he was. He left the DJ booth, he gave me a big hug and said, "Oh, I can't be mad at you" or something like that. But if he was upset with you, I mean, you *knew* it.'

Michael Brody's struggle to pay the bills in the early days of the Garage and Levan's fierce temper and refusal to compromise meant that there were frequent clashes between the two, with one particularly memorable fight ending with the DJ biting his boss in the leg. 'You always lash out at those you love most,' comments Cheren dryly.

But in general, the team saw each other as family, and all had a perfectionist's eye when it came to the club they called 'disco heaven'. The sound system was never complete. Levan would test it continually, looking for holes in the sound, badgering Richard Long to *invent* what he wanted if it wasn't available. Clubbers were frequently kept outside while the DJ made last-minute adjustments, moving a speaker an inch or two, or one night making a packed dancefloor wait patiently while he got out a ladder and polished all six of the mirror balls.

Such perfectionism also showed in his mixes. When he produced the ground-breaking electro-disco duo NYC Peech Boys with Michael de Benedictus, a synthesiser player who often jammed alongside him in the DJ booth, it took a year to complete the mix of the first single, 'Don't Make Me Wait'. Levan constantly tested the latest version in the club, going back into the studio to make adjustments.

As for the music he played, its base was underground disco, the uplifting music played at the Loft, Better Days and the Gallery, but he would throw almost anything into the mix: Kraftwerk, Euro-disco, classical pieces, avant-garde electronica, rock records such as the Clash's 'Magnificent Seven', and later Stock, Aitken and Waterman hits and early house and techno all went on to Levan's three decks. For a while, he had a rocking horse in the booth, and DJ/remixer Bruce Forest recalls a night when he was rocking maniacally, playing along on a keyboard, so off his head that he hadn't realised the record had ended some time ago, and that people were trying to dance to his amateurish doodles.[10]

But if Levan was a virtuoso, his instrument wasn't the turntables, but the whole room. When Chicago house star Marshall Jefferson performed there one night, he saw the DJ standing in his booth, conducting the crowd as if he was controlling their very movements. Some believed he could.

'He would go into the booth and say, "Those people over there aren't dancing, watch this!"' recounts Justin Berkmann, another Englishman who went to New York for a brief visit, experienced the Paradise Garage and ended up staying. 'He'd put on a record, and they would just go off. *That's* how well he knew his dancefloor. Because it was very territorial. Garage people stayed in their areas. You had a speaker, you had your corner, you had your place. After ten years, he knew everyone in the club and he knew what got each group going. That's something very few people get. Most of the big DJs now are flying all over the world, and most of the time you go into a club and you haven't got a clue what people want.'

The sudden availability of cheap flights turned New York into a Mecca for British clubbers in the early to mid-eighties, showing us things we'd never seen, never heard, never tasted, never *dreamed* of before.

There was Eric Goode's Area, which pioneered the idea of the night-club as art installation: I remember once walking in through a corridor of shop windows, each one with its own bizarre tableau inside, leading to a dancefloor that looked like the apocalyptic end of *Planet Of The Apes*, with the huge head and shoulders of the Statue of Liberty emerging tipsily from its centre. There was the Roxy, one of the first big forums for the emerging electro/hip hop scene, where half the crowd danced the night away on roller skates. I saw Grandmaster Flash and his Furious Five perform there once, just after their first single had been released on Sugarhill and rap was still new. Malcolm McLaren went there too, and was later to launch his new protégés Bow Wow Wow with a series of parties in a roller rink in West London. There was the impossibly glamorous and star-studded Studio 54, where an English accent often ensured entry for young club tourists who may otherwise have languished in the queue outside. There was the funk punk of Danceteria, the club that provided the main blue-print for the Haçienda in Manchester and where Madonna handed her first demo tapes to the resident DJ Mark Kamins. There was Kamins' one-nighter the Harem, where belly-dancers entertained the punters and music from all over the world was played. There were endless one-nighters and bars and venues that we brought home and adapted, but most of all there was the Paradise Garage.

Wide-eyed and awestruck, most of the British pop acts who were so successful in the US at the time passed through the Garage. Many young Brits were to try their first Ecstasy there, and Boy George had his first line of cocaine there, in the DJ booth with Larry Levan – an indulgence he was later to feel led him, inexorably, to heroin.[11] Factory records hosted a night there, and Haçienda DJ Mike Picker-ing's first band, the industrial funk crew Quando Quango, performed there several times. Unaware of the colour of the musicians or their history, Larry Levan often championed British dance music that struggled for recognition in clubs back home.

I only went to the Garage once, in the mid-eighties. London DJ Jay Strongman was in the US looking for acts to sign to the fledgling British dance label Rhythm King, and I'd tagged along. The details are hazy now. New York to me then was a dream world, a place I'd seen on TV experienced through a fog of jet-lag. I remember we went to the

Limelight first, and bumped into Jon Moss of Culture Club who offered to get a car to take us to the Garage. I'd never been in a stretch limo before, and I remember trying hard to be cool. I also remember suppressing a laugh when the club turned out to be just around the corner and Moss had to argue with the driver over the fare. I remember the long, sloping and somewhat intimidating ramp up to the entrance of the club. Fruit on tables. A cinema showing cartoons. A beautiful roof terrace offering some respite from the heat on the dancefloor below. I remember how *friendly* people seemed, how joyful, only years later equating their dilated eyes with Ecstasy.

I don't remember the records, or even how long I stayed. What I do remember vividly was the sound. The fact that the music didn't just hang in the air, it came inside you. It was physical. You didn't just hear it, you *felt* it. The music vibrated through the thick cushioned soles of my Doctor Marten shoes, and the bass rumbled inside my rib cage. Yet when my friend leaned over to speak, I could hear every word.

Back in London, the big speakers that fired the illegal all-nighters in warehouses, factories and office spaces across the city no longer seemed so impressive.

The Garage closed on 26 September, 1987. By then, Levan was increasingly using stand-ins on the more demanding Saturday nights, and both his ego and his drug habit were out of control. The remix work had begun to dry up too, with the DJ increasingly likely to fall asleep on the mixing desk or fail to show up at all. When he did show, he often spent so long in the studio that the bills were astronomical. When Michael Brody was diagnosed with AIDS, it was inevitable that the club would close.

'When Larry knew the Garage was going to close, he freaked,' says David DePino, a close friend and frequent warm-up DJ at the club. 'He went on a self-destructive binge. He took drugs to spite people, to hurt them. The more you would say, "Larry, please don't do so many drugs", the more he would do them – right in your face.'[12]

During this period, Levan was so cruel to Michael Brody that he was written out of the dying man's will, never getting the Garage's sound and lighting system as was originally intended. But despite the conflicts, the closing weekend was a spectacular affair. People came from all over the world to be there. Artist Keith Haring, whose work decorated much of the club by then, flew specially from Tokyo to attend. Singer Gwen Guthrie, whose biggest hits were produced by Levan, was carried on-stage on a bier dressed in her best diamonds and furs. 'You know why I'm wearing these?' she asked the ecstatic crowd. 'Because *you* bought them for me.'

'I was there for the last three days almost non-stop,' remembers Mel Cheren. 'At one point I was dancing and Larry shut off all the lights and he put the spotlight on me, and he played the Trammps' "Where Do We Go From Here". And I lost it, because I knew what he was saying.'

Justin Berkmann remembers it as one of the most intense experiences of his life. 'Even with all the drugs I took that night – and everyone was just so fucked up it was a joke – I remember clearly virtually every minute of it. The queue went all the way round the block, until the end of it was where the start was. They said that there were 14,000 people in the club through the twenty-four hour period, which I can believe. There was no space, it was just people solidly jammed in. I'd never experienced so many people. It was a wicked night. But then afterwards New York was empty for us, there was no more. It was very much like your best friend dying.'

For some people, it *was* their best friend dying. The Paradise Garage had hosted the first ever fund-raising event for victims of a disease that was then called 'gay cancer', on 8 April 1982. By the time the club closed, more than 30,000 Americans had been diagnosed with AIDS, and over 20,000 of these had died.[13] But mere numbers cannot convey what was being lost: friends, lovers, many of the people who laid down the roots of the club culture we now enjoy, people who would still be part of it now if they had survived. Michael Brody became another of those sad statistics on 28 December, two months after the Garage closed. Richard Long was already dead. Keith Haring was to die in 1990.

As for Larry Levan, perhaps he knew he could never get that communion with a crowd again. He was, says Mel Cheren, 'a king without a kingdom'. The soaring soul voices and messages of brotherly love that had powered his sound were fading in the face of samplers and programmed beats. Inspired by the music coming out of Chicago and Detroit, Brooklyn-based DJ Todd Terry was starting to make fast, abrasive, sample-based records which mirrored the more edgy, aggressive mood on the dancefloors. Meanwhile, Levan became so unreliable that promoters found it hard to book him. He was sacked from The World club in New York in 1988 after playing the Jackson Five's 'ABC' three times in a row, while screaming at the indifferent crowd for not dancing. He was found asleep in the DJ booth at Trax on another night, in a pool of his own vomit.

Friends began to view his actions as a kind of slow, deliberate suicide. They would see his records being sold on second-hand stalls in the street, and buy them back for him only to have him sell them again to buy drugs days later. 'Larry was adventurous, he was daring, he was a risk-taker,' says Frankie Knuckles. 'He was very, very funny. He was always the odd man out, but he had something about him that automatically drew people to him. He was a dark character, but even today when you go to clubs and listen to the music a lot of young kids are into, they gravitate towards dark sounds, feelings, moods. People were just drawn to Larry like a magnet. He liked the drugs. He liked to play with them. It was a part of what he did. I don't think he ever gave a second thought to the residual effects it could have on him, and that was his downfall.'

Knuckles recalls a night in 1992, when Levan turned up to his Friday residency at the Sound Factory Bar. Former Loft baby David Morales was there too, and they all stood in the booth, playing records and having a ball. 'Larry said, "I'm really proud of you and what you've done with your life. I hope you use what I've done with my life as an example of what not to do." That was a deep statement to make, and I didn't know how to take it – I still don't.

'He said I'd played around with everything, the same drugs as he did, but I'd never got caught up with anything but the music itself. If he had it all to live over again, he'd try to follow my example. But then he said, "Knowing me, I'd still be doing the same thing that I'm doing." '

Larry Levan died on 8 November 1992, just after a successful two-month tour of Japan. Too weak to survive an operation on an injured hip, he died of endocarditis, an inflammation of the lining of the heart that was exacerbated by his excessive drug use. He was thirty-eight.

Mel Cheren still has his remains. He talks about buying back the building in King Street, and restoring it to its former glory, perhaps initially as the set for a film about the club. But then he'd like to install the DJ's ashes in pride of place, throw open the doors, and let the crowd bring it to life again. It's a lovely idea, but it's hard to recreate former glories, especially when they revolved so completely around the creativity of one man and a moment in time, an innocence that is long gone. 'He was very special,' says Cheren. 'He was a genius. I miss him a great deal. So many people do. But you have to go on and keep things going.'

'I miss it and I miss him very much,' adds David DePino. 'It was just like going over the rainbow. Every Saturday night.'[14]

HOUSE MUSIC
ALL NIGHT LONG

3

June 1986. I'm in a studio in Chicago watching the re-recording of Marshall Jefferson's US club hit 'Move Your Body', a track so popular in the clubs of his native city that is has more than earned its alternative title of 'The House Music Anthem'. Local dance labels Trax and DJ International have both found ways to release it, and now it is being re-made in a bigger studio before coming out in Britain.

Frankie Knuckles and Ron Hardy, two of the biggest DJs on the Chicago house scene, are in the control room watching. In the live area, a group of Jefferson's work-mates from the post office are laying down the vocals over a pounding piano riff and a simple, repetitive four-on-the-floor synthesised drum beat. *'Gotta have house music all night long/ With that house music, you can't go wrong/ Give me that house music to set me free/ Lost in house music is where I want to be!'*

Meanwhile Lewis Pitzele, a loud man in a louder Hawaiian shirt who was selling balloons in the street before becoming vice-president of DJ International, is talking incessantly on the phone. Other faces from the house scene have come to hang out too: DJ International's twenty-year-old recording artist and A&R consultant Chip E and Harri Dennis, the vocalist on The It's hypnotic, moaning dance mantra 'Donnie'. Harri is wearing a dog collar and chain and his hair spiked punk-style, which is causing Chicago's man of the moment untold agony.

'Aw God, I wish I could look weird like that!' Jefferson wails, fishing out a little nappy pigtail from under his standard Afro for my inspection. 'My girlfriend said I should grow this so I'd look more like a recording artist.

Does it make me look cool?' He is wearing a black heavy metal T-shirt. I am starting to realise that this is not ironic.

Jefferson has decided to video this, his first interview. Everyone else is trying to persuade me to let them sample my cute English accent. I have been flown to Chicago to write a feature for *The Face* magazine because London Records are about to release the first UK compilation of house tracks from DJ International. People are going out of their way to be helpful and friendly, but I'm still confused.

I've listened to the tracks that are about to come out on the British compilation. Sparse, electronic tracks based around a simple but hypnotic programmed drum beat, a synthesised bassline and often little more on top of this than a repeated sample, a whispered voice or a few soul diva vocals, I'm finding them oddly addictive.

The music seems made for dancing, but I've yet to visit a club that plays it. I've been taken to the Limelight, a club in a deconsecrated church that is even more sterile and soulless than its London counterpart. I've been taken to a black tie chrome-and-carpet disco to watch man-mountain Darryl Pandy unleash his even bigger gospel-trained holler on-stage to a largely indifferent audience.

A series of DJs and artists have been brought to my hotel for brief interviews in which all of them contradict each other and claim to have created the house scene themselves. I've been told that DJ International have signed Kahlid, a fourteen-year-old dreadlocked busker who they are going to mould into their own Michael Jackson; a punkette called Screaming Rachel; Greek and Hispanic pop bands; the Chicago Bears football star William 'Refrigerator' Perry; Salsoul disco diva Loleatta Holloway; a local rap crew; and so many others that they can't quite recall the names, instead giving me a sheaf of publicity pictures so that I can see what they look like.

Now one of Marshall Jefferson's vocalists is trying to convince me that Chicago has its own version of rapping designed specifically to pull in the ladies that is called roping. Everyone seems to be making it up as they go along, jostling for position to ensure that if this thing takes off, they'll be along for the ride. But I still feel I'm no closer to understanding what the house scene actually *is*.

After the singers finish their vocals, they too crowd into the control room, and it seems as good a time as any to drop the question: 'What is house?' There's a brief silence while everyone pauses to consider, and then they all start talking at once.

'It originated in New York, and they don't even know it.'

'Chicago put it on the map, because we didn't have no other music.'

'I couldn't even begin to *tell* you what house is. You have to go to the clubs and see how people react when they hear it. House is more like a feeling that runs through, it's like old-time religion in the way that people just get happy and screaming. It's happening. It's just . . . house!'

'Let me see if I can put it better. It came out of Philly International. It's more like the seventies disco songs in eighties style.'

'It's rock till you drop, that's what it is!'

'All the hippest kids in the city go to CODs and the Music Box. It's a status symbol to party all night at the Music Box. Go there and what you're going to experience is honest-to-goodness, get-down, low-down, gutsy, grabbing-type music. Boom boom boom boom!'

'You'll leave there a changed person. You might go and seek religion afterwards. You're gonna have a great time. It's going to be hot, it's going to be sweaty . . . you're going to love it!'

Later that Thursday night, Frankie Knuckles, ever the gentleman, volunteers to clarify matters by taking me on a tour of Chicago's gay clubs. We start at the more upmarket bars, then pop into a studio to finish mixing a track he's been working on with Chip E and Joe Smooth, whose 'Promised Land' is later to become a house classic. In 1989, Paul Weller's Style Council will take an anaemic version of the song into the UK singles chart. For now, though, Joe is more bothered with another English voice – mine. He gets me to talk breathily into a sampler, listing names of London clubs and exhorting people to dance. He asks me to say, 'Life is strange', and when I ask why, he just smiles inscrutably behind his dark shades. 'Trust me,' he says. For years afterwards, every time I hear a voice that sounds vaguely English distorted through a sampler on a Chicago house record, I wonder if it is mine.

The track complete, our night finally finishes up at a dilapidated warehouse-type building under some railway tracks on Lower Michigan Avenue: the Music Box. It's 5 a.m. by now, but there are still crowds round the door, hoping to get in, listening to tapes in and around their cars. 'Hey Frankie!' a voice yells from a parked car. 'I heard you on the radio last night! You sounded good!'

It takes what seems like an eternity to edge from the entrance up to Ron Hardy's DJ booth. Everyone knows Frankie, and they all want to say hello and shake his hand. Because I'm with him, my presence – the only white face, perhaps also the only female one – passes without comment. To call this dark, dingy club basic would be an understatement. The décor consists of a coat of black paint slapped over bare brick walls. The bar is a tea urn dispensing cold water, surrounded by shirtless youths who have stumbled out of the main room, bug-eyed with exhaustion and dripping with sweat. Crude flyers are taped on to the walls: 'House fever! Let's see the animal in U!' Others remind the regulars of special Sunday-night holiday events. 'No school on Monday!'

The main room is hot as a furnace, making me flinch as we hit the wall of heat, but the scene inside is worth it. It's nearly dawn and the weekend hasn't started yet, but the place is packed. Sweat drips from the ceiling as a sea of bodies jacks up and down to the beat, jumping with hands in the air at a pace that makes the pogo seem like a slow waltz.

The music Ron Hardy is creating on the decks and on the reel-to-reel tape in the booth is equally extraordinary. He mixes Dinosaur L's 1982 New York club hit 'Go Bang' into a treated tape of Aretha Franklin singing her Sixties soul classic 'Respect', then an *a cappella* Latin track leads – unbelievably – into Sade's beigebeat ballad 'Maureen' pitched up on top of a thumping beat without the advanced aerobics on the dancefloor ever slackening. Little more than an hour after it was finished, Frankie puts the track he's mixed on to the reel-to-reel to test it out. The mosh pit under the DJ booth seethes in appreciation.

He takes a look at my face and then grins. 'So now you know about house.'

He was right. And I was hooked.

When Frankie Knuckles moved from New York to Chicago, DJs were a rarity in the city. Most of the clubs used juke-boxes instead, and although Ron Hardy had played at a Northside gay club called Den One in the mid-seventies, he had moved away from the city by the time Knuckles came to play the opening of the Warehouse in March 1977. Initially a series of one-off parties in different venues around the city's warehouse district – hence the name – when they found a permanent venue, the promoters asked Larry Levan to play at the opening. Occupied with the building of the Paradise Garage, Levan recommended his friend instead, and Frankie Knuckles's two-week stint there was such a success that he was asked to stay: not just as a DJ, but as a partner in the club.

He wasn't sure at first, and went back to New York to consider the offer. 'Larry felt it was a market no one had tapped into yet, and I should go and take advantage of it. Being young and stupid, I thought he was trying to get rid of me, get me to move to Chicago so the field would be wide open for himself. But the jobs weren't coming through the way I thought they would, so I figured, "What the hell?" And that move was probably the best thing that ever happened to me.'

The Warehouse was Chicago's first after-hours club, opening at midnight and closing when the last dancers went home on Sunday afternoon. Located in an industrial area on the west side of the city away from any of the other discos and bars, it wasn't aiming to compete but to create something of its own, an underground house party more like the Loft or the Gallery.

'It wasn't a polished atmosphere,' Knuckles recalls. 'The lighting was real simplistic, but the sound system was *intense* and it was about what you heard, not what you saw. We used to do a lot of dancefloor blackouts where you couldn't see your hand in front of your face.'

A small, three-storey building that held about 600 people comfortably, at its peak it would see almost four times that number come and go throughout the night. Free juice, water, sandwiches and munchies were served on banqueting tables on the lower floor, with church pews and couches to sit on. The entrance on the top floor led into a nicely furnished lounge: painted white with comfortable, cushioned sofas, track lighting and house plants, it was designed to be deceptively soothing. At the end of this room was a long, steep stairwell down to the middle dancefloor.

'And that room was *dark*,' laughs Knuckles. 'People would say it was like climbing down into the pit of hell. People would be afraid when they heard the sound thumping through and saw the number of bodies in there just completely locked into the music and everything that was going on. They would say, "I will never come to this place again. You'll *never* get me back into this hell-hole." And then the next week they'd be right back in it. They couldn't resist it.'

The DJ chose his music to be inspirational. 'I was playing all the dance things that were popular at the time, but the voice had to have a nice sound and a message that was more than just "*I met this chick*". Most of the time, it was either really heavy instrumentals or vocals talking about doing something for oneself.' He cites Brooklyn duo D-Train's 1982 hit 'Keep On' as an example: '*I can't let nobody keep me from reaching the top*'.

By 1979, when Larry Levan had his first remix released on vinyl, Knuckles had started to make remixes of his own for the club. As disco gradually died, the records began to dry up and he turned instead to the old Philly and Salsoul records he'd played in New York, re-editing them and making them more up-to-date. A friend called Erasmo Riviera was going to engineering school, and had just learned how to edit and cut tape. Knuckles bought a reel-to-reel tape player, and the two of them would rework records on it, adding new beats and sound effects, making something different every week to drive the crowd wild.

DJs in other cities were doing the same: stripping tracks down, extending the drum breaks, refashioning the raw material they had on record to fit the needs of their crowd. Larry Levan may have been getting most attention for it in New York, but another friend, David Todd, was doing similar things at a gay club called the Catacombs in Philadelphia, and there were others in Detroit and Washington DC. As for Knuckles, 'I wasn't doing anything at that point that other DJs weren't doing elsewhere.'

At the Warehouse, he blended the soaring strings, funky horns and tight rhythm sections of the disco records released by US labels such as Salsoul, Prelude, West End and TK Disco with the more robotic, synthesised dance music coming out of Europe – especially Italy, where dance producers were stubbornly refusing to read the obituaries and accept that disco had died. He also had an ear for the quirky, finding jazz and rock records no one else would have played and making them somehow work in his set.

'Actually mixing from song to song he wasn't the best,' remembers Farley Keith Williams, a young DJ who was later to become better known as Farley 'Jackmaster' Funk. 'But he knew how to put a beautiful set together, whatever it took to drive his crowd crazy. Most of the stuff he played, I would never, *ever* have played. Stuff like the Scatt Brothers' "Walk The Night": hear it and you'd think he had to be an absolute idiot for playing a record like that. But it became one of the biggest, legendary records in the history of early house music.'

It took a while to track down 'Walk The Night', and even longer to decide how to describe it here. Imagine a pounding beat and chanted '*hey*' straight from the Glitter Band. Add rocky guitars. Evil laughs and frightened screams. An eerie male voice threatening violence after dark. Hints of Jamie Principle's 'Baby Wants To Ride'. Now imagine listening to this odd mixture off your head, in the dark, the stereo effects throwing the sound out of different speakers, in that sweaty, crowded room out in the deserted industrial sector of Chicago.

And then there was the train. Old Warehouse regulars still go wide-eyed when they recall the train. Knuckles had an album called *Sound Of A Vanishing Era*, recordings of locomotives made in complete stereo, and he would play it in the club, controlling the speakers so it started at the back of the room and panned down to the front.

'The first time I did it, we had all the lights turned down and no one could see anything. It was pitch black. You could hear the kids out there screaming, because everyone was fucked up [on acid] and when you're high like that and you can't see shit, that just intensifies your high. So they could hear the clanging of the bells faintly in the distance and it got louder and louder until it just came straight through the room. It freaked them all out. Because you really would have thought there was a train coming through and everyone was going to get run over. Right at the end of it we brought the lights up and people were just standing there, their eyes as big as dinner plates. It was so funny.'

Knuckles had told his partners that it would take five years to establish the Warehouse in a city that had no real club culture. In fact, it took him two. By 1980, the club was so fashionable that younger clubbers such as Chip E and Wayne Williams (who was later to record as Dr Derelict) remember trying to act gay, dress gay, even *be* gay to make sure they got in. If they weren't convincing, the music was so loud that they could always hang around and have their own party outside. Club regulars who were high-school teachers started to complain to Knuckles that they couldn't come any more because their students were in there. 'They said that all the kids could talk about in school was last Saturday night and getting ready for the coming Saturday.'

This input of young blood moved the scene to its next level, but it also proved to be the club's downfall. By the end, there was little control of the door. Gang members were getting in, people were being robbed on the dancefloor, and the atmosphere had become ugly. 'They had this open policy of letting anyone and everyone in at that point, so the quality of the crowd had changed,' says Knuckles. 'I realised it was time to move on.'

By then the scene that he had started was spreading across the city's clubs and on to the radio, and it had a name. Clubbers all wanted to hear that mix they played at the 'House. And even after the club closed, it was known as house music.

In 1982, Frankie Knuckles left the Warehouse and started up his own club the Power Plant, catering to an older, more sophisticated crowd. His old venue became a first home for the Music Box, and Ron Hardy came back to the city to play there and take over as king of the underground, toughening up the sound, stripping it down even further to raw, sparse rhythm tracks – and turning up the volume.

'Ron Hardy was just so energetic,' says Marshall Jefferson, who was weaned away from his early love of Yes, Thin Lizzy and Black Sabbath by a visit to the Music Box. 'Frankie played some beautiful stuff, but Ron Hardy would just go berserk. And I mean *berserk*. He was great. And the volume in there . . . whoo! I'd never heard music played at that volume.'

This is a story that will be repeated again and again in this book as the music and the scenes it spawns progress: a split between more sophisticated clubbers and the new young recruits to the culture, between songs, soul and positive lyrics designed to uplift and inspire and a darker, instrumental raw energy that speaks to something deeper, more primal.

The drugs changed too. The Warehouse's spiritual all-nighters were largely fuelled by acid and bags of MDA powder – a similar, if less enjoyable compound to Ecstasy which was common in seventies gay clubs and known as 'the love drug' or 'the Mellow Drug of America'. Now this was replaced by cheaper chemicals more conductive to hyperactive jacking. Apart from the ubiquitous reefer, PCP (phencyclidine, or Angel Dust) and Sherm sticks (cigarettes dipped in formaldehyde) began to help fuel the all-night dancing.

At times, the crowd seemed to transcend physical limits. They would literally climb up the walls. They would fall to the floor, legs thrashing in the air, screaming for Hardy to pump it up more. Nathaniel Pierre Jones, who later made a name for himself as DJ Pierre, vividly remembers his first time at the club, which had by then moved to a venue in an underground car park.

'It was like being baptised into house. It was a different world, the place was real packed and people were dressing different, like in baggy clothes. They wore their hair up and wavy, they wore paisley shirts, satin-type silky pants and riding boots. Ron would play Harold Melvin & the Blue Notes and Loleatta Holloway songs and stuff like that and mix them right in with drum tracks you've never heard, Jamie Principle songs, one after another. You'd see people going crazy, yelling and screaming Ron Hardy's name at the top of their voices . . . He would mess with the EQ and pump the system, and each song he would play for eight or ten minutes. By the time it went off, you'd *feel* that song, you'd know everything about that song, that song would get into us and we would get into it and just allow our minds to go away to anywhere in this world or universe.'[1]

The influence of Europe in all this shouldn't be underestimated. Few of these DJs had travelled (Knuckles didn't own a passport until he first came to Britain in 1986), but throughout the early eighties the music came to them thanks to Imports Etc., a small but influential specialist record shop in Chicago which stocked a wide range of hard-to-find Euro-disco, especially from Italy, and early English synthesiser groups such as Wire, Depeche Mode and DAF.

Farley 'Jackmaster' Funk recalls that punk also had a big impact on black dancers. Billy Idol was massive with the teenage crowd at his club, the Playground, as were the B52s, a quirky, cartoonish new wave band from Athens, Georgia. Young black clubbers would turn up wearing leathers and dyed, spiked hair, and then 'punk out' or pogo to

Italian disco or the Peech Boys – the dance that was later called jacking. Partly – but only partly – because of their name, Frankie Goes To Hollywood were later huge in the city's black clubs. (Monie Love's 'Grandpa's Party' was to become an unlikely club hit in Chicago for similar reasons. Instead of singing '*grandpa's party*' on the chorus, the crowd would chant along, '*It's Ron Hardy!*')

The new technology that was starting to appear on the records also began moving into the DJ booths. Drum machines, keyboards and samplers began to sit alongside the turntables and reel-to-reel tape players to augment the mix, and more and more of the music played started to come from the DJs and clubbers themselves.

In 1980, the Technics 1200 decks were launched out of Japan with an excellent pitch control that was probably first designed so that the key of records could be changed to enable karaoke singers to croon in tune. For DJs, however, it allowed more control over the sound of a record than ever before. (These turntables are still pretty much standard club issue today.) Two years later, Roland released their TB303 Bassline, a reasonably priced box little bigger than this book that was designed to help solo pub performers and learner guitarists, allowing them to create a bassline to play along to. It failed to catch on and was deleted in 1985, making it available cheaply second-hand. This and the relatively cheap drum machines Roland had been putting out since 1979, especially the equally compact TR808, were to be used in ways their creators in Japan could never have imagined.

'We started experimenting, playing with drum machines,' recalls Farley. 'Jesse Saunders was on board with me at the Playground at that time, and he was a musician. In the early days, a kick drum and the electric tom-toms of the 808 was enough to make people dance without even putting any music to it. So a lot of the stuff was just beat tracks in the beginning. Then we came to steal everybody's basslines. See, all we ever did was regurgitate disco again by just stealing everybody's music. Because all the original house stuff that came out was somebody else's bassline.'

But when drum and bass patterns once played by skilled musicians were copied on cheap synths that sounded little like the real instruments, they didn't seem old or stolen. Stripped of their songs, these recycled riffs sounded alien and new, like raw, minimal messages transmitted from another world.

The sound was also spreading via the radio. Farley was one of the Hot Mix Five, a multi-racial team of turntable virtuosos whose two-hour mix slot at 10 p.m. on Fridays and Saturdays on WBMX had developed a massive following in the city since its launch in 1980. By the mid-eighties, up to half a million listeners were said to tune in at some point to the mix shows on this and rival station WCGI – a sixth of the city's population.

At first these mixes were kept fairly commercial, but as the shows grew in popularity, the DJs began throwing in some of the music they'd been hearing in the underground clubs, making their own tracks with drum machines and playing an increasing number of home-made tracks handed to them on tape by clubbers. The mixes became a focus for the house scene, and as a result the insistent, programmed kick drum beat that underlined the music became known locally as 'Farley's foot' – the only black DJ in the Hot Mix Five, he says he tended to get more of the credit.

The mixes were taped from the radio and played again and again, along with the even more highly prized tapes of club sets by Frankie Knuckles and Ron Hardy. 'Somehow their tapes got all over the city,' recalls Marshall Jefferson. 'Kids copied them hundreds, thousands of times over. You would get a Ron Hardy tape that had been copied 400 times. The quality would be horrible. Ron would make a lot of money that way, making tapes. I remember once, someone asked him for a tape and Ron said, "Yes, for $45." When the guy questioned it, Ron said it was worth $75. He had that kind of ego. It was really funny.'

It was only a matter of time before tracks started to appear on vinyl, although there is some confusion as to who actually came first. Some say it was Z Factor, a group centred around Jesse Saunders' friend Vince Lawrence, but their records were fairly pedestrian electro-pop influenced by the lush, polished synth sounds favoured by Frankie Goes To Hollywood's producer Trevor Horn. Others support the claims of Byron Walton, a shy young man with a passion for Depeche Mode and the Human League who claimed that Prince was the only black artist he ever listened to. Experimenting at home with a four-track Portastudio and a synthesiser, under the alias of Jamie Principle he produced 'Your Love' and 'Waiting On My Angel', tracks which were played on tape in the clubs by Frankie Knuckles for some time before they were finally released on vinyl. Clubbers knew them so well that they'd sing along from the dancefloor, and it became a status symbol for other DJs to own a copy on cassette.

But probably the strongest claim is for a simple, synthesised rhythm track released by Jesse Saunders on his own JesSay label in January 1984. The story goes that Jesse had his record box stolen. His signature tune was the B-side of a bootleg megamix, a groove track made of repetitive loops from Lipps Inc's 'Funkytown' and Donna Summer's 'Bad Girls' that his crowd would clap along to. He went into the studio to remake it using an 808, a 303 and a small Korg synthesiser, adding a voice-over to create 'On And On'.

The record may have been basic but it sold well, and others were quick to spot the potential in the local club market. Larry Sherman, a businessman who owned the city's only pressing plant and who had made a good living supplying many of Chicago's juke boxes with new records until DJ culture took over, saw the quantities Jesse Saunders was pressing and quickly set up his own Trax label to release similar material.

Jamie Principle's songs had needed real musicianship, but everyone felt they could do a percussion doodle like 'On And On'. These drum and bass patterns were called 'tracks' since they hardly qualified as finished records or songs. Often pressed on recycled vinyl, the poor sound quality only added to their rawness. No one seriously envisaged that they were creating a whole new music here: their aim was simply to get a track played by their favourite DJ, and perhaps make a little money on the side.

Chip Eberhardt was typical of the new wave of entrepreneurial producers. He became DJ Chip E while still at high school, with guest spots at the Music Box and the Playground, but he didn't get big enough quick enough. A spell behind the counter at Imports Etc. had convinced him that he could make records as good as some of the product he was selling, so he sold his turntables and spent the money in the studio laying down some rhythm tracks. He could only afford a single test pressing of the record, but he knew who to give it to: Kenny Jason from the Hot Mix Five.

'He played it immediately. Then Farley took it and it gained a lot of popularity from that. So by the time I had my first thousand pressed – I borrowed my mother's income tax cheque – we sold 500 in one day, the rest within a week. I ordered another 3,000 and we sold them in a week too. That was the "Jack Trax" EP.'

That summer, local record pool manager Rocky Jones decided to help one of his DJs, Steve 'Silk' Hurley, put out a track he'd recorded with singer Keith Nunally under the name JM Silk. When the first pressing of 'Music Is The Key' sold out, Rocky knew he was on to something big. He drove his hot-rod Corvette over to the pressing plant and gave the car to Larry Sherman in exchange for 10,000 more copies. The DJ International label was born.

These tracks, and the music they have since inspired, are so familiar now that it's easy to forget how startlingly, shockingly new they sounded back in the mid-eighties. But fresh as they sounded, they were assembled from second-hand parts. Just as hip hop in New York used DJs' mixing skills and the new sampling technology to create new music out of old funk sounds, so house rose from the remnants of disco.

The anti-disco backlash that had stirred across America finally reached its peak with a bizarre stunt that took place in Chicago in July 1979. The crowd attending a White Sox baseball double-header were invited by local radio personality Steve Dahl to bring along all their unwanted disco records. After piling hundreds of them in centre field at Comiskey Park after the first game, the DJ had set them alight while leading a chant of 'Disco sucks! Disco sucks!' A mini-riot ensued, parts of the ground were destroyed, and the second game had to be cancelled. The Altamont of disco, to many it signalled the end of an era.

But despite this meltdown, disco never died in the Windy City – it just got eaten alive. The pioneers of the house sound ripped the music apart, cannibalised whatever they needed and assembled it into something new. So Chip E's early club hit 'Like This' was based on an old Paradise Garage favourite, 'Moody' by ESG. Farley 'Jackmaster' Funk's 'Love Can't Turn Around' was a reworking of Isaac Hayes' 'I Can't Turn Around'. Most plundered of all was 'Let No Man Put Asunder' by First Choice, a 1983 Salsoul track championed by Frankie Knuckles.

The label had thoughtfully provided an *a cappella* version on the twelve-inch for DJs to mix with. 'When samplers came out, "Let No Man Put Asunder" got dogged,' laughs Farley. 'It was *barking* by the time it got through getting sampled!'

Vincent Montana, producer of the Salsoul Orchestra and vibes player for MSFB, had voiced his disquiet about the then-new fad of remixing at a disco forum held by the US music trade magazine *Billboard* in the late seventies: 'Making a record is like playing chess; you can have your moves all mapped out, and then an outside mixer comes in and destroys your plan.'

A few years later in Chicago, the game had moved off the chessboard altogether, and the pieces were being used for an entirely different game. Listening now to a compilation of mid-seventies disco tracks from a label like Salsoul is an unsettling experience, like looking at a picture you've always viewed through a prism, and seeing it whole for the first time. All the familiar elements of early house are there, but in the wrong places. Here are all the basslines, the drum patterns we danced to in 1988. There's the '*o-oh yeah*' Todd Terry was to sample on 'Can U Party'. There's the '*burning*' squeal from Nitro Deluxe's 'This Brutal House'. And there, on Loleatta Holloway's soaring 'Love Sensation', are all those glorious vocals you'd later hear on Black Box's 'Ride On Time', but in a different order.

It was only later that sampling started to be seen as theft, and that debates over copyright started to rage. For now, no one cared: few of the people making this music in Chicago were getting paid anyway, and all of them now ruefully tell their own tales of rip-offs and exploitation. Marshall Jefferson and his friend Michael Smith (who recorded as Adonis) would sit around dreaming, convincing themselves that someday the world would sit up and listen to what they were doing. But for now, an appreciative audience in a local club was enough.

Jefferson's story shows how the early house artists were liberated by the new technology they had discovered. Inspired by Ron Hardy's sounds at the Music Box, he'd spent a small fortune on equipment, working the all-night graveyard shift at the post office to pay for it. Since he couldn't actually play any of it, this was a cause of great hilarity to his friends. But the beauty of this equipment was that you didn't *need* musical skills. You didn't need a great soul voice or a full orchestra. You just needed ideas.

Jefferson made his first record within days: simple 808 drum patterns that came out as 'Go Wild Rhythm Tracks' by Virgo. Signing to Trax, he began to produce a prolific number of club hits under different aliases, and after 'Move Your Body' came out a year later with its distinctive piano riff, dance producers all over the States were reputed to be hiring pianists who could play like Marshall Jefferson.

Except he couldn't play. And it wasn't even a real piano.

'Back then, I'd play everything slowed down. If I had a song at 120 bpm [beats per minute], I would record it at 40 bpm so it would be playing real slow. If I couldn't play a whole chord, I'd do one note at a time and stand them on top of each other. Then I'd add it all together and speed it up. Byron from Ten City used to say to me, "Man, I've learned not to mess with you when you're doing something, because it sounds really fucked up, and you're the only one that knows where it's going. I know you're going to come through with something good, but when you start, it's real shady!" '

In bedroom studios throughout Chicago, youths inspired by the sounds they'd heard in the clubs and on the radio were doing the same. Parties were going off all over the city by now: in houses, in school gyms, even in the street, as well as in the clubs. Louis Sims, who DJed under the name Lil Louis, was attracting up to 8,000 clubbers at his monthly parties at the Hotel Bismark. House fever was blowing through the Windy City at gale force.

By 1986 the trickle of records had turned into a deluge. As Mr Fingers, producer Larry Heard introduced fresh, jazzier directions into the music. The records were also becoming more vocal, with some of the city's gospel-trained voices emerging as new soul divas. Marshall Jefferson's friends were no longer laughing. He couldn't make it to the Music Box because of his job at the post office, but his friend Sleazy D would take his tracks down and tell him how often Ron Hardy was playing them. What Sleazy hadn't mentioned was that he'd been telling everyone that *he* had made the records so he could get in free: when Jefferson finally did get to the club, he was astonished to hear the DJ playing nothing but his tracks for a two-hour stretch. 'I was flipping. And people were going crazy, shouting "Sleazy! Sleazy!" '

After the confusion had been cleared up, Jefferson made a track with Sleazy D called 'I've Lost Control' to help him keep face, a track that is now remembered for its inventive use of the Roland TB 303 bass box. Jefferson also went on to work with his mentor. Ron Hardy was to die from an AIDS-related illness in 1992, but he also had a drug problem that may have contributed to the intensity with which he played his music. 'He was into heroin,' says Jefferson. 'He didn't think he was an addict though, because he didn't shoot it up – he snorted it.'

On one recording session, the DJ chopped out some lines of white powder which the engineer, a cokehead, decided to jump in and sample without asking. The engineer spent the rest of the session laid out on a sofa, groaning. Jefferson, meanwhile, calmly took the opportunity to learn his way round a mixing desk.

As the scene intensified, so did the internal rivalries. Different people would claim credit for the same track. Friends ripped off each other's ideas. Farley Keith Williams and Steve Hurley, once best friends and flatmates, fell out over who should use the name 'Jackmaster'. Farley freely admits that the feud spilled over into the music: he may have had the hit with 'Love Can't Turn Around', but the original version was by Steve's group JM Silk. There were even stories of master tapes being stolen from studios and homes, and in one case, from the back of a car. British A&R men like Pete Tong remember the business dealings there as decidedly dodgy. 'You would make an agreement on the phone one night, you'd leave the office at ten at night, and you'd come in the next day to find a fax saying they'd changed their mind and had sold it to someone else.'

By July 1986, the Chicago house scene was ready to break out. DJ International did a showcase at the New Music Seminar in New York, an annual conference that had become a clearing house for new dance music, the place where many deals with British record companies were first brokered. The sound was already trickling into cutting-edge dance clubs across the States, and being played by a handful of DJs overseas. Influential dance producer Arthur Baker had produced a homage to the music in a track called 'Chicago', and as early as 1985 New York singer Colonel Abrams had taken a watered-down version of the sound into the charts with 'Trapped' – a record that was to influence the polished, high-energy pop-dance confections produced by Britain's Stock, Aitken and Waterman. During the Seminar, Frankie Knuckles returned to the club where he started as a DJ, hosting a house night at Better Days in New York and giving the industry a chance to experience the real thing first hand.

Pete Tong was an ambitious young graduate of the suburban soul scene in the south of England, with a show on Capital Radio, an A&R job at London Records and a growing reputation as a club DJ. He was excited by the music, and also keen to find something new to introduce to the UK dance market. Island Records had recently enjoyed club success by signing up most of the funk-oriented Washington go-go scene. Sony had just pulled off the coup of signing a UK distribution deal with the entire Def Jam hip hop label. Determined not to be beaten again, he was quick to pick up on house, making London Records the first to bring the music into the UK charts.

With soaring gospel vocals from Darryl Pandy, Farley 'Jackmaster' Funk's 'Love Can't Turn Around' was the first UK hit for the real Chicago sound, reaching number ten in September 1986. A few months later, Farley's rival Steve 'Silk' Hurley got the first number one. With a bassline taken straight from 'Let No Man Put Asunder' and little else except a hypnotic beat and a distinctive, stuttering sample, JM Silk's 'Jack Your Body' topped the UK charts in January 1987. It was hard to see how the DJ could perform it on *Top of the Pops,* so they showed the video, a hastily-made collage of old black-and-white cartoons taken from a film library and cut up to match the beat. Because of the difficulty in finding many of the artists at short notice, Pete Tong says the video was re-edited and used to promote two further records afterwards. Later still, his label made a video for Lil Louis' 'French Kiss' using wind-up toys.

A few months later, the Chicago House Party toured British clubs, a PA package featuring Adonis, Marshall Jefferson and Larry's Heard's group with singer Robert Owens, Fingers Inc. The Chicagoans found UK clubbers overdressed and reserved after the abandon of the US gay clubs. Asking to see the underground, they were taken to the Wag club in Soho and left distinctly unimpressed. British clubbers were similarly bemused. This was not music designed to be performed live, and both their clothes and the clumsy, cabaret-style presentation seemed terminally uncool in contrast to some of the hip hop acts who were travelling over at the time.

By then, the Chicago underground had already moved on. While Marshall Jefferson and Frankie Knuckles were returning to the music's roots, recording with real string sections and exploring the lush, soulful sound that became known as deep house, a new, rawer sound was emerging from those samplers and synths.

Marshall Jefferson went into the studio with DJ Pierre, a youth from the suburbs who had made his reputation as a DJ at the Lil Louis parties. Jefferson was credited as producer, although he says he did little more than turn on the tape. Most of the music was by Pierre, who'd found a new way of using Roland's 303 bassline machine. The resonant filter knobs were designed to be turned slightly to alter the tones of the bass. However, if you twisted them rapidly in a way they were never intended to be abused, the oddest squelching sound came out. Along with his friends Earl 'Spanky' Smith and Herb Jackson, Pierre had decided to use this noise – a noise he discovered by accident, he says, 'while we were trying to figure out how to use it' – as the basis for a track.

'I thought it was fucking brilliant!' enthuses Jefferson. 'Everyone thought I was nuts, but every time my friends said something was whack, I'd go ahead with it. That's how I was at the time. If they didn't like it, I knew it was cool.'

The sound was a weird one indeed, but also wonderful, tearing a new strand of house away from its disco roots and into something far more left-field and experimental. When they took it down to the Music Box, Ron Hardy played it four times in one night. The crowd were startled at first, but they grew to love it. In fact, the DJ continued to play it so often that many of the dancers assumed the track was his.

There are many stories as to how the record got its title. Trax boss Larry Sherman says it was because it reminded him of the psychedelic rock he heard in Vietnam. The story I like most is that clubbers named the track after a rumour that the water in that urn at the Music Box was sometimes spiked to make the night go with more of a swing. The group themselves say they were going to call it 'In Your Mind' until a friend played them a tape of Ron Hardy's set and told them the name they used for the track on the dancefloor.

Eventually, in 1987, it came out on an EP on Trax under the name Phuture. However it was chosen, Pierre came to regret the record's title and still maintains it was taken out of context. He has always been anti-drugs, and there's a track on the same EP, 'Your Only Friend', that is explicitly against cocaine. But however it was meant, the title and the sound helped define a generation. It was 'Acid Trax'.

MACHINE SOUL

'It's not beautiful or anything. It's strange when we come back here, because it's like home, but without the comforts. There's nothing much happening in the evenings or at the weekends. Nothing ever happens. *You have to make your own culture. We don't believe in music written on paper, we go out to the discothèque all the time and dance.'*

Kraftwerk's Ralph Hütter on his home town of Düsseldorf[1]

'This city is in total devastation. It is going through the biggest change in its history. Detroit is passing through its third wave, a social dynamic which nobody outside this city can understand. Factories are closing, people are drifting away, and kids are killing each other for fun. The whole order has broken down. If our music is the soundtrack to that, I hope it makes people understand what kind of disintegration we're dealing with.'

Derrick May on his home town of Detroit[2]

Detroit was a boom city that grew up rapidly around the automobile factories of Ford, Olds, Chevrolet and the Dodge brothers, a magnet for workers wanting to earn good money on the production lines and who played as hard as they worked. In the thirties and forties, the city had a lively nightlife built around jazz and blues, illegal drinking shops called blind pigs and multi-racial clubs known as black and tans.

This was the energy former Ford worker Berry Gordy Jnr tapped into when he set up his own production line in 1959, building a studio in the basement of his home at 2648 West Grand Boulevard and starting his Tamla Motown label. With a combination of sweet soul vocals, gospel handclaps, irresistible choruses and a stomping 4/4 beat, Motown put black performers into the pop mainstream and changed the face of modern music. Some of the greatest music ever made was created in that basement: the Temptations, the Four Tops, the Supremes, Smoky Robinson, Stevie Wonder, Marvin Gaye and the Jackson Five all recorded in the studio, which operated seven days a week, twenty-four hours a day.

But not everything in Detroit was as harmonious as Motown's backing vocals. The car factories treated its workers as mere cogs in the machinery, there to be discarded when times got tough. In July 1967, unemployment was high, and the tension was increased by police shootings of two black women. When a blind pig was raided during a party to welcome home a black Vietnam veteran, the anger boiled over into one of the bloodiest riots in America's history. By the time paratroopers were brought in to restore order three days later, more than forty people were dead and over 1,300 buildings had been destroyed, leaving scars on the city that have yet to heal. Afterwards, wrote Ze'ev Chafets in *Devil's Night*, the city went 'in one generation from a wealthy white industrial giant to a poverty-stricken black metropolis'.[3]

The oil crises and then increased competition from Japan have continued the decline of the car industry. Parts of Detroit's city centre have never been rebuilt after the riots, with tracts of urban wasteland still littered with burned-out, derelict shells. Most of the remaining white population subsequently moved out to the suburbs. In 1972 Motown moved too, shifting its base to Los Angeles where it began signing white artists for the first time and blanding out in the sun.

Detroit was frequently portrayed in the media as a war zone, the murder capital of America. The city seemed to be in permanent financial crisis, forever teetering on the edge of bankruptcy. As its mayor once declared, 'We are at the edge of an abyss.' Even now the city centre is eerily empty at night and dead at weekends, every attempt at resuscitation failing. Some of the newer buildings on the waterfront may look impressive, but the shops and restaurants inside are sad and desolate.

There was nothing to do in Detroit, nowhere to go. But there was the Electrifyin' Mojo. From 10 p.m. to 3 a.m. every night from April 1977, DJ Charles Johnson launched his *Midnight Funk Association* over the airwaves of Detroit. Five hours a night, every night, he transformed himself into the god-like Mojo, playing without any regard to the normal radio formats and musical pigeonholes and making deep pronouncements about the future that sent his younger fans scurrying for their dictionaries.

Mojo played the Clash, Marvin Gaye, the B52s, Peter Frampton, Madonna, and Devo. He played the hard-edged, futuristic P-funk failed Motown songwriter George Clinton was creating for his bands Parliament and Funkadelic in Detroit's famed United Sound studios, disguising his sharp political comments behind humour and a mock-futuristic language involving Afronauts and Motherships from space. Mojo played James Brown and Jimi Hendrix, the Yellow Magic Orchestra and Tangerine Dream, European synth-pop, strange sound effects and the music to *Star Wars*. He played Prince, who liked the DJ so much that he once called up for a chat on air. He chose an album a week and played it all, even doing remixes and new edits on the tracks so that the listeners got into it more deeply.

Like George Clinton, Mojo transcended restrictions of race and genre by claiming he didn't come from this planet at all: 'He had this great intro about the Mojo coming down from space in the Mother-ship to save Detroit and the world from musical blah,' says Juan Atkins, one of many young fans who stayed up late on a school night, taking in a different kind of education from the radio.

'He definitely was a major force,' adds Kevin Saunderson, who saw Mojo as a lifeline after he moved to Michigan from New York City and its thriving disco mix shows. 'I don't know if he knows how important he was to this day.'

But as well as Mojo, the story of techno is also a story about determined mothers, strong black women who wanted something better for their kids and worked hard to move out to the leafy, middle-class suburb of Belleville, a forty-five-minute drive away from the decaying centre of Detroit. Derrick May and Aaron Atkins were the odd ones out in their class at Belleville High School, former city kids in what felt like the middle of the country, and they soon became friends.

Derrick also got to know Aaron's older brother Juan, an introspective youth who spent a lot of time twiddling with his keyboards and tape machines. Obsessed with theories about the future, Juan had taken a class on Future Studies in high school which introduced him to the ideas of Alvin Toffler. Juan was an optimist. If Detroit was already a post-industrial city, then he felt that surely it would be at the forefront of the revolution Toffler predicted in his book *The Third Wave*. Liberated from the production lines, the city's residents would pioneer information technology, explore the new possibilities offered by the computer.

Toffler had written about 'techno rebels'. Juan set about becoming one. By the mid-seventies, the new synthesisers were there for all to hear. There was the pounding, insistent beat Munich-based producer Giorgio Moroder had placed under American singer Donna Summer on 'Love To Love You Baby' in 1975, a record that revolutionised disco, quickly making large groups of musicians like Philly's MFSB or the Salsoul Orchestra unnecessary. Juan remembers hearing this and the even more epic, orgasmic 'I Feel Love' two years later, and starting to hang out in the music stores in Detroit, playing with the equipment. As soon as the Japanese began launching products that were more affordable, he bought a little Korg keyboard that he used to work on crude home demos, dubbing from one cassette deck to another.

Then, on Mojo's show one night, he heard Kraftwerk. 'I just froze in my tracks. Everything was so clean and precise, so robotic. That's what blew me away. Because I had no access to that kind of sequencer technology, I didn't even know it existed. There weren't any at that time that were affordable for a regular musician.'

After graduating, he studied music at community college and met a student called Richard Davies, an alienated, slightly strange Vietnam veteran eleven years older than him who shared the same visions about synthesised sound, the future and Alvin Toffler's books. For no reason he ever shared with Juan, Davies used the alias 3070, and the two of them began recording together as Cybertron. Mixing Kraftwerk, P-Funk, and ideas taken from science fiction and *The Third*

Wave, they pioneered a futuristic, funky strain of electro that still sounds fresh today but when it was first made must have sounded like it had beamed in from another planet. Mojo loved it, of course.

Kraftwerk came out of the cultural void that existed in Germany after the war. They grew up in a country where the cinemas showed films from France and Italy, and the radio played English and American pop. Ralph Hütter and Florian Schneider were part of an art-inspired movement in the late sixties which aimed to create something distinctively German once more. The past was tainted, so Kraftwerk looked to the future: rejecting their classical training, they used synthesisers to create electronic soundscapes inspired by industrial noise, by motorways and fast trains. Their influence on the British electronic bands that evolved out of punk – groups like Throbbing Gristle and Cabaret Voltaire – was immediately clear. It took a little longer before their equally powerful effect on black American music was noticed.

Cybertron's first record, 'Alleys Of Your Mind', came out in 1981, selling 10,000 copies locally. That year in New York, Afrika Bambaataa and the Soul Sonic Force worked with producer Arthur Baker to lay the melody of Kraftwerk's 1977 hit 'Trans-Europe Express' over the rhythm of a later track, 'Numbers'. The result was the eerie, extended groove of 'Planet Rock' – the record that took hip hop from the era of early rappers like the Sugarhill Gang dressing in dinner jackets to rhyme '*brag and boast*' with '*breakfast toast*' and into the far stranger soundscapes of electro. 'I don't think they even knew how big they were among the black masses back in '77 when they came out with "Trans-Europe Express",' Bambaataa told hip hop historian David Toop. 'When that came out, I thought that was one of the best and weirdest records I ever heard in my life.'[4]

After making his first record in the cultural vacuum of Detroit, unaware that anyone else was pursuing similar ideas, Juan Atkins first heard 'Planet Rock' on a trip to New York. 'It was a very bittersweet type of thing, seeing something along the lines of what I was doing go national like that.' Cybertron continued to record, but it would be years before anything they did would be acknowledged outside of Detroit.

Derrick May had been listening to standard radio fare like Elton John and the Who until he heard the raw-edged, futuristic P-funk of George Clinton's Parliament and Funkadelic on Mojo's show. Later Juan Atkins gave him a tape of English electro-pop acts such as Gary Numan, which turned him on to the possibilities of electronic music. He began helping Juan make extended mixes for Mojo's radio show, using two copies of the same record and a cassette recorder with a pause button. His friend Kevin Saunderson began to hang out with them too, although he says he did more watching than participating.

Kevin had moved to Belleville from Brooklyn with his mother when he was eleven. After New York, the suburb was a culture shock. It was green, leafy, clean. There was space between the houses, and no action and noise on the streets. It was also mainly white, and for the first time in his life, he was taunted due to the colour of his skin. At school he was immediately drawn to Derrick May, another city kid who also shared his aspirations to be a professional football player. They got so close that when Derrick's mother moved to Chicago in their last year at school, he went to live with the Saundersons so that he could stay at Belleville High and keep his place in the football team.

In the long summer school breaks, Kevin would go back to New York to stay with his father and older brothers. His brother Ronnie was involved in the disco scene: he wrote a song for Brass Construction, and worked as a road manager for them, Skyy and BT Express. Kevin had some serious facial hair by the age of thirteen which made him look much older, so when Ronnie and his cousins went out dancing, he went too.

The first club he ever went to was the Paradise Garage: up that long ramp and through the doors into disco wonderland. Later, there was the Loft. David Mancuso had thrown away his mixer by then, and was simply playing carefully selected records, one after the other, with pauses so the crowd could applaud. The sound system was carefully tuned to offer perfect reproduction of what the musicians had intended, the stylus hand-crafted by a Japanese samurai sword-maker. Kevin says he heard some *serious* music there, weird stuff like Cerrone's synthesised disco. Later still, at the Zanzibar in New Jersey, he saw DJ Tony Humphries take up the torch the Garage had lit. 'I was getting educated in the music, and I was falling in love with it. I came in the right way. Once I'd seen all that, I didn't expect anything less.'

Going back to Chicago to visit his mother, Derrick May was also experiencing some intense clubbing. He heard the mix shows there, went to the Power Plant and the Music Box, and after high school the hyperactive youth settled in the city for a while and got to know all the big DJs. 'I think the reason I progressed in dance music or have done the things that I've done is that I had the chance to see a little bit of the future – gay black kids, straight black kids, everybody just going for it.'[5]

It was Derrick who sold Frankie Knuckles his first TR909 drum machine, which was incorporated into the set-up in the DJ booth at the Power Plant and later loaned to Chip E and others when they made their first house records. Later, Frankie was to repay the favour by playing Derrick's records in his clubs and even giving one of his classic tunes its title: 'Strings Of Life'.

Derrick eventually returned to Detroit with tapes of the mix shows to play his friends, fired up to make something happen. There were no clubs in the city comparable to the Paradise Garage or the Music Box, no mix shows like Chicago's Hot Mix Five or the Kiss megamixes in New York. There was, however, a small one-off party scene more like the warehouse scene happening in London at the time: promoters would take over a venue, set up their own decks and sound, and advertise their event by giving out flyers. The crowd usually numbered fewer than a thousand, and even though the flyers optimistically said 'nine until . . .', Juan Atkins says the parties usually broke up around 2 a.m. 'More often than not, we would get the sound cut off on us by the owner of the venue or the police wound up closing it, because we just wouldn't stop.'

To cater for this scene, Juan, Derrick and a few other friends launched their own sound company, Deep Space Soundworks, and also hired themselves out as DJs, playing with three decks, and programming drum machines and later synths into their mix. They billed themselves as 'progressive' and played a lot of Italian disco imports to differentiate themselves from the more mainstream DJ posses in the city.

They also made a few attempts to break into radio. For a while, Derrick blagged them a Chicago-style mix show, *Streetbeat*, taking turns with Juan, Kevin and other friends such as Blake Baxter and

Eddie Fowlkes to create smooth mixes. They were beaten on the ratings by another DJ who sometimes played on the party scene and who would later become a major player in the second wave of Detroit techno. Back then, Jeff Mills favoured a more cut-up, hip hop-based style that the listeners preferred, packing as many different records as he could into his limited time slot – a virtuosity on the turntables that was later to make him the most revered techno DJ in the world, making new music every time he plays in a club from a collection of only about 300 carefully-chosen records.

By the start of 1985, both Derrick and Kevin had built up enough equipment at home to start making records of their own. Cybertron had split due to musical differences; Richard Davies kept the name and made two more albums, although he never attained the same innovative edge alone. Juan Atkins began working with his friends, and all three launched their own labels and began releasing singles under a series of aliases.

Juan recorded on Metroplex as Model 500, a name he chose 'to be as unethnic as possible'. Derrick launched Transmat and recorded as R-Tyme and Rhythim is Rhythim. Kevin went out on KMS under a series of names including Reese. They sold a few records in New York – Tony Humphries played the odd track on his Kiss FM mix show – and Kevin even licensed his first record, 'Triangle Of Love' by Kreem, to a small British label. 'I had no idea what licensing even meant back then. It was only $700, but it was like, "Hey, I made my money back, already!" '

But their main market outside of Detroit was Chicago. They would pile their latest pressings into the car and make the four-hour drive on a weekend, dropping off their new records at Imports Etc. and collecting the cash for anything the shop had sold. Then they'd sit in the car and listen to the Hot Mix Five on the radio, hoping to hear one of the DJs play their tunes, before going to check out the mayhem at the Music Box.

Ron Hardy liked the Detroit sound, but by then Kevin Saunderson says the atmosphere in the club was so fevered that he had to use disco and old tracks to calm the crowd down: 'He couldn't play too many house records in a row, or the club would just explode. For real. People would just go crazy.'

The Detroit boys were constantly blagging and improvising. Promising to pay the pressing plant in thirty days' time, and hoping to sell enough records in the intervening period so that they could. Taking orders for records then borrowing the money so that they could actually get them made. There was no safety net to catch them if they fell, says Derrick May, so they worked hard.

'Every day was a new experience,' remembers Kevin Saunderson. 'You were always learning something new about your equipment, about the business, and all the time people were playing your music and you were getting all these telephone calls. Then we started getting calls from Europe. From 1985 to 1988 was a very fast, unplanned period of learning. And very creative too. We were just doing our thang and not knowing what was ahead of us.'

Chicago was an influence, but the sound they were creating was different. If Chicago was a celebration of dance, of the power of the crowd, Detroit's music was more about alienation and a yearning to overcome. Techno had no soul. Not in the sense of the gospel-derived handclaps and vocals that had informed Motown, the Philly sound that followed it and even the most synthesised of disco tracks. The soul in techno was hidden far deeper, embedded into its circuits, in the spaces between the bass and the beats.

There were few vocals, and even these were deliberately disembodied, whispering, emotionless. Yet paradoxically, the best techno conveyed an intense emotion that connected instantly with the dancefloor and was understood. Derrick May says he cried while making 'Strings Of Life', and even though there is nothing but programmed machines on the sparse, hypnotic track, you can hear it. The basic equipment they were using meant the music had to be kept simple, and the formula has been deceptively easy to imitate. The hidden soul in the machine has proved rather harder to reproduce.

'I want my music to sound like computers talking to each other,' said Derrick May. 'I don't want it to sound like a "real" band. I want it to sound as if a technician made it. That's what I am: a technician with human feelings. This music is like Kraftwerk, the tension between emotion and coldness typified by "Computer Love". I think some of their music is very emotional.'[6]

Kevin Saunderson's best music bore the lush, soulful influence of the music he'd heard in his early teens in New York, but Derrick and Juan weren't interested in the past. They were techno rebels, the vanguard of Alvin Toffler's third wave. For a while, Derrick had a job in one of Detroit's first video game arcades, and their group would spend hours in there, playing the machines: *Pacman, Defender,* and Derrick's particular favourite, *Stargate.* They loved *Tron,* a computer-animated science fiction film about a man trapped within a computer, and saw their lives like a video game, where they too had to overcome all obstacles put in their path. They didn't want to look back. They were the future.

Nonetheless, it was Detroit's past that finally got them noticed. The first real interest in the UK was from another motor city in decline: Birmingham. Neil Rushton was a graduate of Britain's Northern Soul scene who had started releasing British-made house tunes on his label Kool Kat, as well as searching for US product to license. Everything from Chicago was going straight to the major labels by then, but when he noticed a few records from Detroit, home of the sixties soul rarities he had danced to, he was intrigued. He arranged for Derrick May to come over and do a remix, and the twenty-four-year-old arrived in the Midlands with a bagful of cassettes which Neil at first assumed were copies. In fact, they were the original recordings of what would become the classics of Detroit techno.

The techno rebels may have liked to see themselves as working on the cutting edge, but by the mid-eighties British pop producers like Trevor Horn were using synclaviers, Fairlight computers and state-of-the art digital studios that they could only dream of. Their equipment cost hundreds rather than thousands of dollars, and Derrick May made most of his classic records on a four-track tape cassette.

Neil Rushton fell for 'this brutal, but at the same time really evocative music'. He persuaded Virgin that there was enough to make a marketable compilation, and they paid him to go to Detroit and sign up tracks, accompanied by two journalists who would write about the scene for *The Face* and *NME.* By 1988, Juan Atkins had moved to Los Angeles. He'd been there for a few months when he got the call, and rushed back to be interviewed. Kevin Saunderson was at university studying TV and radio broadcasting and paying his way by working as a security guard, protecting scabs as they broke through picket lines. Neither Neil Rushton nor Mick Clarke at Virgin had envisaged a chart hit on the twelve-track compilation, which came out that summer under the title *Techno! The New Dance Sound Of Detroit*. But this was before they had heard 'Big Fun', the song that was to enable Kevin to quit both his depressing job and his degree course. Made with singer Paris Grey under the name Inner City, it went into the top ten of the UK charts in September 1988, the first techno hit.

But in the meantime Derrick May had a new audience for his ideas, and was in his element. Keenly aware that they were expected to have a story behind the music, a scene to sell, they worked hard to connect the sound to the landscape of their city. 'The music is like Detroit – a complete mistake,' Derrick May told Stuart Cosgrove in *The Face*. 'It's like George Clinton and Kraftwerk stuck in an elevator.' He drove *NME*'s John McCready round the city, showing him the dereliction that had inspired their sound. By then he was living back in the centre, and was keen that the journalist understood the view from the apartment at 4841 Second Avenue where his records were made: 'I would see the city waking up. I could see the face without the make-up. At night you would see the heat rising in the air from the stacks of old factory buildings. When I listen to those tracks, I see that view. The confusion of the view from the window. Juan and the rest of us are all part of the third wave, the future.'

Fans of British electro-pop like Depeche Mode, New Order and the Pet Shop Boys or the more industrial sounds of Skinny Puppy and Nitzer Ebb, the Detroit boys were bemused that the Brits wanted to see the Motown Museum. Derrick May didn't know where it was, and was puzzled by their obsession with second-hand record stores and old seven-inch singles. Neil Rushton was thrilled to hear that at school Kevin's mother had sung with the girls who later became the Marvelettes. At the pressing plant the techno crew used, he sat talking to the owner's retired father, who had pressed many of the independent soul rarities the Northern scene coveted. While Derrick May was finishing a track on his home studio one night, the visitors were upstairs playing the old soul records they'd bought. Derrick had to shout at them to turn the crap off.

'Mute records [in England] had been much more of an influence on them than, say, Stax,' says Rushton. 'That was what they wanted. The people I grew up with, if we saw a David Bowie record or a Tamla Motown record, we'd play the Motown. They almost had the opposite attitude.'

Juan Atkins perhaps best summed up their indifference to their city's soul heritage: 'Berry Gordy built the Motown sound on the same principles as the conveyor belt system at Ford's. Today their plants don't work that way – they use robots and computers to make the cars. I'm probably more interested in Ford's robots than in Berry Gordy's music.'[7]

'It's the soundtrack to the decay of a city,' said Blake Baxter, a friend who also contributed a track to the compilation. 'To every end there's a beginning.'

5 KEEPING THE FAITH

'It was something else in there . . . always full to bursting and never far away from the long arm of the law. It used to get up their noses that so many people were having such a good time with the minimum of aggro. On a hot summer's night, the buzz was electric. The dancefloor was packed and gear would be going around the place like there was no tomorrow. The drug scene was uncontrollable and the plod knew this. Every now and then, they would keep us on our toes with surprise visits in the hope of catching a few people either dropping gear or selling it. They would burst in and the dancefloor would rapidly empty. All that was left on it was hundreds of assorted capsules and crushed tablets.'

Pete McKenna, *Nightshift*[1]

Some seem to believe that club culture didn't come to Britain until 1988, but the extract above describes the Highland Room at Blackpool's Mecca Ballroom in 1973. All-nighters, all-dayers, banging four-on-the-floor beats, baggy clothes, sweat-plastered dancers, travelling huge distances for parties in strange venues, dodging police roadblocks to get there with a wrap of powder or a pocketful of pills . . . all of this was already happening in the UK in the seventies, on the Northern Soul scene.

Northern Soul grew out of a British passion for the up-tempo sounds produced in the golden era of Tamla Motown, for its strong, uplifting melodies and stomping 4/4 beat. As progressive rock crept into the discothèques towards the end of the sixties, as hair got longer and acid more popular, the Mods in the north and the Midlands especially kept their sharp mohair suits, their short hair, and their faith in the Motor City soul sound. Collectors would strive to own everything the label ever released in the UK, and then to find records that only came out in America, before turning their attentions to the similar-sounding music released on other small labels in the Detroit/Chicago area in the sixties.

Club culture as we know it grew out of this obsession, out of all-night sessions in R&B clubs fuelled by coffee, amphetamines and melodic American soul. To be specific, it has its roots in a Mod/R&B club at the far end of Whitworth Street in Manchester called the Twisted Wheel. At the Wheel's all-nighters, the bar upstairs served Cokes, coffee and milk. In the dark warren of a basement below, DJ Les Cokell served esoteric soul to a knowledgeable crowd. *Blues & Soul* columnist Dave Godin coined the name Northern Soul after a visit to the club in 1970, giving the scene an identity and a fierce regional pride that would outlast the Wheel by decades. In a later column, he wrote about one of the last all-nighters there:

> The dancing is without a doubt the finest I have ever seen outside the USA. Everybody there was an expert in soul clapping. In the right places, and with a clipped sharp quality that adds an extra something to appreciation of soul music. Les kept the records coming one after the other – each a soul classic, and each loved and respected by the crowd. Between records one would hear the occasional cry of 'Right on now!' or see a clenched gloved fist rise over the heads of the dancers.
>
> There was no undercurrent of tension or aggression that one sometimes finds in London clubs, but rather a benevolent atmosphere of friendship and camaraderie. Everyone seems to know everyone else, and if they don't, then they don't stand on ceremony. For one thing they know they all have in common is a love and dedication to soul music.

During the beat boom of the Sixties, Manchester had come to rival Hamburg as the Fun City of Europe, with over 200 clubs playing live music until chief constable J.A. McKay pledged to deal with a culture he believed to be 'a public scandal'. Many of these venues were coffee bars which charged membership and so qualified as private clubs, needing no licence for music or refreshment and appealing, McKay noted in his annual report in 1964, to 'individuals of exaggerated dress and deportment, commonly known as mods, rockers or beatniks'.

These clubs were apparently ill-lit, unsanitary, provided a haven for homeless youngsters who wandered endlessly from club to club under the influence of hashish and speed, and – most horrific of all – were often also frequented by 'men of colour'. The moral panic he subsequently provoked was enough to persuade Parliament to pass the Manchester Corporation Act of 1965, giving his force wide new powers to close clubs. By 1968, the Twisted Wheel was one of the only two clubs in the city catering exclusively for young people. Situated directly opposite a police station, it suffered frequent raids by the police and fire departments, and was finally closed in January 1971.[2]

This was not particularly unusual. Soul clubs were regularly raided by the police, and in the same *Blues & Soul* column, Dave Godin talked of dancers at the Tiles club in London being strip-searched by officers looking for drugs. 'Young people have become too much a target for police harassment in Britain,' he mused darkly, saying that all-nighters were becoming as furtive as American speakeasies during Prohibition.

British club culture has always existed just on the fringes of the law, mainly because there was, until recently, very little that the law actually allowed. Right up until 1988, the hours in which alcohol could be served to the public were restricted by a law passed to stop munitions workers frittering away their time drinking during the First World War. Many of the laws governing playing music and dancing date back even further. As a nation, Britain tends to be suspicious of fun, and as a nation with a strict class system and a deep distrust of its own young, it disapproves of the leisure activities of working-class youth most of all.

Far from controlling our consumption of alcohol or anything else, this has led to a culture of excess that baffles our fellow Europeans, and the energy we have put into circumventing the restrictions on all-night partying has left us with one of the world's most inventive and innovative club scenes. Where there's a will, there's a way, and the

British have developed a will to dance and indulge ourselves that can defy belief – given the chance, we tend to go mad. William Blake once said that the road of excess leads to the palace of wisdom. If we can take this literally, then British clubbers are very clever folk indeed.

Throughout the seventies, the back pages of *Blues & Soul* and *Black Echoes* were filled with advertisements for all-nighters and all-dayers and other Northern Soul events. These were members-only (membership to be applied for at least forty-eight hours in advance) to get around the licensing laws. But even then, the police were not averse to setting up road-blocks or sending out massed ranks to try and stop clubbers invading their patch.

The venues were basic: rugby clubs, working men's clubs, church halls and faded dance palaces. The floors were often so sticky that dancers bought their own talcum powder to sprinkle before they attempted their most athletic moves: backflips, twists and fast footwork that was also tight and self-contained, designed for crowded clubs. They danced at the Golden Torch in Tunstall near Stoke-on-Trent, at Samantha's in Sheffield, at the Catacombs in Wolverhampton, in halls and rooms in Nottingham, Derby, Bolton, Blackburn, Doncaster and Cleethorpes. But the most revered venues have entered club legend: the Blackpool Mecca and the Wigan Casino.

The twin temples of Northern Soul developed two distinct personalities. At the 1,000-capacity Highland Room above the main discotheque at Blackpool's Mecca Ballroom, Ian Levine and Colin Curtis were known for having records no one else had. They attracted a more fashion-conscious crowd and eventually added esoteric soul and funk tracks from the seventies into the mix. To the Wigan fans, this 'modern' soul was anathema: they stuck firmly to the sixties, but introduced forgotten pop records made during that decade by white artists with a similar stomping 4/4 beat.

Ian Levine's parents owned a casino in Blackpool and took their summer holidays in the States. While they lay on the beach, their son would be trawling through the racks in record shops in the black areas of town, buying up forgotten records for twenty-five cents knowing he could sell them for £20 at home. He says the music they revered and played in the Highland Room from the spring of 1973 was the soul strain that was to lead to disco: 'Swirling strings and lots of girl backing vocals, very happy and melodic, not earthy soul like Otis Redding or Aretha Franklin. It was more in line with the Supremes and the Four Tops and Martha and the Vandellas. Very sweet chord changes.'

At the end of 1973, the Wigan Casino began its legendary all-nighters, with Russ Winstanley and Richard Searling heading the DJ line-up. Members from all over the north, the Midlands and Scotland would squeeze into the crumbling ballroom when it opened at 2 a.m., carrying Adidas sports bags on their shoulders and dancing until 8 a.m., when Winstanley would play the same three records – the 'three before eight' – to close every week.

In between, sweat-soaked clothes would be discarded for the fresh outfits carried in the bags, girls stripping unselfconsciously in front of the lads. Sex was the last thing on anyone's mind, and considering the temporary shrinking effect prodigious amounts of speed tend to have on the male genitals, this was probably for the best. Because of this asexual atmosphere, many young gays felt comfortable there too, although Wigan was never an easy club to join. Although friendly once you were accepted, to newcomers it was as terrifying as it was exciting, full of speed freaks who showed clear contempt for anyone who didn't know the moves and the music. Respect had to be earned, out on the dancefloor.

The Casino closed in 1981 to make way for an extension to the town's civic centre that was never built, and the building was destroyed by a fire soon after. When Russ Winstanley played his three before eight for the last time, people were seen to weep. The rare soul scene is still popular now, and its influence has echoed through British pop ever since. Electro-pop duo Soft Cell's first hit was 'Tainted Love', a Gloria Jones soul stomper popular on the scene. Ian Levine went on to invent the post-disco dance sound Hi-NRG and to produce boy band Take That. More importantly, the devotion to the music, the awesome consumption of illegal substances and the emotional intensity of the night set a blueprint for UK club culture that anyone involved in the house boom will recognise.

If the Northern scene was – still is – about collecting rarities, an obsession with the past, then the south was all about newness. British record companies were far slower to pick up on American dance music in the seventies, with records often taking months to come out on this side of the Atlantic, if they were released at all. So in the clubs the import was everything, and the best DJs were those who could get the freshest sounds off the plane and on to the decks first.

But like Northern Soul, the southern scene was based in suburbs and satellite towns, and people had to travel to dance in venues like the Goldmine on Canvey Island, the Lacey Lady in Ilford, the Royalty in Southgate, the Rio in Didcot, Frenchies in Camberley, Tiffany's in Purley. Like the Northern scene, it was based on insider knowledge: only certain shops stocked imports, and the best tunes would be put aside for their most prestigious customers. The south also had its own road to excess, in the form of all-dayers which peaked in 1978 with a spectacular event for 7,000 clubbers at Alexandra Palace in north London; and then with soul weekenders which started at Caister in 1979.

Held in holiday camps in the off-season, the weekenders pulled together all of the suburban soul DJs and their crowds in a forty-eight hour orgy of dancing, drinking and debauchery. They were dominated by a group who became known as 'the soul mafia': DJs like Chris Hill, Robbie Vincent, Chris Brown and Sean French who were supported by a B-team of up-and-coming young DJs including Pete Tong, Bob Jones, Nicky Holloway and Mick Clarke (who was later to work at Virgin, where he signed up the first Detroit techno compilation as well as UK dance acts like Soul II Soul).

Although serious about their music, the DJs also played the fool, telling jokes on the mic, organising games and contests. When the cheesy US sitcom *Happy Days* was on TV, Chris Hill would run competitions for the best Fonz lookalike and the crowd would dress up fifties style. Fashion fads like this were common. When the film *The Great Gatsby* came out in 1974, the crowd at the Lacey Lady in Ilford started wearing beige suits, cricket jumpers and spats, some even carrying canes. In 1978 Chris Hill began playing the odd Glenn Miller and big band swing record in his set at the Goldmine, and overnight the crowd turned to GI uniforms and forties frocks.

This kind of club culture was often seen as the natural enemy of punk in the late seventies, but the reality was more complex. Malcolm McLaren, the Sex Pistols and their friends would go drinking in West End gay clubs like Louise's and Chagarama's where they could wear their outlandish clothes without fear of violence, and some of the most fanatical early Pistols fans came out of the suburban soul scene. In the mid-seventies, people who were into punk for the fashion and the attitude still went to dance to Roy Ayres at the Lacey Lady wearing bin-liners and safety pins. Mohair jumpers, pegged trousers and jelly sandals were worn by both punks and soul boys, and at times it was hard to distinguish one from the other.

West London soulboy Norman Jay remembers happening upon an early night at punk club the Roxy in Covent Garden just after it took over the venue that had been Chagarama's. 'Don Letts was DJing and playing a lot of dub, so there were Rastas dancing alongside punks. And because it had recently been a gay club too and gay style hadn't become so macho and cruisy by then, it was hard to tell who was what. We were all young then, and very confused.'

A schoolboy from the suburbs of south-east London, Jeremy Healy remembers being fascinated by local soul fans and Bowie boys wearing purple trousers, purple winklepickers and purple hair in 1975 and '76. He began wearing the clothes in his early teens and befriended another outlandishly dressed, slightly older boy he met on the bus. He and George O'Dowd – later better known as Boy George, the name he chose when he formed his group Culture Club – would go to the punk clubs to pose but found the music boring; at weekends, they danced in a Kensington gay club called Sombreros, where odd clothes were not just tolerated but encouraged.

As the first thrills of punk began to fade at the end of the seventies, a new kind of club emerged in central London, with outside promoters taking over a venue for the night and bringing in their own crowd. In 1978, Rusty Egan moved into the Soho gay club Billy's on Tuesdays and started up a Bowie night for post-punk poseurs who wanted to dance. Steve Strange was drafted in to control door in 1979, and an incestuous group of 200 or so faces began to form, all trying to outdress each other and stay one step ahead.

Journalist Robert Elms described the scene in *The Face*:

The still dominant black leather of the post-punk depression was rejected in favour of gold braid and pill box hats. It was toy soldiers, Cossacks and queens to the outsider, an odd fantasy world down the stairs; to the participants, it was a mutual admiration society for budding narcissists, a creative and competitive environment where individualism was stressed and change was vital. Looks came and went as fast as the innovators could construct them.[3]

The music widened to include Iggy Pop, TV and film themes, Kraftwerk and new British electro-pop like 'Warm Leatherette' by the Normal and 'Being Boiled' by the Human League, and then the scene started to move: to the Blitz in Covent Garden (where the mix became known as 'electro disco'), to St Moritz in Wardour Street for two months of bossa nova, swing, Edith Piaf and dancing cheek-to-cheek, and then to a night called Hell back in Covent Garden.

Dubbed The Cult With No Name, New Romantics and then futurists, the scene gradually spread to other towns: the Tanschau in Cardiff, the Rumrunner in Birmingham. Pip's disco in Manchester had a Bowie room at the back which also became a big favourite with Gary Numan clones. To club owners struggling to come to terms with the end of the disco boom, it was a gift. In April 1981, the trade publication *Disco International And Club News* celebrated the 'futurist movement'. 'All the signs suggest,' wrote editor Peter Harvey, 'a major teen boom which could bring the half-filled clubs bouncing back to life.'

Trying to stay one step ahead of a growing media, but also courting their fifteen minutes of fame, clubbers began frantically trying on different styles, eras, musical genres. With vast back catalogues of music being made available again on the newly-launched compact disc format, suddenly there was a wealth of new sound to explore, and the Soho set spent as much time rifling through the record racks as the dressing up box. It was a time of experimentation: be-bop, African pop, rumba, rockabilly, salsa, ska, blues. Zoot suits, cowboy hats, fifties Americana, berets and braces. Soon there were clubs every night of the week in W1, catering for everyone from Goths to rude boys, jazz dancers to rockabillies. It seemed that youth culture was fragmenting as never before: Teddy Boys lasted years before the Mods came along to usurp them in the early sixties. In West Wonderland in the early eighties, styles lasted months, sometimes just weeks. But the theme kept returning to the mix DJ Steve Lewis had introduced to the Soho preen scene at Le Beat Route in 1979, to the cutting-edge dance music flooding out of black America.

To differentiate themselves from the cheesy discos and tourist traps around the West End, most clubs operated a strict door policy. The cool, the connected and the outlandishly costumed got in; everyone else queued and hoped. It has been said that these clubs, with their élitism and VIP rooms were a reflection of Thatcherist values, but it is doubtful that the Iron Lady would have approved of many of the freaks and misfits who found a home in the Soho clubs of the eighties. No one who has seen Taboo promoter Leigh Bowery dancing in a costume fit for Mr Blobby with light bulbs strapped to his head, or Mud Club promoter Philip Sallon rustle across a crowded dancefloor in an outfit made of knotted plastic carrier bags, could believe that everyone on the scene took themselves seriously.

Despite the rediscovery of black dance music, the crowd in the West End clubs was still predominantly white. In London at any given time, there was always one, perhaps two central venues where black soul fans who were not part of the hip élite felt welcome – Crackers in Wardour Street and the 100 Club. Sometimes they could get into the suburban clubs too, but this was often a game of chance. Although he'd been admitted to the club in the past, Norman Jay was turned away from the Lacey Lady with his friends on his twenty-first birthday. Calling the Goldmine one night to check that he and his friends wouldn't have a wasted journey if they drove out to Canvey Island, Hackney soul boy Trevor Nelson was told not to bother.

For these young Britons, the sound system was often the most reliable source of music, just as it had been for their parents. A kind of mobile club with huge custom-built speakers and everything needed to run a dance including technicians, DJs, MCs and singers, the sound system travelled over to the UK from Jamaica with the first great wave of immigrants in the fifties, and continued the same function of providing entertainment where there would otherwise be none. Sound systems are about neighbourhoods, about local pride, supported like football teams. They set up in houses, in halls, in clubs, wherever a party is needed, and 'clashes' in which two or more rival sounds compete for the approval of the crowd have long been used to add spice to a night.

While respecting the reggae roots, however, this new generation of black clubbers wanted something more funky to dance to. Norman Jay borrowed his Rastafarian brother Joey's sound system Great Tribulation to play soul and funk, renaming it Good Times after the Chic disco hit. Trevor Nelson built his own system and called it Madhatters to discourage the conservative reggae crowd from attending his soul and funk parties in east London.

With names like Rapattack, Freshbeat, Soul II Soul and Good Grooves, similar systems began to emerge across London and in many other British cities from the late seventies onwards, playing parties in private houses and flats, in hired halls or in buildings that had simply been broken into. In the weeks before the annual Notting Hill Carnival in London, huge empty houses in Westbourne Grove would be commandeered for these blues dances or raves: four floors of music from the sound systems, and more people crammed in than could be thought possible.

'The warehouses came out of the house parties growing so massively popular,' says Norman Jay. 'This is where the term roadblock came from. It was about black guys pulling up outside the blues dance in a car, blocking off the road so the police couldn't get down.

'We did a huge party in a mansion on the top of Hampstead Heath once, in an old girls' school we called the Haunted House. That's the first time we had the Chelsea Sloanes turn up, all their jeeps parked over the heath at dawn and music just booming out. We were doing big parties around Ladbroke Grove, Westbourne Grove, Maida Vale, those big four-storey houses plus massive basements. I had a mate who worked in Notting Hill Housing Trust who used to slip me the keys.

'We charged 50p or £1 to get in, my dad ran the bars, all the local hoods would work the door and promote it. It was like a community thing, everyone would work to make it good.'

Trevor Nelson remembers travelling parties too: up to twenty-five coaches setting off from east London to a hired hall or hotel function room in Margate, Yarmouth or Blackpool to dance to their local sound system for a few hours before driving all the way back again. He and his friends treated the hip one-nighters with suspicion: 'We had this real anti-West End feeling. We all thought it was extremely racist. They wanted to play black music, but they wouldn't want black club-runners to control it in any way. And I didn't want to do a club where I would have to turn a lot of black people away.'

As these new soul sounds began building links with each other throughout the early eighties, promoting joint parties, playing shows on the same pirate radio stations, they built an infrastructure that later club promoters would use for their own parties. If the DJs who were later to pioneer the acid house scene in London were mainly white, the music they were playing boomed out of sound systems lovingly built and operated by black clubbers like Joey Jay and Carl Cox.

As the trendy one-nighters continued to proliferate across central London, Chris Sullivan was the first to adapt the culture of illegal all-night raves to this crowd, with three parties at Mayhem Studios in Battersea, south London, in 1978 and '79. At the first, there were fifties blue movies shown on the ceiling, a snake dancer and a funk sound-track. 'We did it because they wouldn't let us in anywhere else,' he told *i-D* years later. 'We couldn't get into normal clubs, so the only thing to do was organise our own.'[4]

It was the Dirtbox, however, that popularised the idea. Phil Dirtbox opened up above a chemist's in Earls Court in 1982, the same year Chris Sullivan took over the Whiskey-à-Go-Go in Soho and renamed it the Wag. To get into the Wag's nights, you had to pass the critical stare of Winston on the door, to prove yourself one of the élite. To get into the Dirtbox, you had to know where it was and pay the entry fee of £1. Inside, DJ Jay Strongman offered a mix of rockabilly and raw-edged funk. 'The police didn't notice it for the first few weeks. On the sixth week Pride [later to become Sade] played live and the queue went around the block. The police raided it and there was a big punch-up, fire hoses were set off, people were arrested and a pinball machine was pushed downstairs.'[5]

Nonetheless, the Dirtbox continued, moving to an assortment of venues and inspiring a host of similar outlaw club nights over the next two years. Amongst them was the Circus, a series of parties promoted by Jeremy Healy and Patrick Lilley which set new standards with lavish décor that included banks of TVs showing scratch videos by John Maybury. They held a party for Blondie's Debbie Harry, and Bianca Jagger once paid her £5 to get in. The popular all-nighters promoted by the hip clothes shop Demob even attracted early tabloid attention in 1983, when *Daily Mirror* columnist Paul Foot accused them of paying off the police.

The crowds grew: Dave Mahoney's Wharehouse night built up enough of a following to go legal at the Electric Ballroom in Camden in 1984, a night that fused rockabilly and funk styles and helped establish a sharp flat-top and pair of Levis 501s as the regulation club issue. Jay Strongman ruled the decks there, and also bought his credible funk mix to the kitsch and high camp of the Mud club on Fridays.

Slowly the strands began to converge around a new consensus, a shared passion for the dance music of black America. As Jay Strongman said, 'I can't imagine a kid who's grown up through punk, or kids who've been to rockabilly clubs, being satisfied with anything that isn't raw and heavy.'[6]

The music pouring out of the States in the mid-eighties seemed impossibly exotic, fresh and new to British clubbers. All these wonderful *noises*. Electro, hip hop, rap, Latin freestyle, underground disco, mutant funk, Washington go-go: the coolest dancefloors consumed it all, with little of the segregation between styles practised in American clubs. If America's black population were the creators of the music, then we were the archivists. We carefully catalogued and collected, and were often instrumental in marketing the music to the rest of the world.

British record labels would sign artists or put together compilations, then fly journalists from the music press and style magazines to the city involved to write about the local scene. Often, this would be the first media attention these artists had ever enjoyed. When I was in Chicago to write about the house scene, a local music journalist called to ask why on earth *The Face* was interested in it. 'It'll never cross over,' he said, citing a commission to write about Chicago rock bands for the US music paper *Creem* as the best thing to come out of this sudden burst of interest from Britain.

The suburban soul DJs began to look outmoded. The younger DJs who had been making their way up the hierarchy began gravitating more to the West End style of clubbing instead. In Southwark, just south of the Thames, a cheeky young DJ called Nicky Holloway took over the Royal Oak pub in Tooley Street, dressed the venue with colourful painted banners like a West End club, and began building a bridge between two worlds. DJs like Gilles Peterson, Bob Jones and Pete Tong played there, and Holloway began hiring off-beat venues for one-off parties he called Doos – Doo At The Zoo in the function rooms at London Zoo, a Googly Doo at Lord's Cricket Ground, Doos in Chislehurst Caves and amongst the dinosaurs in the Natural History Museum. He even began running his own alternative week-enders for those bored of shaving foam, whistles and drunken lads, and club holidays to places like Ibiza and Crete.

At the same time, two more imports were slowly creeping across the Atlantic to affect our club culture. The American concept of mixing records took a while to catch on in Britain, where DJs were still fond of talking on the mic. The first commercially-available twelve-inch singles in the UK came out in 1978: 'You Plus Me' by Undisputed Truth (in a limited edition of 3,000); and Goodie Goodie's 'No 1 DJ'. Greg James was probably the first DJ to mix records in a London club: an American who had been trying to make a name in the New York clubs, he played a residency at the Embassy Club in London in 1978.

Ian Levine began mixing at Angels in Burnley later that year, and in 1979 when the Embassy's promoters opened Heaven in London, a vast club modelled on the New York disco Infinity, he was offered the main DJ slot. Meanwhile, Levine berated his fellow jocks for being slow to embrace the concept in *Disco* magazine, but the soul mafia insisted that they weren't impressed with American fads.

It was Ilford DJ Froggie who introduced the concept to the suburbs. On his regular pilgrimages to the Paradise Garage in New York, he befriended Larry Levan and began to learn this new way of playing records. To DJs still used to blending records one after the other, or announcing their next selection on the mic, it was a revelation. Soul guru Bob Jones, then an up-and-coming DJ from Chelmsford, remembers: 'He'd put two copies of "Stomp" by the Brothers Johnson together and they'd be running one beat behind the other, so you'd get an echo like '*stomp, stomp, all night, all night*'. I'd never seen anyone do that before.'

Meanwhile, other clubbers travelling to New York came back not with a new technique but with a new drug. Introduced to MDMA while recording their debut album in New York in 1981, the Leeds synth-pop duo Soft Cell were so besotted that they even got their dealer to contribute a rap praising Ecstasy on the remix of their track 'Memorabilia'. 'Nobody knew what we were talking about at all and we got away with it completely,' said Soft Cell's David Ball. 'When we got back to London, nobody had ever heard of it.'[7]

But slowly, the word got out, and as the pills and capsules made their way into the UK they became an occasional new delicacy for pop stars, fashion folk, and well-connected club promoters.

Ecstasy was rarely used as a dance drug in Britain at that point. A photographer friend who travelled frequently to New York for fashion shoots told me that he used to have a sweet jar full of pills at home in west London. The drug had been illegal in the UK since 1977, but since no one really knew what it looked like, it was easy enough to bring through Customs. He and his friends would drive out into the country, take it and wander round enjoying the natural beauty, or use it in small, informal parties at home.

The first in-depth article on MDMA in the British press appeared in *The Face* in 1985. Journalist Peter Naysmith had been introduced to the drug by a circle of therapists and New Age explorers very similar to the people who originally experimented with the drug in the States. But by then the main people using it were the Soho élite: those who could afford £25 a pill, and more importantly had the contacts to acquire such a rarity.

One night at a warehouse party in Old Street, I was taken into a VIP room where a handful of eighties faces were lolling about listlessly on cushions. One of them was stroking a fake fur coat. Another was rubbing a cheek against a velvet curtain. All of them had smug, dreamy, self-absorbed smiles. I'd heard about Ecstasy and been mildly curious, but this didn't look like fun. To me, clubs were for drinking, dancing and talking, and these people weren't doing any of that. I retreated hastily back to the noise and funk of the main room, to a warm can of lager, a dab of speed and my friends.

By the mid-eighties, we had a fixed weekend routine. Meet in a Soho pub at about 10 p.m., drink our beer on the pavement outside whatever the weather, and wait for the promoters to come round with the flyers for that night's illegal action. After last orders, we'd hit the clubs until 3 a.m. then jump into a cab to Old Street or Southwark or Kings Cross or wherever else the party was meant to be. The address was often deliberately vague, but you'd look for other people dressed in the regulation club uniform of flat-top haircut, black MA1 flying jackets, Levis and DMs, listen for noise and look for a cluster of people standing round an unlit doorway, pleading their case to get in.

There was the odd spectacular event to match the increasingly spectacular décor and production in legal clubs like Raw in the basement of the YMCA, but warehouse parties were rarely glamorous. The bar usually consisted of cans floating in a plastic dustbin filled with what had once been ice but was now dirty water. We were used to dancing in puddles on concrete floors, taking care not to lean against filthy walls and looking carefully in dark corners for unseen hazards and dangerous drops.

There were illegal parties in empty office buildings, in warehouses, factories, gyms and hotels. There were one-off events in theatres, cinemas, mansions and swimming pools. Much of the scene was hidden, underground. Most of it was constantly shifting. Popular nights would move from venue to venue; popular DJs would often change nights, taking their crowd with them. There was a seething, restless energy that couldn't settle down to sleep when the clubs closed at 3 a.m.

The London *Evening Standard* picked up on the story in July 1986, their report focusing on both the allegedly huge profits made by the organisers ('as much as £13,000 in one night') and the spectre of drug-dealing gangsters: 'Cannabis and amphetamine sulphate – commonly known as speed – were openly on sale as 1,800 danced to loud pop music.'[8]

When house music came along in 1986, it was seen as just another music to be added to the mix. The hip hop label Def Jam was massive in clubs across the UK that year too, with artists like Run-DMC, the Beastie Boys and Public Enemy managing to appeal to everyone from B-boys to *NME* readers, flat-topped funkabillies to students. Unlaced Adidas trainers and medallions made from Volkswagen and Mercedes symbols became part of the club uniform, and a liaison between black and white, rock and rap was forged that laid the ground for the merging of the tribes in acid house.

Flyers for clubs in London that year promised house as part of a musical menu that might also include go-go, hip hop, jazz, funk and whatever else was flavour of the month. In the Midlands and the north-west, DJs like Mike Pickering in Manchester, Graeme Park in Nottingham, and Winston and Parrot in Sheffield explored it more fully, still mixing the music with hip hop and current dance but devoting longer sections of their sets to house and including some of the harder, weirder Chicago and Detroit mixes as well as the more accessible vocal tracks. Perhaps prepared for house's repetitive 4/4 beat by the stomping 4/4 dance tracks so revered on the Northern Soul scene, clubbers in the north took to the music with a passion.

'What we were doing in Nottingham, Manchester and Sheffield would never be mentioned in the style magazines,' says Graeme Park. 'We were always reading about rare groove and warehouse parties, Jay Strongman and Nicky Holloway, and I wanted to get people off their arses and see what *we* were doing, to realise that the end of the tube line wasn't neccessarily the end of the country. Now all the magazines have regional correspondents and people travel everywhere to go out. Then, it was a real struggle.'

By 1987 I was writing about a north–south divide measured not in cash and jobs but in beats-per-minute. Scotland favoured the frantic rhythms of hi-NRG (just as it now is the only part of Britain to have taken to the frenetic, machine-gun rhythms of gabber), the north and the Midlands moved to the 120 bpm rhythms of house, while the south had become obsessed with a slower, retro funk they called rare groove.

The music had come from the sound systems. Norman Jay had started playing his old seven-inch singles at his warehouse parties to try and get the older, seventies soul crowd dancing again. But through the massive bass bins of his brother's reggae-tuned speakers, the music sounded different: 'Those dirty, funky records hadn't been played that way before. A lot of those records used to amaze me when I heard them on the sound system – and I *knew* them. The crowd would go mad, and the more I played them, the more they responded.'

Graham Ball had already introduced concepts like funfair rides into clubs as one of the promoters behind the legendary, lavish Westworld events. Now he added a fashion element to rare groove by demanding that the crowd dress up for parties like Starwash, a night in a car wash in Holborn that attracted 600 clubbers in flares and Afro wigs.

By 1986, Norman's sound system was called Shake'n'Fingerpop and he was promoting parties with Soul II Soul and with Family Funktion, a crew that had no rig of their own but a big following of trendy students from their college parties and clubbers from their home patch in north London. DJ Julian O'Riordan was a white law student at the London School of Economics, which also came in useful for putting up squatters' notices in future venues and bluffing it with the police if they came down. Norman called him Judge Jules, and the name stuck.

Norman and Jules began travelling to New York to search out rare records to sell back home in London, staying with Justin Berkmann who had been part of the Family Funktion posse before moving to Manhattan. He took them to the Paradise Garage and both DJs began collecting house and garage records, although at home they stuck with the increasingly lucrative rare groove scene. They began bootlegging rare records that had proved popular on the scene, using some of the proceeds to bring over artists such as the James Brown associates Bobby Byrd and Vicki Anderson to play live, and eventually inspired the re-release of rare groove classics like Maceo and the Macks' 'Cross The Tracks' and the Jackson Sisters' 'I Believe In Miracles'.

They put on all-night parties for 1,500 to 5,000 people in empty buildings around London. '*Don't tell anyone,*' Norman Jay would whisper on his show on the weekend pirate radio station Kiss FM, '*but there's a rave tonight.*' He'd then casually mention the venue. The sound and lighting would be hooked up to their generator which, if it ran out of petrol, would plunge the building into silence and darkness. At a party in a former British Rail depot near Paddington one night, they couldn't get it started at all, so Joey Jay wired everything up to a lamp-post outside. At 5.30 in the morning when the street lights went off, so did the party.

Many of the stories they tell about these times echo the later experiences of the acid house and rave promoters: friendly police moving them on from their patch but pointing out empty buildings controlled by another force nearby; leaning on the door of the office they were using to count the night's takings to try and convince the police outside that it was locked, ankle deep in money; and, towards the end, the threat of take-over from criminal firms.

'The rare groove scene was very much part of the growth of what became acid house,' asserts Judge Jules. 'It was the same people. Now I'm constantly approached by your Meccas, Ranks and First Leisures and asked to DJ, but it was their attitudes in the first place that forced us to do what we did. They wouldn't *entertain* the idea of putting on a big dance event in the West End.

'The parties were also a reaction to the archaic licensing laws at the time. Most clubs shut at two then and clubs in London all shut at three. So did we all go home? I don't think so.'

By 1987, the imports that had been the backbone of the culture for so long were losing their appeal. Record companies were becoming quicker at picking up on the music and releasing it in the UK. Astute entrepreneurs like Morgan Khan at Streetsounds had begun to license hot US dance tracks for compilations, producing an album of choice cuts for little more than the cost of a single imported twelve-inch. After the success of these, Streetsounds bought in DJs to compile collections of jazz dance tracks, old disco, new hip hop and electro, and suddenly tracks that had been hard to get were available in high street shops. If DJs wanted something exclusive to play in their club, then they'd have to make it themselves.

The new sampling technology meant that you didn't necessarily need musical skills to make a new track; you just needed a large record collection to steal from, and DJs began to make the move from being curators to creators. Jonathan More, a DJ who had made his name with the Meltdown, an all-nighter in London's Docklands, teamed up with a friend to form Coldcut. Influenced by the hip hop collages being made in New York by a nerdy-looking white duo called Double D and Steinski, he and Matt Black put together their own record, 'Say Kids What Time Is It?'. 'It was such an outrageous idea, that you could take whatever you wanted and put it together to make something new,' enthuses More. 'It just hooked into all my art school training, and it was so punk.'

They pressed 500 copies of their first record for £250, and sold it out of the back of a van for £15. A few records later, they were asked by Island records to remix Eric B and Rakim's US hip hop track 'Paid In Full', and their radical reworking of the tune with weird wailing vocals and other samples from their collection went into the charts. They were only paid £700, but their credit on the record was unusually prominent. Remix culture, the notion that the DJs remaking the records could be as important as the original artists, was beginning to take hold.

Until then British dance music had rarely been anything more than a pale imitation of American styles, but now it was finding a new confidence, a new irreverence, and a voice of its own. As the Justified Ancients of Mu-Mu, Bill Drummond and Jimmy Cauty made two guerrilla albums of scratches, samples and stolen beats that set the scene for what was to come when they discovered acid house and became the KLF. *1987 (What The Fuck Is Going On)* and *Who Killed The Jams?* snatched sounds from the likes of Petula Clarke, the Beatles and Whitney Houston. When Abba sued, the duo seemed genuinely surprised.

Then in September a faster, more energetic medley made by DJs Dave Dorrell and C.J. MacIntosh with members of the indie group Colourbox went to number one. 'Pump Up The Volume' by M/A/R/R/S opened the floodgates, and soon every club DJ in the country was signing a deal or booking out a few days in the studio. The first British house records began to appear too, although they were not always regarded as such. 'Carino' by Mike Pickering's band T-Coy is now regarded as an early Brit-house classic; then, many saw it more as a lively Latin jazz workout.

In the capital, house music was being played on pirate radio, most notably by Jazzy M, whose show *The Jackin' Zone* went out on from nine till twelve every Tuesday and Thursday evening on LWR – raids permitting. In the clubs, however, the main places playing house were the Jungle and Pyramid, gloriously mixed club nights 'for gay people and their friends' with Colin Faver and Mark Moore behind the decks and an assortment of colourful characters on the dancefloor. (Kevin Millins was involved with the promotion of both nights, and had been Faver's partner in the hip post-punk concert agency Final Solution, who promoted near-legendary gigs by the likes of Joy Division. Later, this experience of promoting both concerts and clubs would serve him well as a promoter of big, legal raves.)

For the straight crowd there was Delirium on Saturdays, where brothers Noel and Maurice Watson mixed garage and house with hip hop, pop and dance tracks. Graduates from the warehouse scene who had managed to bring 2,000 people to their weekly all-nighter behind King's Cross station for an extraordinary seven months before the police finally stopped it, they were now playing in a legal venue known for its extravagant décor. Its walls covered with graffiti art, the Astoria had a new theme every few weeks. Once, the dancefloor was painted green and marked out like an American football pitch. Another time, a fairground ghost train ride was set up on the stage.

But house was tolerated only in small doses at these kind of clubs. When Mike Pickering came down from Manchester to guest at a funk/soul night called Fever at the Astoria, the bpm divide was still in force: when he began playing house records one after the other, the dancefloor ground to a halt. Both he and Graeme Park remember taunts about 'gay boy music' when they played down south. At many of LWR's club events, Jazzy M got a similar response, sometimes backed up by flying glasses and bottles.

When the Astoria closed for refurbishment and a short-lived launch as a live music/cabaret venue, the Delirium team split. Robin King kept the name and moved to Thursday nights at Heaven, where he continued to promote house music. Derrick May played there once, and Frankie Knuckles came over for a two-month residency in 1987, quickly becoming intimate with the motorway between London and Manchester as he travelled up for guest spots at the Haçienda. Nick Trulocke opened Discotheque, an ironic take on tacky disco culture where the DJs played requests from the crowd.

King may have seen the future, but it was Trulocke who had the full house. Delirium was a club before its time. It closed in December 1987, finally bowing out with a one-off Delirium Deep House Convention at the Empire in Leicester Square two months later. Frankie Knuckles, Fingers Inc., house diva Kym Mazelle and Marshall Jefferson came over to play the event, and Patrick Lilley was asked to help with promotion. A bald Buddha of a man from Birmingham who had lived in the Warren Street squats which had sheltered Boy George, Jeremy Healy, and many more of the early faces on the Soho club scene, he now did PR for club events like Westworld. Lilley arranged for sponsorship by Uptime, a caffeine and vitamin supplement, so that pills could be given out with the flyers. They were aiming for something suitably trippy and psychedelic, but, he says with characteristic drollness, 'It ended up more caffeine and op-art than acid house.'

After the House Convention on 18 February, Lilley was invited to go out to Chicago to meet some of the house artists and advise them on media opportunities in Britain. Once there, he gave his usual forthright opinion. Ten City were wearing glittery outfits and make-up in their press shots and looked more like a seventies glam rock band than deep house artists. Kym Mazelle and Marshall Jefferson favoured stone-wash denim. 'I told them their fashions were totally inappropriate for London and that they would never get anywhere with it, and then ripped up the press biographies and the photos.'

Lilley arranged make-overs and new pictures more suited to the UK market, and then devised a plan of action for his new clients. His assistant Jak had grown up in Streatham, right out on the southeastern fringes of London. Jak had been enthusing about a new club scene coming up from these suburbs via Ibiza, and which apparently involved house music. Lilley was starting to think it could be the Next Big Thing.

6   FANTASY ISLAND

A popular package holiday destination once dubbed Margate in the Mediterranean, the island of Ibiza may seem an unlikely place for the forces that had been gathering in the clubs of Europe and America to finally come together. But the Balearic island has a long history of cultural assimilation and hedonism, and by the eighties it was a pleasure-seekers' paradise, its economy built on not just a cheap fix of sun, sea and sand but also the rhythms of the night.

Despite a long history of invasion and colonisation, the inhabitants of Ibiza have always kept their rights to the land, holding on to a fierce pride and independence, a tolerance of other cultures, and an attitude that life is something to be enjoyed. The Carthaginians, who occupied the island for a thousand years from 740 BC, even gave the island its own deity. Tanit was the most sacred of their goddesses, representing love, death and fertility. Ibiza was considered a holy island, its earth believed to radiate positive energy. Since then, there have been Islamic and Christian invaders, and more recently Buddhists, Hari Krishnas, followers of the Baghwan Shree Rajneesh and almost every New Age cult. All have seemed to hold the same views of the island's special energy.

By the middle of this century, however, Ibiza had declined. Forgotten, isolated, and almost medieval in terms of its development, its economy was largely based on trading salt. There was some tourism, notably *viajes de novios* – literally trips for fiancés, a kind of pre-marriage honeymoon tester for couples from the mainland. Later came a handful of Americans and Brits, mainly wealthy bohemians and artists, who were attracted by both the island's beauty and its unspoilt isolation.

Irishman Sandy Pratt ran a bar in Santa Eulalia for twenty-five years, entertaining actors such as Nigel Davenport, Diana Rigg and Laurence Olivier there. 'It was like having a cocktail party in the morning and a cocktail party in the evening,' he reminisced in Paul Richardson's book *Not Part Of The Package*. 'The Fifties and Sixties were a wonderful period. The war was over and there was this great feeling of relief and goodwill. When I first sailed here in 1955 there were a handful of foreigners. Ibiza was every Northerner's idea of what the Mediterranean should look like. There were two paved roads and very little electric light. It was an *Alice In Wonderland* world.'[1]

In 1960, the island's hotels registered just 30,000 visitors. This had increased to 102,538 by the mid-sixties, by which time it had become an essential stopover on the hippie world tour. Known locally as *peluts* (hairies), they found welcoming locals, deserted beaches and cheap accommodation, and soon set up communes on old *fincas* (farm estates), a circuit of parties, 'happenings' and plentiful supplies of drugs.

Novelist Joan Wyndham remembers a sixties full moon party in her autobiography *Anything Once*: 'The huge courtyard was lit by flares, and by children who ran around like fireflies waving torches. All around were black bearded freaks banging away on African drums and Tibetan bells, while in the centre of the square the rich French poseurs gyrated slowly in their ethnic robes.'[2]

When Spain's fascist premier General Franco decided that tourism might be a good source of revenue and encouraged the building of the island's international airport in 1967, he also shipped over police to deal with the hippies. Public meetings and late-night parties were banned, and twenty-seven hippies were thrown off the island that year. Sebastian Brockley, a Briton who has been a regular visitor since the mid-sixties, remembers one man being arrested in 1967 for giving his girlfriend a piggyback. He personally spent a short spell in Ibiza Town's prison that year.

'Basically, it was for having long hair. It was then the age of Franco, and "untourist-like activities" covered a multitude of sins. There was a

Dutch guy called Mario who was an outrageous out gay and wore satin pants. They tried to arrest him, there was a push-and-shove battle, and they came down in the evening and just arrested a dozen of us. They put us away for four days, but they'd arrested a French girl whose father was an international lawyer who then got us out.'

But overall, the islanders' attitude of tolerance prevailed. If the numbers of hippies dropped, it was due more to increasing commercialisation than to repression. The clubs that now form the centre of the island's nightlife grew organically out of this counter-culture. Amnesia was an old *finca*, a working farm a little way back from the road between Ibiza Town and San Antonio. A cheap, bohemian party venue for hippies and artists, it didn't even have electricity at first, the revellers dancing round bonfires in the house and grounds.

Pacha opened just outside Ibiza Town in 1973, playing reggae and psychedelic rock to a similar crowd. By then, the annual number of visitors had rocketed to half a million, and the island was starting to develop two distinct and separate personalities: families on package holidays gravitated towards Playa d'en Bossa and Es Canar, and younger holidaymakers to the growing numbers of bars and clubs in San Antonio, while the island's more alternative or sophisticated visitors stayed either in Ibiza Town or in villas in the hills.

As disco took hold, clubs like Pacha, Amnesia and Club Raphael (later to be renamed Ku) began to add on dancefloors, bars and massive sound systems. By the eighties, they had evolved into ornate Moorish fantasy palaces, their many levels hung with white drapes, planted with palm trees, decorated with fountains, pillars, balconies and plush cushioned areas. If they were film sets, Hollywood would have rejected them as too flamboyant. Es Paradis had fountains that could be turned on at the peak of the night, soaking the dancers. Amnesia had its weekly foam parties, where the dancefloor would be pumped with *espuma* until the dancers stood neck-deep in bubbles and all kinds of activities would be going on under its cover.

The biggest of them all, Ku had a capacity of 8,000 and a swimming pool in the middle of the main dancefloor. Dancers and musicians were flown in specially from Rio for its annual Brazilian carnival, and

Spandau Ballet, Kid Creole & the Coconuts, James Brown and Talk Talk once played live in just one season. Before new noise regulations forced the clubs to build roofs in 1990, it was said that Ku's spectacular lasers could be seen from the mainland.

In all the clubs, there were lavish theme parties, constant redecorations, extravagant one-off events. There was a rumour that the owners of Studio 54 in New York had visited the island to take ideas from Pacha. Even if untrue, certainly the same people were dancing in both clubs. The crowd in these exclusive, expensive Ibizan clubs were not package tourists, who wouldn't notice the venues from the road in the daylight and had no reason to drive across those parts of the island at night. The clubs were for the celebrities and socialites who viewed the island as an ideal holiday spot. For gays who had come first to escape the repression of mainland Spain, but who later came from all over Europe to enjoy the decadent atmosphere. For the international jet-set who saw Ibiza as another stop-over on the party circuit.

All of these mingled in the streets of Ibiza Town, shopping in the designer boutiques, eating in the expensive restaurants on the harbour front, posing in the numerous cafés and in bars that grew wilder as the night drew in. It was a cosmopolitan place, attracting people of all nations: models, film stars, designers, musicians. A place where local matrons in traditional black dress simply smiled when confronted with a near-naked transvestite, where the wealthy moored their impressive yachts in the marina and impoverished gypsies peddled drugs in the streets.

Long before British clubbers started travelling there *en masse*, Ibiza was a fantasy island. Living there is like living on a boat, says long-time resident Alfredo Fiorito: people get on, people get off, but while they're there, they have to get along. 'I think that's far more important about Ibiza than the music. It's a meeting place. You meet people that change your life completely or blow your mind, and you go back home and you start something different. That's the magic of the place. Most of the people who come to Ibiza are the centre of attention in their own area, the superstar of their own town. Even if they're little places. And then they come to Ibiza and realise that what they were doing is not so easy here. So they have to grow.

Everybody in history wanted to come here, and they're going to keep on wanting to come here, so something's always going to be happening here.'

Alfredo – he never uses his second name – left his native Argentina after the 1976 military *coup d'état*. He was jailed for a while for promoting rock gigs, although he's keen not to make too much of this. 'They jailed many people, I was nothing special. I'm not an ex-revolutionary turned DJ, even though it's a good story.'

He headed straight for Spain and then, on a friend's advice, to Ibiza. After the repression of Argentina, the free and easy attitudes he found there made the island seem like paradise on earth. Alfredo knew he was going to stay, and immediately set about spreading roots: within a week, he owned two dogs. Within a year, he was a proud father.

He did whatever he could to earn money, and through clubs like Pacha, he slowly got involved in the dance scene. The first record he danced to in Ibiza was Led Zeppelin's 'Stairway To Heaven'. Which, he adds dryly, was no mean feat, even on acid. But the clubs played reggae too, a music which became a lasting passion.

In 1982, a friend decided to return to South America and left his bar in Ibiza Town to Alfredo. Known for its free jazz soundtrack, the bar was equipped with two turntables and a mixer and, at the age of thirty, Alfredo set about learning to DJ. Finally, he had found his calling. He went back to Argentina to get his record collection, and began agitating to play in the clubs. In 1983 he worked at Amnesia. For a week. 'I'd been playing Culture Club records, which wasn't the best thing to do at the time.'

The next summer, he played there again, this time for the whole season. Amnesia wasn't popular. Some nights he'd play for six hours straight to a crowd of about twenty. Friends would pass by *en route* to Ku, tell him how much they liked the music, then continue on their way. British DJ Trevor Fung played there too, for six weeks at the height of the season: 'It was dead, completely empty. There was no big scene. I went on to work for other clubs there throughout the summer, smaller places like Glory's.'

It was a depressing summer for Alfredo. After finishing at 6 a.m., he had to wait another hour before the manager turned up to pay him his £20 wage. At the start of September, his girlfriend suggested he play records to pass the time. He did, and people started to call in on their way back into town after Ku closed. Within three days, he had a thousand people there. After two weeks, the place was packed, and the managers decided to close the club at night, and open up instead at 5 a.m. Ibiza had its first big after-hours club.

'At the end of the summer of 1984, that place was beautiful,' recalls Alfredo. 'It was the most incredible thing I ever saw. It was young and old people, black and white, any language, cool and relaxed. Obviously there were drugs, but the people there were perhaps more used to taking drugs. They weren't kids going mad. It was open-air, in the sun, and it was beautiful. The music was Bob Marley, all my musical roots.'

By the 1985 season, Amnesia was *the* club on the island. Alfredo had spent the winter in Madrid, where he'd met a New Yorker who used to bring over underground disco records to sell. There were no vinyl importers in Spain then, and Alfredo describes their meetings as being more like illicit drug deals than record purchases. Certainly, the dealer got him hooked. The first record he gave Alfredo was 'Donnie' by The It, a track made by Chicago producer Larry Heard with the punk-styled singer Harri Dennis. 'It was incredible! It was completely different – the noise, the sound, everything was different. I really loved it. And that guy brought me most of my DJ International and Trax records.'

Back in Ibiza, Alfredo began building his sets round this new house sound. Adonis' 'No Way Back' was his favourite, but he was playing to a crowd whose main exposure to electronic experimentation was Depeche Mode. The big Amnesia tracks were 'Shout' by Tears For Fears, Donna Summer's 'Love To Love You Baby', and anything by Bob Marley. Somehow, however, Alfredo managed to shoehorn house into the mix, alongside a growing collection of European club tunes garnered from DJing trips to France, Germany, and especially Italy. 'I got all these tracks that I'd found in record shops around Europe. Most of them had already been hits in Europe, and became hits in Ibiza. "Jibaro", "City Life" – these weren't new records, even at the time.'

But the blend was fresh. Alfredo is the first to admit that his choice of old and new records from all over the world was a naive one. Later, he was to educate himself about the origins of this music, about the scenes in New York, Chicago and Detroit. But for now, he just threw it into the pot with chart pop, British synth bands, indie rock, Euro disco, reggae and anything else that seemed to fit. The Ecstasy that had started to come in via the hippies, cultists and jet-set clubbers was another ingredient. And, on a dancefloor illuminated by the dawn and then warmed by the Mediterranean sun, the recipe worked. 'In Ibiza, we were the kitchen of music. Because we'd been more free, and we had the best public, the most open-minded, the most mixed culturally. I used to play "Moments In Love" [an ambient electronic track by the Art Of Noise] and people would dance.'

There were other DJs. Jean-Claude, the Belgian DJ at Glory's was a big influence. Massimo, an Italian. A gay man from St Lucia, who also played Sombrero's in London and had a big box of records covering the whole history of disco. Pippi and César Di Malero played at Ku, and at the Café del Mar on the beach in San Antonio, away from the beer boy excesses of the West End, José-Marie Padilla had been playing his eclectic, atmospheric sets while the sun set into the sea ever since he first moved to the island from Madrid in 1973.

The DJ wasn't revered then, points out Alfredo. 'There wasn't a star system at that time. There was only people wanting to have fun. And people are serious about fun. It was like a religious service. They used to clap, but not because of me, they were clapping the music, saying thank you very much. I cried so many times in Amnesia because there were really emotional moments. People were getting something they'd never had before. I think they were the most romantic times of my life. And they didn't last so long.'

With no photographers to bother them, celebrities could come and dance alongside everyone else without fear of exposure. Alfredo met Grace Jones, Freddie Mercury (whose parties on the island were legendary for their decadence), George Michael, Stevie Wonder. Prince Albert of Monaco used to come to Amnesia, surrounded by bodyguards. He once offered the DJ 50,000 pesetas to keep the club open for one more hour. 'I said to him, "All right, everybody here wants the same thing and you have a lot of money. Why don't you give me 500,000?"' laughs the DJ. 'It was too much money for him!'

Ibiza was an appealing holiday destination for young Brits in the eighties. Wham! filmed their 'Club Tropicana' video round the pool at the upmarket hotel Pike's in 1983, and the island's clubs became a summer playground for the new pop, fashion and club glitterati: Boy George had a birthday party there, groups like Animal Nightlife and Spandau Ballet played at the Ku, and *The Face* ran a feature in 1985 in which writer Don MacPherson wondered at the club's £15 admission price and at the diversity of people partying there.[3]

For working-class youths unaware of or unable to afford this other world, the booming resort town of San Antonio had a similar lure: cheap alcohol, plenty of small clubs and bars, and a party atmosphere. In the late eighties, San Antonio was one of the settings for the British tabloids' periodic horror stories about 'lager louts'. Danny Rampling, then a young painter and decorator who was struggling to break into DJing, remembers it somewhat more fondly: 'It was a free and easy place, a good place to have fun and meet members of the opposite sex. That's what young people do on holiday.'

'I went to Ku once in the mid-eighties,' says Nicky Holloway, another young package holiday visitor. 'It was too expensive, and full of bloody foreigners – because that's how you thought in those days. So while Wham! and Spandau were at Pike's and Ku, me and Danny were doing the Star Club in San Antonio with all the girls.'

Although both Londoners, Holloway and Rampling first met each other in Ibiza, outside the Tropicana Bar in San Antonio's raucous West End. Holloway had hoisted himself out of the south London disco pub circuit Rampling was playing by putting on his own events, combining the kind of soul and jazz-funk soundtrack played in the big suburban clubs with a hipper, more West End style of presentation. Rampling began to help him out, putting up banners, handing out flyers, carrying record boxes, playing warm-up: the kind of DJ apprenticeship that hardly exists any more. He also painted Nicky's house.

A born entrepreneur, Nicky Holloway ran his first club trip to Ibiza in 1985, taking over San Antonio clubs to put on nights for his crowd. 'I did this really bad flyer. We cut a picture out of a magazine, typed some of the wording out, and finished it with Letraset. It was wobbly and all over the place, yet we got 200-odd people to go. Now people would look at it and think, "I'm not sending any money there!" But it was all so naive then, no one had upped the ante.'

But some came to the island for more than just a holiday. By the mid-eighties, unemployment in Britain had reached a record high. Prime Minister Thatcher was fond of telling us we'd never had it so good, but despite the stories of champagne-swilling yuppies in the City and loadsamoney lads in the property and building trades, for many young Britons the reality was the dole or pointless job schemes.

Some took another path: they simply left. Not everyone travelling around Europe by thumb and by InterRail was a student on their year out. Unnoticed, unmissed at home (many in fact still finding ways to collect their dole cheques), significant numbers of young Brits were on the move. You would see them selling snacks on the beach in the south of France, smoking weed in the coffee shops in Amsterdam, hanging out in Spain in the summer or in Tenerife in the winter, working, blagging, thieving, dealing – doing whatever they needed to avoid going back to the boredom and the complete lack of hope that was all England seemed to offer.

Ibiza was as attractive to these travellers as it was to the package tourists, but giving out flyers for the clubs, working in the bars, or on the clothes and jewellery stalls that litter the streets of the wild Sa Penya district of Ibiza Town at night, they stumbled into the other side of the island's nightlife. They blagged in at the door and relied on others to buy them drinks, but experimented with trips and Es as they stood on the sidelines and marvelled at the wonders they had found.

These weren't Taboo kids, used to the flamboyant dressing-up games of the London élite. The mix of gay and straight, the extraordinary poses and costumes, were all new to them. Dancing in the same club as actors and singers and people they'd seen on TV, alongside an international mix of beautiful people of all ages, all races, all languages, they felt as if they had walked through the looking glass and found themselves in wonderland.

Alfredo became aware of these young Brits in 1986, when he got to know Nancy Turner, who was working on the island for her second summer along with her friend Joanna McKay. Joanna's dad worked for British Airways, where cheap flights are a perk of the job. After Joanna told her younger sister about the scene there, Lisa came out as often as she could to enjoy it for herself. A year later, for reasons obvious to anyone who has ever seen them in a club, the younger McKay and Turner were rechristened Lisa Loud and Nancy Noise, and became key faces in the Balearic summer of 1987. But the real foundations, Lisa says, were laid the summer before.

'That was a really significant year for all of us because we made a lot of friends. There were a lot of guys that were your typical travelling InterRail-type northern lads who would just stop off in Sweden or Switzerland, then bomb off to France, travelling here, there and everywhere and probably having quite a lot of shady dealings that would get them from A to B. You could just tell they were relevant faces from a scene that was about to explode. They really looked out for us, so there was a real element of loyalty in this scene that was suddenly materialising. We all stuck together, went out clubbing together, and ended up spending summers together.'

Ibiza, she says, was like a fantasy world. 'It was more exciting, more colourful, more worldly. It might have been because I was young, but the things we saw! Guys walking round on stilts with wedding cakes on their head. A guy wearing a swimming hat with Barbie and Cindy dolls attached so their legs all stuck out. This French couple who were always in luminous Lycra with high-rise platform shoes. The madness and extravagance and outwardness of gay people you never really saw in Britain. Those scenes were separate. Ibiza brought that all together, and I just thought it was so amazing.'

In June 1987, Mrs Thatcher was elected for a third term. Britain seemed depressed, moribund, incapable of change. The club scene was stagnating. It had been a long, grim winter. More young Brits than ever went over to the island, hoping to stay for the summer. And this time they had a focus, a place to meet. Trevor Fung and his cousin Ian St Paul, south Londoners who had both spent seasons working on the island in the past, this year decided to open a bar of their own in San Antonio. They called it the Project, in homage to the club night Fung had been running in Streatham with their friend Paul Oakenfold. It was a small place, and the location wasn't ideal: about 300 yards out of the town centre, away from the main bar area in the West End. In fact, Fung says that this became the making of the place. 'You really noticed it if you went past it, because it was the only bar there with hundreds of people standing outside it. If it had been in the centre, it would have just looked like all the others.'

This year, Ecstasy was part of the scene from the start. And the Project became a focus for the young Brits out there for the season, with Ian St Paul at their centre. ('He's the chief of the acid revolution,' says Alfredo. 'He's the ideologue.') Soon there were regularly 200–300 people standing outside the bar in the evenings, people from all over the UK talking to each other, making friends, listening to anything that was thrown on to the decks, from Prince's *Sign O' The Times* album to early releases on Trax: 'Nothing was mixed, we just put them on.'

Ian St Paul went to Amnesia early in the season. He and Paul Oakenfold had lived in New York for a while at the start of the eighties, and had spent many nights at the Paradise Garage. Unexpectedly, St Paul now found the same kind of atmosphere out in Ibiza. 'I was totally shocked. It was that feeling that something had been awakened inside me. That serotonin. When you dance all night for hours and hours, something in your body gets released that's equal to an orgasm, but it only happens when your adrenaline gets to a certain peak. That buzz is *the* buzz. Once you've had it, you can't explain it. And once you're hooked, you're hooked. The Garage was my first serotonin leap. Then, seven years later, there was Amnesia.'

In the sun, away from dreary England, the normal rules ceased to apply that summer. Reality had been suspended, and life seemed like one long holiday. Ecstasy had broken down the barriers, and this small band of Brits were building their world anew: looking after each other, sharing money, food and beds, watching sunset at the Café del Mar then gathering at the Project before hitting the clubs together, they were closer than family.

'We were there to dance! And dance, and dance, and dance! And not stop!' said Adam Heath, then a nineteen-year-old clubber from Bromley. 'We got into this ideal, the E-ed up, loved-up thing; we wouldn't have been so close without it. At one stage, eighteen of us lived in one apartment with six single beds. We all got into the clubs for nothing. They knew us, they called us "the crazy English" and they loved us. Everyone was quite young and well-travelled. We all had the same mentality, which was to have a really good time and try as hard as possible not to think about anything else. When we all came back from England, it really struck me that we'd got some kind of . . . it felt like a religion.'[4]

'We used to just talk to the bouncers for an hour until they let us in, then steal drinks when people put them down because we couldn't afford to buy them,' says another summer clubber who asked to remain anonymous. 'We thought it was the coolest thing on earth, because not everybody knew about it. You had your 18–30 tourists in San Antonio doing pub crawls, and we felt like we were in this whole different, secret world. You would do things that you wouldn't do in England. You could pretend to be someone else.

'We took trips and Es and met all sorts of weird people out there, these gay Spanish men who were so pretty and so different. I don't know how we got by. I was eighteen, nineteen. We used to steal from supermarkets to eat. Chat up the 18–30 guys to get them to buy us something to eat and drink then walk off. Some of the guys we met would catch fish from the sea and we'd cook it with a lime picked off a tree.'

In this escapist paradise, even those with something to lose were shedding their old lives like dead skins. Lisa McKay was working as a financial consultant at a time when the City was booming, earning a ludicrously high wage for an eighteen-year-old and going to Ibiza as often as she could. Her boss took holidays on the island too, and in the summer of 1987, McKay bumped into her at Glory's, an after-hours bar in Ibiza Town with a terrace for eating breakfast and lounging in the sun and a dancefloor inside for those who weren't ready for the night to end. 'I was sitting on this swing in the garden, and my boss said, "Lisa! See you in work on Monday!" And I was like, "Yeah!" But I knew that was it. I never went home. I just didn't want to. I phoned my mom and said, "I'm here, I'm loving it, and I'm not coming back!" '

'It was like a magnet, you got drawn into it,' adds Trevor Fung. 'And also the sheer number of people that were all feeling the same, from all over the world. I was having such a great time, I thought, "Sod England. What is there in England at the moment?" I think that's what shocked Paul and the others. They were really shocked when they saw us.'

Paul Oakenfold and Trevor Fung had known each other for some years by 1987. Both were from the outer edges of south London – Fung from Streatham, Oakenfold from Thornton Heath. Both were into soul, jazz-funk. Fung worked as a warm-up DJ for Steve Walsh, a massive man who was big in every sense of the word on the southern soul scene. He did a lot of coach trips, and on one Fung ended up sitting next to Oakenfold, a chef who was hoping to break into the music business. Fung got him his first gig as a DJ – at Rumours, a wine bar in Covent Garden – and introduced him to his cousin Ian, who also became a good friend.

Now working in club promotions, pushing hip hop records to DJs and writing a column in *Blues & Soul* under the name Wotupski, Oakenfold couldn't leave Britain for the summer like his friends, but he planned to go out at the end of the season to spend his fortnight's holiday there with them just as he had in previous years. He and Trevor Fung had even tried to launch an Ibiza-style club in London in 1985, but the time wasn't right and Fun City had bombed.

It was Oakenfold's twenty-sixth birthday on 30 August. Johnny Walker, another DJ, who had just got a job working club promotions for Phonogram, was to turn thirty two days before. Since Steve Walsh would also be on the island at the same time, it seemed a good chance to have a party. A villa was hired and Nicky Holloway was also invited. He in turn bought a plane ticket for his friend Danny Rampling, who had just returned to the UK after an extended trip to the US – waiting tables, working on building sites, doing whatever he could to escape the boredom of London.

All of them were surprised at what they found in Ibiza. 'We'd definitely all changed,' says Fung. 'We'd taken our British reserve, that guard down. Wearing black, sitting at the bar, too cool to talk to anyone – all that had gone. Over there everyone was talking to each other, you were a different person. Happier, because of the sun as well as the Es. It wasn't *just* drugs. We didn't have drugs all the time. Es were just an excuse. We probably needed it to express ourselves then, but it was all in us all the time. It was fun. We'd all just come out of ourselves.'

'I didn't know what was going on,' says Oakenfold, admitting he was taken aback by how much his friends had changed in a matter of months. 'They seemed a lot more open-minded and just ... free. There was no pressure to do anything, it was just go with it, and everyone lived for the night. The day wasn't important, the day was for recovery. Of course I got there, and I wanted a bit of a tan, to hang out. And they were like, "No no no! It doesn't work that way. *This* is what you do." So of course you run with it, you take the pills, and then it just went on from there.'

When Oakenfold heard about the new drug his friends were doing, he was determined to try it. Rampling, who had read about Ecstasy in *The Face*, was also keen. The four of them went to a San Antonio club called Nightlife, Oakenfold and Rampling swallowing the white capsules while the others waited to see what happened.

Nicky Holloway was strongly anti-drugs, and known for berating even the DJs at his events if they indulged: 'I was always worried about getting slung out of venues because of people smoking draw.' He wasn't going to take his capsule, but then his friends seemed so happy that he decided to have a go. 'By the time we left Nightlife to walk over to the Star Club, I was on cloud nine. I found these two girls I knew from Special Branch, and I was like [*floaty voice*], "Come with us, come with us, we're going to Amnesia!" '

Johnny Walker was still a little apprehensive. 'I hadn't tried any drugs, apart from a dab of speed. They all took theirs, and I saw them all running around the club, hugging each other, big smiles, and I thought, "Oh well, this doesn't look too bad." So I had mine.

'From there we went on to Amnesia, and it was a completely new experience. Just feeling absolutely wonderful. Sparkly vision and colours, and everything felt much warmer and larger than life. We were lucky that we did it in the perfect environment. We were dancing all night in the open air, under the stars. That warm, Mediterranean night air was so much part of it.

'I'd been going to Ibiza just as a normal holidaymaker since '82, but I'd never actually ventured to other parts of the island. So it was all new. And then to hear Alfredo play this complete eclectic mixture of music, it just blew me away. It was something that I hadn't heard in London, having been involved in the soul, funk and hip hop scene. To hear house music played against Cyndi Lauper, the Woodentops, Thrashing Doves, Prince and George Michael was just amazing. And the whole thing was enhanced, obviously, by being on a really good E for the first time, being with good friends, and being in a club full of beautiful people.'

Trevor Fung, who had seen his friends looking at him 'as if I was a nutter' only days before, went along to watch them hold hands and skip round the club, sit on and inside the speakers, dance and open themselves to the experience. Almost everyone who has taken the drug has a similar conversion tale to tell, and has then kept a watchful eye while friends they've introduced to the drug have theirs. But this was also a more innocent time: the MDMA was pure, the setting was perfect, the open-air clubs meant that overheating was a danger yet to be discovered. Many of those taking it that summer weren't even definite that the drug was illegal.

'I sat on top of the speakers or in front of the boxes the whole night, having a ball,' remembers Danny Rampling. 'It was an amazing experience. There was a feeling in the air, generally, in Europe at that time. A great release, I think, of people's anxiety with the political situation.

'I hadn't seen a club as *international* as that before. There were buffalo boys, boys with skirts on. There were the wildest transvestites from Barcelona. There were club kids from London. All the Europeans were represented, and it was such an egalitarian mix of people inside. It was quite an elitist door policy, but most clubs at that time were. And that wasn't such a bad thing, because if you had a heart, if you were enthusiastic towards the place and you looked OK, you came in.

'But it was also Alfredo's music that night. He was mixing up everything, in the same way Larry Levan did at the Garage. And hearing that played in the open air in a glamorous club is something I'm never, ever going to forget in my life. Whenever I look back on it, it warms my heart to think about it, because it was such a special moment.'

The four of them spent the next day at their villa discussing what had happened. How they'd felt. The things they'd seen. The music they'd heard. Finally someone suggested they get into the pool, and they held hands and floated in the water, the Art Of Noise's ethereal 'Moments In Love' playing on the tape they'd acquired of Alfredo's set.

'I felt spaced out,' remembers Johnny Walker. 'Very tranquil, very peaceful. When someone suggested we all get into the swimming pool, we didn't have to think about it, it wasn't a conscious thing. We just got in, lay there, linked hands and transcended off somewhere, just floating. It felt so good.'

'I felt as if I'd been to heaven and back,' says Danny Rampling. 'We discussed the whole thing, and I just said, "This has *got* to happen in London!" '

It was only the start of the holiday. There was a birthday party at the villa, pictures of which were later published in *Mixmag*, then a subscription-only publication distributed to DJs and the industry by the Disco Mix Club. One of the captions has a dig at Paul Oakenfold, for only drinking water. There were other nights in Ibiza's clubs – and plenty more pills, despite their initial fears.

'I remember us saying, "We mustn't do it every night. We'll just keep it for special occasions," says Nicky Holloway wryly. 'Because we were worried about the drugs. So what happened? Every night. By the end of the week we were doing two.'

But what would happen next was decided that day, sitting round the pool, listening to the tape of Alfredo's set.

'That was the mission then, to get back to London, find these records and carry on that vibe,' says Johnny Walker. 'It really was such a genuine, wonderful experience that we'd had that we all wanted to bring that back and share it with other people. It wasn't contrived. I don't think anyone immediately thought, "I can make a lot of money out of this." It really was a true feeling – "This is so good, we want it to go on and on and on." '

'We all got involved in what went on,' says Paul Oakenfold. 'It became probably the most important – as well as the best – holiday all four of us have ever had.'

PART II
1988-90

MAD FOR IT

No Way Back

'Too far gone / Ain't no way back'

Adonis, 'No Way Back'

If the summer had felt like a dream, then the autumn of 1987 was a harsh return to reality. On the night of 15 October, a hurricane lashed across the south of England, uprooting mature trees, destroying buildings and killing seventeen people. In the pictures that dominated the news that week, the countryside looked devastated, as if it would never be the same again. Three days later, Black Monday signalled the end of the eighties boom, with the British stock market suffering its biggest drop this century. The values of the time can be summed up by a survey conducted by the advertising agency McCann Erichson, who found that compassion was out and conspicuous consumption was in for the country's under-twenty-fives. More than anything else, the report concluded, Thatcher's children wanted to work hard and earn money.

Coming home from Ibiza into all this was a cruel comedown. No one wanted the summer to end, even those who'd only been part of it briefly. Two days after Nicky Holloway and his friends came back to England, there was an offshoot of his Special Branch night in Kingston. 'We all had our XTC and Amnesia T-shirts on,' he remembers, 'and we were playing the records we'd heard on holiday. Everyone who

105

had been in Ibiza the week before came that night, but the rest were looking at us like we were lunatics. It was clearly divided into those who got it, and those who didn't.'

As the season ended and they made their way home that autumn, the Ibiza crowd were determined not to lose what they had found. They had taken a leap into the unknown. There was no going back. The northern lads went back to Sheffield, to Manchester, or off on further adventures, but they all arranged to meet up for a reunion weekend in Amsterdam.

Many of the southern contingent came from the south-eastern fringes of London. Quiet, suburban areas that are tantalisingly close to the glittering glamour of the capital and yet a world away, they have long been a breeding ground for inventive, aspirational youths who worked hard to be different, reacting against cool London but also longing to be embraced by it. Mick Jagger and Keith Richards grew up in Dartford. David Bowie came from Beckenham and ran an 'arts lab' in the back room of the Three Tuns pub there. The most enthusiastic of the early punks were the Bromley Contingent. Boy George is from Eltham. This is the area that nurtured the suburban soul scene, and now the Ibiza gang gathered up their friends from Bromley, Beckenham, Bexleyheath, Hornchurch and Dagenham and quietly, unnoticed, began sowing the seeds of a new movement in the capital.

'There were about fifty of us,' says Lisa Loud. 'That summer we'd all slept in the same beds, washed in the same washbasins, used each other's toothbrushes. We felt like we had really good friends. Everyone started to get into a really happy life of clubbing. It was a word-of-mouth thing, everyone bringing their mates.'

The Converse baseball boots and colourful, baggy holiday clothes stayed, and felt even more liberating contrasted with the monochrome clubwear everyone else in the capital was sporting. Loud, boisterous and completely unconcerned about what anyone else thought of them, they were regarded with suspicion in the clubs. The word went out that they were drugged-up football hooligans, and in the diary I kept sporadically in 1988, I dismiss people who were later to become some of my closest club friends as 'Millwall fans on Ecstasy'.

'It just looked different to the club uniform that everyone was used to in London,' recalls Johnny Walker. 'People were wearing that in Ibiza because it was comfortable, it wasn't planned. That little hard-core crowd came back still wearing the same things, wearing their hair longer. I suppose it was a bit of an eighties hippie look. It wasn't soul boy or hip hop. A lot of them were into indie guitar bands before. They liked doing E and dancing, but they weren't from a club background.'

Keeping to the resolve made round the villa pool in Ibiza the month before, Paul Oakenfold talked to the manager of Ziggy's, the wine bar in Streatham where he played funk, hip hop and soul every Friday at the Project. It was agreed that after the club had emptied at 2 a.m., he could reopen the doors for a small, private Ibiza reunion party till 6 a.m. All of the Ibiza gang was there. So were the pills, bought in via Amsterdam with little hassle: Ecstasy was still so rare in Britain then that neither Customs officers nor the police were looking for it.

Oakenfold played the records they'd heard at Amnesia. 'Kaw-liga' by experimental US band the Residents, indie tracks like 'Why Why Why' by the Woodentops, 'Join In The Chant' by Nitzer Ebb, the Fini Tribe's 'De Testimony' and the Thrashing Doves' 'Jesus On The Payroll' mixed in with Chicago house and New York dance records. Odd, obscure tracks that would be puzzling even to an *NME* reader, to DJs who came up from the soul and jazz funk scene, they were radically new. As Nicky Holloway says, 'It took Argentinian and Spanish DJs in Ibiza to make us listen to records that had been made by bands right next door to us in Basildon.'

The sound system at the Project and the illegal after-hours gathering was supplied by Carl Cox, a South London DJ who was popular at house parties but was still trying to break into the club scene. He confesses to being bemused by the clothes, by the intensity of it all, and by a music they called 'Balearic' but he saw as the same mix of pop and dance he'd once played as a mobile DJ at weddings.

'Not having experienced E myself at that time, I was like, "How can they dance like this, all night long?" It was pretty hardcore to see it. But I loved the energy, how they brightened everything up. People dressing how they wanted to dress, dancing how they wanted to dance, sweating and not giving a shit what they looked like. I've seen this scene grow from 100 people all in tie-dye, Kickers and flares, really getting into the music and trance-dancing.'

Paul Oakenfold invited some of the West End faces he knew from his work in club promotions. A Chelsea fan, he also invited along some of his friends from football. Amongst these new recruits were a group of fashion-conscious lads from Windsor and Slough whose fanzine, *Boy's Own*, had started to get them noticed in the clubs. The sporadic magazine was inspired by *The End*, a hip terrace fanzine written by Peter Hooton and his friends, Liverpool football fans who also had a group called the Farm. The mixture of football, music and humour and the obsessive cataloguing of casual fashion details had appealed to Chelsea fan Terry Farley, and he took it to his friends Andrew Weatherall, Steven Mayes and Cymon Eckel, proposing they did something similar. Their first issue came out at the end of 1987, with a clear declaration of intent: 'We are aiming at the boy (or girl) who one day stands on the terraces, the next day stands in a sweaty club, and the day after stays in reading Brendan Behan whilst listening to Run-DMC.'

Instant converts to this new scene, Farley and Weatherall were to become important DJs and later producers, while *Boy's Own* quickly became the nearest the nascent movement had to an in-house publication.

By the sixth week Alfredo came over to play, but he never finished his set. Someone had left their car parked over the goods entrance to the Safeway supermarket opposite. When the delivery vans started to arrive during the night and were unable to get in, the police were called, and the party was brought to a halt. The Project's Ibiza nights were over.

Alfredo's West End debut at the Limelight in Soho the night after was no more auspicious. 'The promoter came over and said, "This is kids' music!" And I said, "Yes, thank God." But they took me away from the decks.'

In November, Oakenfold and Ian St Paul found a new venue for the parties, this time in central London. Many of the Ibiza crowd had been congregating at Heaven on Thursdays for Delirium, still one of the few London club nights to specialise in house music. Now they came to an even better arrangement, hiring out the Sanctuary, a small, intimate space at the back of the main club. The hire fee was only £300, but they couldn't initially afford to pay it upfront. They waited outside the main entrance to Heaven until the first sixty Ibiza refugees turned up, took their £5 entrance money, stamped their hands, then all ran across the main club together to get to their Balearic haven.

The club was called the Future. The name was heartfelt: it genuinely felt as if they were at the vanguard of a new way of life. The small, dark venue tucked in at the back of Heaven's pleasure palace had been designed to feel clandestine. With its black walls, tiny dancefloor and endless shadowy nooks and corners, it now seemed like their private playground, a place where they could all get on the same buzz, open out to each other and express themselves freely. The membership card exhorted 'Dance you fuckers!' but no one really needed telling. People whooped and screamed with joy on the dancefloor, their white clothes flashing under the ultraviolet lights. The heat was so intense that on some nights the sweat literally hung in droplets, in the air.

Nancy Noise and Lisa Loud made their DJing débuts behind the decks there, a move that felt as natural as playing records at a party at home. 'Future was a club full of friends,' says Lisa. 'If we ever saw anyone in there we didn't know, everyone would be asking who they were. It was that small. You're weren't intimidated, you felt comfortable, you didn't feel you were going to go up to anyone to say hello and them just blank you. It just made *everything* easier. You weren't surrounded by inhibitions and barriers and bad attitude. It was just one great big group of people that were just hanging out.'

Happy Happy Happy

Danny Rampling had also been busy. Of the original four DJs on that holiday in Ibiza, he perhaps felt the experience most deeply. Unlike the others, he wasn't an insider with an established career in dance music. He was still working his way in, and here was a scene he felt he could make his own. But there was also another factor.

'I'd come back from America in a much more spiritual frame of mind,' he explains. 'I nearly lost my life in a car crash there, which totally turned my life around. So it wasn't solely taking a pill. That enhanced it, but I had a great *positive* feeling after this accident. I was reborn, I had a second chance with life, and I was having a great time. My spirit was totally free. That was part of the catalyst that sparked the revolution, definitely.'

Just before going to Ibiza, Danny had met his wife-to-be, Jenni, and now they too set about opening a Balearic night. Together they secured a Fitness Centre just south of the river by Southwark Bridge, a popular area for warehouse parties. A basement gym with mirrored walls and a small bar to the side, the space held 250 people. They booked Carl Cox to supply the sound system and to play alongside Danny and a second funk DJ, and the first Klub Schoom was on a Saturday night in November.

The name was supposed to convey the feeling of coming up on Ecstasy. 'Sensation seekers, let the music take you to the top', said the flyer, but the night didn't really gel. The plan was that the Ibiza crowd and Cox's funk following would together fill the place. About 150 people turned up, but both factions regarded the other with suspicion. The funk fans failed to be converted, standing round the sides nodding to the beat while the others danced.

Still, the couple felt optimistic enough to hold a second night a month later, before splitting with Carl Cox and bringing in Norman Jay's brother Joey to do the sound system. This time they filled the basement with dry ice and strobe lights, invited older DJ Colin Faver along to play the house mix he had pioneered in London's gay clubs, and went unreservedly for the Ibiza vibe. 'We gave out flyers in Delirium, Pyramid, Jungle. The clubs where we thought people were compatible. And the King's Road, all over London, on fashionable streets. That was the way to build a club, select people on the streets.'

Inspired by the tongue-in-chic retro of Nick Trulocke's Discotheque club night and by writer Alan Moore's use of a bloodsplattered smiley icon in his hip graphic novel *The Watchmen*, *i-D* magazine had decided to make their January cover a winking version of the seventies yellow smiley. Their eccentric stylist Barnsley had made a jacket festooned with them, which he was wearing round the clubs. When Danny Rampling saw him, the beaming, beatific faces seemed to symbolise everything the Balearic crowd were feeling. By January his night was simply called Shoom, and the flyer had smileys bouncing across it like a shower of pills: the scene may have involved only a couple of hundred people, but the identity of acid house was already being forged.

This was a period of experimentation, of discovery. In the small, enclosed worlds of Shoom and Future, people reverted to childhood, even babyhood. There was no one to criticise or sneer, because everyone was on the same level, sharing experiences and exploring similar feelings with the help of the drugs. They wore dungarees, romper suits. They carried teddies and cuddly toys. They made gifts for each other, gave out flowers, hugged and kissed and declared their love for each other.

Dancing moved from the hips to the knees and elbows. People would trace fluid patterns with their hands through the smoke and flickering strobe lights. Others perfected a jerky, chopping dance like kung fu fighters. There was no showing off of fancy moves: the clubs were too dark, the bodies packed too tightly together, and besides, nobody cared about impressing anyone else. Many would simply hold their hands in the air as if trying to touch the energy there. One night in Shoom Charlie Colston-Hayter, whose older brother Tony had introduced her to the club, remembers standing with her hands stretched up, convinced that the love in the air was so real she'd be able to touch it.

'It was the most magical night. Everyone was just so happy. And you could feel the love, the energy in the air. When they turned the lights on, I started crying. It was like going back to your childhood, that's why it was great. It was all right to wear whatever you liked – I'd make a potato print T-shirt, and then give it away to someone I liked. You wanted to be all bright, to just get away from that whole black and white designer fashion thing. Now you can walk into Our Price and buy the music and into any shop to get clubwear, but then it was all new and you just wore what you wanted.'

Many were using acid as well as Ecstasy. This, the longer hair, Ibiza's hippie past and the feelings of peace and love they felt they were sharing all invited parallels with the sixties, although without the radical politics. When Ian St Paul invited two friends to Future who were genuine hippies, veterans of free festivals and the Peace Convoy, Maggie and Roger Beard were eagerly questioned. Was it better back in the sixties? 'No, no, it's better now,' they replied. 'We didn't have the drugs.'[1]

People talked about the dawning of a new age, about opening new doors of perception, but there was no real philosophy behind these vague notions, no thought-out strategies or directions; this was a movement about *feeling*, about friendship and fun rather than serious thought.

'I always was disappointed that it didn't get a bit more angry or political,' says Mark Moore. 'The thing is, it never had a leader – no one would *be* a leader. It was so linked with drugs, and you saw what had happened before to people like Timothy Leary and Ken Kesey from movements that were linked with drugs. It wasn't going to be easy, and I guess no one wanted the job!'

Inspired by Double D and Steinski's cut-ups and by the house music he was mixing in with Italian disco and kitsch at mixed gay nights like Jungle and Pyramid, Mark Moore became the latest British DJ to make a record at the end of 1987. He gathered together snatches of old disco tunes by the likes of Rose Royce, the sampled voice of New York performance artist Karen Finley and vocals by his motley crew of club friends in a mix that caught the mood of the time perfectly. Long before it was released, Moore was playing 'Theme From S'Express' in his clubs, and one night Danny Rampling came up to ask for a copy and invite him down to Shoom, which had gone weekly in mid-February. Moore told me about it, and we went down one Saturday towards the end of the month, after Discotheque.

Shoom was a hot, sweaty, claustrophobic space with low ceilings, a full-on assault on all the senses. The strawberry-flavoured smoke made it difficult to see, and even people who went there week after week would often walk smack into the steamed-up mirrors or find themselves talking to a reflection. The music was loud and exciting, and the relentless strobes made the movements of the dancers seem even more jerky than they were. The thing I remember most was that people I knew only vaguely threw their arms around me like long-lost friends, then tried to remove my clothes. I was wearing a Levi's jacket that I rarely took off in clubs (cloakroom queues were too long, floors too dirty) and a zipped-up tracksuit top, and it seemed that everyone

Larry Levan at the Paradise Garage, New York, 1983 (*Patricia Bates*)

Frankie Knuckles (right) and Ron Hardy at the Music Box, Chicago, 1986 (*Simon Witter*)

Dancing to Northern Soul at the Wigan Casino, 1974, originally reproduced in *Soul Survivors*, an account of Casino history by Russ Winstanley and David Nowell (Robson Books)

Post punk Boy George (left) and Jeremy Healy, March 1980 (*Graham Smith*)

Paul Oakenfold, Lisa Loud and Ian St Paul at Shoom, London, April 1988 (*David Swindells*)

Lisa Loud, Nancy Noise and the Future posse photographed for *i-D* in April 1988 (*David Swindells*)

Shoom, April 1988 (left to right): Spike from MFI, club face Johnny Rocha and Gary Haisman (*David Swindells*)

Chill out area of the main dancefloor at Spectrum, April 1988 (Danny Rampling in centre) (*David Swindells*)

Reading the latest tabloid coverage of the club scene outside the Café del Mar, Ibiza, 1989 (*David Swindells*)

The Energy rave team at their weekly club night Fun City (left to right): Anton Le Pirate, Jeremy Taylor, Tintin Chambers (*David Swindells*)

Mike Pickering (left) and Graeme Park at the Haçienda, Manchester, 1990 (*David Swindells*)

Dawn at Joy, the first outdoor rave near Blackburn, August 1989 (*Peter Walsh*)

Freedom to Party demo in Trafalgar Square, London, January 1990 (*David Swindells*)

Ibiza-style foam party at the Haçienda (*Peter Walsh*)

The Illusionists, professional
bodypainters from Amsterdam, at
Chuff Chuff's 'Christmas panto' party
in Harrogate, 1996 (*Rob Farrell*)

Around the DJ booth at Metalheadz,
1996 (left to right): the back of
Cleveland Watkiss, Grooverider, Rob
Playford, Peshay (*Gus*)

that walked by seemed to want to help me off with the jacket, unzip the top, help me loosen up a little.

The crowd was already starting to broaden from the original Ibiza crew. There were clubbers from the suburbs who were barely in their teens (some of Shoom's regulars were fourteen and fifteen, although so street-smart that it would have been hard to tell), but also several faces I recognised. Actor/comedian Keith Allen. Dancer Michael Clarke. Paul Rutherford from Frankie Goes To Hollywood. Patsy Kensit. A member of a then-current teen pop band became a regular there, despite being banned by his record company, who were terrified that the tabloids might pick up on his newly acquired drug habits. He would sometimes appear out of the smoke, bug-eyed and grinning conspiratorially, before putting a finger to his lips to ask me to keep quiet and disappearing back into the fog.

Part of the appeal of Shoom was that these faces weren't assured entry. They were made to wait outside with everyone else, and often had to come back a few times to show willing before Jenni would let them in. 'If there was a Malcolm McLaren for house music, it was Jenni,' says West End club veteran Patrick Lilley. 'She was the one that would have the nerve to challenge the former nightclub gods and say, "No. You've got the wrong attitude. You can't come in." When you do that, you leap about forty places in the trendy nightclub league automatically.'

When Boy George and Jeremy Healy first came they were left outside, noses pressed up against the steamed-up glass. 'All you could see through the tiny little windows was strobe lights and smoke,' remembers Healy, a note of incredulity still creeping into his voice. 'The doorman told us he couldn't be responsible for our safety in there. This was the first club I had ever been turned away from in my life.'

Of course, this made it all the more desirable, and after Paul Rutherford took them in, they quickly became regulars. 'The drug was familiar, but the music wasn't at all,' says Healy. 'It was really exciting, and having seen the start of the New Romantics, the punks, I could tell that it was going to be massive.' After his club the Circus had ended in 1985 he had made a good living creating music for ads, but he was soon telling friends that he wanted to go back to the clubs and DJ again, and play like Danny Rampling.

This mixture of the original crowd and the very West End glitterati they felt they were rebelling against quickly began to cause tension. The venue was tiny and suddenly there was a queue outside at 11 p.m., clamouring for Jenni Rampling to let them in, and people who had been there from the start were no longer assured admission. 'One night at Shoom, I saw friends of mine that were major friends of the scene, very instrumental in keeping us all going, getting turned away,' says Lisa Loud. 'How could they not see the significance of these people? We all started with like twenty of us.'

Jenni became a hated figure to those she excluded, but it is also fair to say that none of the clubs the Ramplings were to run in the next few years would have been as influential or have lasted so long had she not been on the door, carefully picking her crowd. And the new faces were just as sincere in their conversion to this new lifestyle. Many had tried Ecstasy before, but the music, the bright, baggy clothes, the lights, the sheer emotional *intensity* took it to another level. 'People were walking round like they'd found Christianity,' says Jak, a Streatham girl who worked with Patrick Lilley at Victory PR and had been introduced to the scene early by Paul Oakenfold. 'You could express how you really felt instead of worrying about image.'

Years after the event, people still talk with wonder about their own conversion experiences, the first time the drug and the music and the atmosphere came together and they felt themselves opening to a new way of life. Most people can remember exactly what they were wearing, because it instantly felt wrong. 'That first night was *the* defining, life-changing moment of my life,' says Helena Marsh, now one half of dance group the Beloved, but then a buyer for the designer fashion shop Brown's. 'All my values, my opinions, everything changed. I went down there in all my designer clothes and by the end of the evening they had gone. I was wearing wool Gaultier pants, and it was so hot in there I had to take them off. So I went into the toilet with my friend, we ripped off our trousers, he took off his polka dot boxer shorts and I put them on. They were all sweaty, but it felt right.' She laughs. 'I don't know what I did with my trousers but at the end of the evening I did get them back.'

For the *Boy's Own* posse, it was similarly enlightening. 'We'd already taken pills, but we didn't really come alive to the potential of the drug until we walked through the door of Shoom,' says Cymon Eckel. 'It wouldn't have developed into what it was without Ecstasy. There wouldn't have been the same intensity and positivity. I'd just come out of the polite West End and all of its finesse and fashion and walked into this complete devil of a club where it was dark, there was a smoke machine constantly on, and people sat in the bass bins and didn't worry about getting their clothes dirty. There were these kids in ponchos, Kickers, and dungarees with no tops. It was the anti-Christ of clubland. From then on I went every week, and it changed my life.'

After their conversion, the *Boy's Own* crew became evangelists, and their fanzine quickly became the nearest the scene had to a mouthpiece. 'The politics of acid house were no sell-out, no commercialisation, let's keep this for the people,' explains Eckel. '*Boy's Own* was the only tangible thing that the press and record companies could drop into.' The Ramplings were ambivalent about the media – simultaneously courting the attention their scene deserved and determined to keep it underground and unspoilt. Jenni had asked me not to write about the parties at the Fitness Centre, but by then they had also approached Victory PR to help with strategy.

Patrick Lilley persuaded his other club client, Graham Ball, to let Shoom do the VIP room at Supernature, a Westworld event at the Brixton Academy. The Ramplings decked out the space with carpets and cushions, decorated the walls with ethnic hangings, and booked belly dancers. As a way of spreading the word about Shoom, the ploy worked brilliantly – everyone in the massive main club was clamouring to get upstairs, unsure quite what was happening up there but convinced it must be good.

Lilley also arranged a party in the basement of the hip members-only drinking club Fred's in Soho, inviting all the DJs involved in the scene, forty or so Shoomers and some of the house artists he'd met in Chicago. Much to the bemusement of the media and fashion folk drinking in the bar above, a smoke machine and strobe were set up while Danny Rampling played, and the creators of house got their first inkling of what the UK was about to do with the music they'd made.

In the following weeks, Chicago house star Bam Bam performed at Shoom, standing on a milk crate in the middle of the dancefloor.

Fingers Inc. played there too, Larry Heard and singer Robert Owens tucked away in a corner, almost invisible in the smoke. Marshall Jefferson, over in the UK to produce an album for house diva Kym Mazelle, came down to the club with a group of us one night and finally found a British club that had the same kind of energy he'd seen at the Music Box. 'I thought Danny Rampling was the greatest DJ I'd ever seen in my life. He was tearing up some shit at Shoom. I was surprised because he was white, and I'd never heard a white DJ play like that.'

'Everyone there sensed something special was going on,' adds Jak. 'I used to look around and see all age groups, all cultures, pop stars dancing alongside estate kids, and I felt I was witnessing something really powerful. I had big optimism. I was thirty-two, and it was like I'd been injected with this new energy. I just wanted to give myself over completely to the hedonism, and I'd never felt that before in my life. It was very liberating, to really go *beyond*. Before, you might get drunk or whatever in a club but there was always that boundary. Here, it was like the boundaries had been broken.'

When she left her Filofax in a cab one night, with all her work contacts in it, she found herself wondering if it wasn't a sign that she should quit her job in PR and give herself up to the feeling completely. So many others felt the same that at one point the Ramplings had to add a note in the hand-written newsletter they sent out to members pleading with them not to give up their day jobs.

'You really felt at the time almost like that old lifestyle wouldn't exist any more,' says Jak. 'I'd been very much into clothes and recognising that you were judged by what you wore, but suddenly it didn't matter as long as you were expressing yourself. I started wearing saris and no make-up and not feeling like other people's opinion mattered, because I felt fine.'

'A lot of people did think, "This is it, this is the big change coming on"', says Danny Rampling. 'Which was partly due to drug use as well, the same as in the sixties. But it did change things, for a moment. Enormously. It broke down everything, it pushed down most of the barriers that were in the way. But some people took it like a religion. I started to become a messiah to some people, which was quite scary. They'd been touched by it even deeper. I don't know, but maybe they'd been using a lot of LSD too because that does alter one's state of mind.'

'But it was very spiritual. Some of those moments in the club were unbelievable. People literally went into trance states, including me. Not from the use of drugs, but through that music and the human energy that was going around. That was most unique and special. It happens on the plains of Africa and South America, but it's not something that's happened in Britain for centuries. And that feeling in that small space was so *intense* some nights.'

At the Prestatyn soul weekender that April, Nicky Holloway, Paul Oakenfold, Johnny Walker and Pete Tong – who had gathered up the tracks coming out of Chicago into an acid house compilation as early as January 1988 – decided to take the sound to the soul establishment. Johnny Walker says they were horrified.

'The older generation of DJs didn't really relate to it. Chris Hill, Robbie Vincent and a few others came in to listen, and decided we were completely bonkers. They weren't having any of it. The next day they hung up a big banner saying "No acid house" and there were a few jibes and comments: "This is a soul weekender, we're going to keep it this way." '

Walker chuckles. 'And how wrong they were.'

Theatre of Madness

'Let the music take control.'
                    The Nightwriters, 'Let The Music Use You'

Heaven had approached Ian St Paul to say that the Monday night in the main club was about to become vacant, and he decided to take it on. It was a giant leap of faith: one of the biggest clubs in London, with the best sound system and lights, Heaven had a capacity of 2,000. Monday was traditionally a night for recovery, not for mad clubbing, and few thought he could succeed. But St Paul believed the scene was capable of growing. To pull in more of the West End crowd, he brought in Gary Haisman as his partner, a likeable jack-the-lad who promoted a club night called the Raid and knew everyone.

Geordie designer Dave Little had already made the flyers for clubs like the the Raid, and the distinctive boy-and-dog logo he had drawn up for *Boy's Own* had been turned into a popular T-shirt. Now he was offered £200 to do a flyer for this new venture. The brief was simple: the club was to be called Spectrum – Heaven On Earth, and Haisman had an idea about an all-seeing eye. Little was a fan of Ken Kesey, and saw parallels between this emergent scene and the LSD-inspired happenings in Haight-Ashbury in the sixties. He reflected this in the artwork, an unusually lavish full-colour production featuring a huge, slightly bloodshot eye that was to become the first brand logo of acid house.

'Ken Kesey experimented with strobe lights and wibbly wobbly sounds in 1962. I saw this as the second acid wave, which is why I copied the psychedelic sixties art for the flyer. On the back I put, "Have you passed the acid test?" I was fascinated by that kind of art. But it was also a gut reaction.'

Everyone from the emerging scene came to the opening of Spectrum on 11 April. The northern posse travelled down, bringing friends, and the southern contingent were out in force. Free Ecstasy was handed round amongst the group to help the atmosphere. But there were still only a few hundred of them: fine in a small space like Shoom or Future, but a little sad in the huge, lavish environs of Heaven. The next few Mondays saw little improvement, and by week four Haisman had left and St Paul was running the club alone, looking at a mounting debt he would be unable to pay off if his faith proved misplaced. With the cost of the flyers, production and security, he owed well over £15,000.

'Ian, being top blagmaster, got us into this situation, but if you actually thought it through, we were in a lot of trouble,' says Oakenfold. 'We hadn't got fifteen grand. And if it fell through, we were dealing with Richard Branson – Virgin owned Heaven. But we had this belief in what we were doing, that if one person comes and brings someone else, they will love it so much that they will then bring another person.'

They were right. The word got around, and almost out of the blue, the place was full. By week eight, there were 2,000 clubbers inside and the same number outside trying to get in. The flyers began calling the night 'Theatre of Madness', and it was an apt description. People danced on speakers, on podiums, arms stretching out of the smoke reaching up to the green lasers that cut across the dancefloor, streaked with sweat, hair awry. With girls wearing minimal make-up, everyone stripped down to shorts or dressed in clothes designed for dancing rather than posing, this was beyond fashion. It was beyond anything anyone had ever seen before. The quietest night of the week in clubland was now the most extraordinary. Gary Haisman started the chant on the dancefloor, but soon everyone took it up: 'Acieed!!'

Ian St Paul remembers standing in the DJ booth next to Paul Oakenfold, looking down at the lasers and thinking, 'This is the best. How could it be better?' When he danced, he would move under the DJ booth so that his friend could see him. 'Paul would always put on the tracks that he knew I loved, my favourites.' And he would go off. Lost in music. No way back. And the people around him, the ones standing by the bar unsure how to dance because the music was new to them, they would go off too, watching his moves, feeding off his energy, feeling the same freedom.

'That was the early days, when every moment counted. Towards the end, you just knew that next week would be a good night, that it would be packed, whatever. Those days, we weren't sure. What I remember most about that time is being with Paul, being a part of the most happening thing in London, and sharing that moment with my best mate.'

Added to the atmosphere, Spectrum was a spectacular club in terms of production. There were frequent décor changes. Snowstorms and explosions of silver confetti, leaves scattered on the dancefloor, a spaceship coming down from the roof. Jak, who had moved from Victory PR to work at Spectrum, says Ian St Paul's energy was hard to keep up with. He would roam the office shouting out ideas, details, grand themes. 'There weren't any real rules,' she says. 'There wasn't anybody that had gone before to tell you how it was done, so it was all being made up on the spot.'

There were different bands every week. Flowered Up, Guru Josh, Happy Mondays, the KLF. One week Kenji Suzuki from Bomb the Bass stood on a podium in the middle of the dancefloor in a white suit playing along to the records on a white guitar, the lasers bouncing off it. Another week Haçienda DJs Mike Pickering and Graeme Park set up decks at the opposite end of the main room and played a sound clash against Paul Oakenfold and Colin Hudd.

Everyone passed through there: rock bands, actors, models, design-ers. Bros, David Bowie, U2, Prince. The Pet Shop Boys bought Liza Minelli along once: the balcony was shut off so she could view the action undisturbed, sitting at a table with a bottle of champagne.

Then as now, Oakenfold was a master of the grand entrance. When he played a record like the Nightwriters' 'Let The Music Use You' (made by Frankie Knuckles) or 'Big Fun' by Inner City, people clutched their heads and danced like they were losing their minds.

'I came to England early in 1988, and there wasn't really a lot going on in the clubs,' says Inner City's Kevin Saunderson. 'Then I came back in the mid-summer and I went to Spectrum. "Big Fun" was played, and I'd never seen such a reaction in my life. The energy, the response. It was just wild.'

'You'd see the whole place come alive,' says Carl Cox, who was still on the sidelines, a spectator standing on the walkway and watching the madness below. 'It brought everybody into it. You could go to that place on your own, and when you walked out, you'd know ten people from Manchester, Ireland, Scotland. It really did break things down.'

The gentle wash of Balearic had been replaced by the full-on sonic assault of acid house, those expanding frequencies and warped basslines taking on new nuances when played through Heaven's huge sound system. Every day was a discovery: there was, by then, a huge back-catalogue of music from Chicago, Detroit and New York to be played, with new stuff coming out of Britain too by the day. As the club took off, Mark Moore's 'Theme From S'Express' moved up the charts to number one. A DJ and his colourfully dressed club mates cavorted on *Top of the Pops*, making no attempts to mime instru-ments, to look like 'real' musicians or even like a band, and no one quite knew how to take it.

Mark Moore remembers being interviewed on breakfast TV, and being asked during an ad break whether there was anything new in music he'd like to talk about. He mentioned acid house, and the presenter looked doubtful, asking if it had anything to do with LSD. Moore denied that the music had any association with drugs, joining what was to become a long tradition of lying to defend the scene. The presenter still thought the subject was best avoided. The ad break ended, and as they came back live on air Moore looked straight to camera. 'There's this new thing called acid house . . .' he said. The presenter blanched.

This was our time now. The lunatics were taking over the asylum.

Bringing Down The Walls

Not everyone involved in the acid house scene in London had been to Ibiza. Shock were one of a growing number of younger sound systems who were playing soul, funk and hip hop as well as the traditional reggae. Some time at the start of 1986 they played a sound clash in Northampton, and Nottingham-based DJ Graeme Park was on the bill. He played Adonis' 'No Way Back'. Ashley Beedle was a junior member of the crew, and none too impressed. 'I really couldn't get my head around it, but the rest of the guys were into it. They were saying it was like jump-up reggae. That's the way they used to look at it. They never even used to call it house.'

The Shock crew started to play some of the Chicago records in their sets at parties in London, even though they often cleared the floor. They travelled down to Mi Price in Croydon to buy the records from Jazzy M, whose LWR show *The Jackin' Zone* was now getting the station's biggest mail bag. He was also getting sent tapes of music his listeners had made themselves. 'It was a very simple music to make,' he says. 'The early stuff is just a simple beat or rhythm together with a catchy sample. But because it was upbeat and raw, it was very exciting too.'

Richard West was another convert to the Chicago and Detroit sound who listened avidly to the LWR show. A CB radio enthusiast from Holloway, north London, who went on-air under the name Chelsea Boy, he had also been involved in the capital's nascent hip hop scene. He had been a body-popper, but when the style changed to break-dancing, he dropped out. There were dancers who were younger, more supple than him, and with his hair already prematurely thinning, he worried about spinning on his head. Instead he turned to rapping, adjusting his old CB radio tag to became Mr C.

'At sixteen, seventeen, I was rapping over Salsoul, Montana Sextet and electro. But when people like Eric B and Rakim started coming through, I didn't like that slow, bad attitude stuff. I was always more into your upbeat party music. From 1986 onwards, I refused to rap on anything but house.'

Styling himself on Malcolm McDowell's character in the film version of *A Clockwork Orange*, he would go out dressed in a leather bomber jacket and a bowler hat and blag his way on to the mic in clubs. In the summer of 1987, he went to Colin Faver and Eddie Richards' night at the Camden Palace, a grand folly of a club erected during the New Romantic period in homage to New York's Studio 54. He asked Faver if he could rap, but the DJ asked him to wait until his set moved back from the house into hip hop. 'He'd just cued up Nitro Deluxe's "This Brutal House", and I started rapping about jacking your body, pure house lyrics, and it blew them away.'

Eddie Richards had a label, Baad Records, and that September he released a house track called 'Page 67', recorded with Mr C under the name Mister E. (There was no drug reference in the name: the Mister came from Mr C, the E from Evil Eddie Richards). Lawrence 'Kid' Bachelor, one of the first black DJs from the sound system tradition to commit to house in a major way, helped out on the mix, and Mr C went on to rap with him live as well as at Soul II Soul's influential Sunday-night jams at the Africa Centre in Covent Garden.

The parties that brought all these strands together were called Hedonism, the first big Ecstasy warehouse parties which happened between February and May 1988 in Alperton Lane on the outer fringes of west London. They were free parties, held in an empty warehouse owned by the father of one of the promoters, four friends who were inspired not by Ibiza but by a trip to the Paradise Garage. Only a few hundred people turned up to the first one, which was advertised on flyers given out at Delirium's Chicago House Convention in February. 'It made a change to have a warehouse party that had no funky music,' says Norman Jay. 'In one night, everything that went before it was gone, redundant.'

As the word spread, the parties soon became huge celebrations of a scene about to break big, lasting all night and well into the following day. The walls were decorated with painted day-glo banners with slogans like 'Party People' and 'This is Acid' picked out with UV lights. At one, a group of Indian musicians entertained exhausted dancers in the chill-out room.

'It was more sophisticated than the warehouse parties we were used to,' recalls Nikki Trax, a clubber who went to every Hedonism party. 'They had the first chill-out room I'd ever seen – a basement with mattresses, cushions and tables so people could flop down and roll spliffs, and then a big room with the most kicking sound system outside of Heaven. The next morning, Soul II Soul would play football in the industrial estate outside and people would be swinging on the banners, carrying on the party long after the music ended.'

Everyone came. The sound systems, the rare groovers, the Balearic posse, the West End trendies. Danny and Jenni Rampling got married on the afternoon of 26 February, and celebrated that night at Hedonism. Promoters, DJs, bands, MCs like Mr C and most of those who were to become major players in the summer of '88 passed through the parties.

'It was raggas, mad estate kids, uptown kids, everyone in one place without any grief whatsoever,' says Ashley Beedle, who took his first E there and finally got into house.

'House music dominated, proper 'Trax stuff, the real nasty stuff,' remembers R&B DJ Trevor Nelson. 'We were all dancing to it, and it was a pretty cold night so we had layers on, and everyone was peeling their clothes off bit by bit. It became almost like, *let's see if we can keep this going all night*. It went on and on and on. My shoes were in a mess, my clothes were in a mess. The next one, it was like everyone dressed in the worst possible clothes they could find. They all turned up looking like New Age travellers. That for me was the start of the whole dressing down thing that followed in the clubs.'

At one of the final parties, the sound system was only hired until 6 a.m., after which it needed to move to do another booking. Soul II Soul brought their rig to fill in, and as one system came down, they were putting theirs up at the other end of the warehouse. In the time it took to swap over, the crowd bashed bottles and cans on the walls and floors, clapped, stamped and chanted to keep the beat going and carried on dancing to the music they were making themselves. None of those present had ever felt this kind of unity in a club before.

Eventually, the local police warned the organisers that they would be forced to act if the illegal parties continued, and so Hedonism bowed out on 29 May with a fifth and final event. Inspired by what they'd seen there, anarchist punk couple Lu Vudovik and Paul Stone had already opened an alternative. The first RIP party was in the basement of a transvestite shop just behind Euston station on 14 April. I went there after going to Future and Heaven, and spent most of my time talking to a group of DJs and ecstatic clubbers who were worried about an article that my friend John Godfrey was about to write about the scene for *i-D*, taking it public for the first time. 'There seems to be some concern over the effect it will have on the Shoom-type clubs,' I wrote in my diary.

There were few journalists covering clubs in central London then. *Mixmag* was a subscription-only publication, and magazines like *Blues & Soul* largely regarded the antics of trendy clubbers with disdain. David Swindells was ever-present with his camera, and compiled the club pages for the London listings magazine *Time Out*. John Godfrey and I had worked together compiling the clubs and music sections at the now-defunct rival listings magazine *City Limits*, and had just started work at *i-D* and *The Face* respectively. Magazines which had found a new niche market in the young and hip, both publications were starting to run into trouble: they had catalogued the styles and tribes of the eighties brilliantly, but the decade was running out of steam, the style was getting stale and the readers were getting older or losing interest. We were both searching for something new, but it was John who saw a scene building where I saw only a few disconnected clubs.

A few weeks later, Vudovik and Stone secured a new venue, a decaying building in Clink Street in Southwark that now houses London's prison museum. RIP (Revolution in Progress) opened up on Saturdays just round the corner from Shoom, and soon there were parties there on Fridays and even Sundays too. Eddie Richards, Kid Bachelor and Mr C were amongst the DJs, and the atmosphere was dark, shadowy – more like a reggae blues dance. People would rap or sing on the mic, plug guitars and synths into the sound system and play along, and bring harmonicas and drums. Soul II Soul supplied the sound system at first, but then Shock moved in, finally finding an appreciative audience for their house mix in a barely lit back room draped with camouflage netting.

The nights had different names, but most of us simply called them Clink Street. 'The place was a complete dump, really,' says Mr C. 'That's the best way to describe it. A nasty, sweaty dump of a venue. It was the raw edge of it that kicked it off. Nothing but a strobe light and a fog machine. You'd see the most horrible, frightening and ugly ragamuffins you'd ever seen next to the most beautiful, warm and welcoming people you'd ever seen. It was just a total mix-up, a big melting pot.

'I went to Shoom, but only when I rapped with Colin Faver, because it was far too namby-pamby for me. It was all that light, fluffy poppy stuff, whereas Clink Street was always very dark, dangerous and intense. It was a totally different thing, like trying to compare cheesy happy house with dark hardstep jungle. Shoom just didn't have the edge that was required, especially on drugs. When you're taking pure MDMA and LSD, you want the real deal.'

We went to Clink Street quite often after or instead of Shoom. In some ways, I preferred it. No one tried to loosen your clothes or massage your shoulders there, the crowd was more racially mixed, and it was easier to get in (although that didn't stop people desperately offering bribes to the doormen, trying to rush the door or climbing up the external walls on nights when it was full). Perhaps because it was a family affair, Shoom always felt cliquey, despite its often-voiced aim to be open to all.

Clink Street was more comfortingly anonymous. It was the first place where anyone pointed out groups of rival football fans, lads I was told would once have been cutting each other with Stanley knives, mixing in the same club together. Whether they really were hardcore hooligans or just a group of casuals who supported different teams I don't know. But Clink Street's dank labyrinth of rooms were places of strange alliances, a dream-like, subterranean world where reality often seemed to have been suspended.

'Once they just had a red light on, there was this intense music playing, and we just went to another planet,' remembers Danny Rampling, who would go there on nights Shoom wasn't open. 'We were on Mars or somewhere – there was just this feeling that we were not on earth. That was a very, very strange feeling. A great feeling. And all of us shared it.'

Strangest of all was the night when Ashley Beedle was in the back room with Shock playing the Fingers Inc. track 'Bring Down The Walls', and the crowd began chanting singer Robert Owens' words and then taking them literally. 'There was cladding on the walls which was quite easy to break,' says Beedle. 'I remember them actually digging a hole through like four levels of this stuff and actually reaching the last wall, which was made out of brick. Then they wanted to take the bricks out as well. It was really funny. They just demolished it. Completely demolished the room we were in.'

To many who were there, it felt symbolic. There were no longer any barriers holding us back. The old élitism was finished. The walls were coming down.

The Summer of Love

As the year drew on, time seemed to be accelerating as the movement spread ever faster. Everyone who got involved talked sagely of the need to protect the scene, to keep it underground. Then they all told their friends, who in turn invited other people they knew. Nothing this much fun could be kept secret for long.

In May Shoom moved to Raw, a club in the bowels of the earth way under the YMCA building off Tottenham Court Road. They promoted it with a booklet of poems and cartoons portraying the happy happy happy Shoom vibe. 'The greatest thing that Shoom creates is the freedom in which we can be ourselves,' wrote Lisa. Another contributor, Claire, declared: 'Shoom has never been a club. It's just like one happy family who care about each other.' But the disquiet that had already been building amongst the original crew was compounded by the fact that the Ramplings had chosen Thursday, the same night as Future. For the first time, people were forced to choose. The illusion of one big, happy family was already beginning to shatter.

John Godfrey's piece came out in *i-D* at the end of May, with pictures of Gary Haisman dancing in a *Boy's Own* T-shirt, of Lisa Loud and Nancy Noise and their posse, and plenty of smileys. It called them 'the Amnesiacs' and 'beach bum hippies', deliberately downplaying the role of drugs, although there were plenty of clues for those in the know: 'Peace and love mateys and get on one right now,' the piece ended. 'Aciieed!!'

A few days after *i-D* had come out, on Saturday 4 June, acid officially went overground with the launch of Nicky Holloway's club the Trip at the Astoria Theatre on Charing Cross Road, bang in the centre of the West End. The Astoria had been a glorious venue for Delirium, but had since been refurbished into a rock/cabaret venue. The top balcony was seated with tables supper-club style, each one furnished with a glowing orange lamp. The bars were done out with tacky neon signs naming them after rock stars like Keith Moon.

Holloway had been offered the venue for a five-week stretch while a successful black theatre production took a summer break, and he wasn't at all confident he could fill it. He stretched white drapes from the balcony to the top of the stage to recreate the look of the Ibizan club Es Paradis but also to block off the balcony, which he had assumed would stay empty. The music in the main room would be acid house, with Mike Pickering's group T-Coy playing a live PA on the opening night. In the bar area upstairs, Andrew Weatherall and Terry Farley from *Boy's Own* were to play a more eclectic, psychedelic mix. Holloway himself came back early from a Special Branch holiday he'd organised to Ibiza in order to give out flyers at Spectrum.

'At that time, I still stood outside doing all the flyers myself. People forget that. You'd have to run round all the pubs and the bars with your black flying jacket on. The thing was just gathering steam, snowballing all the time, and the timing was perfect: *i-D* did the front cover the week we opened. It was the week it went overground. And that was it. Whoosh! It was get on board or get run over by it.'

The first week, the queue stretched around the venue and into Soho Square behind it. By the second week, it was impossible to get anywhere near the door of the Astoria for the crush of bodies around it, all clamouring to get in. Inside, the scene had to be seen to be believed. The dancefloor was a heaving mass of day-glo-coloured humanity, all moving together to the beat. On the balcony, illuminated only by the eerie orange glow of the table lamps, people climbed on top of the tiered tables and fused into a writhing, wriggling mass of arms and legs that resembled a painting by Hieronymus Bosch. When the right record was played, there was no sense of *individuals* dancing any more: the club felt like one living, breathing organism.

'I always felt like someone should stay straight and watch what was going on,' says Pete Tong, who had a family at home and so avoided the chemicals everyone else seemed to be indulging, despite the prominent notices warning that drug users would not be tolerated. 'But oddly, I never felt tired at that club either.' When I suggest that it was the energy of the place carrying him along, he just smiles, suggesting that the amyl nitrate rising up from the dancers around the DJ platform may also have played a part.

Many of the original crew resented this encroachment on their scene. They accused Holloway of spoiling their party, of selling the scene out and being motivated solely by money. But in the end, he was just a convenient target for their anger. It was too late to keep it all small, and the business of acid house had already begun. Shoom now appeared in the club listings and was leaving flyers in fashionable West End shops. The same week the Trip opened, *Time Out* nominated Spectrum as its club of the year and ran a two-page feature on acid clubs. That week, Spectrum opened up in its usual venue of Heaven, but also in a marquee on the opposite side of the Thames as part of a dance festival sponsored by the magazine. Both Holloway and Paul Oakenfold had already made Ibiza-influenced singles for release during the summer, under the names Beats Workin' and Electra (one of the other members of Electra was the exotic-sounding Nic Divaris – as plain Rob Davis, he'd played guitar with the seventies pop group Mud). Holloway's tune was 'Sure Beats Workin', a Balearic reworking of 'Stone Fox Chase', then the *Top of the Pops* theme tune; Oakenfold's was a cover of the Amnesia favourite 'Jibaro'.

The Trip was successful enough to have its run extended, but still it only stayed open for ten weeks. In that time, clubland changed completely. You either rode the roller-coaster, or it ran over you. Overnight, people who had been the hippest people in London looked like dinosaurs, obsolete. The eighties were over. One night, three of the decade's major players in central London came to check out the Trip – a club promoter, a magazine editor and a journalist. I remember seeing them standing near the ground-floor bar looking immaculate in their designer clothes, staring at the scene before them in undisguised horror. When I looked back again, they were gone.

That summer, it seemed there were parties everywhere. When the clubs closed at 3 a.m., no one wanted to go home. Those in the know would trek down to after-hours clubs like Mendoza's in Brixton, an illegal drinking den where local pirate radio DJs Fabio and Grooverider played acid house five nights a week after the clubs closed. Less connected clubbers would stream into the Charing Cross Road after the Trip, dancing around cars in the middle of the road, or on top of the fountains near Centrepoint opposite. One night a police car turned on its siren to try and clear the crowd, and to the officers' amazement everyone went mad, dancing even more. The wailing sounded like the siren sample on the acid anthem 'Can U Party', recorded by Todd Terry under the name Royal House. When the same thing happened outside Clink Street, the siren wasn't even needed. Clubbers danced around the patrol car's flashing light singing the record's hookline 'Can you feel it?'. For a few weeks a Mini pulled up outside Spectrum at closing time and played acid house on its sound system while a thousand clubbers danced in the street around it. There was even a spontaneous street party in Trafalgar Square at closing time one night.

Yet despite the numerous dealers now working openly in the clubs and already starting to organise into gangs, Ecstasy was still our secret. It felt like we'd opened a door and stepped into the future, leaving the dull reality of eighties London behind us. Other initiates were instantly recognisable: the bright, baggy clothes, the beads and ethnic accessories, the music blaring out of their cars, the girls without make-up and the boys growing out their hair. (It's easy to forget now how shocking, how taboo it had been for men to sport hippie-style locks in the eighties.)

People were shedding their black clothes and opening out like brightly coloured flowers. The traditional English reserve seemed to have disappeared. Once-surly security men laughed and joked with the queues outside clubs. Strangers would talk to each other freely. The regulation cool club pout was replaced by ear-to-ear grins. The most extraordinary music was being made, some of it by people who were dancing alongside us, like Baby Ford's abrasive acid anthem 'Oochy Coochy' or 'Everything Starts With An E' by the E-Zee Posse – an alias for Jeremy Healy, working with MC Kinky, a white girl who rapped in a Jamaican reggae style.

You would end up in the unlikeliest places, with people you'd only met an hour before on the dancefloor, in the toilet queue, in the street outside. A grand house in Stockwell owned by a foreign diplomat. A squat in Hackney. A penthouse overlooking the Thames owned by someone who did something in the City. A house available while someone's parents were on holiday. Sometimes you'd be driving and pull up alongside another car full of people drinking water and shaking their heads to the music, you'd make eye contact and smile and simply follow them to wherever it was they were going.

Tintin Chambers, a public schoolboy who promoted his first big acid party, Hypnosis, at the end of August in the Brixton Academy, was another tie-dyed T-shirt in the crowd at clubs like Spectrum at the start of that summer. He remembers the atmosphere in London late at night. 'I'd be coming back from a party, walking down the King's Road where I used to live. A car would drive past and you'd hear some acid house music, and you'd just put your arms in the air. They'd stop, you'd get in the car, you'd go and have a smoke and a chat with them. Because it was such a small thing then. There were a few thousand people in the whole of London going to these parties. You'd meet someone on the street, and you might not know who they were, but you'd be wearing exactly the same style of clothing – baggy, day-glo, Mambo-style tracksuits, pink-tinted glasses. And you'd get talking. That sort of thing happened all the time.'

One night after Future, almost everyone in the club piled into a convoy of cars and went to carry on the party in a gym in Dagenham owned by one of the members. 'Every time one car stopped, we all stopped and got out,' remembers one clubber. 'Not in service stations. Just on the A13. That unity that was so embedded. If one stops, we all stop! Whether it was for a wee, a water, a fag or a chat. It was like a party on the motorway. How we got away with some of those journeys . . . I mean, obviously, the police weren't thinking that everyone was drugged up and off their knackers on E.'

Danny Rampling remembers a party in a flat above a café in Chapel Street market in north London which started on a Sunday night and finished around Tuesday. 'On Monday morning the market was setting up, and there were just people dancing on the rooftops and out in the street while everyone else was going about their daily life. London was swinging, for the second time since the sixties, with different groups of society mixing with each other in different areas of London. There were parties every night. It was quite a special, underground thing.'

Acid nights began to spring up everywhere as DJs abandoned the funk beats and cranked up the bpms. Westworld opened Enter The Dragon and MyAmi. The Wag's Love night spawned one of the summer's best T-shirts: a beatific image of the Virgin Mary under the words 'Love. Love. Love.' Club MFI (Mad For It) at Legends showed the change most clearly: in the ground floor bar, the monochrome set sat talking and drinking in designer suits just as they had before. Downstairs, the once-cold chrome dancefloor area was transformed with smoke machines and strobes while clubbers danced in tie-dye, beads and cut-off jeans.

Ecstasy was a drug that worked well in crowds, giving users the sense that everyone was feeling the same warmth and joy, moving in the same direction. It quickly spread to the football terraces, and it was common to see younger fans going to the match wearing smiley T-shirts and dilated eyes, and to see them later on the dancefloor in the same state. Some referred to them, somewhat patronisingly, as 'love thugs', but this also reflected a genuine belief that everyone could be changed for the better if they just got right on one.

The extraordinary optimism of the time is perhaps best illustrated by the story of Cymon Eckel of *Boy's Own*. He had a job building film and theatre sets, and was working on a set for a George Michael video one morning when he was involved in an industrial accident and lost all the fingers on his left hand. He was in hospital for six weeks.

'What is amazing to this day is how positive I felt. I'd always wanted to study furniture design, but I'd never been able to give up the money, because I liked going out, buying clothes and taking drugs. So I had an operation, and when I came out of the anaesthetic my mother started talking about the future. I was saying, "I'm all right. It's great, now I can go to college. Fuck working, I'm never going to work again!"

'I came out of hospital, I had a week in Windsor convalescing and then I went to Ibiza, dancing with my hand still in bandages. It didn't matter, because I was in this whole new world. What should have been a very traumatic period didn't seem at all traumatic to me. That was the gift it gave me. Whatever you were doing, it grabbed hold of you, gave you a shake and made you look at yourself.'

The élite, the people who had started this movement, had already lost control. Now that Future was full of people they no longer knew,

Lisa Loud and Nancy Noise opened up on Tuesdays at the Sanctuary as Loud Noise, then later another night in Camden with the self-explanatory title Us. Shoom held one-off parties for their inner circle, including a memorable Ibiza-style foam party in a barn near Brighton, and a boat trip. *Boy's Own* started promoting acid parties too, taking coachloads of clubbers into the countryside for one-off events that have become part of club legend.

Some of the inner circle were starting to find ways to make a living out of their new lifestyle. By offering to work for free initially, Lisa Loud had talked her way into a job doing promotions in Virgin's dance department. Others had begun to fund their clubbing by selling drugs. It was easy money, and contrary to the popular image of the pusher, enticing innocents into their evil clutches, this was not a drug that needed hard sell. The demand seemed insatiable.

The days of one single dealer, known to everyone in the club, handing out the pills to an orderly queue were long gone. Many of the people who had once danced in the middle of an empty dancefloor in the first weeks of Spectrum were now standing round the edges, selling pills. Rivalries were starting to develop, and there were rows about money. By then, any ambiguity about the legality of Ecstasy had been ended too: a week before Spectrum even opened, Adam Heath, one of the original Ibiza crew from 1987, had been arrested. One of the first people in the UK to be convicted for possession of Ecstasy, he was eventually sentenced to a year in prison.

It was only a matter of time before the tabloids ran with the story. By July, the weekly music press – who have never been as close to club culture, and therefore as protective of it, as the monthly style magazines – had all run detailed stories about the widespread use of drugs, and seemed almost indignant that the national press hadn't yet picked up on it.

On 17 August the *Sun* finally got there, with a story headlined 'Scandal of the £5 drug trip to Heaven'. It was Richard Branson's ownership of the venue that made it newsworthy, and the reporter still got it badly wrong, taking the name of the music literally and assuming everyone there was on acid. Which was odd, considering that by then it was hard to move far in any club without being offered Ecstasy.

The summer was over.

Love and Money

'It's not over, between you and me.'

Tyree, 'Acid Is Over'

October 17. Bananarama party at the Novello Rooms. I wore a white shirt printed with big yellow roses from Christopher New. Got a cab down with Mark Moore. When we got out, the paparazzi turned on us, the flashes blinding. Weird. I've never thought of Mark as a celebrity. Inside, there were some tacky fairground bits, a few people dancing, everyone else milling aimlessly around.

Left quite quickly for Spectrum, which was hard work. It's over. It closes in two weeks. Mark argued with someone who's trying to sue him over a sample he used on 'Theme'. Left depressed, and went to Bangs [which then had a reputation as a tacky gay night] for a giggle. It was brilliant, like the old Jungle but with aciieed. Bought some poppers and danced till chuck-out time.

October 18/19. The opening of Pyramid in Paris. Bernard Sumner came, said New Order have recorded their new album in Ibiza and it's Balearic. The club is packed, but the best dancers came with us from England. A lot of the French clubbers are wearing tacky English acid house T-shirts. Meet a Danish DJ called Kenneth Baker, who works at the Koma club in Copenhagen. He says he's teaching them to shout 'aciieed' there.

Saw Laurent Garnier too. He's left the Haçienda and come back to France to do his national service as a cook in the army, but he's still playing house. Mark Moore plays, then Colin Faver. David Cabaret, one of the dancers, falls off the podium twice. The second time he needs stitches, and as the ambulance men take him away, he tells them they'd look great in ruffles. At 6 a.m. the bar staff start throwing trays on the floor to try and make Laurent stop playing, but he carries on.

Arrive home in time for the 6 p.m. news and find we're living in a police state. It's now illegal to broadcast the views of the IRA or anyone sympathetic to them on British TV and radio, including Gerry Adams – an elected MP. Nice to know we're importing South African censorship laws as well as supporting their government now. How can we think clubbing is important compared to this? Surely I should be writing about something more than the next new trend? It seems appropriate to go to [Kid Bachelor's Sunday night acid club] Confusion. Stand disorientated in the smoke and crowds clutching a Perrier and feeling . . . confused.

By autumn, even though the music was clearly spreading across Britain and beyond, it felt as if acid was over. The Trip had closed. Spectrum was about to do the same. *Boy's Own* had long been contemptuous of the new crowd getting into the music, wearing their smiley T-shirts and bandannas like a uniform, dismissing them as 'acid teds'. In the August issue of *i-D*, the club column bemoaned the spectacle of 2,500 people at the Camden Palace every Friday screaming 'aciieed'. 'It's definitely going wally,' said Nicky Holloway. Amongst the *cognoscenti*, everyone was talking about Belgian New Beat – a dense, electronic beat created when DJs from Antwerp and Ghent began playing electro-pop and industrial synth bands on slow speeds – as the Next Big Thing.

Holloway and Oakenfold's singles had failed to set the charts alight, and outside London the whole Balearic concept had been received with suspicion by many clubbers, especially those already converted to house. 'It's got beyond a joke,' Nottingham-based DJ Graeme Park told *i-D* in September. 'This morning I got a Cyndi Lauper record through my letter box with a press release saying it was a Balearic Beat. What's going on? This is one club craze that nobody up here wants anything to do with.'[2]

For Spectrum, the *Sun*'s story turned out to be 'not such a bad thing', says Paul Oakenfold. Richard Branson came down to look around, and didn't seem overly concerned by what he saw. Later, word came down that the night should close for a few weeks, then reopen under a new name. 'Furious pop tycoon Richard Branson is axing acid house parties at his nightclub', said the *Sun* afterwards, claiming victory. In fact, Spectrum was to hang on until the end of 1988 until relaunching as Land of Oz. (It had initially been going to change the name to Phantasia in November, but press reports about a new drug apparently called Phantasy meant the flyers they had printed had to be pulped.) At the relaunch on 12 December, a yellow brick road led into the packed club and Snap played live. The night was to continue for another two years.

Nicky Holloway soon had the Astoria back too, and reopened as Made On Earth, and then early in 1989 as Sin: 'We changed the name because of all the press attention, like everyone else.' While the club was closed, he had taken the chance to get his nose reshaped with cosmetic surgery. As news of this spread, there were sniggers on the dancefloor. Behind the decks one night, the DJ took the needle off the record and turned the joke back on his crowd with characteristic cheek. 'Yes, I've had a nose job,' he announced on the mic. 'But you know what's really funny? You lot paid for it!' The laughter silenced, he continued with the music.

'No smileys, no tattooed terrace boys', said the flyers for Made On Earth, and door staff there and elsewhere weeded out the newcomers in their new desperately uncool smiley T-shirts. Inside, though, the party continued pretty much as it had before. The Clink Street parties also continued undisturbed until the New Year, when they followed many other promoters into the East End and carried on there.

Meanwhile, the national press were finding it hard to decide whether acid house was a danger to the nation's children or a wacky new youth cult they should jump on. Many opted for both approaches. In mid-September the *Sun* ran an acid house fashion story, with a model clad in an enjoyably naff ensemble of smiley gear designed by Pink Soda for Top Shop.

The use of Ecstasy was by then widely reported, with much of the early coverage pruriently focused on MDMA's power as an aphrodisiac. It is true that many of those taking the drug in private were using it as an enhancement to sex (although many men also find themselves unable to get an erection or ejaculate on the drug). But Ecstasy has a different effect on the user depending on the setting in which it is taken.

Many people who had used the drug in the eighties had done so in small groups in tranquil settings, where it heightened the sensitivity to such a degree that they couldn't imagine enjoying it in a sweaty club crowded with people. In these clubs, however, it had a different effect: people felt the same opening of the spirit, the same joy and empathy, the same loosening of inhibitions, but they also experienced a loosening of the body. On E, the insistent rhythms of house seemed to pulse inside you, become part of you, urging you to dance, and dance, and dance.

People would tell each other they looked beautiful, there was touching and hugging and a great joyful feeling of belonging, of being at one with the crowd. But this was a generalised, unspecified kind of eroticism that was perfect for a generation who had been drilled to fear casual sex by the Government's AIDS campaigns. Just as in the sixties, a pill came along and liberated a generation, but these users were more gregarious than they were promiscuous.

By October, however, the mass-market tabloids had decided this all was pretty much a bad thing and had whipped themselves into a frenzy. London Records had released a single which producer/DJ Danny D had made under the name D Mob, using Gary Haisman's chant of 'acieed'. By the time 'We Call It Acieed' had reached number three in the charts, *Top of the Pops* had caved in to the pressure, and on 24 October producer Brian Whitehouse informed record company promotional staff that BBC TV would no longer be showing any videos or playing any records that featured the word 'acid' in the title. The directive had apparently come from James Moir, the BBC's head of Light Entertainment. High-street clothing chains like Top Shop, Miss Selfridge and Chelsea Girl got in on the backlash by announcing they would no longer be stocking smiley gear.

The ban did little harm: D Mob's record finally sold around 250,000 copies. For Paul Oakenfold, this in itself was a wake-up call. Danny D had been one of many industry friends who had come down to survey the Theatre of Madness. When he returned a few weeks later to say he'd made a record that mentioned Spectrum and Future and that the chorus was the chant he'd heard coming from the dancefloor, Oakenfold didn't think much of it. Later, Pete Tong played him the record after he'd signed it, and Oakenfold liked it.

'But still I didn't think that *I* should have been making this fucking tune until Danny D made a fortune. That's when I actually woke up and realised that if we didn't get on it, people were just going to come and take this all away from us. We started off Spectrum PR, Spectrum the label, and we did the university tour, the club tour. We had everything the superclubs were later to have. But because we weren't really doing it for the money, it all eventually fell apart.'

Dave Little, who had designed the original Spectrum artwork, got his wake-up call too. 'I went into Hyde Park on a Saturday afternoon, and I saw about 200 people wearing Spectrum T-shirts. That's when I started to realise that there were vast sums of merchandising money being made, and I didn't get a penny for it. There were tens of thousands of bootlegs around the country. It began to spread. I made bugger all.'

By the end of the year, Shoom was also suffering a comedown. A collection had been made amongst the regulars to buy Jenni Rampling a computer to automate her mailing list. One of the original Shoomers, who had previously been a heroin user and who had recently drifted back into his habit, took the money for himself. 'A Christmas collection was done in Shoom a couple of months ago,' said the next newsletter, 'but alas, we didn't receive the pressie. So for all those kind, generous people who did think about us, thanks for the contribution. To those who stole, spent or borrowed everyone's money, find yourself another club to go to – because you're not welcome at ours!'

'It was disappointing,' remembers Danny Rampling. 'That special feeling was becoming lost, the dream disintegrating. You just had to let go of that dream then, and push forward. It wasn't to become a reality.'

In his book on the E generation, *Altered State*, Matthew Collin maps the cycle of Ecstasy use.

The first rush begins the honeymoon period – the beatific, loved-up, evangelical phase. Within a year or so, that early excitement begins to fade and many experience diminishing returns. A few accelerate into excess, abuse sometimes leading to the emergence of physical or psychological problems. The third stage is the comedown: disillusionment, reduced use, and attempts to readjust to the fact that the initial high is gone forever. Finally comes the re-entry into the post-Ecstasy world, a time of reassessment and the regaining of equilibrium.

For the original Balearic crew, the honeymoon was over. Few of them now believed that they were going to change the world. 'That was always one of the great tragedies of it in a way,' notes Cymon Eckel, 'that it didn't motivate people politically, that it was too much of a pleasure zone.'

But for many others, of course, the game had only just begun. DJs wishing to distance themselves from acid but keep with the faster rhythms the dancefloor now demanded turned to deep house and garage – a more structured, soulful sound which took its name from the Paradise Garage in New York but was now being played by Tony Humphries at the Zanzibar in New Jersey. With PAs from acts like Blaze, Phase II, Adeva, Ultra Naté and En Vogue, Patrick Lilley's High On Hope night began to reassert the music's black roots and gave Norman Jay a chance to leave rare groove behind and air the garage records he'd been collecting on his trips to New York.

Frankie Knuckles and Marshall Jefferson were amongst the Chicago producers now working in this area – 'Someday', the song Jefferson wrote and produced for Ce Ce Rogers, was played everywhere in the second part of 1988. But the main impetus came from New Jersey, where Tony Humphries was mixing it at the Zanzibar and producer Kevin Hedge was creating music for his group Blaze and others like Phase II which paid homage to the long Friday nights he'd spent at the Paradise Garage, sitting by the DJ booth to study how Larry Levan controlled the moods and peaks in the music.

As the initial idealism faded, it was replaced by a cheeky irreverence, a sense of fun that was still a breath of fresh air. When Canadian 100 metre champion Ben Johnson was stripped of his gold medal in the Seoul Olympics at the end of September after failing a drugs test, the T-shirts were on the street the next day: a picture of Johnson crossing the finishing line, arms held up like an acid dancer, and the slogan 'Get right on one, matey!'

T-shirt sellers weren't the only ones seeing new opportunities. 'This whole new opening for everyone had emerged,' says Danny Rampling. 'It just all snowballed: record companies, promotion companies, fashion, merchandise – everything. It was very positive. There was this huge chance for people to try something else, things they wouldn't perhaps have considered before, and that's what a lot of people did.'

And while the first wave of the E generation were busy consolidating, moving on from acid house, a new breed of promoters were already at work, laying the ground for something that would be far bigger than any of us could have imagined.

8 FIELDS OF DREAMS

Apocalypse Now

If spinning a good yarn were an Olympic sport, then Tony Colston-Hayter would be a national hero. He is a champion talker, full of tall tales and outlandish anecdotes that are all the more entertaining because the most unbelievable of them tend to be true. Slight, baby-faced, with a hyperactive manner and an endless supply of enthusiasm and ideas, this is the man who was to dominate the tabloids in 1989 as 'Acid's Mr Big', held responsible for corrupting our youth, despoiling our countryside and threatening the very fabric of British society.

Yet he is also very much a child of Thatcherism, part of a generation raised to believe that there was no society, no safety net, and that if they wanted to live well they had to grab it for themselves. In a bulletin for the Libertarian Alliance, one of his best friends was later to describe him as 'an imaginative, entrepreneurial technocrat with a relaxed attitude to legal formalities'.[1] This was meant as praise: despite the Conservative calls for a return to Victorian morality in our personal lives, in business the prevailing ethic was that it was only wrong if you got caught.

The son of a history lecturer and a solicitor, he was born into a comfortable middle-class home in Hampstead. Money got tighter after his parents separated when he was nine, and Tony and his two sisters moved with their mother to a village just outside Milton

Keynes. Perhaps because of this change in circumstances, he wanted to be noticed, he wanted to get on.

He developed a passion for computers, gadgets, and especially video games. At Stantonbury Campus, a progressive comprehensive in Buckinghamshire, he gained an O level in technology by building his own fruit machine. The same year, he formed his first company, Nebular Adventure, with a £500 loan from his local bank. He had already been allowed to set up a youth club at his school, painting the walls black and hiring in some arcade games. Now he bought his own Atari Tempest and secretly installed it alongside the others. It paid for itself in three months.

By the age of seventeen, he was importing logic boards from Japan and selling them through the trade press, and when he left school a year later he opened his own arcade in Milton Keynes, and then a second in Plymouth. He soon had three companies: Colston Leisure operated machines in cafés, pubs and arcades; Colston Marketing sold machines and logic boards; Colston Micro-Electronics concentrated on repairs and new designs. Together, they claimed a turnover of £1 million before going bust.

Undeterred, Colston-Hayter developed a method for counting cards at blackjack and began playing the tables, donning wigs and disguises but still gradually getting banned from casinos across the country and later across the world as his winnings mounted. After the casinos closed at night he would hit the clubs, his pockets stuffed with cash, his entourage all drinking champagne. In Milton Keynes, he would go to cheesy discos with his friends in dress suits and ball gowns, all handcuffed together and relishing the stares.

In London, it was inevitable that he would eventually be drawn to Ecstasy, and then to the after-hours pleasures of Shoom. He booked Danny Rampling to play at his birthday party and soon became a face on the scene, at first celebrated as another colourful character, then later derided as impossibly vulgar in his flamboyance. 'I was twenty-two, twenty-three,' he says now. 'I *was* a flash git. I used to go to Spectrum and they wouldn't let me in because I had a dinner suit on and a bow tie, so I gave the doorman £200 and he was like, "All right, in you go. Sweet." '

One of his late-night clubbing friends was Dave Roberts, another ambitious young entrepreneur with a relaxed attitude to legal formalities. At first sight, they were an unlikely pair. Dave was one of six sons born to Grenadine parents in Finsbury Park, north London, before his mother finally got the daughter she had wanted. They grew up literally and figuratively in the shadow of the Arsenal stadium. The Roberts brothers became well-known faces on the terraces, men you didn't mess with lightly, and Dave spent short spells in various approved schools and homes for taking and driving cars before ending up in Borstal for six months at the age of fifteen for being the driver at a robbery. It was here he finally learned to read and write, so that he could send letters to his mother and girlfriend: 'I didn't need it before that, it didn't bother me.'

But it would be a mistake to see this as a lack of intelligence. Determined to succeed, with a strong will to make things happen no matter what, he was quick and resourceful and began dreaming up an array of money-making schemes. 'When I came out, I realised then that I was on my own and I had to make it on my own. I wanted to get involved in anything that made money, whether it was legal or illegal.'

A father at the age of seventeen, he says he skipped the teenage stuff and went straight into adulthood. He would hang out in the West End funk clubs and in after-hours drinking clubs, but never danced: 'Dancing was for soul boys, and soul boys smelled of sweat.' If Tony Colston-Hayter was a middle-class kid who enjoyed the idea of slumming it, of deliberately searching for the sleazy, Dave Roberts did everything he could to rise above his working-class origins.

He would stand at the bar in his bespoke suits, posing and watching. He passed his driving test at the age of fifteen (his licence still bears the wrong birth date) and was soon driving Jaguars, Porsches, a Jensen Interceptor. Property was booming and lenders were throwing mortgage deals at anyone who asked, so he got into property scams. Some would call what he was doing fraud. Others would call it bending the rules. But this was the mid-eighties, when bending the rules was a way of life in the big financial institutions themselves – the mis-selling of pensions, insider dealing, financial scandals which are only just coming to light over a decade on.

Roberts had been told about this young man from Milton Keynes who was making serious money through gambling, and in 1987 he arranged to meet Colston-Hayter. He had a proposition he thought might interest him, involving the movement of a large amount of cash through the banking system. 'We set a meeting up, and he brought a security man along with him, which I immediately told him was not at all necessary when dealing with me. We clicked straight away. We both love girls, a good time, and both earned money from business scams. And we could both spend it!'

Although initially interested, Colston-Hayter couldn't deliver on the deal in the end, but by then it didn't matter. They'd been out clubbing a few times, and become firm friends. Colston-Hayter took his friend to Shoom and introduced him to Ecstasy. It was a wild weekend, and one that Roberts now says was to change his life for the better, although he dismisses the Shoom crowd as 'too snobbish'. When the door policy began to tighten and it became harder for them to take down their friends, they moved to the Trip. 'That was where I felt most comfortable. The people were more real. Nineteen eighty-eight was the first time I really danced. Back then, all I wanted to do was take drugs and party.'

After the clubs, there were late-night sessions at Colston-Hayter's home in Winslow in Buckinghamshire, attended by many of the big promoters, DJs and club faces. He had smoke and bubble machines there, and strobe lights in the front room. Although subsequently portrayed as sleazeballs who simply saw the scene as another chance to turn a quick buck, the friends' enthusiasm was genuine. It soon became all-encompassing for them, as it did for everyone touched by its fever.

'Going out and going to those clubs became the only and most important thing in the world,' says Colston-Hayter. 'And then doing those clubs, and doing them differently, and taking them out of London and throwing the doors open to everyone became my whole life and everything that I believed in, totally. We just went on this mad, fantasy trip of the more the better and everyone's welcome. *Boy's Own* and Shoom wanted to keep it as their own secret little thing, and we just wanted to give it to everyone.'

With his entrepreneurial flair, it was inevitable that Colston-Hayter would get involved in promoting parties of his own. The first big event was Apocalypse Now, a well-received party at Wembley Film

Studios which he organised with Roger Goodman at the end of August 1988. The walls and floor in the smoke-filled room were painted white, leading disorientated clubbers to bump into the walls just as they often walked into the mirrors at Shoom. They did a second successful weekend of parties together on 9 and 10 September before falling out, after which Colston-Hayter went to Amsterdam for a weekend and sat up all night in a stoned Purple Haze with his girlfriend writing an exhaustive list of possible names for a new party organisation. The one he liked best was Sunrise, and he set up his first Sunrise party in Wembley on 8 October.

When he went to give out flyers for his event at the next Apocalypse Now at the start of October he found he wasn't welcome, and ended up in a running battle with Goodman and his security that, by Colston-Hayter's own account, involved kicking down doors, climbing through windows, and a potentially murderous stand-off with a CS gas canister. Peace and love only went so far.

Although they failed to film this fracas, the TV cameras that had been allowed into the party that night were filming pretty much everything else. After the *Sun* story on Spectrum, the Balearic élite were still busy trying to regain control of the roller-coaster, to protect their scene from sensationalism. Jenni Rampling had already turned TV crews away from Shoom; now she stood at the door of Apocalypse Now warning her regulars away from the presence of the TV news.

On 4 October, ITN transmitted a report showing blank-faced dancers pumping their arms in the clouds of dry ice and blanked-out faces handing over money and taking pills at Apocalypse Now. A strange, American-accented 'dealer' offered some dialogue that seems stolen straight from TV cop series *Starsky and Hutch*'s stereotyped black informer Huggy Bear; Richard Branson gave a spirited defence of something he called 'acid rock'; and Professor Griffith Edwards of London University quoted valid research about the possible neurotoxicity of Ecstasy before somewhat oddly warning of bad trips worse than those experienced on LSD. At the time the report was devastating: E culture was no longer our little secret. It was taking up six whole minutes on the lunchtime news.

The first Sunrise event the following Saturday was raided by the police, who had been tipped off about the event and could hardly turn a blind eye to another acid party in their area after the ITN report. It was the last time Colston-Hayter was to print the address of one of his events on the tickets. He was £7,000 poorer, and more importantly he now had something to prove.

His next move was a characteristically bold one. In 1988, few clubbers were willing to travel far across London for a night out, let alone out of town to an unknown destination. But if promoters and DJs were willing to make the fifty-seven mile drive down to his home in Buckinghamshire for a party, he reasoned, then why not clubbers too? It was a gamble, but gambling was his profession. He hired an equestrian centre not far from his home, and on 27 October he and his team set about installing a bouncy castle, lasers and strobes, and transforming it into wonderland.

'I borrowed money to do it with, and while we were building it the team I had doing the production couldn't look me in the eye. You could just *see* them thinking, "We know this isn't going to work, but we've got to make him happy." There were horses riding round, and at 8 p.m. there was still some show-jumping event going on. I'd given this equestrian centre £500 and told them we were doing a little garden party. They had no idea.'

Eight hundred clubbers gathered at designated pick-up points in the capital to be driven on his magical mystery tour, the hired coaches finally winding down a wooded lane lit with flaming torches to reach their destination. All of the strobes in the building were turned on as they arrived, the lights flashing out of the windows and roof to make it look like an alien spaceship landing in the beautiful English countryside. Party-goers streamed in, eager to be transported to another world. Colston-Hayter stood on the door, taking names and addresses for the mailing list he'd decided to start. Wham's Andrew Ridgeley was amongst the guests, but when Colston-Hayter tried to wave him through, he claims the star insisted on handing over his £10: 'No no, I *want* to pay!'

At the peak of the night, the lights went off, the place filled with dry ice and DJ Steve Proctor played the opening bars of Richard Strauss's *Also Sprach Zarathustra*, better known as the theme to *2001: A Space Odyssey*. As the music built towards a climax, a green laser cut across the smoke-filled room, and all the DJ could see was disembodied hands reaching towards it through the mist, like an entity from John Carpenter's film *The Fog*. All of the London club promoters who had advised Colston-Hayter not to waste his money were there, awestruck. The agenda had changed: this was no longer about club nights, one-off parties. It was about *events*, about spectacle.

When the music finished at 8 a.m. with the Beatles' 'Magical Mystery Tour' and jazz vocalist Bobby McFerrin's upbeat 'Don't Worry, Be Happy', people still lingered, unwilling to wake from the dream. 'We were sitting there cross-legged and plaiting each other's hair and singing and dancing,' remembers Tony's sister Charlie. 'It was beautiful sunshine, birds singing, dew on everything and it was sparkling and wonderful, a new day. And all of a sudden this tractor came round the corner. This bloke had probably driven that tractor round that corner every day for forty-five years, and now he's hit by bedlam. Boys and girls in tie-dye, dancing with flowers in their hair. You should have seen his face. Can you imagine what he'd go back and say to his wife?'

Sierra Mark – named after the massive sound system he'd installed in his Ford Sierra – opened up the boot and the doors of his car to let the sound out, and the party carried on in a car park overlooking the road. As the congregation began to arrive at the church next door, they simply stared in disbelief as 300 misfits in baggy day-glo clothes clambered on to the roofs of parked coaches and danced like people possessed to these strange, psychedelic beats.

'Obviously, nobody had seen anything like this before,' observes Tintin Chambers, who was soon to be organising similar parties of his own. 'This was 1988, there hadn't been much press. It must have been a shocking thing to see.'

But the time of innocence was all but over. Soon, everyone would have heard of acid house. At the end of October, twenty-one-year-old Janet Mayes died after taking a second E – one more than she usually took – at the Jolly Boatman pub in Hampton Court. The first death to be attributed to Ecstasy in the UK had gone almost unremarked: 19-year-old Ian Larcombe swallowed eighteen tablets after being stopped by police, and died in July. But Mayes's tragic death came in the same week as the ban on 'acid' on *Top of the Pops* and received the full treatment in the tabloids. On 3 November, Scotland Yard formally declared war on the acid parties, and in Operation Seagull the day after, the police raided a small party on a pleasure boat on the Thames at Greenwich using frogmen, four launches fitted with powerful searchlights, undercover officers dressed in smiley T-shirts and dozens of riot police. Nine people were subsequently charged, including the party organisers.

On the freezing cold night of 5 November, Tony Colston-Hayter held the Sunrise Guy Fawkes Edition – in Greenwich. The venue was a former gas works on some open wasteland near the mouth of the Blackwall Tunnel, where Stanley Kubrick had filmed parts of his Vietnam movie *Full Metal Jacket*. Three thousand tickets had been sold, but police arrived at the meeting point at Bishopsgate car park in the East End and threatened the coach drivers with arrest if they moved to take clubbers to the venue.

They blocked Blackwall Tunnel and the entrance gate of the road leading to the venue, turning revellers away and saying that the party was cancelled. But when Colston-Hayter shone a laser into the sky to show that it was on, clubbers began scrambling over fences and walls and running across the vast tract of wasteland towards it. He eventually got around half of the ticket-holders in, and when riot police charged inside, the crowd simply ignored them and kept on dancing. But when the music was then shut off, they began shouting their displeasure. After it was explained that there would be no coaches to take the revellers back to their cars until 10 a.m., the police finally withdrew at 5 a.m., fearing a riot.

The event went ahead, but nothing could be done about those who had left after being told the party was off. Colston-Hayter needed to change strategy again, to find some way of communicating with clubbers and giving them regular updates. Something else happened that night to change the agenda: he had been snapped through a telephoto lens orchestrating the action and the tabloids finally had a face on which to focus their outrage, someone to demonise. Dubbed 'the acid king' by the *Sun*, he was to live the next year-and-a-half in the often uncomfortable glare of the spotlight.

The rest of the winter of '88 was spent in evasive action. Tintin

Chambers and his partner Jeremy Taylor tried to run their own coach mystery tours to warehouse venues, working with Brandon Block, a DJ from the suburban fringes of West London who had been amongst the dancers captured on camera by ITN at Apocalypse Now. Most of them were ended by the police, and one was filmed for a report by *World In Action*.

Kevin Simpson, now Jamiroquai's manager, organised the Freedam weekenders to Amsterdam, taking DJs like Judge Jules, Danny Rampling and Harvey and a few hundred clubbers to party in the more liberal atmosphere of the Netherlands. Reading the British tabloids on the plane home from one such jaunt, they were surprised to see that their weekend had made the front page. Judge Jules says quite a few clubbers made hasty trips to the toilet to get rid of souvenirs: which turned out to be wise, as every one of them was searched going through Customs.

Tony Colston-Hayter, meanwhile, began scouting venues in the East End, where the acid house scene had already begun to spread. Tony Wilson was an old friend of Paul Oakenfold who soon began to DJ at Future, introducing many East End faces to the scene. By the autumn of 1988, he had taken the music back on to home ground with his Adrenalin night at Echoes nightclub in Bow.

The area's many empty warehouses and industrial buildings were also prime ground for illegal all-nighters. Colston-Hayter began working with Genesis, an outfit who were starting to make a name for themselves by pulling off guerrilla-style acid events, breaking into venues and convincing any police who came along that they had been hired legitimately for a music business party. Reverting to the name black Londoners had used for years for illegal dance parties, when the parties started to move eastwards and attract a more racially diverse crowd, they began to be called raves.

By then it was widely rumoured that the notorious West Ham football crew the Inner City Firm (ICF) were moving in on the east London scene, and there were whispers about large-scale drug-dealing, about thugs taking a share of the ticket money and taking over security arrangements, about threats and serious violence by the ICF and shadowy other gangs.

Wayne Anthony of Genesis has documented this violence in *Class*

Of 88, his frank, raw memoir of this period.[2] As well as the euphoria of the parties and the numerous scams they pulled off to acquire venues, he describes bags stuffed with bank notes, security men demanding increased money with menaces in the middle of the parties, armed ex-army mercenaries arriving to demand their cut, and kidnappings and brutal beatings by various gangsters.

The police were convinced that the ICF were involved in such activities. But despite a long surveillance operation against alleged ICF members, Echoes nightclub and the pirate radio station Centre Force, the police were unable to build a case that stood up in court. Those who were arrested after this operation insist that this is because there was never a case to enter.[3]

Financially, the raves Colston-Hayter did with Genesis under the name Sunset were his most successful to date. He walked away with £7,000 from the New Year's Eve bash, and quickly did two more. But the organisation wasn't up to his standards – one night a youth climbing over the warehouse in an attempt to get in without paying fell sixty feet through a glass roof and landed at the feet of the security crew, miraculously unharmed.

And there were warnings. 'I went to see a very dear friend of my security manager who'd been in jail for a very long time, and he said, "You don't know what the fuck you're doing. You're in Hackney. You're just some little idiot white boys thinking that you can go there." '

Soon after, the ICF 'sent a message that it wasn't right'. Colston-Hayter would, he admits, have lost control of his organisation then had he not brought in his old friend as a partner. 'The ICF mugged off all the promoters like Genesis,' says Dave Roberts simply. 'I saw Tony losing money. I was his closest friend in London, so I put my name up as his partner to protect him.'

The last thing the West Ham team wanted at that point was a confrontation with some of Arsenal's top boys. There was room for everyone here. In fact, the police surveillance was starting to reveal unprecedented co-operation between some of the old football crews when it came to organising raves and the sale of drugs.

Since the Greenwich stand-off, meanwhile, Colston-Hayter had been considering some sort of live communication that he would be able to update to guide people towards his events and stay one step ahead of the police. Mobile phones had only become available to the public in 1986, and were still relatively rare, caricatured as yuppie accessories for loud-mouthed City whiz-kids. Colston-Hayter, of course, had one. Now he bought a whole set of chunky Vodaphones, and began printing the numbers on his tickets. This meant he could keep the venue secret until the last possible moment, but it still wasn't ideal.

'People were ringing up off their nuts to ask where the party was, and I had these four poor girls trying to cope with speaking to all these lunatics. Then I found this thing, British Telecom Voice Bank, which had ten lines into it. I called it TVAR – Telephone Venue Address Releasing. You didn't even have to put a meeting point on the ticket any more, because that mobilised the old Bill in that area.'

All they had to print from now on were phone numbers. He hired seven voice banks, seventy lines in all, and now had the power to just dial in from his mobile at any time and change the message being released to clubbers calling the numbers. When even these became overloaded, he moved to 0898 numbers, which could deal with 100 callers at once and also paid a commission of about eight pence for everyone who dialled in. Ever the canny businessman, he kept complete control of this system: any promoter over the next year who wanted to use his lines to give out their address had to rent them from his organisation, at often extortionate prices.

Everything was in place for what was to come. All he and his new partner had to do now was wait for the weather to change.

The Sun Rising

The spring of 1989 was a dress rehearsal, a time to get out in the field and practise manoeuvres. The M25 orbital motorway had finally been completed the year before, running in a circle around outer London and so offering easy access to the countryside around the capital. Using their new TVAR system, Tony Colston-Hayter's World Wide Promotions could guide clubbers to a meeting point on or near the orbital while their team set up at the venue. When everything was ready, the full address was released on the phone and clubbers could arrive with such speed that it was difficult for the police to mobilise against them. By the time the local force realised anything was happening, there were already too many people inside for them to bring the party safely to a halt.

World Wide Promotions now had two brand names for their parties: Colston-Hayter's Sunrise and Dave Roberts' Back to the Future. Sunrise held a couple of parties at the Ivor Heath Equestrian Centre near Slough that spring, while Back to the Future made its debut at Linford Film Studios in London before moving out to the countryside on 29 April.

This party proved more problematic: they were unable to find a venue until late that night, by which time their production manager had given up on them and gone out on a date. After finally getting their team mobilised, they set up within hours. The grain silo on a farm in Surrey was still half full of stinking cattle food pellets, but the revellers thought it made a great slide. The local police seemed equally amused, helping ferry people between car park and party in their vans.

'That was when it started getting really good,' grins Dave Roberts. 'Everyone believed we were going to get that party on. We had some wicked parties after that.'

Their next event was a Sunrise in an aircraft hangar at Santa Pod speedway on 20 May and included a fairground amongst the attractions. It attracted a crowd of 5,000, and World Wide were triumphant. 'All we wanted to do was have a good time, and we couldn't see what was wrong with that,' says Roberts. 'We were fighting for a cause, we really felt that.' And for now, it felt as if no one could touch them.

The other big rave promoters were also honing their operations. Working out of the office at the back of Jazzy M's record shop, Jarvis Sandy held his first Biology rave in February, on the night Mike Tyson was to fight Britain's Frank Bruno for the world title. The flyers had claimed the match would be screened as part of the party at Linford Film Studios, and Jazzy was behind the decks at the appointed time.

'I had to turn all the music off, and the satellite projector was to show it on this huge white wall. But because it was so hot in there the projector failed, and the whole crowd of 4,000 people started booing me. Awesome. It was so full it was dangerous, very claustrophobic. I couldn't even get off the stage. I'd have had to walk across the sea of heads. Believe me, I was very frightened. So I put Nitro Deluxe on, "This Brutal House", and the whole crowd went bananas. They didn't give a fuck after that. The Bruno fight got shown in the VIP room next door, and we carried on raving.'

As the weather warmed, Biology's next event on 10 June was open-air, held in a field off the M25 near Elstree in Hertfordshire. When the sun came up and the lasers no longer strafed the sky, the raised stage, the stalls round the edge of the field and the large crowd of long-haired, tie-dyed clubbers made the event look more like a hippie festival than a club, and there was talk of 'Woodstock revisited'.

'It was pretty amazing to be on a stage, DJing to 12,000 people,' recalls Johnny Walker. 'I'd done the soul weekenders to three, four thousand people which were amazing as well, but this was one big open-air arena with everybody going wild. Lasers going off everywhere, projections and lightshows all around the area. It was a fantastic thing to experience.'

Energy were the last to appear, with an event that immediately established them in the premier league. A well-spoken young man with a public-school education, a flat in Chelsea and a sharp eye for a business opportunity, Jeremy Taylor was the son of a millionaire. His family home Cricket St Thomas was used as the setting for the late-seventies sitcom *To the Manor Born*, and its thousand-acre estate in Somerset encompasses a successful wildlife park.

He already had experience of organising large-scale events with the Gatecrasher Balls, grand parties for fourteen- to twenty-year-old Hooray Henries and Henriettas which had given the tabloids endless opportunities to print pictures of suited and gowned young toffs lying about in a state of advanced inebriation or feeling each other up. Tony Colston-Hayter used to run the blackjack and roulette tables at these parties, but when Gatecrasher fell apart, it was Quentin 'Tintin' Chambers who pointed Taylor in the direction of acid house.

Taylor describes his friend as 'the long-haired trendy type who got off with all the girls at the Gatecrasher events'. Keeping the hair length, Chambers had since become an enthusiastic devotee of acid house, sharing a flat with an equally enthusiastic club character, a flamboyant, dreadlocked white man who had become well-known in the acid clubs as Anton Le Pirate.

151

Working as Karma Productions, Taylor and Chambers organised a large-scale party called Hypnosis at the Brixton Academy in October 1988, but their first real success was Fun City, a weekly club night at Shaftesbury's in the West End which ran on Fridays from the start of 1989. They transformed the somewhat tacky club with elaborately painted backdrops and 3D scenery props of futuristic cityscapes, left free popcorn and jelly babies on the tables, gave out specially recorded flexi-discs as flyers, and did everything they could to make the night stand out. Hardly a corner of the place was left untouched: they even brought their own sound system to install in the venue.

For Taylor, essentially a businessman who never got into the drugs side of the scene (working on the sensible assumption that if he tried it, he might like it), such expenditure still made sound financial sense: 'A lot of these events that we'd been to, it was just an empty warehouse and a sound system. No lights, no booze, nothing. The better the events were, the more likely people were to come back. Certainly as far as I was concerned, it was always a business thing.'

Anton Le Pirate did the door, and the resident was Fabio (Fitzroy Heslop) a Brixton-based DJ who had played hip hop and funk on pirate station Faze One before building up a following for his hard-edged, energetic, largely instrumental blend of house at after-hours gatherings at Mendoza's in south London. Every two weeks, a young squatpunk called Adam Tinley would come and plug his keyboards into the PA system and create spontaneous, sequenced live techno for the dancefloor. Chambers had seen him play at a small boat party and thought it might add something novel to the night, although at first Adamski wasn't even considered enough of an attraction to warrant a mention on the flyers. Later, he was to become one of the scene's first genuine stars, the keyboard wizard who launched Seal's career on his 'Killer' single.

Mixing Fabio's Brixton rave crowd and Karma's Chelsea set, the night was an instant success. After building up an impressive mailing list they felt confident that they could pull off something bigger, and hired the Westway Film Studios in Shepherd's Bush, west London, for a party on 27 May. Tintin Chambers was determined it would outdo anything that had gone before: 'Jeremy was always worrying about the money side, whereas I just wanted to spend as much as possible putting on the best show. Artistically, nobody had put much effort into these events. I wanted to do something more spectacular. I guess it was my ego taking over.'

No one had ever seen a party like Energy. Five rooms, each with its own lavish theme: a set from the cult science fiction film *Blade Runner*, a Greek temple, Stonehenge, a pyramid room and a sushi bar. They sold out two weeks in advance, 5,000 tickets at £15. On the night, there were hundreds, maybe thousands more people outside, trying to get in. The studios had a small central office tower which overlooked all of the rooms, and the Karma team spent much of the night in there, watching the mayhem they had created.

'People were just climbing up the walls to get in,' remembers Lynn Cosgrave, who had just started working at their office in Taylor's Chelsea flat, setting up ticket sales across the country. 'It got out of hand, and we were all really scared. The money was all done, that was with the record shops and other outlets, but we had no control whatsoever. We just sat there going, "Oh God, what's going to happen now?"'

Jazzy M played the temple room, his decks wobbling on a platform high above the dancefloor. 'I was playing two copies of "Strings Of Life" and hyping everybody up as you would in a jam, getting on the mic and just sending them completely crazy. Everyone's on top of this temple, dancing on top of the columns, and the lasers are firing straight into the middle of it, hitting a prism and just shooting everywhere. Every single person in that room had their hands in the air. It was the best gig I've ever played.'

After Jazzy's set, at around three in the morning, Adamski came on and played a set that was to make him a fixture at all the big raves that summer. Seeing the music created in front of them there and then, the crowd went wild. 'I'd never seen a crowd rock like that!' says Chambers. 'He had an ability to just destroy people on the dancefloor. They would be just physically exhausted after one of his sets. It was crazy. I still think that was the best acid house party ever thrown.'

A week later, Westworld held a party called the Secret of the Golden Flower in a large, empty mansion on the exclusive Coombe Park estate near Kingston. Compared with Energy it was an intimate gathering for 700 people with a beautifully lit garden and a heated swimming pool in the grounds, but it still caught the eye of the tabloids: the *Sun* report afterwards made the first reference I'd seen in print to M25 'orbital parties'.

Boy's Own were to continue to hold similar small, deliberately low-key events throughout the summer, keeping the spirit of '88 alive. At their party by a lake near East Grinstead, clubbers greeted the dawn lying on the giant hay bales scattered round the field. The party provided the inspiration for the Beloved's first hit 'The Sun Rising', a song which for many summed up the awe and joy of the second summer of love. But it was the Energy party which set the standard for 1989, became the benchmark the other big promoters felt compelled to beat.

As if to underline the changes in club culture, at the start of 1989 the pirate radio stations Kiss FM and LWR, the main voices of London clubland since the mid-eighties, voluntarily went off air. It was the end of an era. Ever since Radio Caroline began transmitting from a ship off the British coast in 1964, playing a mixture of current pop and R&B that was then rarely heard on British radio, the pirates have catered to audiences ignored by the BBC. From the seventies on, they moved from the sea to the inner cities and became more focused on black dance music, their car stickers and T-shirts often more common in inner London than those of the legal stations.

The kind of current club music now played on national radio every weekend was still hard to find in 1988, heard on only a few specialist late-night shows. Apart from the pirates, the main sources of music were recordings of DJs' club sets, or highly prized tapes from the US: a tape of Tony Humphries' mix show for Kiss in New York was a sure way to win friends and influence people.

LWR was on-air full time, had a mainly black staff, and catered to the soul and reggae clubs. Kiss ran on weekends only, had a more mixed roster, and catered more to the West End/warehouse scene. Tim Westwood, Danny Rampling, Judge Jules, Trevor Nelson and many more from Radio One's current dance roster served their apprenticeship in studios set up in tower blocks and empty offices, forever on the move in an attempt to stay one step ahead of the DTI officials. One memorable Christmas, Kiss set up the decks on a bow-legged paste table at the home of one of the DJs, with his mum interrupting the show to serve the turkey.

Fines then averaged £100–£200. 'Up till now, there have been no sentences,' LWR's manager Zak told me in 1987. 'In their heart of hearts, the judges know it's harmless.'

But now the rules were changing. New legislation had been announced that would allow higher fines, sentences of up to six months, and the confiscation of equipment including not only the records DJs had in the studio at the time of the raid, but the collection they kept at home and used to earn a living in the clubs. It was also announced that twenty new local stations were to be launched across the country, but that anyone broadcasting illegally after 1 January 1989 would be unable either to apply for one of these new franchises or to work for a legal station for five years. As a result, at midnight on 31 December, both Kiss FM and LWR went off-air to prepare their applications.

Yet the house boom and the can-do attitude it had spawned meant that new stations proliferated. Advances in technology had made broadcasting cheaper and easier, and the transmitters easier to conceal from the DTI. In May 1989, a group which included some well-known faces from the West Ham terraces launched Centre Force, blasting out the frantic, clattering sound of the rave on 88.3 FM twenty-four hours a day, seven days a week. It was soon followed by a host of others: Sunrise, Fantasy, Obsession, and later Dance FM, all of them advertising the numerous raves and clubs, giving out updates on the night or, if it served their own interests, merely adding to the confusion.

By June, when the new London radio franchises were awarded to a jazz and a classical station, these new renegades were the sound of the city: drifting out of open windows and blasting out of passing cars, providing the music for small gatherings of people who had been out partying and didn't want to go home. Pirates like Kiss had prided themselves on their professionalism. 'Don't talk any shit' said a sign on the wall of their last makeshift studio. 'No drug stories, no sex or sexist comments.' But the new breed gloried in their rough-edged amateurishness. Listeners would phone in their dedications to the stations' mobile phones, and MCs would scream out their messages on air, big shouts going out to anyone who wanted them.

For a while in July and August, Clapham Common became an informal Sunday meeting place for Londoners who had been out in the clubs and fields all night, a place to dance and chill, share a spliff and a drink and come down from the weekend. When the police began stopping sound systems setting up on the grass there for impromptu parties, people turned up carrying small generators and home turntables or tape machines. If that didn't work, then the pirates could provide the required soundtrack. 'Are you ready London?' asked one of Centre Force's best jingles, as Rhythim Is Rhythim's 'Strings Of Life' swelled under the manic MC's voice. 'Let's go . . . *mental!!'*

Looking back at it now, that summer has the quality of a dream: warm, shimmering, unreal. The weather was glorious, the hottest since the record-breaking heat wave of 1976, and under the blue skies and baking sun, the British cast off their traditional reserve and put on smiles as well as shorts and sandals. Restrictions on drinking hours had finally been eased the year before, allowing pubs and restaurants to serve alcohol all day providing it came with food. As a result, London took on a relaxed, almost Mediterranean feel in the heat, with tables starting to creep out on to the pavements and people drinking, talking and laughing in the middle of the afternoon.

The bright colours favoured by the class of '88 were now everywhere, loud prints, bagginess and informality replacing the neutral colours, sculpted tailoring and uptight attitudes that had gone before. Their faces often free of make-up, girls wore pretty much the same as the boys.

'Where we come from, girls sit behind the mirror for eight hours before they go out, they're into glamour,' said Brooklyn's Frankie Bones, a popular guest DJ on the UK rave circuit that year who was surprised at what he saw there. 'The field and the girls just wouldn't mix. In England, it's more of a comfort thing.'

Clothes were practical and layered, an eclectic mix of ethnic prints, African hats and pendants, loud shirts with huge spots and flowers, embroidered waistcoats, ponchos, oversized jumpers, garish tracksuits and patterned surf or skate shorts. Black DMs and brogues had been replaced by Timberland hiking boots, brightly coloured Kicker shoes and pastel-shaded suede Wallabees.

Fashion designer Nick Coleman had been to Shoom, Spectrum and *Boy's Own* parties and now ran his own Sunday night house club, Solaris. He began adding strange items like ponchos to the more traditional shoulder pads and frills in his mainline collections, and began producing T-shirts with slogans. 'Why can't we live together?' asked one, while another declared 'Come on, this is it, right now' with all the letters in different bright colours, *ooh* running down one long sleeve and *aah* down the other. Now all the big design houses do diffusion ranges, sportswear and casual clothes. Then, this seemed like madness.

'People looked at me as if I'd just lost it totally. It was such a shock to them, so contrary to everything they were into. They were unable to just shift everything they believed in, everything they'd been doing for ten years. But because I'd never really enjoyed standing around in the Wag drinking Pils, when something came along that felt totally me, I embraced it.'

In May, Prime Minister Thatcher celebrated ten years in power and announced in regal style that 'we are a grandmother', but it still felt like a time of change and of optimism. A new decade was round the corner, a millennium was drawing to an end. Around the world, power blocs that had seemed invincible began to tremble and crack, even crumble.

In China, pro-democracy students occupied Beijing's vast Tiananmen Square in a demonstration that was eventually crushed with brutal military force. Yet the image that endured was a hopeful one: an anonymous young man standing alone in the road in front of a line of tanks, forcing them to stop rather than roll over him on their way to the Square.

Mikhail Gorbachev was giving the Soviet Union a human face, and a tide of restlessness was starting to wash over Eastern Europe. In Iran, Islamic fundamentalist the Ayatollah Khomeini was dead. In South Africa, President P.W. Botha went to meet the jailed ANC leader Nelson Mandela in prison and began to admit that apartheid could no longer be sustained. By the end of the year, the Berlin Wall had fallen, and Hungary, Czechoslovakia, Romania and Bulgaria had exchanged communism for what seemed then to be a new freedom. For a brief, heady time, it felt as if a new world was opening before us and that anything was possible.

The fight for the right to party may seem trivial compared to all this, but it really *did* feel like a cause. The promoters who followed Sunrise, Back to the Future and Biology into the countryside to hold all-night raves were seen as crusaders, as heroes. Spending £15–£25 on a ticket felt like an act of defiance. Clubbers would go to extraordinary lengths to ensure the party went on, and were endlessly tolerant when it did not.

Tony Farsides was working at Black Market Records in Soho, which became one of the main ticket outlets in central London as the summer warmed up and the scene broke big. 'It's a very working class attitude. You'd get these kids coming in to buy these £25 tickets, they'd buy four and go, "God, £100!" But it wasn't, "What a rip-off", they were actually quite *impressed* that they were spending it. They bought into the whole thing, they were up for it. I don't think they ever felt they were being ripped off.'

People had begun to live for the weekend, just as they did with disco during the recession of the seventies. But now they wanted more than a mirrorball and a few flashing lights. They wanted all the new technologies of pleasure, and they wanted them now. They wanted 15K, 20K, 30K, 40K, 100K of turbo sound, water-cooled lasers in different colours, big-screen projections and fairground rides. They wanted bouncy castles, jugglers, magicians, stilt walkers, fire eaters and mime artists. They wanted candy floss, fruit stalls, ice cream and burgers. They wanted big-name DJs and exciting live acts performing their hits. Most of all they wanted MDMA, and lots of it: pleasure in pill form, an instant escape.

The psychedelic, full-colour flyers handed out at clubs at closing time and stacked on the counters of record and clothes shops promised all this and more (although most put a token warning about taking drugs somewhere in the small print). Printed over New Age, cosmic images of babies and fractal patterns, flowers and planets, the names captured the optimism of the second summer of love, the sense of new possibilities unfolding: Sundance, Joy, X'Pression, World Dance, One Nation, One Family, 2000 AD, Harmony, Empathy, Humanity, Infinity.

Saturday night fever had spread, and no one wanted the weekend to end. At the start of 1989, Phil Perry and Charlie Chester opened a Sunday-lunchtime session for those in the know at the Queen's Club near Slough, overlooking a reservoir with a view towards Windsor Castle. On a sunny afternoon, clubbers would laze on the wooden decks outside, chatting and chilling. Inside, though, the scene was as frantic as any Saturday night: many of those on the dancefloor had been out since then, and still looked for somewhere else to go when the music ended at 5 p.m.

Yet if this was a mass movement, it was still without leaders, without a manifesto, without any articulated aim except to have fun and stick up a finger at authority. Around the time of the Greenwich débâcle, Tony Colston-Hayter had been approached by activists from far-left organisations who were keen to get involved. 'They were saying fuck the old Bill, fight the old Bill, and started infiltrating the scene, giving leaflets out, trying to lead us in that direction. We were about to get involved in this illegal rally, but I suddenly thought, "What am I doing? This is the last thing we need. These people want it for their own ends, they don't come to our clubs."'

Yet in its own vague way, it was also about more than making money, about drugs and dancing. Prime Minister Thatcher had been fond of fighting talk about 'the enemy within', but after the defeat of the miners in the strike of 1984–85, the threat supposedly posed to Britain by its own trade unionists and workers had effectively been crushed. A new enemy was needed, and the young have always been a convenient scapegoat.

The young were often stereotyped by the media and by politicians as lazy, violent, immoral. There was anxiety about city yuppies with too much money, and council-estate joy riders with too little. Lager louts and football hooligans had become the new folk devils. Meanwhile apprenticeships, training and other ways into meaningful work had been slowly replaced by an array of pointless job schemes. Benefits had been cut to make it far harder to leave the parental home. The former sixties radicals who had voted the Conservatives in were fond of whingeing that the young had become reactionary, apathetic, not at all inclined to demonstrate in the streets as they did. What they forgot was that no one believed that the world could be changed by marches and slogans any more. Least of all them.

In this climate, the defiant hedonism of the raves was all the more exhilarating. Running through fields, climbing walls and fences, dodging police dogs and road-blocks, a generation that had been taught to stand alone and look after themselves began to learn the power of numbers.

The raves began to gather up all the disparate threads of youth culture and knit them back together. Black and white, male and female, rock and soul fans, crusties and Sloanes. It was a cliché often repeated but generally true that bankers were dancing next to barrow boys, Sharons next to Selinas. There were no elitist door policies here. Anyone could go on an adventure to wonderland: all they needed was the price of a ticket, some access to transport, and a pill if they wanted it.

The addresses on the mailing lists covered every postal district in London, every big city in the UK. There was room for everyone in the fields that summer, a sense of unity, warmth and belonging that few of us had experienced before. In 1987, Mrs Thatcher had declared that 'there is no such thing as society' and that we should all rely on ourselves first. In fields and warehouses and aircraft hangars around Britain, for a while it felt as if we were building an alternative society of our own.

What was to astonish the police and authorities again and again was that many of the people consuming vast quantities of class-A drugs at these parties and so openly defying the law were not deprived. And much as the tabloids liked to portray them as innocent victims swayed by mind-bending music and evil acid barons, it was clear to anyone who came near one of these events that they were willing, even voracious, participants. They didn't fit the stereotype of joy-riding, ram-raiding, shop-lifting, drug-pushing, estate-dwelling lost youth. These were nice kids. The kids next door. *Their* kids. And it seemed as if they had all gone mad.

The Magic Roundabout

The scam was everything that summer. Getting the party on at any cost. On 3 June, Back to the Future III took place at Biggin Hill airbase, a venue that was not ideal owing to the fact that it backed on to a middle-class housing estate. As they moved their gear on site that afternoon, the crew told residents that they were setting up a funfair for the kiddies, inviting them to bring their families when it opened on Sunday afternoon.

When the police arrived that evening, Tony Colston-Hayter went to meet them wearing a suit and carrying a clipboard with fake headed notepaper from a film company and his usual carefully prepared story. This time they were shooting a Michael Jackson video and Colston-Hayter was the location manager, a put-upon soul who was as concerned as the police about the choice of venue and keen to get the nightmare over as quickly and efficiently as possible. The speakers were all covered in drapes, and opera was playing quietly as he showed the officer around, taking his address so that he could send him tickets to Jackson's next British concert.

Meanwhile, the cast of rainbow-clad 'extras' were filing through the security checks, patiently waiting until the hangar was full enough for the party to start. 'As the last people came in, I shook the officer's hand and said thanks. I got on stage, took my suit off, turned up the sound and *bang!* Fifty thousand watts. And I was in the middle of the crowd in a tracksuit, and the police never saw me again.'

The anger of the local residents is understandable. After Dr Anthony Hayter was quoted a few weeks later in the *Daily Mail* praising his son's inventiveness, he received an angry anonymous letter from someone whose weekend had been ruined by the Biology party in June:

The sound levels – which went on unremittingly for twenty-four hours – must have reached 10,000 watts-plus of output. Indeed, the noise was so great it could be heard six miles away . . . I don't know if you know the music style, but its chief attribute appears to be an intense baseline beat which really seems to climb inside one's skull making sleep or any other distraction impossible. This was enlivened for us by the addition of 'rapping' DJs whose technique involves a moronic scream which rises above the level of the music – yes, it *is* possible – with exhortations to 'get down' and 'clap your fucking hands together'. These raps are given out every fifth or tenth record, and make life worth living at five in the morning.

One resident was happy, however. An eighteen-year-old girl who had been grounded by her parents because she'd expressed interest in going to a rave was astonished to be woken up by the sound of one going off at the end of her garden. She climbed from her bedroom window and turned up at the entrance in her pyjamas. Sunrise and Back to the Future weren't known for their generosity, adding ultra-violet markings to their tickets to avoid forgeries and meticulously checking each one. But even they couldn't resist this blag: the pyjama girl got in free.

The next Sunrise event was the biggest yet. The Midsummer Night's Dream in an aircraft hangar at White Waltham airfield in Berkshire on 24 June attracted around 8,000 people. A passing patrol officer estimated there were 3,500 cars and thirty coaches parked outside. It was a spectacular night: lasers strafed the crowd, smoke machines belched out clouds in a variety of colours, and psychedelic images were projected on to two giant balloon-shaped screens hanging from the roof.

'It was just so much bigger than anything else that had been before it,' says Judge Jules, who played at most of the Sunrise events. 'The DJ booth was on a huge scaffold mount right at one end, so it gave you a real sense of perspective. It was a lovely warm summer's night, so some of the hangar doors were open as well. It was like the funeral scene in the film *Gandhi*, just people as far as the eye could see.'

There were only a handful of police in attendance, two of whom climbed up on to the DJ platform at the peak of the night, then stood nodding their heads to the beat. But amongst the revellers was a team of reporters, and on 26 June the *Sun* went front page with 'the scandal of the M25 drugs parties'.

The British tabloids and the country's vibrant youth culture have an oddly symbiotic relationship: they love to loathe each other, but also need each other. Scandal sells papers, but it also helps spread trends and validate new movements. Rebellion only works if there's someone to be shocked by it. Picking over these reports, gloating over the details they have wrong, is part of the joy of being involved in an underground movement. So while those involved will usually show disgust at the media's sensationalism, they also spend a lot of time anticipating tabloid involvement, then reading and analysing their coverage when it comes.

The *Sun*'s Ecstasy Airport story was a classic of its kind, still quoted lovingly today by the class of '89, many of whom know sections of it by heart: 'Drug-crazed kids – some as young as 12 – boogied for eight hours at Britain's biggest ever Ecstasy bash. More than 11,000 youngsters paid £40 each to flock to the amazing "secret" acid house party in a huge aircraft hangar.' Tickets were £15. World Wide estimated the crowd at 7,500. The 'thousands of Ecstasy wrappers littering the floor' were the remnants of the silver foil pieces that had showered down over the dancefloor, glittering in the lights, during the night. 'Beheaded pigeons littered the floor of the hangar after Sunday's party,' elaborated the tabloid a day later, zooming off into the realms of the absurd. 'Youngsters were so high on Ecstasy and cannabis that they ripped the birds' heads off.'

The voice of middle England, the *Daily Mail*, also splashed the story front page: 'The evil drug derivative Ecstasy was easily available,' it thundered. 'So were LSD and marijuana. They were sold, bought and taken to degrading effect ... No decent parent could have been anything but revolted and afraid for the children there.'

Tony Colston-Hayter had enjoyed his games with the media before, revelling in his status as 'acid's Mr Big', a mouthpiece for an outlaw culture. But this was no longer such fun. His sister Charlie had tabloid reporters camped out on her doorstep in Camden. Their parents were being phoned for comments. Home Secretary Douglas Hurd had ordered an enquiry into unlicensed parties, a move enthusiastically endorsed by his opposition shadow, Roy Hattersley.

'It's a nightmare,' Colston-Hayter says now of the media attention. 'They're looking for you all the time, writing anything they feel like about you, winding the police up by saying I'd said they couldn't catch me, camping outside my mum and dad's houses, asking ex-girlfriends what I did in bed.

'I was always the one saying "There's no drugs" on TV, which was a hard line to take when there obviously was. Not everyone was on drugs, but the more the press said it was all about drugs, the more people came to sell drugs. They totally generated that. And I would never have got those crowds if it hadn't been front page news.

Nowhere near. [*Sun* editor] Kelvin MacKenzie promoted it for us. Massively.'

Colston-Hayter knew he was in trouble. He also knew who to call. 'He had no idea how to handle it,' says the man who took over that day as World Wide's PR. 'He didn't know what it was like to be doorstepped, chased around. And he sensed intuitively that he could turn this to his advantage, but he didn't know how to do it.'

Colston-Hayter had met Paul Staines when they both competed in the UK Asteroid Tournament in their early teens. The Harrow school-boy won, Tony came second and the two vid-kids soon became firm friends. 'Even then he was a bit of a rogue,' recalls Staines. 'He taught me how to diddle 50p coins into the Asteroids machines and get extra goes. I was thirteen or fourteen. He thought nothing about hopping into a black cab and I lived in London paying five pence on the tube. So he was quite good fun. I smoked a bit of dope with him. He led me astray, I had a good time and I liked him immediately.'

At university, Staines was drawn into the Federation of Conservative Students, right-wing libertarians whose antics were so extreme that even the Tories eventually shut them down. 'I wasn't so much a Conservative. I didn't like all these tweedy guys in pinstripe suits. That wasn't where I was from. I'm not anti-gay or racist. I really did believe that capitalism was the best way of doing things. Free enterprise. I was very, very anti-communism. I thought communism was about Stalin keeping people in concentration camps and the Berlin Wall, that socialists were people who conformed and wore all the same clothes. So it was individualism.'

Afterwards, he worked for right-wing think tank the Adam Smith Institute, and became a political aide to David Hart. A wealthy property developer, right-wing maverick and adviser to Margaret Thatcher, Hart played a key role in the Conservatives' 1983 election victory, and in the defeat of the subsequent miners' strike. Since Mrs Thatcher was deposed as leader of the Conservative Party, he has worked as an adviser to Michael Portillo, the pin-up boy of the Conservative right.

According to Staines, Hart's Committee for a Free Britain organisa-tion received funding from Rupert Murdoch, James Goldsmith and – indirectly – from the CIA. It produced two publications, the Cold War bulletin *World Briefing* and *British Briefing*, which aimed to smear Labour MPs and left-leaning lawyers and writers.[4] Staines worked on the latter, stressing that to him it was all a bit of a laugh: 'Hart is completely round the twist, you know.' But their mailing list included names like George Bush, and his boss would also chat at length to senior figures in British intelligence.

It was all great fun. The twenty-one-year-old got to travel the world, going on 'missions' for Hart to Washington, South Africa, South America. He got to fire off AK-47s while supporting anti-communist movements in Nicaragua and Angola, and to drive around East Berlin in a limo just before the Wall came down, contacting dissident students and taking them out to lavish meals.

In the meantime, encouraged by his old video gaming friend, he was also going out to the raves. He took his first E at Apocalypse Now in Wembley, and with characteristic extremism immediately followed up with his first tab of acid. 'It was brilliant, the usual *whoosh* experience. I thought, "If this is brilliant, maybe acid is great." That was it, I turned into a whiff of smoke, lost for two days.

'I had to give a speech the next day. I had just been to Panama on some kind of fact-finding mission, and I was going to say what it was like there and how [military dictator and alleged drug-trafficker General Manuel] Noriega was a real bad guy. Obviously, I had done loads of drugs the night before so it was very appropriate. I had a shower, put a suit on and I can remember standing up there with the E just getting out my body, saying something like, "Noriega; real bad. Panama; nice place, bad government." Just complete bollocks. It wasn't the kind of thing you would expect.

'I didn't see it as incompatible with raving. You probably think we were all wearing pinstripes, but it was jeans. We had this office in Buckingham Gate which was a complete nut house. We were given loads of money and we'd got nothing to do but pick up wheezes. What shall we do now? Let's campaign for legalising drugs. Let's see if we can get some guns to Nicaragua . . .'

For the next year, Staines was to lead an odd double life, still working for Hart but also troubleshooting for World Wide – writing press releases, accompanying Tony Colston-Hayter to an increasing number of TV appearances, co-ordinating legal actions and attending the events.

'When I was in politics I used to wear multi-coloured rave clothes, but at the parties I would have a suit on, carry a clipboard. So the police would be at the door, and I would be pushed up the front because I was quite articulate. When they see someone like that, they think: "Oh fuck, lawyer." That way you probably stop them cutting too many corners. Although sometimes the road-blocks came out.'

Even this had its irony. 'Hart was the guy who financed the Union of Democratic Mine Workers that helped break the miners' strike, where the tactics of road-blocks first started. And then here I was on the other side!'

Tony Colston-Hayter was charged after White Waltham for holding an unlicensed party. By then civil rights organisations such as Liberty (then still the National Council for Civil Liberties) were voicing concerns at some of the police tactics, especially their restricting the freedom of movement and the sometimes arbitrary nature of the arrests.

Both sides were minutely examining the statute books to find ambiguities in laws that were never written with events like this in mind. Like the underground American clubs, the raves didn't need a drinks licence because they didn't serve alcohol. A loophole in the 1982 Public Entertainment Act meant that they could avoid the need for an Entertainments licence by claiming to be a private, members-only party on private land.

It was a game of nerves. Promoters had to ensure that they really did have a contract from the landowner (difficult, when many venues were found by third parties and passed on in exchange for a lucrative commission, and when the children or employees of the landowners and estate agents with keys were all keen to cash in). They then had to make sure the owner honoured this contract, despite pressure from the police – often, they would be sent away for a weekend break with their family to keep them away from both the authorities and justifiably angry neighbours. Then, providing they got enough people on site before police were able to stop them, it was difficult for the authorities to intervene without causing a full-scale riot.

After the press hysteria the stakes had been raised. MPs had begun to ask questions and the police to allocate resources to this perceived new threat. At the start of July, Energy were the first to feel the heat. Their second party was to be in a disused airfield on the Berkshire/ Wiltshire border, but their contract proved to be with the wrong person. They'd spent more money on the production for this event than on their first: a twenty-foot polystyrene replica of Stonehenge and a row of surreal laughing houses stood waiting for an audience that was never to see them. Two hours before the party was due to start police swarmed the site, closing service stations along the M4 and blocking exits along a 20-mile stretch of the motorway to prevent clubbers getting access after the address was released. A few hundred did eventually find a party in a scrap dealer's field just off the A34 in Oxfordshire, where the dancing went on until a police helicopter broke it up at 9 a.m.

After the triumph of their open-air event in June, Biology too found themselves losing venue after venue, and a week later ended up leading their ticket-holders up the M1 to a tacky disco in Birmingham, where the doors opened at 8 a.m. It was a mystery tour all right, but hardly magical.

On 22 July, the hottest night of the year, Energy fought back with another party just behind Heston Services on the M4, allowing those with tickets from the cancelled party in free. 'Having been stung once, we did a much more tactical operation,' says Tintin Chambers. They took to disguising themselves with baseball hats, pony tails, glasses and changes of clothes, running into Tube stations to lose police tails, and buying cheap run-around cars to store in strategic places so they could swap vehicles to move around.

It was cheesy spy movie stuff, great fun to play, but it all fell apart when a security guard walked into the venue as they were setting up and informed the police. Determined not to be beaten again, they immediately released the address over the phone lines, with police racing against the clubbers to block the M4 and the access roads from Heston Services. The perimeter fence of the warehouse was surrounded by officers with dogs and tactical support vans, and inside fire officers immediately demanded that an axe be taken to Stonehenge on safety grounds.

But this time, people weren't giving up so easily. Unable to get into the service station car park, they simply left their cars on the hard shoulder, scrambled up the bank into the service station, and began climbing over walls and fences to get into the venue. Those parked on the wrong side of the motorway ran across six lanes of traffic.

'We were all inside in the courtyard, and suddenly there were masses of people coming over the back,' says Lynn Cosgrave. 'As soon as a few people parked, everyone did. There was a massive fight with the police and the dogs and people were running towards the fence in these mad dashes. Eventually they had to open it, because there were so many people it was impossible. It was just better to let it happen than not.'

It was, says Tintin Chambers, like being in an action movie: 'But instead of *Escape From* . . ., it was *Escape Into* . . .' It wasn't Energy's best production: the décor had been pulled down, one side of the sound system wasn't working. When they feared the police were going to storm the venue at one point, the 10,000-strong crowd were asked to converge together in the centre of the building, while the MC chanted, 'If they come in, don't let them take us!'

Outside, the motorway had to be closed while the parked cars were towed away, causing delays to flights from nearby Heathrow. 'It was utter chaos,' laughs Chambers. 'Absolutely mad. But it was a good party.'

A few day later, two plain-clothes policemen dressed in smiley T-shirts and beads arrived at Taylor's Chelsea flat to take him and his partner back to a police station near Heston in a Citroën 2CV. 'They were nice coppers, they didn't give us a hard time at all,' remembers Chambers, who feels the choice of transport was deliberate. 'They were just having a laugh with us. It took a long time to drive there. It was hysterical.'

There were no charges. Taylor told the police he just wanted to organise parties, and if there was no route promoters could follow to get a licence, then events like these weren't going to stop. 'I'd been done for a licence breach during one of the Gatecrasher balls because an exit wasn't big enough, pathetic stuff. You get fined £1,500 and that's the end of the story. So if I made more than that, then it was worth doing it.'

Planet Ecstasy

'*I never had an agent, I just dealt with everyone directly. They'd tell you vaguely what time you were on, and you'd agree a price. The journey was always fantastic. They'd never tell you where it was, just give you a list of instructions, so it was very spy movie. When you got there, you'd be like, "Oh, this one seems like a real dud, it's really quiet." We'd drive round the corner and it would be like opening a box of diamonds. My God! There'd be all these cars nestling out of sight in the valley, lasers, a funfair, and you could just feel the energy. The organisation was equivalent to an army-scale operation.*

'*I never had a bad time, ever, and I was playing raves every single weekend, all over the country. There was never any violence or aggression. It didn't matter what you were, what you wore, nothing mattered at all. You could do what you wanted, say what you wanted. You could just take your clothes off and jump on top of the car, and people would just hug you and tell you how brilliant you were.*

'*I loved it. The buzz of singing that track to thousands of people. And then afterwards getting changed, dumping your bag and joining the crowd. The record company weren't around, it was nothing to do with them then. Later, they tried to get their acts on at the raves, but we weren't doing it because we had something to promote. You didn't see it as work. It was a laugh:* Wicked, we're going to play Sunrise!'

MC Kinky from the E-Zee Posse, whose 'Everything Starts With An E' was still popular at the raves

Once the newspapers began printing their front-page advertisements for the scene (secret rendezvous points! mind-bending music and lasers! gyrating bodies! drugs that can boost sex-drive! loud music all night! youngsters dancing till they drop!) everyone wanted to try this new leisure concept.

Flyers and tickets were being distributed all over the country: shops and private numbers, some of them belonging to the very DJs you were paying to dance to. Carl Cox was the main Brighton agent, and remembers days of chaos before an event with clubbers phoning and knocking on his door round the clock. Vendors would get one ticket free for every four they sold, with the choice of selling the fifth for profit or using it to take friends.

Buying the ticket was part of the fun, your entrance into a secret society. Charlie Colston-Hayter was an agent for Sunrise and Back to the Future and often had people in her flat for hours, chatting about the parties and hanging out while they bought their tickets. She also handled last-minute sales on the evening of the event itself. As the parties got bigger, the queues outside her sixth-floor flat on Camden Road in north London got more ridiculous.

One night, she had a bouncer on her door upstairs and another with a dog on the ground-floor entrance to the block, the line snaking down the stairs and then outside. When her bemused flat-mate arrived home from work, the bouncer tried to make her queue with everyone else. Charlie would keep the door on a chain and simply throw the cash into a cupboard in her bedroom until Dave Roberts or her brother arrived to stuff it in a sports bag and take it away; a croupier in casinos when she wasn't working the raves, she was used to handling large bundles of notes.

The summer developed its own language: *wicked, mental, pukka* (good); *moody, Jekyll, snide* (not so good). It had its own rituals. Rushing home after work on Saturday to get ready, before cramming into a coach, a hired van or a car with all the night's requirements: a change of clothes, coins for the phones, chewing gum, munchies, mix tapes, Ribena, Rizlas.

'We used to travel really early,' recalls Lee Garrick, now one of the team behind the Birmingham club Miss Moneypenny's but then an assistant in the Depot, a clothes shop which also served as a Midlands ticket outlet. 'It was incredible because you'd get so excited and you really didn't know if it was even going to be on. You never knew who you were looking for, you never knew anything. All you had was this phone number. You'd hit the service station, and there'd be all these young people hanging around, and you'd be like, *Is it on? Is the rave on?*

'It was really exciting, really naughty,' agrees Michael Ryan, co-owner of the Depot. 'Whenever we had a coach going down, everyone used to come in the shop and buy something. We were manufacturing our own clothing – shirts with big, long collars and polka dots; big, wide trousers. When the papers picked up on it, it just made it even cooler. Everybody wanted to say they'd been to a rave. It was just a big crowd of people sticking two fingers up. The whole thing was rebellion, wasn't it? Just like punk.'

Except the numbers far exceeded anything that had come before. In 1988, a party for 3,000 people at the Brixton Academy was feature material for the London listings magazine *Time Out*. By the summer of 1989, unprecedented numbers of young people were on the move, driving to massive parties in fields, barns and aircraft hangars. Motorways had traffic jams after midnight, cheerful log-jams of hooting, waving party people. Garages and service stations were bustling, with rainbow-coloured clubbers grinning at each other from open car windows, swapping news and clues. 'Where are you from?' 'Where's that?' 'Heard anything?' 'What you on?' 'Be lucky, have a good one!' Every phone box had a cluster of anxious youths around it, waiting to hear the latest news.

Finally, someone would run from a phone box or wave a chunky mobile, screaming, 'It's on! It's on!' and people would scramble to their vehicles. The first cars roared off on to the motorway, everyone else following as closely as they could.

Then, after winding down a dark, unpromising country lane, suddenly it was there before you, a glittering one-night fantasy world constructed for your pleasure. The chaotic parking arrangements meant it would be almost impossible to leave early, even if you wanted to. You might have to trek a mile or more over muddy fields after leaving the car. But on a good night, none of this mattered. You were part of it. And being there, being in that field with thousands of others who all seemed to be feeling the same as you, who all seemed to be on the same buzz, was the best feeling in the world.

For the small group of people organising these parties, the summer of 1989 was even more dreamlike. 'We were like rock stars,' says Dave Roberts. 'Girls used to ring us for sex. Tony thought he was Elvis.'

It's impossible to estimate exactly how much money was being made at the peak of the parties. Less than the tabloids claimed. More than the tax office was ever told. The biggest events of the summer were probably netting the organisers somewhere between £50,000 and £100,000. Parties stopped at the last minute were probably losing a similar amount by then.

In a well-researched piece for Q magazine that autumn, Lloyd Bradley outlined the costs of a typical event: sound system £10,000; lights £5,000; marquees and staging £3,000; security £5,000; DJs £2,000; flyers/radio ads £3,000; power supply £500; toilets £500; coaches from pick-up points £1,000; hire of the land, anything up to £10,000.

By the time they were published, even these figures were conservative. As the crowds got bigger, DJs who had been happy to play for £100 were suddenly demanding £1,000 for a two-hour set. In the space of two parties, Lynn Cosgrave remembers Energy's DJ bill jumping from £1,500–2,000 all night to £7,000–8,000. Similarly, Tony Colston-Hayter was paying £1,500 for venues at the start of the summer but up to £20,000 for a field by the end.

The cost of sound and lighting went up, with hire companies often charging double their fee with the logic that, if the rave was cancelled and they only got the half they'd been paid upfront, they wouldn't lose out. As they struggled to get the parties on, the big promoters often had two or three venues on hold, and two sets of light and sound in case one was detained by the police. There would also be dummy vans and lorries which would leave to circle the M25 in opposite directions in the hope of distracting the police while the real crews left for the site.

All of these people had to be paid on the night, all of the money counted and processed. A frequent live PA at the raves, MC Kinky remembers Portakabins filled with mountains of bank-notes, where loved-up promoters celebrating their success would pay her with dreamy MDMA smiles and so much cash that she was convinced it must be counterfeit. Energy would have money stuffed in bin-bags in a coach parked on the site. Ever efficient, World Wide would establish a safe house on a strategically positioned housing estate, knocking on a door and asking to use a room for the night. 'We would take all the neighbouring households a case of champagne, for the noise,' says Dave Roberts. 'We'd then offer one of them £500 for the night. We'd be counting out all the money whilst being served cups of tea by some old dear whose house we'd rented!'

From the security to the sound hire companies, the DJs to the farmers, the profits were being shared between far more people than the tabloids implied, and it's hard now to pin down who walked away with what. What is certain is that substantial amounts of cash were floating around, and most of it was being spent.

There were cabs and stretch limos and cars and drivers. There were wild parties in hotel suites, long weekends in Amsterdam and jaunts to Spain and Ibiza. There were champagne and cocaine parties, Es for everyone and all-night sessions most nights. It was a fantasy world, where life was one long party and nothing felt real.

'I hate to think what I did with so much money,' says Lynn Cosgrave now. 'I wasn't sharing in the profits, but I was still earning about £2,000 a week and spending more. It wasn't real money. We'd eat at Pucci's every night. We'd drink every night. We'd go to clubs in the week, raves at the weekend. You never got back till Sunday night. Then you'd go to bed, get up late on Monday, go out to dinner and then go to another club. Tintin had a chauffeur. He had a Porsche for two weeks. There were always drivers around. There was always money, drugs, a bar.'

'If I were to be in the same position now, I'd do it very differently in terms of how I'd manage my affairs,' admits Tintin Chambers. 'I was young. I spent the majority of it on my mates, buying drugs for everyone, going out, nice cars. Easy come, easy go. It was the buzz of organising a party that was best. There's so much adrenaline, especially when you know you're in a running battle against the authorities, against the police, and you're a bit of a modern-day revolutionary. Doing it for dance, doing it for the cause. Just attending your own party and seeing people go mental, knowing you put it together . . . it's quite an egotistical thing, a hell of a vibe. It was just a really good laugh.'

'We loved the partying, the buzz of doing it,' agrees Dave Roberts. 'We just wanted to do it right. If Tony had the choice, he would have spent every penny we had. Every penny.' He pauses, marvelling at the wonders they created. 'Just think how good we would have done the fucking party if we'd had loads of time.'

The long, hot summer peaked with the Energy and Sunrise festivals in August. Both events looked shaky at first. Energy found a site at the last minute in fields in Effingham, Surrey, on the Bank Holiday, but the event wouldn't have happened if they hadn't hired a tough lawyer to stay on site. A judge was pulled out of bed that night to rule that the party had to go ahead. By then the police road-blocks were already up, but Energy had announced over the phone lines that the first 5,000 to turn up would get in free, and the whole area was jammed with cars.

At one point, the security team decided to expedite matters by telling around 500 ravers to leave their cars in the country lane and stand behind one of their men. He then led a charge towards the police vans blocking the road, causing officers to jump into the vans in terror of the mob and lock the doors. The security then lifted the vans to the side of the road, allowing the clubbers to return to their cars and drive through.

The fairground was arranged all round the edge of the field, bathing it in a magical, twinkling light while people danced under the stars. As the police stopped parties elsewhere, Taylor's mobile kept ringing with promoters pleading for their ticket-holders to be allowed to join in, and the crowd swelled to something like 20,000. Lynn Cosgrave was caught in a traffic jam about two miles from the venue with Fabio, who was already due on stage. Two lads in another car saw her distress, took the DJ's heavy record boxes and ran with them across the fields. Everyone pulled together, because the party had to go on.

The Sunrise/Back to the Future Dance Music Festival took place on 12 August at Longwick, near Aylesbury. This was the climax, the moment when all of the energy crackling across the country came together for one electric night. Again, the police found the site, their helicopters landing early in the morning to stop the lorries carrying equipment into the field. A war of nerves with the land-owner followed, with the police changing his mind and Sunrise's lawyers persuading him to honour his contract. But the party went ahead.

A crowd of 25,000 people danced in the fields. Speakers blasted out 100,000 watts – twice what U2 had used at Wembley. A massive, state-of-the-art Diamond Vision screen had been flown in from the States and erected over the stage, flashing messages to the crowd and showing the live acts: Raze, 'Break 4 Love'; Doug Lazy 'Let It Roll'; CrySisco, 'Afro Dizzi Act'; and of course MC Kinky. The music could include anything from the shuffling two-step beats of Soul II Soul, through De La Soul's eclectic, trippy Daisy Age rap and the hypnotic instrumental mantra of Lil Louis' 'French Kiss' to the manic, stadium-size acid of the KLF's 'What Time Is Love' and '3 AM Eternal'.

For Tony Colston-Hayter and Dave Roberts, this was the climax to a year in which at times they'd felt as if they had been charmed: 'We did have some kind of supernatural magic with us. Every party has some mental unbelievable story. Every time, the sun came up. Every time, miracles happened.'

Colston-Hayter took the stage just before dawn, talking through the PA to give the crowd the latest weather report, and just as he was saying the words '. . . and a beautiful sunrise' the sun came up behind him and the crowd erupted. They knew then that it would never be this good again. How could it get better?

Near noon the next day Carl Cox went on, playing hip hop and acid house on three decks. His eyes shine at the memory. 'It was in open countryside, the best sound you've ever heard, visually it was amazing. Half the crowd were sitting down in the sun, so I decided to pick them all up again.' He got the whole crowd dancing again, while his girlfriend handed out his business card to the promoters at the side of the stage. They all called to book him in the following weeks. 'Since then, I've never looked back.'

But the real impact was on the charts. At the end of August, 'Ride On Time' by Black Box went to number one, where it stayed for six weeks. An Italian-made cut-up of Loleatta Holloway's old Salsoul disco hit 'Love Sensation' with added house beats and a jangly piano, its components may have come from the music's history but its success signalled the beginning of a rave new world.

'That's when I realised,' says Tony Colston-Hayter. '*The music!* And I missed it. I could have been the Motown of acid house. I loved the music, but at the time it was more about the trip and the buzz. We didn't realise it was going to be so big. I just gave them £50, £100 to play on-stage.'

By September, more than a quarter of the singles in the top thirty were dance records, many of them rising to the charts with no mainstream radio play at all, promoted through the raves and the pirates. By October, dance records stood at numbers one, two and three in the chart. This was no surprise to the dance shops, who were used to a deluge of clubbers on Monday mornings coming in singing the hook to A Guy Called Gerald's 'Voodoo Ray' or whatever else had been that weekend's big tune.

'People would bring in tapes for us to play and tell them what it was,' says Jazzy M. 'You'd get loads of kids come in off their heads, still humming this tune. And some of the things they thought the lyrics said . . . Some of them were hilarious.'

Major labels who had dismissed the music as a fad suddenly became more interested. DJs were quickly offered A&R jobs and their own labels. Artists were offered major deals. Tony Colston-Hayter says he was later introduced to the head of a major label who told him he'd sacked his entire A&R department in the autumn of 1989 because none of them understood how these cheaply made records were suddenly shooting up the charts. Colston-Hayter then asked if he could do a compilation for the label, but the executive just laughed. 'He said, "No, too late, we've done it all now. I just wanted to meet you because you fucked up for us for a little while." '

Police and Thieves

On 31 September, Tintin Chambers attended two raves. At Helter Skelter, near Oxford, a crowd of about 4,000 turned up despite the soft rain to dance to PAs including Ce Ce Rogers and Salsoul disco diva Loleatta Holloway. The KLF asked for their £1,000 fee in Scottish pound notes, wrote 'We love you children' on as many as they could and then threw the lot into the crowd during their performance on top of a high tower which had previously been used to bounce the lasers off. After the KLF came offstage, Chambers and his friends piled into a car to drive to Woodhatch near Reigate in Surrey for Phantasy – a rave that was using Strikeforce, the same security company as Energy.

'There was a really weird vibe as we came into Heston. Police all just standing by their cars, scratching their chins and talking quite heavily to each other. The closer we got the more police there were. Then we hit a road-block. This was about six in the morning – late to be having a road-block, because usually they'd give up. They let us through because we were with someone who lived locally. At the party Carl Cox was playing and it was absolutely storming. But there was this strange vibe there, as if something really terrible had happened, but everybody was so high they hadn't registered it.'

Ten thousand people attended Phantasy, and few of them saw the incident that was to mark a turning point in official attitudes towards the raves: a battle between the police and Strikeforce involving Rottweilers and CS gas that left sixteen officers injured, seven of them in hospital. Douglas Hurd, playing the law-and-order card as Conservative Home Secretaries tend to do before the party's annual conference, promised action.

Even those involved had to concede that the atmosphere at the raves had changed. As the events had got bigger, it was impossible for even the most reputable security firm to provide enough trained men: friends were being invited along for the night to make up numbers, and stories were now rife about bouncers confiscating drugs from ravers to sell them to others, of them letting ticketless clubbers in for a backhander, of dealing and extortion. With the tabloids talking of profits in excess of half a million being made from one party, everyone wanted to put on an event of their own. If the tickets weren't profitable enough, promoters could always control the drug dealing, or franchise it out in exchange for a cut of the take.

The Soho record shop Black Market had begun to hold back the ticket money until after the event, so that they could refund their customers if the party didn't happen. Already coping with a massive demand for tickets at the shop, with filling out membership cards, getting clubbers to sign contracts as 'movie extras' and all the other attempts to side-step the law, Tony Farsides says some of the new promoters made his life a nightmare.

'When I started, it was three or four events. The occasional Sunrise or Energy party. Then we had every petty criminal in London coming through the door, putting on their own rave and wanting us to sell their tickets. These people were putting up a lot of money, so when the events were busted they'd try and get the ticket money off us because they were facing such heavy losses.

'I was in the office with one promoter, and he had this giant East

End tough guy with him who kept patting his jacket intimating that he had something more than a packet of Tic Tacs in it. There was a sense that something really bad could happen. There were battles between the bouncers, you heard stories about people disappearing. I didn't want to be involved.'

The big promoters had also noticed a change. 'All the villains suddenly thought, "We've missed this for a year here",' says Tony Colston-Hayter. 'At the festival we took something like £300,000 on the ticket sales, but a million pounds changed hands in the field which we had no part of at all. I just remember whole lines of dealers working together, walking in synchronised lines, combing backwards and forwards across the field.'

Well-spoken public schoolboys, the Energy team were prime targets. Even for their own security. 'Strikeforce were so into making sure the party happened that they'd do *anything* to stop the police,' says Tintin Chambers. 'They could turn against you, though. They did have a habit of turning round and demanding more at the end of the night. But we still kept on using the same guys. You don't want to piss off 100 security men. You need them on your side.'

In the middle of August, two men appeared at Jeremy Taylor's flat wearing long macs despite the heat. They said they wanted a large pay-off, or they'd make sure the next party wouldn't happen. 'Once someone rang the doorbell at 6 a.m. I've got a video camera on the front door so I could see that the guy had a hood on. Five minutes later all the windows at the front of the house were smashed. That was nasty, not knowing who it was and whether it would happen again. There were definitely situations where you were scared, but it was something you suddenly found yourself in, and once you were in it was too late and you just had to deal with it.'

A business associate of his father's recommended a security team headed by ex-SAS soldiers. 'They came down and gave my flat a complete security check, gave me a twenty-four hour security guard. I never saw it, but I suppose he was armed.'

The next Energy event was planned as a benefit for the families of the victims of the *Marchioness* disaster. Sixty people had been killed after a pleasure boat they were using for a twenty-sixth birthday party on the Thames was hit from behind by a dredger. Both Taylor and

Chambers had lost friends in the tragedy. They had hoped to be allowed to hold Dance '89 in an inner London park, but the council involved backed out. Instead they went back to the countryside, and after police helicopters discovered their first venue, they ended up on a day-long chase round the M25 on 23 September, their juggernauts driving in circles while Chambers sat in the office in London frantically co-ordinating the search for a new venue.

Eventually they began setting up in Raydon airfield in Suffolk in the early hours of the morning, and were ready to admit revellers at 6 a.m. The party went on till around eight that night and was enjoyed by most of the 10,000 attending, but the last-minute organisation was chaotic. The hangar was still full of heavy machinery, crops were trampled, and four cars parked near the stage were set on fire – although far from being concerned, most of the ravers seemed to treat it as just another sideshow, with one vehicle doing handbrake turns between the burning cars to cheers from the watching crowd. Unsurprisingly, Taylor was charged with conspiracy to cause a public nuisance. After the distressingly bad press coverage made them out to be exploiting the tragedy for profit, they were also disowned by the *Marchioness* appeal – something which genuinely hurt both of them.

To add to their woes, after another series of threats their safe was stolen with £9,000 in it. 'We started to get newspaper reporters following us around, which scared the shit out of me,' says Lynn Cosgrave. 'It wasn't funny any more. This was really serious. As much as it had been our campaign to keep dancing, I didn't want to be in prison. People around you were getting arrested, going down for being caught with drugs. And I just thought, "No, this isn't worth it any more." '

Energy went back to legal venues indoors. They reopened Fun City in the West End and began organising parties at the Brixton Academy. Lynn Cosgrave left soon after, going to work for Nicky Holloway at Sin and setting up as a booking agent for Fabio, Grooverider, David Morales and Frankie Knuckles – one of the first DJ agencies.

Inspector Ken Tappenden, soon to become the nemesis of the rave promoters, watched the climate change as the summer peaked. The divisional commander of North West Kent, an area crossed by the M25, he had been keeping a careful eye on the pay parties. Now his superiors felt it was time to act. 'Tony Colston-Hayter and Jeremy Taylor weren't villains in the true sense of the word, they were looking at a buck. When it all became serious is when the real villains got into it from east London. Then we knew it was bad news. It became extortion, it became brutality. It was almost like the Krays again.'

The police crackdown began in earnest the week after Phantasy. Before, says Tony Colston-Hayter, the different forces were rarely co-ordinated against the parties: 'There's so much rivalry. You could do the same moves on different areas, because they wouldn't help each other. They didn't *want* the next lot to stop it. They wanted it to look just as bad in the next county as it did in theirs.'

A career policeman with twenty-two years' experience in CID, Ken Tappenden had an unblemished record in the thirty years he had served with the force, except for one incident during the miners' strike, when he was reprimanded by a judge for blocking the Dartford Tunnel to prevent flying pickets moving up from the Kent coal fields to Nottingham. On 7 October, he used similar tactics to prevent a Paranoia 2 party taking place in Chatham, Kent. Recognising that it was impossible to halt a party once it was in progress, he aimed to seal off the venue before it started and prevent clubbers getting in, finding the location by buying tickets and calling in on the phone lines just as they had. Operation Jute took three weeks of planning, and involved 250 officers waiting at strategic motorway junctions and services. Fighting the parties was never easy, and Tappenden learned to respect his adversaries.

'If I was to set up a team of military generals, I'd want half of them on my team. They were strategists, they could get in when you thought you'd stopped them. And when they got in, you couldn't tackle them. We clearly would have needed an army, a regiment of police to stop a party. Once that fairground got up and the music started, all you could do was contain it. To go in would have been folly. I had a lot of admiration for the way they operated, the way they were able to dictate the scene from mobile telephones.'

Amongst the other parties stopped that night was Back to the Future's Late Summer Dance Party. Lorries carrying equipment were turned away from the Biggin Hill site, and clubbers calling in for directions heard a message saying the event had been cancelled due to 'over-reaction from the Government, local authorities and the gutter press'.

Paul Staines persuaded Tony Colston-Hayter that the best place to fight back would be at the Tory Party conference in Blackpool the following week. 'I was going to be there anyway, and we did some deal where Tony got the lasers for David Hart's gig, then we had them to launch the Freedom To Party campaign. Our press conference was in all the round-ups of the conference that night: MTV, Japanese TV, ITN, all the press was there.'

A loose alliance of all the big party organisers – Sunrise, Energy, Biology, World Dance, Ibiza – the campaign presented them as Thatcherist entrepreneurs, catering to a demand in the market. Lobbying to bring the laws controlling drinking and dancing closer to those of the rest of Europe, and for the introduction of one-night music and dance licences for warehouse-style events, they claimed that the authorities were pushing Britain's youth into the arms of criminals: 'Whatever happens, the dancing will go on,' said the briefing paper written by Staines and Colston-Hayter. 'The choice facing politicians is simple. Do they prefer to see young people dancing under licence, or dancing with organised crime?'

At Hart's fringe meeting, Paul Staines distributed a Committee For a Free Britain pamphlet written by *Sun* columnist Dr Vernon Coleman and supporting the decriminalisation of all drugs. In his briefing paper for Freedom To Party, however, he tried to minimise the association with illegal substances, inventing a novel explanation of the term acid house. In Chicago slang, he contended, 'acid burn' meant to sample, to steal a snatch of music in a mix. This lie has since been repeated in Parliament, in the press, and can often be found in otherwise authoritative histories of the music. Only once has he ever been challenged on it – at a convention run by the Disco Mix Club, one of the Chicago DJs attending got up to say he was talking bullshit. Which of course he was.

Meanwhile, the crackdown continued. On 13 October, three of those arrested in the police swoop on the Greenwich pleasure boats in Operation Seagull in November 1988 were found guilty. Clive

Reynolds, who was caught in possession of fifty-eight Ecstasy pills, was immediately sentenced to four years. In the following weeks, party organisers Robert Darby and Leslie Thomas were sentenced to ten and six years respectively for 'conspiring to manage premises where drugs were supplied'. It was an excellent result, crowed Detective Chief Inspector Albert Patrick on the TV news, 'the first conviction of its kind in the country'.

Ten years. More than most rapists or muggers ever serve. For organising a small party where no one was forced to do anything against their will. If it was intended as a warning, it worked.

That weekend, 200 officers were used to stop clubbers getting to an event in a field at South Ockendon, Essex: there were eighty arrests, and the police made sure the media were informed that three firearms were seized as well as drugs. The police also announced that a Pay Party Unit had been established in the main conference room at Gravesend station, and that Ken Tappenden was now co-ordinating the battle against the parties.

The unit was set up at a cost of £95,000 with a staff of six and four computers. Within months, it was the central resource for the whole of England and Wales, with sixty staff and thirty computers connected into the HOLMES (Home Office Large Major Enquiry System) database established after the Yorkshire Ripper fiasco. (Serial killer Peter Sutcliffe had been interviewed on nine separate occasions by the police, but lack of pooled information meant that he managed to murder thirteen women before finally getting caught.)

At the same time, the promoters began to lose the communications systems that had made them so effective. Tony Colston-Hayter's phone lines were cut off after the telephone watchdog ICSSTIS ruled that they breached its code of practice – unlike, say, sleazy sex lines. He was allowed to continue using them for information, but had to move any announcements about venues to another phone system.

On 20 October, a two-month operation based at Plaistow police station came to a head when officers simultaneously raided the studio of the leading pirate station Centre Force, its associated club in Bow, and several houses in east London. Set up in August after a series of violent incidents at parties in the area, including the stabbing and scalping of a bouncer, the operation had only circumstantial evidence that those running the station were involved in the violence or in drug-dealing in association with the ICF and other ex-football firms. Much of the evidence was ruled inadmissible and the case eventually fell apart, but in the meantime many of the station's DJs left for new pirate Dance FM, and Centre Force was finished.

Now retired from the force, Ken Tappenden has admitted that he wasn't averse to bending the rules a little at the Pay Party Unit. Although not as much as he may have wanted: 'I was frightened to because it was so much in the eye of the politicians.' He operated in the same grey area as the promoters themselves, fighting their high-tech operations with a few of his own. Phones were tapped. Mobile phone networks in certain areas were shut down on Saturday nights. Light aircraft and helicopters were sent up at weekends to spot sites with suspicious activity. Scanners were used to monitor the pirates. They even set up a pirate of their own for a while, broadcasting loud music and disinformation from the Pay Party Unit itself. Learning the language had been hard at first – they had to compile a glossary of terms – but the younger officers got into it all with gusto.

Since it was difficult to charge promoters with anything that would result in more than a fine, they aimed instead to disrupt as many parties as possible, to take the thrill out of the night with road-blocks, spot checks, petty arrests. The police even staged their own phantom raves, calling in to the pirates with false locations and sending clubbers on pointless journeys to darkened fields. One night, they put the word out that a party had been moved to Brand's Hatch. Around a thousand clubbers turned up. 'We shouldn't have done, but we then immobilised them by putting a whole block round them with vans and police cars so they couldn't move for five or six hours. It was the only way we could stop them going to . . . I think it was Colchester that night. We did it a number of times.'

Few of the parties were pursued over the abuse of drugs simply because it was impossible to prove without massive manpower: even if hundreds of officers swamped a party at once, most of the evidence would end up in the grass. Indeed, the one time they did try it, officers filled three plastic bags with the illegal substances they picked up from the field afterwards. 'The number of arrests for the amount of trouble was minimal. And even then, you would not be blessed by the courts for taking 300 people up for being in possession of a few pills. You clog the courts, you clog the system, and why go for kids who were having £10, £15 taken out of their pocket on a Saturday night for almost nothing when there was such out-and-out villainy?'

Instead, the unit concentrated on environmental offences, noise pollution and local by-laws, scouring the statute books for any obscure legislation they could use. Health and safety issues were the most effective means of attack. 'They used to get into buildings and rewire them back up again from live fuse boxes with all the wires hanging everywhere, dripping with water,' says Tappenden. 'They would take over warehouses round the M25 and knock out middle walls which were load-bearing walls to make it twice as big. They'd get in bulldozers over the weekend. That's the kind of thing I admired, because it would take me a week to start thinking about that, let alone do it.'

The police collected flyers and fanzines, bought tickets and attended raves, and had 200 intelligence officers across the country collecting information for the HOLMES database. By early 1990, it held 5,725 names and 712 vehicles. The unit had monitored 4,380 telephone calls and made 258 arrests. But still the parties persisted: all over the Midlands and the north now, as well as the south-east.

Laws are generally enforced by consensus. Faced with thousands of young people who ignored their authority, the police were often at a loss as to what to do. One night Ken Tappenden was policing a rave with 100 men under his command, when fifty people simply got out of their cars and threw the keys into the bushes to stop police moving them on. It was dark. The officers couldn't have found the keys even if they'd tried, let alone have matched them to the vehicles and then moved them. 'I felt absolutely helpless,' says Tappenden. 'For us that was . . . it was another kind of policing. It was entrapment of us, almost. We'd never been subjected to that. We'd never been subjected to mass numbers you couldn't deal with.'

Watching the surveillance videos of one rave, he was astounded to see dealers loading pills in costermongers' barrows to satisfy the demand. At others, they were carried in buckets. When he spoke to authorities with no experience of the scene, few would believe what he was telling them. 'It was a period where people were finding themselves, and losing themselves,' he says. 'They were nice kids. If you ever got a group of them on their own, they were lovely.' Once he saw youngsters being sold pills in the queue outside a rave and then having them taken off them again by bouncers with dogs, and the thought crossed his mind: *that could be my son being ripped off.*

When the first Balearic clubs had opened two years before, most of the pills coming into the country were smuggled in by small-scale operators: photographers, clubbers, promoters, an accessories designer who used the proceeds to finance his (now thriving) fashion business. But now the emphasis had shifted to criminals with the means to finance huge shipments. By the end of 1989, HM Customs & Excise reported record seizures not only of MDMA but of speed and acid – something they directly attributed to the rise of the house movement.

But even Ken Tappenden learned to love the music. 'I hated it at the beginning, but eventually I was like a little kid jigging about to it. That's true. It got to us all in the end. I used to think it was trash, the way it used to bang on all the time. But by the end we used to stand on the edge of the field, having a dance about.'

Party Politics

Biology, 21 October. This is to be the season's grand finale: US rap stars Public Enemy, EPMD and Big Daddy Kane live. DJs Paul 'Trouble' Anderson, Kid Bachelor, Fabio and Grooverider. A venue built for 40,000 people. Free drinks all night, even a raffle for a brand new G reg BMW. It sounds unbelievable, but when I talk to Biology's office on Friday afternoon, they assure me it is on.

We finally get through on the phone at midnight, and are told to go to the Byfleet services on the A31 for further instructions. We get there an hour later to find the service station under arrest. Police ring the Happy Eater to protect it from crazed clubbers demanding hamburgers, and a small group blocks the entrance, waving cars on.

Following processions of similarly packed cars, we drive on to Farnham, but there's nothing there. Bemused but friendly local bobbies; clusters of clubbers round pay phones listening to the same recorded message we'd all heard hours ago; cars parked in rows while people run anxiously from window to window asking for news. Some aren't even looking for the same party: they have tickets for a different rave, but just followed the crowd. Drive decisively in any direction and you find yourself the leader of a convoy; pull up and people assume you're a guide waiting to give out instructions.

For hours, we play the clubland version of a treasure hunt, winding down country lanes, circling the same roundabouts again and again, then on to the Fleet services on the A3, which have also been swamped by police. But by now it's 5 a.m., and the car park is all but deserted. In the shop, a few would-be ravers queue quietly for Coke and crisps. No one seems angry. In fact, for people who've just spent £25 each on a futile drive around the countryside, they seem positively benevolent. The search is part of the pleasure: in fact by this point, the search is often the *only* pleasure.

Back in London, we tune into a pirate to hear that the party has been cancelled. On the TV news the next day, the only raised voice belongs to a motorist trapped in the services by a police road-block. 'This is ridiculous!' he screams. 'All these kids want to do is enjoy themselves. Why is the law trying to stop them?'

New Year's Eve fell on a Sunday in 1989, bringing the absurdities of the UK licensing laws into even sharper focus. It was the start of a new decade, a time for celebration, yet the Academy in Brixton was the only London venue to be granted an all-night licence. Many clubs in the capital weren't even allowed to serve alcohol after 12.30 a.m. In Manchester, the Haçienda was offered an extended licence on Christmas Eve *or* New Year's Eve, but not both. Too much fun in one week could not be tolerated, even during the season of goodwill.

Glasgow had been nominated European City of Culture for 1990 and had announced that pubs could open till 2 a.m. and clubs until 5 a.m. that year. But elsewhere in the country, clubs closed between 12.30 and 3 a.m. depending on the area. Freedom may have been sweeping across Eastern Europe, but it didn't extend yet to Britain's dancefloors.

Yet clubbers were still determined to dance, their persistence astonishing those whose job it was to stop them. On Christmas Eve, 300 clubbers assembled in a disused warehouse in Leigh-on-Sea, Essex, only to find that the police had got there first. They moved on to a semi-derelict house in nearby Westcliff, where sixty-six of them were arrested for burglary. Yet they still went on to a disused restaurant back in Leigh-on-Sea before finally being dispersed.

After getting a police injunction overturned, Sunrise had held a small, showcase event at Santa Pod racetrack on 21 October. A month later, after Tony Colston-Hayter handcuffed himself to chat show host Jonathan Ross on live TV to protest the planned new restrictions, he enjoyed another triumph in court in Maidenhead. He was accused of organising an illegal party at White Waltham in June, but the magistrates again accepted that his membership cards made the event a private party. Now Sunrise planned to kick off the nineties in style.

On the afternoon of Sunday 31st, three big tops and two smaller marquees stood on private land at North Walsham in Norfolk all with specially laid wooden dancefloors and interconnected by tunnels floored with matting to keep out the cold. Lasers, sound systems, and special effects such as a giant strobing Christmas tree were in place, plus a huge Diamond Vision screen that would show the celebrations in Trafalgar Square at midnight. There were to be spectacular fireworks, and an artificial snowstorm. It was going to be one hell of a party. But it never happened.

After their successes in court, World Wide printed the address of their New Year's Eve megaparty on the tickets for the first time since 1988, but the first venue – a former army depot in Harlow, Essex – fell through. They moved to the back-up location in Norfolk after Christmas. The police arrived at their farmhouse base there at lunchtime on the 30th, waiting for hours to try and see the land-owner before presenting Tony Colston-Hayter with their injunction.

World Wide's lawyers prepared to appeal. After twice proving themselves in court to be a private party, they felt positive that the injunction could be overturned. 'We stayed up all night, writing statements about safety, noise levels and parking,' says Colston-Hayter. 'We were 100 per cent confident, lulled into a false sense of security . . . I didn't realise they were so determined.'

At a special three-hour hearing at the High Court in London that Sunday afternoon, Mr Justice Potter upheld the injunction, ruling that if his decision was subsequently proved wrong, Norfolk District Council could afford to compensate World Wide for their losses. Despondently, they guided their followers to a free party thrown together at the last minute with Genesis and Biology in a brand-new, freshly carpeted warehouse near Slough. Instead of ushering in a new decade, they were going backwards, cutting locks and breaking in as they had the year before.

We spoke a week or so later for an article I was writing in *The Face* about the crackdown on raves, and Colston-Hayter was full of fighting talk about suing Norfolk council for £200,000. But for the first time, his words sounded empty, deflated. Everyone involved sounded tired. 'It's not worth putting money into illegal parties any more,' Jeremy Taylor said wearily. 'It doesn't make sense when they're likely to be stopped. It's more like gambling than business.'

The Government's new measures against the raves had been announced in December. Graham Bright, the Conservative MP for Luton South, was given the task of pushing through the new legislation as a private member's bill. Describing himself as 'always interested in protecting young people', he had been responsible for the Video Recordings Act against 'video nasties' in 1984. He was later to become a Parliamentary Private Secretary to new Prime Minister John Major, a loyal servant who was ultimately rewarded with a knighthood.

The Entertainments (Increased Penalties) Bill was cleverly written. It didn't give new powers or create a new criminal offence, it simply raised the existing fines from a maximum of £2,000 to £20,000 plus six months' imprisonment. When this became law, the Home Office announced that it would also use powers given to them under the 1988 Criminal Justice Act to order the confiscation of 'criminal proceeds' from illegal parties. Meanwhile, the Association of District Councils urged its members to adopt the Private Places of Entertainment (Licensing) Act of 1967. A measure intended to restrict Soho-style private sex clubs even if they operated a membership system, it had only previously been adopted by councils in Greater London and other inner cities where such clubs were considered a problem. The loophole that had enabled the promoters to claim that they didn't need a licence for a private party would thereby be closed.

In January, helped by Douglas Smith, another of David Hart's young aides, Tony Colston-Hayter and Paul Staines launched a professional body, the Association of Dance Party Promoters, trying to distinguish themselves from the gangsters and cowboys and present a respectable front to apply for licences.

Their first Freedom to Party rally was held in Trafalgar Square on 27 January. David Hart offered help and resources, and even allowed a temporary pirate radio station, Freedom to Party FM, to broadcast from his office to publicise the afternoon. 'The rally was organised by John Galt, who doesn't exist,' smiles Paul Staines. 'The name comes from an Ayn Rand book – he's a mystery character that leads a revolution. Because the law had changed. The named organiser was responsible if it broke up into chaos, and I didn't want to get nicked for organising a demo that got out of hand. I had no intention of being a martyr.'

The day was shambolic, showing none of the ingenuity that had gone into organising the raves. Only voice amplification was allowed into the Square, leaving a crowd that had come hoping to dance standing in the rain listening to rambling speeches, rapping and *a cappella* singing. 'I want to give you a party,' shouted one promoter, 'but I don't want fourteen years. Child molesters don't get that!'

The Square was full, but as ever on demonstrations there was a difference of opinion as to the numbers: 'I can't understand it,' said Colston-Hayter afterwards. 'We have a private party, 4,000 people come, it's all over the press and the police say there was 12,000. We have a public demo, 10,000 people come, there's no coverage at all – and the police say there were only a thousand.'

Afterwards, there was a free party in a warehouse in Radlett, Hertfordshire, organised by a group called the Freedom Fighters – a last chance for the original rave organisers to get one over on Ken Tappenden and his troops, if a little pointless and half-hearted. 'We did have our last laugh, where we fucked the Pay Party Unit totally,' says Colston-Hayter. 'But we were finished by then, really.'

After a small event in Manchester, there was another demo in London on 3 March, but the bill passed its second reading shortly after with little opposition. Labour's worries mainly extended to how the legislation would affect 'genuine' music events like Glastonbury or even Glyndebourne's opera festival. 'This is a very authoritarian government,' Labour's Home Office spokesman Barry Sheeman told *The Face* apologetically. 'Their liberalism is only an economic liberalism, and even that is a bit fuzzy in this case.'

'It was never going to work,' says Paul Staines, admitting that the sale of Freedom to Party hats and T-shirts and calls to its phone lines were one of the motives for keeping the campaign afloat by then. 'I was taking it seriously on one level, but I knew it was futile. Where were we going to get parliamentary support? If it hadn't been for the drugs it would have been completely different. But they couldn't be seen to be soft on drugs.'

The bill became law in July 1990, when it was quickly used against the growing rave scene in the north of England. As for the original class of '89, Energy continued to promote Fun City, and put on two massive concerts at the 12,000-capacity Docklands Arena with impressive line-ups of current dance stars. But they ended at 11 p.m., with the all-seater stadium reducing the crowd to passive spectators, rather than active participants in the show. Jeremy Taylor was eventually sentenced to 240 hours community service for the Dance '89 event, and spent most of it gardening in north London. 'We were doing really well with Fun City then, and I used to turn up with a Jaguar XJS convertible. It was great fun because half the people there were drug dealers who had been to the club or the parties.'

A series of eight parties in the Brixton Academy featured some of Energy's best production ever. They used Pink Floyd's lighting rig one night, and built up an impressive stock of scenery and props. But Tintin Chambers says the joy had gone out of it.

'We had so many threats of violence against us. We had a well-known gangster kick our door open, knock Jeremy and me to the ground, and put a sawn-off shotgun in our mouths. To combat that, we then we had to get involved with . . . heavy people. It started out as a happy, family affair where everybody had respect for each other, and turned very much into a money thing. But the gangsters got there too late, because all the money had already been made by then. People weren't doing large illegal parties any more.'

They finally gave up at the start of 1992. 'Because we'd gone out in the beginning and taken the big risks, the people that came after us were cleaning up,' says Jeremy Taylor. 'They were coming along with a clean record and doing big parties without the kind of police objections we had to face.'

Tired of fighting, he went home to launch the Crinkley Bottom theme park for TV presenter Noel Edmonds and manage the wildlife park at Cricket St Thomas, where he also puts on classical concerts. Tintin Chambers became a DJ, and now plays trance parties in the countryside: small events, spread by word of mouth and run for fun rather than profit, they're the nearest thing left to the open-air parties of 1989.

Biology's Jarvis Sandy resurfaced later too with the two Desert Storm parties in Peckham in 1994, landmarks in the development of the breakbeat-based music then known as jungle.

World Wide ran two profitable weekly club nights at the Park nightclub in Kensington while they negotiated the comedown from the heady highs of 1989. They tried to buy a venue in central London, and made a few expensive attempts to apply for licences before they realised it was futile. 'It was sad to let it go, but by then I didn't believe in it all anyway,' says Colston-Hayter. 'The crowd was getting younger, and the drugs were so shit. We never had any serious fights at Sunrise, we never had any deaths, and it felt like only a matter of time before something like that happened to us. I thought I'd get out while I was relatively unscathed – apart from my name and my health.'

Paul Staines went to work in the City. We met to talk for this book at the office he'd just moved into with the new company he had launched – a penthouse with its own swimming pool overlooking Tower Bridge. Dave Roberts went into the music business with the successful *Havin' It* compilations, and is planning a film about the raves of 1989. Tony Colston-Hayter drifted back into the casinos, disappearing to Spain for a couple of years to negotiate his way back into the real world.

Nine years later, he has yet to get there completely. 'What do you do after all that?' he asks. 'What do you do for excitement? What do you go into? Every night was a brilliant night then. There were really strong friendships made, really strong bonds . . . And all the letters we got, thousands of them, about who they'd met at our parties. People got married and had their reception at Sunrise. There was a girl in a white wedding dress at the Festival, dancing in the mud. You'd get girls who went to private schools who'd never talked to a black geezer before. Some friends of mine, their son was conceived at a party.'

The battle was lost. And the battle was won. Without the acid boom of '88 and the raves of '89, without the ingenuity of the promoters and the defiance of the clubbers, without the influence, benign or otherwise, of Ecstasy, it is doubtful we would have the thriving club industry we have today. Before it closed in September 1991, the Pay Party Unit and its clones around the country may have been successful in curbing the raves, but they hadn't stopped them.

'We didn't win,' says Ken Tappenden. 'All we did was displace it. What was happening around the M25 then broke out in Manchester, Blackpool, Harrogate, Skegness. Wherever you could imagine, it just came up like a boil.'

The cost of fighting this every weekend ran into the millions. 'The police authorities were getting worried. They were asking the Government for more money. The Government was saying no, you've got to run it out of your own contingency funds. It was beginning to get painful.'

If it couldn't be killed, then the culture had to be taken back into a controlled environment. Clubs began finding it easier to gain late-night licences. 'It wasn't a coincidence,' says Ken Tappenden. 'It was a co-ordinated plan.'

On 16 December 1989, Gordon MacNamee of Kiss FM was out walking his dog with his parents when his mobile phone rang. It was the *Observer* newspaper's media correspondent, wanting his reaction to the news but ending up breaking it to him. Kiss had shut their offices early that year, so the letter finally granting his station its franchise was still unopened. The capital was to get its first ever legal twenty-four hour dance station, and since its launch in September 1990 it has been the most successful of the new London stations.

In the first months of 1990, local councils began granting licences for raves to new organisations such as Raindance in London, Dreamscape in Slough, Amnesia House in Coventry. And just after the final

Freedom to Party demo that spring, a DJ and his business partners went to Southwark Council for a hearing on their application to open a twenty-four hour dance club in south-east London. The Labour councillors listened to their arguments carefully and decided to grant one of the first such licences in London. The team from the Ministry of Sound were thrilled.

NORTHERN
EXPOSURE

If You Build It, They Will Club

On 18 November 1989, Manchester rock group the Stone Roses played a triumphant gig to an audience of 7,000 at the Alexandra Palace in north London. Dave Haslam, the DJ at the Haçienda's long-running Temperance night, provided support. Just before the band came on, he wanted to lift things as high as he could, so he played Inner City's Detroit techno hit 'Good Life'. The crowd pogoed up and down in approval.

Indie rock fans. Dancing to disco. Only two years before, Manchester indie stars the Smiths had been exhorting their fans to '*hang the DJ*' on their hit single 'Panic', a chorus that had been taken up by readers of the weekly music press with gusto. But now the Stone Roses were talking about an end to grey introspection. Aligning themselves with the hedonism that was sweeping the nation's clubs, they wanted to dance and have fun. 'Why be glum?' they asked. 'Why celebrate sitting lonely in bed-sits?'[1] Something was happening.

Five days later the Stone Roses and another Manchester indie group, Happy Mondays, made their *Top of the Pops* débuts in the same week. 'The nineties actually began during the six weeks that Black Box was number one in England,' Factory Records boss, Granada TV presenter and sharp-suited Manc motormouth Tony Wilson told *The Face* that day. 'Happy Mondays and Stone Roses entering the charts together the same week and getting their first *Top of the Pops* together

195

makes the decade well and truly open. This makes it official.'[2]

Manchester mop-tops Inspiral Carpets were also in the charts in November, as well as Manchester dance group 808 State. 'It felt as if Manchester was taking the nation,' says the Stone Roses' charismatic singer Ian Brown. 'We felt fantastic. Justified. Like we were on the right path. All the others were wasting time, they had to completely look at their thing and re-invent themselves.'

The two bands turned their BBC dressing rooms into their own private party, dance music blaring out of their tape machines, hanging out with each other and as many friends as they could blag in.

Something was happening. And it didn't take a genius to pinpoint the location as Manchester. On their away-day trips to the city to observe these colourful northerners in their quaint flares and their humorous T-shirts showing the brilliant graphics the city had been renowned for since punk, it seemed clear to visiting media folk that the source of this new energy could be narrowed down still further. All roads led to the Haçienda.

As the eyes of the media not just in Britain but all over the world came to rest on the Manchester nightclub in 1989–90, it was made to seem like an organic part of the landscape. It seemed natural, normal, that such a venue existed in England's third-largest city. But this had not always been so.

Galvanised by two seminal early Sex Pistols gigs at the Lesser Free Trade Hall in 1976, Manchester had been one of the most important centres for punk outside of London, producing influential bands like the Buzzcocks, the Fall and Magazine. It was also a leader in the explosion of DIY activity that came afterwards. Factory Communications was one of the most successful of the independent labels which rose from the ashes of punk, their band Joy Division one of the most successful of the new groups who began experimenting with synthesisers. Most used them to make electronic noise at first, but those programmed beats proved seductive and many were soon dabbling with dance forms. Even in the Gothic gloom of Joy Division, there's a rhythm struggling to get out from under the angst on some tracks.

'[Producer] Martin Hamnett told me that every change in music which I see as being cultural, he can point to the change in technology, or the piece of equipment that comes of age,' says Tony Wilson, citing the Factory band A Certain Ratio as another example. 'They were all starting to experiment with these early synths and the first computers, and beginning to get those weird machine rhythms.'

When Joy Division's singer Ian Curtis succumbed to the depression that his lyrics had so eloquently expressed and killed himself in 1980, it was the end of an era. Afterwards, the remaining members formed New Order, making their US début at Hurrah's in New York that autumn as part of a Factory showcase and beginning a love affair with US club culture that was to lead them to produce the monumental, synthesised beats of 'Blue Monday' in 1983. The first great indie dance record, it is still one of the best-selling twelve-inches ever released in Britain. What they saw in New York also led to the building of the Haçienda.

Opening such a venue in Manchester in 1982 was an extraordinary act of faith – some would even say folly – although all New Order, their manager Rob Gretton and the Factory team claim they actually wanted was a club in their home town where they felt comfortable. So, while many mainstream British clubs were foundering after the decline of disco, they created a venue modelled on New York clubs like Hurrah's and Danceteria – sleek, modern spaces which doubled as live music venues and dance arenas. Designed in a radically stark industrial style by Ben Kelly (who had helped design McLaren and Westwood's shop Seditionaries during the London punk boom), the Haçienda was housed in a former yacht warehouse by the canal. In a run-down former industrial area to the south of the city centre, it stood at the opposite end of Whitworth Street to the venue that had once been the Twisted Wheel.

There were no sticky carpets. No mirrorballs and dark recesses. Light and spacious, with a high roof, bare brick walls, pillars painted in hazard stripes and traffic bollards around the edge of the dance-floor, it was as far from a traditional British nightclub as could be conceived. It even had a catalogue number – Fac 51 – to confirm it as a Factory product. Britain had never seen anything like it, but in its early years it was a club more talked about than visited.

Just before it opened, someone asked Tony Wilson what the club was for. 'The kids,' he replied. It was then pointed out to him that since most of the kids were still wearing long grey raincoats and listening to Echo and the Bunnymen, a New York funhouse might not be top of their wish lists. The walls were still wet on the packed, invite-only opening night, which featured the left-field New York disco divas ESG. The notoriously reactionary comic Bernard Manning had also been booked, but his mic didn't work. 'I've played some shit-holes in my time,' he said as he left the stage, 'but this is really something.' The next night, Sheffield electronic experimentalists Cabaret Voltaire played, and just seventy-five people turned up to watch.

The Haçienda has rarely been profitable. At first it opened seven nights a week, and for many of those it was almost empty. The acoustics left much to be desired in the early years, the DJ booth was tucked away out of sight downstairs, and like most British clubs of the time, it was poorly equipped. In 1983, the long-suffering regular DJ Hewan Clarke wrote a memo asking for a light in the booth and 'a pair of monitor speakers to aid in the mixing of records'. Now, the lowliest of bedroom DJs wouldn't dream of mixing a tape for their friends without such basics.

But it was still a better space than anything the capital had to offer except perhaps Heaven. It hosted some legendary live gigs, provided the perfect space for up-and-coming New York club kid Madonna to flirt with the cameras for the cult TV music show *The Tube*, gave Factory bands and the city's hipsters a great bar to drink in, and doggedly continued to play Troublefunk to people who on the whole would have preferred Prefab Sprout. Trusted because of its impeccable indie associations – *these people brought us Joy Division, how could they be wrong about Cameo?* – the Haçienda slowly pulled white Manchester past the Student Union disco and into the black technological futures of electro, funk and mutant disco celebrated in smaller specialist dance clubs such as Legends, Berlin and the Gallery.[3]

The bands were booked by Mike Pickering, who was born in Stockport in 1958, and with his friend Martin Fry danced to Northern Soul at the Highland Room and saw the Sex Pistols gig at Manchester's Free Trade Hall. After punk, Fry fronted glam pop ironists ABC, while Pickering ended up playing Chic and Crown Heights Affair in a squatted venue in Rotterdam before returning home to work at the Haç. His own band Quando Quango were one of a string of quirky dance-influenced bands signed to Factory in the early eighties, and were popular in the New York clubs. There, like New Order, he was exposed to a whole new world.

'That was the golden age. Danceteria was the meeting place, you'd go there from ten till two. Then there was the Roxy, with Africa Islam and Africa Bambaataa DJing. The Funhouse was a bit heavy, but we knew [DJ/producer] Jellybean [Benitez]. The Paradise Garage was amazing. Larry Levan was the best. And the Loft, I couldn't believe that place. They had a big marble font full of water with cups all around it, the most incredible sound system, and people were doing all this really creative dancing. It was only in 1987, after Paul Oakenfold had been to Ibiza and we played a club in Barcelona together that the penny dropped. *Ecstasy.*'

In November 1984 Pickering joined up with Martin Prendergast and as MP2 they started a Friday night they called Nude, because you didn't need much on you to get in: admission was 50p, bar prices reduced. If the Saturday night was for strange haircuts and student posing, Fridays appealed to a more local, working-class crowd. At first Pickering played everything from Motown and Northern Soul to British electro-pop like Yazoo, as well as the Latin break that would be his signature for years. But the emphasis was on cutting-edge black dance music: electro, hip hop, and then in 1986, house.

The pounding 4/4 beat of house worked well with a crowd accustomed to Northern Soul, although the athletic style of dancing that had been used for records no more than three minutes long had to be adapted to suit Chicago mixes that could go on for ten minutes. Responding to the music's commands to 'jack your body', cool young dancers like Foot Patrol would come in suits and spats and entertain the crowd with fast, synchronised moves on the raised stage in the middle of the dancefloor, while the smell of weed in the air was so intoxicating that you'd be stoned whether you smoked or not.

When Paul Mason moved from Rock City in Nottingham to become the club's first professional manager in 1986, Nude was the only successful regular night. There was no stock control in the club and the organisation was shambolic: 'All the best-furnished flats in Hulme were full of stuff from the Haçienda. People just walked out with the stools.'

The club had been too cool to publicise its events before, preferring news to spread by word of mouth, but Mason immediately took on Paul Cons to do promotion. A Londoner who had come up to Manchester to study drama and who had attempted an unsuccessful gay night on Mondays at the Haç, he was to be instrumental in the club's subsequent success.

'We had to rebuild the club from scratch because apart from Friday it was empty,' he says. 'Saturday was about 200 people. We did some marketing on it, and within three months, it was full. It was nothing spectacular: Vidal Sassoon fashion shows, things like that.'

Mason had a successful student night at Rock City, and brought in Dave Haslam on Thursdays to tempt a similar crowd to the Haç. Aiming to provide something for everyone, he played an eclectic mix of rock, funk, hip hop and electro-pop and quickly drew a capacity crowd to Temperance. But although Haslam's name was later to become synonymous with indie dance, he was hardly revered at first.

'The DJs were anonymous then. Mike Pickering was called MP. In black music circles, the guys who played the records were respected, but in rock circles the DJ was the enemy. It needed that black culture to come in to give us more standing. We didn't spend years in our bedrooms practising and sending out demos. We were probably the last generation of DJs who were just punters with big record collections.'

Although completely separate scenes in America, in Britain hip hop and house were played together in the clubs, seen as similar fusions of new technology and black club culture. On his *Bus Dis* show on Manchester's Piccadilly Radio, DJ Stu Allen played an hour of hip hop, an hour of house, and local musicians with access to the right machines began dabbling in both.

At the start of 1987, there were two live shows which in their own ways were as influential to the emerging scene as the Pistols had been in the seventies: New York hip hop star Mantronix played his innovative sample-and-steal dance mix at Nude, followed a month later by the Chicago House Party revue. Musicians from Manchester and Sheffield who would later play a crucial role in the development of British house were there in the audience, checking what these

Americans were doing with samplers and sequencers.

'It was a real event when Mantronix played the Haç,' remembers Graham Massey, whose industrial funk outfit Biting Tongues had been signed to Factory. 'That's when you realised there was a culture for that kind of thing, because before that it was all in people's bedrooms, there wasn't a lot of occasion for people to get together around it. I remember the house revue being really cheesy. They all wore leather and did one-handed press-ups on stage. We knew that music was beginning to shoot off in a more left-field direction that we liked, but there were very few English bands doing it.'

By February 1988, there was enough music being made for Mike Pickering to stage a Northern House Revue. Pickering's latest band T-Coy performed their Latin-house workout 'Carino', and in his first appearance at the Haçienda, Nottingham DJ Graeme Park brought some jazz-funk dancers he knew from the Midlands all-dayers on-stage with him while he sheepishly mimed the keyboards on his sparse, disco-derived northern club hit 'Submit To The Beat', released under the name Groove.

The venue was ready, the music was there, the key DJs were in place. The stage was set. Only one ingredient was missing for the performance to begin. And the Happy Mondays and their friends were about to provide it.

Freaky Dancing

'The Haçienda didn't change us. We changed the Haçienda. It all went off under the balcony in the left-hand corner.'

Bez[4]

Manchester's geography is determined by its economics. The few grand, red-brick Victorian Gothic buildings left in the centre are a monument to its role at the centre of the Industrial Revolution. The city expanded rapidly after the introduction of steam-powered cotton mills and machine looms in the 1780s, and its achievements in the following century included the construction of the world's first passenger railway and later the Ship Canal, which turned a land-locked city into the country's third largest port. But this progress had a human cost, seen in the poverty-stricken, diseased slums that ringed the centre. Friedrich Engels, co-author of the *Communist Manifesto*, used Manchester to illustrate the effect of capitalism left to run unchecked. More than a century later, areas like Cheetham Hill to the north of the centre, Moss Side to the east, and parts of nearby Salford provide an equal insight into the consequences of a blind faith in market forces over four successive terms of Conservative rule.

Shaun Ryder met his best friend Mark 'Bez' Berry in the dole queue at Little Hulton in Salford. Both had wide experience of illegal drugs by their mid-teens. Both had fallen foul of the law and spent periods in custody – Bez had served six months in prison when he was seventeen after his father, a CID officer, had handed him in for robbery; Shaun had been caught after crashing a stolen car. Eventually, Bez was to join the band Shaun and his brother Paul had formed with three other local lads in 1980, his function being to dance, play maracas occasionally and add 'vibes'.

When Happy Mondays first played the Haçienda on a talent night in 1983, they came last. But Factory eventually succumbed to their shambolic charm – Mike Pickering produced their first single 'Delightful' in 1985, oddly making them sound more like a traditional indie rock band than they ever did live. Their next single 'Freaky Dancing' was produced by New Order's Bernard Sumner and allowed their loose, funky forms more room to breathe, but it took the acid house explosion and the subsequent rise of the DJ remix to give them their real voice.

In the meantime, the band was a means to an end, another way of supporting their delinquent hedonism. 'We aren't musos,' said Shaun Ryder in an early interview. 'We're just drug dealers who happen to be in a band rather than the other way around.'[5] Manchester was too small to contain their restless energy, and like the young Britons who ended up in Ibiza in 1986/87, they travelled constantly.

Charlie, a self-confessed bootlegger, ligger, and one of the Mondays' extended entourage, described the life to one of Ryder's biographers:

It was the wildest of times. Some of us were into pirating. Printing up posters and T-shirts of bands who were touring

Europe, and we'd pile into a van and just take off. Throughout the early Eighties a whole network of faces from Salford and Wythenshawe began to spring up. You'd see these people all over the place. You'd go into some stupid little bar in some god-forsaken village in Spain or somewhere and you'd find Bez asleep in the corner. Or you'd see some van speeding along a really dangerous mountain road and you'd know it was a Salford van . . . I'd say the Mondays grew out of that weird, loose scene rather than the other way around. In Amsterdam, Shaun and I would just be bouncing from coffee bar to coffee bar, totally in a dream, but not just for a weekend – it was for months on end. That joke about Bez living in a cave in Morocco, well it's true . . . Suddenly there was a whole lot of Salford and Manchester lads, none of whom had any money and most were on the dole, who would exist on a world-wide scale. You'd see some cunt stagger-ing down a dusty Spanish lane in the middle of nowhere on Monday, and then you'd see the same person at the dole office on Thursday. How did they do it? Just jibbing, blagging, scrounging. It was street logic.[6]

On these travels, it was inevitable that they were to discover Ecstasy – Ryder has said he took his first pill in Amsterdam in 1986. By the start of 1988, they had established their own supply routes to Man-chester and forged links with the Balearic contingent in the south. Before he opened Spectrum, Ian St Paul often came up to Nude to dance with friends he'd met in Ibiza, and the Mondays and their friends quickly became regular visitors to St Paul's London nights.

In early 1988, their activities in the Haçienda were confined to an area under the balcony that became known as 'E corner', and the attitude towards these lads with their weird drugs and strange dancing was pretty much the same as that in London – although instead of 'love thugs' or 'Millwall fans on Ecstasy', these pioneers were dismissed as mad scallies, pilled-up Perry boys. But they were only too happy to share their discovery with anyone who had the requisite £25, and within months everyone at Nude was dancing on the spot with their hands in the air Bez-style, while the man himself could often be seen out front conducting the crowd.

Flares had made a comeback on the Manchester football terraces in 1983–85, and the Mondays crew had been wearing them ever since their first manager, the Northern Soul DJ Phil Saxe, bought a job-lot cheap and began selling them from his clothes stall in the Oasis market in the mid-eighties. To punks, flares were a symbol of the hippie enemy. To the eighties style set, they represented the ultimate in seventies bad taste. But worn with the requisite delinquent swagger, they became a defiant statement of pride, flipping a finger at ageing punks, fashion victims and condescending Cockney football fans alike. And just as the Ibiza fashions spread across London, so the wide trousers, hooded tops, old school trainers and designer casualwear in E corner gradually became the Manchester uniform.

'All the posh kids from Cheshire who were wearing Yojhi Yamamoto suits were suddenly going, "All right, double top!" and pretending they were from Ancoats,' laughs Justin Robertson, later to become an important DJ in Manchester but then just another student in the crowd. 'The scene was very snobby before, but suddenly you'd be talking endlessly to people you'd just met – and I wasn't really doing drugs, early on. It was just the prevailing atmosphere.

'I think a lot of people felt really *relieved*. The economic situation was so appalling for most people, and we all felt relieved that here was something we could be *part* of, rather than just watch the country go down the pan. It was a release valve, a reaction against yuppies and go-getter Thatcherite politics.'

By the end of June, the queues would stretch down the street at opening time. Evangelists even began picketing the club, urging the regulars to turn away from their hedonistic, sinful lives. 'As a director, I'm all for anything which entertains the queue,' quipped Tony Wilson, never short of an apt soundbite.[7] But the emphasis at Nude was still house more than acid; the summer of love kicked off for real with a rumble of thunder at Hot on 13 July.

In May 1988, Paul Cons had been down to London, where his friend Patrick Lilley had taken him to Shoom and Hedonism on a long, lost weekend tour of the emerging acid scene. For the summer, Cons had planned to transform his successful, tongue-in-chic Wednesday night Zumbar into the Costa del Zumbar with a tacky holiday theme, and the Haçienda's maintenance man was already building a set of palm trees. Now Cons went straight for the Ibiza vibe instead. He bought in podiums, smoke and strobes, installed a small, high-sided swimming pool on the edge of the dancefloor and called the night Hot.

At first it had the same kitsch cabaret acts that had enlivened Zumbar along with holiday videos, beach balls, bubbles, ice pops and whistles. But by the time the Muscley Dream Boys took the stage on week three, the club had gone beyond camp. Only weeks after Balearic/acid house had gone overground in London, Manchester had shrugged off its grey indie coat and gone day-glo. 'It was unbelievable,' says Cons. 'It just spread like wildfire, literally from week to week, enveloping everyone from scallies to queens to students.'

The DJ at Zumbar had been Laurent Garnier, a local chef who had handed Cons a tape of well-mixed disco. But with Garnier leaving for France to do his national service in the army, Jon Dasilva got his chance to DJ alongside Mike Pickering and give Hot an identity of its own. He would do New York-style 'slow mixes', playing two records simultaneously, laying *a cappella* vocal tracks over instrumental acid house. Playing Shalor's pretty electro garage track 'I'm In Love' over Londonbeat's 'There's An Acid House Going On' was a particular favourite: he'd leave both records running together for five minutes, creating a live acid house mix of Shalor. Having read articles which mentioned Larry Levan and Frankie Knuckles' use of sound effects, he also began to set off thunderstorms over the oppressive heat of the dancefloor, while the sweat dripped down the walls of what had once been seen as a cold, unwelcoming venue.

'It was very much a Zumbar crowd at first, a bit glammy,' says Dasilva. 'Acid fever took over from the third week in. I remember just walking out of the DJ box and realising that everybody in the place was completely off it. And being quite scared, actually. The crowd had changed. There was a Rasta guy shaking his head with all his dreads flying round in a big arc, crying and smiling at the same time. The old English reserve was gone. People had always jumped on the dance-floor when they liked a record and then left when they didn't, but now they started at nine and they were on the floor till two.'

The atmosphere in the club that summer has been described as though a goal was being scored for four hours on end. Many places were to be transformed by an Ecstatic glow in 1988, but none more so than the Haçienda. It was a venue that had finally found the purpose for which it suddenly seemed custom-built. A cathedral of dance, the high roof no longer made it look cold and empty. People would stretch out their hands towards it, climbing up on the podiums, turning to face the DJ booth upstairs like worshippers at an altar and *reaching,* as the Phase II song said, *reaching for the top.*

'You'd be trying to concentrate on playing your records, but every time you looked up you'd make eye contact with someone on the dancefloor,' says Graeme Park. 'Probably because everyone's eyes were like saucers.'

When Mike Pickering took his holiday in July, Park filled in on Fridays. 'It was three of the most incredible weeks I've ever had in my life. I was playing the records I'd been playing for the past few months, but getting this unbelievable response. I'd get there at 9 p.m. and there'd be a queue. This was unheard of. At the Garage in Nottingham, between nine and eleven it would slowly fill up and people would sheepishly edge on to the dancefloor. But here at ten the club was full and the atmosphere was *so* intense. It was electric. Every time I went to light a cigarette, I was worried I was going to make the place ignite.'

Afterwards he stayed, forming a successful partnership with Mike Pickering that was to last to the end of 1990. The tapes of their sets sold from the DJ booth are still treasured today, and began a trend that led inexorably to today's mix CDs. 'People still come up to me now and go, "The Haçienda, 17 July 1988, side B, fourth track in – it's banging, what is it?" ' laughs Park.

There was the same sense of intimacy that the London crowd had experienced, the same amiable mix of estate kids, students and trendies. 'You used to get new records, and think, "Oh that's fantastic. I can't wait for them to hear this"; says Mike Pickering. 'And you felt you were talking about almost all of your friends.'

'There was something the matter with you if you were a lad dancing in the early eighties, but now it's become there's something the matter with you if you're not,' observes the Stone Roses' Ian Brown, a regular at Nude since 1986. 'People felt like they were showing themselves up if they couldn't get into it that night, if they weren't dancing.'

'I remember looking down from the DJ box and thinking what a *democratic* art form it was,' adds Tony Wilson. 'Rather than four people in the spotlight on-stage, everybody was the show. You danced wherever you were, you didn't have to be on the dancefloor. In E corner everyone would be sitting down rolling joints or whatever, but still moving. That's what I loved about it. Everyone moved.'

The same playfulness that had emerged in London quickly appeared on the Manchester scene too. 'Manchester E posse' said the first T-shirts, and soon the Identity T-shirt stall in Affleck's Palace was turning out many more only half-ironic statements of local pride: 'On the sixth day, God created Manchester', 'Born in the north, live in the north, die in the north'. Local entrepreneur Shami Ahmed set up his Joe Bloggs jeans company to meet the demand for flapping flares and later Chris and Anthony Donnelly, two brothers from the Wythen-shawe estates and well-known faces on the Manchester club scene, set up the successful men's casual label Gio Goi. Members of the Stone Roses and Happy Mondays were their first models.

It was an intense period of creativity. Tapping into the energy that seemed to course not just through the clubs but through the city itself, Graham Massey, Martin Price and Gerald Simpson formed 808 State (named after the Roland TR-808 drum machine) and would spend all day in the studio making tunes which they would then take along to the Haçienda for the DJs to play. After the club closed, they'd often rush back again to make more. 'We used to fill a C90 and they used to play thirty minutes of it,' says Massey. 'We were just staying up all night in the studio churning it out like wallpaper. I've still got loads and loads of tapes.'

As A Guy Called Gerald, Simpson made the spooky, shimmeringly beautiful 'Voodoo Ray', which was a hit in Manchester long before it became a crowd-pleaser at the big raves in 1989. Later, 808 State's soaring instrumental 'Pacific State' became an anthem at the Haçi-enda, its synthetic sax ending the night there for months before it even came out on record. 'That's when we started really taking ourselves seriously,' says Massey. 'It was a hit before it was released, as far as we were concerned.'

When they did put it out on their own label, it was picked up by Radio One immediately (by DJ Gary Davies, who heard it while on holiday in Ibiza) and they were quickly offered a major record deal:

'Now you'd have to go with a plugger and get it on a playlist. It just by-passed all that, because of the excitement of what was going on.'

'Obviously a lot of it was the drugs, but everyone was really in awe of the music as well,' remembers Liverpool-born journalist John McCready, who would make regular pilgrimages to Manchester to buy records and go clubbing. 'We'd never heard anything like it before. You'd go into record shops and you'd find that this American whose record you'd heard in a club and loved had also made seven other records three years earlier. It was just flying at you every week.

'You'd go into a shop like Eastern Bloc and you couldn't get near the counter on Saturday afternoon, because they were eight or nine deep and it was just, *Give me this music, I've heard it in a club, I want it now!* Just the passion of people, how much they wanted to know about it . . . It felt like a secret society, that information was being withheld from you. It was so exciting. A lot of people found something in themselves they didn't know was there, talents they didn't know they had before this music brought them out.'

Alexander 'Sasha' Coe had recently moved with his family from Kent to south Wales and was supposed to be studying at college there, but soon the Haçienda became a consuming passion. 'It was an hour and a half's drive, so we just went for the Friday nights at first. Early 1988, they were "jack your body" nights. Quite black, with posses on the dancefloor showing out and doing all the fancy moves. I didn't go for a couple of months, and then when we went back acid house had arrived. It was like being struck by lightning. All that twisted music from Chicago, and the energy in that room was just incredible. By 2 a.m. the atmosphere got so intense that if they ever did go over and play the extra record, it was like a huge moment and so exciting.

'It became like a place of worship for me. If I missed a Wednesday or a Friday, I'd really feel there was something missing from my life. It is like seeing the light or something. I knew this was what I wanted to do. Jon Dasilva was the first DJ I've ever heard doing key mixing, really crafting a set. He mixed two records together in the same key or in keys that worked together so they worked *musically* rather than just the beats matching.'

Everyone came to the Haçienda that summer. Students, trendies, estate kids. Happy Mondays, the Stone Roses, New Order, the Inspiral

208

Dancefloor of the Trip, London 1988 (*David Swindells*)

Dancing in Charing Cross Road, London, after closing time at the Trip, summer 1988 (Dave Roberts, later of Sunrise/Back to the Future, in car) (*David Swindells*)

The sun rising at a Boy's Own party, East Grinstead, summer 1989 (*David Swindells*)

Sasha at the Haçienda, Manchester, 1989 (*Peter Walsh*)

World Dance rave off the M25, July 1990 (*David Swindells*)

Ravers at the
Roller Express,
Edmonton, 1991
(*David Swindells*)

Game for a laugh:
Bob's Full House,
London 1992
(*David Swindells*)

'Playing a big record was like scoring a goal at the Kop', Quadrant Park, Liverpool, 1991 (*Mark McNulty*)

Still raving at Rezerection, near Edinburgh, 1994 (*Mark McNulty*)

Gaychester: Flesh at the Haçienda,
1992 (*Peter Walsh*)

Trade in London, 1993
(*David Swindells*)

Fireworks at the Haçienda for Flesh's second birthday party, 1993 (*Peter Walsh*)

Dressing up and showing out at Vague, Leeds, 1994 (*Peter Walsh*)

Club face Shettika and Lee Garrick from Miss Moneypenny's at a 'God Bless America' Chuff Chuff party near Bristol, 1995 (*Rob Farrell*)

Goldie standing out in the crowd at Metalheadz, London, 1996 (*Gus*)

Carpets (and their guitar roadie, Noel Gallagher, who would later rise to prominence with Oasis and shock many by singing on a dance track by fellow Haç regulars the Chemical Brothers). Manchester's centre was small enough to feel like a community – 'It's a village!' declared Tony Wilson in a celebration of his city's creativity – but the club's catchment area was vast. Around 3.5 million people lived within a fifteen-mile radius of the Haçienda, with the major cities of Liverpool, Sheffield and Leeds not much further away on the motorway.

'It became a tourist trap very quickly,' says Paul Cons. 'We completely lost control of the door. We were absolutely hopeless. We were under siege. Until then the Haçienda always had a bit of a weird reputation. It was sort of a trendy club: people had heard of it, but it didn't attract big crowds. And suddenly there was 1,000 people outside the club at 9 p.m. They always felt it was a bit élitist, a bit of a poncey southern notion to have a door policy. But the consequence was that we lost it fairly quickly in terms of the crowd.'

The queues reached down the road by 6 p.m. The doors sometimes opened early, before the music began, so that as many people as possible could be in when it started. 'It was like walking into a circus or a fairground,' says Justin Robertson. 'It sucked you in. You just couldn't wait. You'd throw them your money and just run straight through the plastic sheeting that used to hang over the entrance and on to the dancefloor. The first time I went to the Haçienda it was very cool, people standing looking at each other. But now it was a friendly, inviting place. I used to go by myself sometimes, which I would never have done before.'

Tom Rowlands and Ed Simons, now the Chemical Brothers but then also students at Manchester University, would take sandwiches and make a night of it: 'Friday was a good day, because you didn't have to go to college. So we'd queue up outside at about 6.30. You met all these people from Bradford and Bolton, real characters like Chris the Fireman and his mate Monkey. He always used to go on about being a fireman and years later we discovered it was just a fantasy. He used to tell us these horror stories about pulling little kiddies out of burning cars, stories which would go on for about forty minutes while we were queuing. That was a good Friday ritual. It was so exciting to get in. It was brilliant.'

By the summer of 1989, the queue even had its own magazine, *Freaky Dancing*, photocopied sheets which were handed out free to the waiting clubbers by Nick Speakman and his friends, who like everyone else simply wanted to do something, *anything* to express the excitement they were feeling.

The energy was too much for one club to contain, and soon began to spill across the city. At 2 a.m. people would mill around the Haçienda's exit, exchanging addresses for parties. A bleak inner city housing estate in nearby Hulme became a regular destination for those in the know, its crescent-shaped concrete blocks overlooking a desolate wasteland sparkling with broken glass. Charles Barry Crescent housed the Kitchen, two flats whose adjoining walls had been knocked through to make a recording studio which now also became an illegal after-hours venue. At first just a chill-out session, soon there were hundreds packed inside for a full-on acid party. When Danceteria DJ Mark Kamins came over from New York to visit, he was astonished that it was so hot that steam rose out of the pores in the concrete walls.

'It never ended,' remembers Graham Massey. 'The weekend started on a Wednesday and ended on a Tuesday. There were a lot of parties at people's places. We used to put on parties at the basement of Eastern Bloc. It was two red light bulbs and the sound system, but it used to be rammed. Thinking about it now, it was no wonder the police shut us down all the time – it was a health and safety nightmare. No toilets, no fire exits. But it all just roller-coastered along. I remember going to one party in a barn just outside Manchester where the lighting system was four sunbeds.'

In October, club faces Eric Barker and Chris and Anthony Donnelly acquired a railway arch under Piccadilly Station, brought in a generator and held a party called Sweat It Out after the Haç closed. 'It sold out,' remembers Mike Pickering. 'The police raided it about 7 a.m. when it was over. There was just a mountain of cans, but no alcohol. They didn't know what was going on. They confiscated our records, but we got them back. That was a fantastic party.'

New Order held a wild all-nighter in the Haçienda's large, unlicensed basement after their December 1988 show at G-Mex. Less well-known is the party they held earlier that year during a recording

session at Peter Gabriel's Real World studio near Bath. 'It was completely mad, with coaches going down from the Haçienda,' says Mike
Pickering. 'We all descended on this place and we were there for two
days. People were going round with trays of Es. At one stage, Graeme
said, "Mike, I'll go on now right?" And I'm like, "I've only just come
on!" But I'd been playing for four-and-three-quarter hours. That was
the first time that it was excess for me, because before that I'd only
taken one.'

By the end of 1988, Eric Barker and two more bohemian blaggers
with a background in T-shirts and fly-posting, Jimmy Shelock (Jimmy
Muffin) and John Kenyon (John the Phone), had opened up the
Thunderdome in Miles Platting, a deprived, decaying area to the
north of the city centre. Formerly called the Osbourne, it was a dark,
low-ceilinged venue that had been used largely for Irish dances and
wedding receptions. The crowd was mainly drawn from the surrounding estates. The music, played by the Spinmasters, Jam MCs and Steve
Williams, was harder, darker, less song-based than the joyous anthems
favoured at the Haç: Detroit techno and Belgian hardbeat formed the
soundtrack in a club that could be frightening to outsiders, but which
was loved by its regulars with a passion.

Ian Brown describes the atmosphere at the Thunderdome and at
Konspiracy, a warren-like club which opened up on Fennel Street in
the centre a year later: 'Thunderdome was north Manchester, so that
was nearly all scallies, working-class lads. And it *was* nearly all lads.
Konspiracy was a bit rougher, because it was later so there were more
gangsters in there. The Haçienda was the most . . . beautiful place.
There was less money in clubs like the Thunderdome or Konspiracy, it
was more dole kids. So it was all trips. There were times when
everyone in the place was tripping. When we used to do acid in '84,
'85, it was like a dream for us, a club where thousands of people were
tripping at the same time.'

The Haçienda opened up nights in Blackpool and Blackburn as the
scene spread, and Graeme Park was ideally placed to watch the culture
take hold in house nights across the Midlands too. 'On Saturday I'd go
down to Nottingham after the Haçienda, usually a bit the worse for
wear, and do the same thing at the Garage, except without Mike. The
difference was everyone in Nottingham was pissed, and everyone in

Manchester was completely off their knackers. But as time went on, enterprising young men from Nottingham introduced the concept of Ecstasy to the Garage. At first people were suspicious, but like everywhere, they slowly began to dip their toes in the water, see that it wasn't too cold, and dive in.

'For about two years, I had four nights a week that were incredible. I had Wednesday at the Leadmill in Sheffield, Thursday at the Fan Club in Leicester, Friday at the Haç and Saturday at the Garage. Bizarrely, the money I got for all of that would be about a quarter of what I get for one gig now. I'd get a taxi back from Leicester and Sheffield because I didn't drive, and get the train up with my box. Times have changed.'

The Future's Mine

'Kiss me where the sun don't shine / The past was yours but the future's mine'
The Stone Roses, 'She Bangs the Drums'

Jeff Barrett had been enamoured of the Mondays ever since he first heard 'Freaky Dancing'. He had promoted their first London gigs, and by 1988 was in charge of their press. 'They looked like this great gang, who were totally up to no good. And the music was the same: totally up to no good, an exciting mish mash of everything.' But it wasn't until another London PR, Philip Hall, played him the eponymously titled début album by his charges the Stone Roses early in 1989 that Barrett realised: something was happening. 'I thought, *Jesus Christ, something's going to go here!* Much as I loved Primal Scream and New Order, the Roses were just amazing. It was a glorious record, a call to arms for people who hadn't had anything for a long time.'

The Stone Roses had been regulars at the Haçienda's Nude night since 1986. Singer Ian Brown and guitarist John Squires grew up in Timperley, a suburb between the satellite towns of Altrincham and Sale, in the same leafy street – Sylvan Avenue – the Bee Gees had lived in two decades before. Like the Mondays, they took their pleasures where they could: reggae blues dances, Northern Soul nights, a Mod

212

scooter club, records which spanned everything from the Beatles to Van Halen to Parliament/Funkadelic. The Roses achieved a certain outlaw notoriety in 1985 when they painted graffiti of their name all over the city, provoking a storm of complaints; they built their following by promoting two all-night warehouse parties in 1985/86 with themselves as the live attractions. Then, like everyone else, they got swept up by acid house.

'It was one big community in the Haçienda,' enthuses Ian Brown. 'Everyone was your friend. There was no fear there, just pure love, pure positive thinking. It felt like anything could happen, like everyone was going the same way together. We used to go to Spectrum and Shoom because we were down in London recording in '88. They used to call us roundheads [because of their pudding-bowl haircuts], but we ended up meeting loads of kids we definitely wouldn't have met a few years before.

'All that rowing between Manchester and Liverpool, Manchester and London just finished. All the bully kids that would go in clubs and throw their weight around, suddenly you'd see these psychos E'd up and throwing their arms around some student. It was great.

'Two or three weeks before Mandela was released, the *energy* from everybody! When he was doing those speeches we were watching on TV and there was that feeling of, *Oh! It's going to go, this!* When you saw South Africa fall . . . it really did feel like the world was changing with us.'

Neither the Stone Roses nor Happy Mondays actually *played* acid house. The Mondays sound was a loose, shambolic funk rock topped off with Shaun Ryder's compellingly poetic stream-of-consciousness lyrics. The Roses were largely sixties-influenced rock with basslines and sometimes breakbeats borrowed from their funk record collections. With both bands, it was their *attitude* that made them part of the E generation.

This was a time when the Wedding Present, House of Love and the Mission were big news. When bands still earnestly debated whether appearing on *Top of the Pops* would be selling out, even when they sold so few singles that the question was purely theoretical. Then along swaggered the Stone Roses, cocky little rock gods with a singer who made the music seem sexy again and an ambition to take over the world. They said they wanted to be bigger than Michael Jackson. They turned down a support slot with the Rolling Stones, asserting that they should be the headliners. Ian Brown told the US music paper *Rolling Stone* that the last good record made by white musicians was the Sex Pistols' début LP. 'Pop music was saved by the advent of acid house and rap because whites have done nothing for ten years.' In a *Melody Maker* interview, John Squires name-checked Love, Parliament, Isaac Hayes and Adrian Sherwood while asserting, 'I'm not really into white guitar bands. They're boring.'[8]

If the Roses were working-class kids with attitude, then Happy Mondays were even more exciting: a thrillingly loutish gang who liked their football, music and clothes, talked openly about thieving and taking drugs, and above all seemed to be having a wonderful time. Going to survey his charges while they were recording their *Bummed* album in Hull in the summer of 1988, Tony Wilson was taken aback by the atmosphere they had created in their time off from feeding Es to their producer Martin Hamnett and to the squaddies from the local army base.

'They were doing a rock album, but the lounge room where the band hang out and usually play pool or whatever was completely black. I couldn't see and I was stumbling over the vinyl strewn all over the floor. There was this incredible beat going on and they were all lying on the floor in the dark, playing these obscure house records, soaking it all in.'

'The Happy Mondays and the Stone Roses brought a sense of rhythm into guitar music that had been lost,' adds DJ Dave Haslam. 'They were keen to be seen as part of rave culture. That's how they saw their generation being defined: against Morrissey, and for dance music. It felt liberating, because a lot of the indie values then were very restrictive: you cannot chat up women, you cannot enjoy reggae, it was a bit like that. If you wanted to be a Smiths fan, you almost felt like you had to sign up to Morrissey's Ten Points of How To Behave As a Human Being.'

These bands provided the faces the music press had needed to personify a scene that to them lacked figureheads, real stars, and they also finally provided many journalists with an entry into E culture. Clubs rarely had PRs then; bands did. Jeff Barrett could get journalists on the guest list, give them safe passage into this strange new world. When Happy Mondays held the launch party for *Bummed* in Spectrum, it was the first time many of those invited had ever been to the club.

'They did a gig at Dingwalls the same night,' says Jeff Barrett. 'And that's when I saw it happen. This ... merging. You saw lots of very disparate people: journalists and so on who were more of the indie persuasion, and then the well-dressed, different-looking guys, the club crowd. Something I exploited quite a bit in my job were the voyeuristic people who'd heard about Ecstasy, who knew about this scene, but were too scared to go down to Spectrum. They really believed it was about football thugs.

'The gig that night was a great rock'n'roll show. They weren't an acid house band as such, they were the rock'n'roll band that scene needed. The music press weren't interested before because as far as they were concerned, there were no personalities involved. They never got it, and they still don't get it.'

There had been a lot of *talk* about an indie-dance crossover in 1988, but not much music. There were a handful of pop and rock records that worked in the clubs, and later a few bootleg remixes of hoary old stadium anthems, but very few rock records had the requisite beat. So the Happy Mondays asked Paul Oakenfold to provide it (with assistance from Terry Farley). In retrospect this seems like a bold, prescient move, although it is usually conveniently forgotten that 'Wrote For Luck', the first single Oakenfold remixed, also came with a makeover by Erasure's Vince Clarke.

Oakenfold and his studio partner Steve Osborne stripped the original drums and bass from the track and replaced them with sounds from the DJ's collection. 'We had a rhythm section that everybody could dance to and was familiar with – four-to-the-floor and on the beat – but we kept the integrity of a band with guitars,' says Oakenfold. 'I didn't know if it was going to work, to be honest, so I took the drum loop from [a record by gangsta rappers] NWA and the bassline from somewhere else to give me a real tough rhythm to work from, and then kept everything else from the original.'

Titled 'WFL', the remixed track came out with a flickering, strobe-lit video filmed by the Bailey Brothers, aka Phil Shotton and Keith

Jobling. Two Newcastle lads the Mondays' manager Nathan McGough had brought into Factory work on an idea for a film called *The Mad Fuckers*, it was they who were to give the baggy scene its brand name. In their office one night during the Manchester T-shirt boom, they began playing with new slogan ideas. To hoots of laughter, they suggested 'Just say no to London' in homage to the Government's latest anti-drug campaign, 'Nigel Madsell from the isle of Mad', and then 'Madchester'.

Tony Wilson takes up the story: 'I liked Madchester a lot, so I asked if I could use it for the new Mondays EP. I raced over to Dry bar, found some of the Happy Mondays and got their approval. Five days later when, as all musicians do, they changed their mind because it wasn't their idea, I lied and said it had gone to press.'

Factory issued postcards of the city's most tedious buildings, the captions subtly altered to 'Madchester'. They plastered posters for the EP all over the expensive new offices they had acquired in Oldham Street, creating a new Madchester landmark, and when the Mondays' 'Madchester Rave On' EP charted at the end of 1989, the scene was branded: even the prestigious American magazine *Newsweek* was to use it in its cover report the following July on the city's youth culture.

There were other guitar bands working in the same areas. Primal Scream collaborated with *Boy's Own* DJ Andrew Weatherall on the glorious 'Loaded', played concerts that felt like club nights, and with 'Screamadelica' somehow managed to distil the essence of 1988–90 into a classic album. The Farm, the Liverpool group whose fanzine *The End* had inspired *Boy's Own*, teamed up with Terry Farley and Pete Heller to enjoy brief crossover success, and Scottish baggy wannabees the Soup Dragons had a notable chart hit with 'I'm Free'.

But Madchester had the edge. It was more than just a few records or bands, it was a *scene*, with its own clubs, clothes, slang. Soon every A&R man in the country was in Manchester signing up bands in wide trousers, and teenagers everywhere were affecting Bez's stoned gait. Local groups like the psychedelic garage band Inspiral Carpets and James were swept along by the tide, and the Inspirals' 'Cool As Fuck' T-shirts became best-sellers. Suddenly bands could become famous and make money through their merchandise as much as their music.

Both the Mondays and the Roses were quick to distance themselves from Madchester. Shaun Ryder pointed out that they'd spent much of the eighties away from the city, travelling. At their show at London's Alexandra Palace, Ian Brown silenced the Manchester chants with the announcement, 'It's not where you're from, it's where you're at!'

The Happy Mondays' third and best LP, *Thrills, Pills And Bellyaches,* was recorded in Los Angeles. Producer Paul Oakenfold got a weekly residency in a club there for the eight-week period, and the band would come down and hang out when he played. 'One night Julia Roberts had a soft spot for Bez and sent her security guy over,' he recalls. 'He didn't know who she was and he blanked her. It wasn't until afterwards that he realised it was the actress from *Pretty Woman.* But he was in his own little world, Bez. He reversed up the freeway once. He missed the turning, and he just put the brakes on and reversed. Can you imagine being in the car when he's reversing down a motorway? But he got away with it.'

For dance producers like 808 State, it was galling to suddenly be written out of the story, for it all to be about bands and not beats again. For the DJs who had kicked off the scene in the first place, it also became an irritation. 'One guy asked how long I played for,' recalls Mike Pickering. 'When I said five hours, he asked if I had enough records from the Roses, Carpets and Mondays to fill that time. There was a really distorted idea of what was going on. A lot of the bands were hanging around the Haç, but only because they were there anyway and that was where they lived. Most people were just into house.'

The record that perhaps saw the peak of Madchester was a collective affair, pulling together many of the disparate strands. Bad football records were then as much a part of the game as rancid meat pies and managers in car coats. But somehow, the record the England team made for the World Cup in 1990 got hijacked by baggy, becoming a glorious in-joke for the chemical generation. Actor Keith Allen, a Shoomer who had also become a regular at the Haç while filming the TV series *Making Out* in Manchester, contributed lyrics to 'World In Motion'. New Order made the music. Mike Pickering and Graeme Park mixed one side, Andrew Weatherall the other. And as the England team sang along to that catchy chorus, many of us wondered how many of them actually understood: '*It's E for England!*' It got to number one, and somehow the whole spectacle of Italia '90 – the record, the foreign football T-shirts that became standard clubwear, Paul Gascoigne's tears, England's near-triumph – seemed part of that summer's euphoria, part of this huge merging of all of youth culture's formerly separate strands.

From August 1989, when they took over the Empress Ballroom in Blackpool to give 4,000 Manchester clubbers a big day out to crown the second summer of love, the Stone Roses had specialised in *events* more than live gigs. 'We didn't feel separated, we didn't feel like a band with fans, we just felt like four kids from Manchester who could supply the music for all of us,' says Ian Brown. 'Our shows weren't like a traditional show, it felt like we were putting parties on.'

But they were always better at generating a sense of occasion rather than pulling off the occasion itself, their productions often marred by bad sound and bad organisation. Still, after the Happy Mondays sold out Manchester's vast G-Mex hall in March 1990, a gig promoted by Jimmy Muffin and John the Phone and featuring 808 State in support, the Roses knew they had to do something special to top it. And so, on 27 May, they brought 28,000 people to some barren grassland in the middle of an ugly industrial estate at Widnes near Liverpool, to kick off the third summer of love.

Spike Island was to be the Woodstock of the E generation, the point where baggy would greet rave, club would join concert in a great meeting of the tribes. The signs were there from the beginning that it was not to be, but most of us were too hyped up with anticipation to notice. A group of us travelled up by minibus and went to the Haçienda the night before. I hadn't been for a few months, and it had changed: the atmosphere was oddly muted.

At the site the next day, the security staff were searching everyone, confiscating food and drink at the gate to leave the crowd at the mercy of the foul-smelling burger vans that ringed the site inside, and an under-staffed beer tent. I'd expected a funfair, lasers, side-shows, all the trappings of the big orbital raves, but there was nothing but plumes of pollution from the surrounding factories.

The sound system was muted as the DJs played, and the crowd just sat in the sun as Paul Oakenfold, Frankie Bones and Dave Haslam did their best. A hail of bottles greeted On-U Sound's Gary Clail when he played. The whole day felt as if we were waiting for it to begin, for something to happen, and when the Stone Roses took the stage after dark for a triumphant set that ended in spectacular fireworks, something did. But it wasn't enough. Many of us left with a sense of anti-climax, feeling let down. 'I was disappointed,' agrees Paul Oakenfold. 'Maybe I just expected too much. But it didn't happen as it could have.'

'For me it felt like the end of Madchester, the end of my indie dance career, and the end of it all,' says Dave Haslam. 'I can't really work out why, but it did feel like it then. Everyone was still quite naive about it. Now, the list of DJs for a big outdoor event like Creamfields is prepared and advertised months before, it's all themed, sponsors are organised, and it's all done in a much more professional way.'

After the euphoria had worn off, the band themselves suffered the same comedown as everyone else. 'At the time, arriving there and seeing all those people, it felt fantastic,' says Ian Brown. 'But the next day we found out that people had their sandwiches taken at the gates. The PA was tiny, we thought it was going till dawn and it closed at 11.30. So we felt disappointed, ripped off. Angry that it was done in our name.'

This was to be the Stone Roses' moment of triumph, their first step towards finally toppling all the old stadium dinosaurs or at least taking their place alongside them. In fact, they didn't release another album for five years. There were contractual battles with their old label Silvertone in court, a high-profile signing to the huge US label Geffen and then . . . silence. When their *Second Coming* album finally did come out in 1995 it was rather good, but no longer buoyed up by that great wave of energy, they became just another band.

Those who remembered 1990 felt angry, let down that the Roses had somehow failed to bring all that excitement and optimism back with them. Those who didn't wondered what all the fuss was about. Besides, by then another band were rising up from Manchester with all of the Roses' old swagger and ambition and the Mondays' bad boy poses. In Liam Gallagher, Oasis even had a frontman with the same combination of arrogance and unease on-stage, a mix of discomfort and charisma that came straight from Ian Brown.

By the end of 1990, the Happy Mondays had also peaked. Shaun Ryder now admits he barely remembers their triumphant shows at G-Mex, Wembley and Glastonbury. The heroin he had been using 'chill out' since his teens had become a problem he was no longer able to conceal, and in December he checked into the Priory Clinic in Cheshire for the first in a series of attempts at rehab. Journalists who had revelled in the Mondays' laddish bad behaviour and prodigious appetite for illicit substances now recoiled in horror. Smack was still a taboo too far, and a backlash that had begun with interviewer Steven Wells portraying them in *NME* as reactionary, homophobic yobs gained momentum.

'They got a lot of new friends,' remembers Jeff Barrett. 'There was a lot of money around, a lot of girls, and suddenly these quite scary people appeared. That group were up to a lot of tricks. They were grabbing the moment. Selling their own tickets outside, forging their own tickets for the gigs, their own guys doing T-shirts. It was a cottage industry.

'There was a dodgy side to it. The stories I was supposed to deal with as a publicist . . . You were on your toes all the time. There came a point when you decided to milk these stories, and you found yourself talking to the tabloids, which I was never that comfortable with. But Shaun got the best angle on that, because he got friendly with a few people and made a bit of money out of it.'

On the way to Barbados to record the group's fifth album in January 1992, Ryder dropped his maintenance methadone at the airport, smashing the bottles on the floor, and so resorted to smoking crack in the Caribbean. He was unable to record his vocals there, and the album they finally finished failed to justify the £250,000 it was said to have cost. On 23 November, Factory went into receivership with debts of around £2 million; a deal was done with New Order to keep the Haçienda open. The Mondays split soon after, although Shaun Ryder was to make what one critic dubbed 'the biggest comeback since Lazarus' with his band Black Grape and their glorious, ironically titled 1995 album *It's Great When You're Straight . . . Yeah*.

Meanwhile, in 1991, 808 State headlined G-Mex alone. Established promoters wouldn't touch the event, so Jimmy Muffin and John the Phone put up the money – it was a sell-out. Dance bands were learning how to present themselves as spectacle, and in the following years bands like the Prodigy, Orbital and Underworld who had learned to play to large crowds at the raves were to headline festivals like Glastonbury. Once considered as ephemeral acts who sold one-off singles and didn't – couldn't – play live, within years they would be selling albums by the million and performing in stadiums. Having mingled on the dancefloor, the old boundaries between rock and dance would remain blurred; and though it is true that many a rock band has benefited from the remixing touch of a DJ, many dance acts too learned from their new friends with guitars.

Hardcore Uproar

It started, as so many things did, in a corner of the Haçienda. The third alcove along on Wednesday and Friday nights was for the Blackburn posse, and like everyone else converted to this culture, they were keen to spread the word. They soon began holding their own Saturday night events upstairs at a gay bar in Blackburn called Crackers, and by the end of 1988 were organising small free parties after the club closed at 2 a.m. The first was in an empty shop and drew about fifty people, and from there it grew gradually, organically, into weekly events in garages, lock-ups, work units and empty warehouses – wherever the space could be found. By the summer of '89, they'd taken over the Sett End, a social hall attached to the Red Parrot pub in Shadsworth Road. Local DJs Shack and Lee Stanley would play to a crowd of about 400 inside the club, and outside even more would gather in the car park, waiting for that night's after-hours action.

Within easy reach of Leeds as well as Manchester, the small industrial town that ravers began to call Boomtown was an ideal party location. It was outside the jurisdiction of Greater Manchester's chief constable James Anderton – a strict disciplinarian who once infamously claimed to have a direct line to the Lord, and had come down hard on parties on his patch. The Donnelly brothers had pulled off Joy, an M25-style spectacular in the countryside on 5 August, but Mike Pickering had been served with an injunction banning him from the area and legal action was taken against shops in Manchester, Liverpool and Birmingham for selling tickets.

The Blackburn scene was always underground, organised by a loose collective based around Tommy Smith and Tony Creft who called themselves – when they bothered with a name at all – Hardcore Uproar. More about ideology than making money, the parties were initially free, then cost £3 and finally £5. For many, the first sign that the scene existed at all was Live the Dream, an impressive illegal rave in the countryside at Great Harwood in September 1989 with around 5,000 clubbers enjoying two dance marquees featuring DJs from London, Manchester, Liverpool and Blackburn, and an alternative tent overseen by Tommy Smith, a thirty-year-old Scot who had been living in Germany as part of a travelling theatre group. A lifelong socialist, he went to an acid party on his first night back in England, and felt that it was the start of the revolution he'd been waiting his whole life for.

'The drum was beating and people were tuning in on it, it was something primal inside us,' he said in *Altered States*. 'You had euphoria spilling out all over the place, genuine happiness. The law of the dance was stronger than the law of the land.'

After Live the Dream took the Blackburn scene to another level, it was impossible to get into the Sett End after 10 p.m. By 1.30 a.m. there were massive crowds milling around outside, while the promoters plotted from the safety of the club's back room, secure in the knowledge that the police could never get near them through the throng. At 2 a.m., a car would roar off and everyone would follow, at first in one great convoy, later in several that set off in different directions to confuse the police.

'You hadn't got a clue where you were going, it was a complete magical mystery tour,' says Jane Winterbottom, who met Tommy Smith at the Haçienda one night in 1988, fell in love and soon moved in with him. 'Early on it wasn't such a race against the police, because East Lancs. was quite a country force. They let it happen for a long time. Then later, you'd see a police presence in the centre as you were in the convoy, driving along, ignoring the red lights.

'At the warehouse you'd dive out the car as quick as you could, because it was a race against time. Inside, usually it was in complete darkness or just one little light. No music, people just talked as it filled up. Then after about half an hour, the generator would start up and everyone would just scream. It went wild when the music came on. The record jumped every ten minutes, it was such a primitive set-up, thrown together so quickly.'

'It just started growing and growing,' says Sasha, who became a regular at the raves. 'Blackburn city centre would be busier with cars at one in the morning than it was at one in the afternoon. Towards the end when I started playing at those parties, there were 10,000 people there. Only a few thousand at the front could hear the music, but the vibe in the room . . . it was just amazing energy.'

A bright, red-haired youth from Liverpool with the gift of the gab and the restless spirit of the times, James Barton had travelled round Europe following rock bands, selling bootleg T-shirts and posters, touting tickets and doing whatever he could to soak in the glamour not so much of the music but of the *show*, the spectacle. He'd been taken to Spectrum and the Trip early on by some fellow touts from London, and went back home fired with enthusiasm. He quickly started a Thursday-nighter called Daisy at the State in Liverpool, and was instrumental in spreading acid house into Merseyside in 1988.

'It was a really exciting time. I was nineteen, twenty, and my brothers had come through punk. I caught the back end of that, seeing the Clash before they split, then the Jam, and I was into a lot of local bands like Echo and the Bunnymen. But acid house felt like a music which my brothers hadn't loaned me. It wasn't handed down, it felt like *ours*. We were in the middle of what felt like a revolution. It was wonderful, I loved it.'

By the time the Blackburn scene kicked off, his night at the State has closed (the police objected to the word 'acid' appearing on its promotional posters) and he was running the Underground with DJ John Kelly, a small but much-loved Liverpool club with a copy of the London tube map painted on the wall, marking not underground stations but key moments in the development of the local house scene. Barton and Kelly played at Live the Dream, and became Blackburn regulars. After the Underground closed at 2 a.m., that week's venue would be relayed to them, and they would lead a convoy up the motorway to the party.

'Every week without fail, we'd be up to Blackburn till seven or eight in the morning. We always brought a crowd. The Underground only held 400 people, but outside there would be a thousand people in cars – the police were always on our case about it. The night we were at Live the Dream, it was like coming out of a football match, all these crowds and cars and even a coach.

'It was dangerous going to those parties, they were in some really horrible places. But the challenge was always to get in regardless. Because we had the club we'd never get there until around 3.30, and by that time it would be surrounded by police. There was one in a warehouse in Skelmersdale, and when we pulled up this kid came running up saying, "There's police everywhere. You won't get in." So we went round the back and climbed up through a window. All of our crew got in, and I remember it because that one got a bit heavy, the police smashed down the door and gave a few people a couple of whacks.

'That was always weird, because people just didn't understand what they were doing wrong. I mean, obviously some of the warehouses had been broken into, but I remember coming out of so many parties to hundreds of police in vans and dogs and lights, and it would be like, "For crying out loud! We're just dancing around a sound system with a few DJs and dodgy lights!" '

Unlike the promoters in the south, the Blackburn crew made no attempts to find legal loopholes, no bids for respectability or acceptance from the authorities. There was a reward of £100 for anyone finding a suitable venue, and these would usually be checked out a few days before and then broken into on the night. As for decorations and special effects, there were a couple of Hardcore Uproar banners, a few basic lights, a generator and the decks. But equally, there was none of the intimidating security of the orbital raves, no high prices, and a glorious feeling of solidarity amongst the crowd. 'Our day shall come' proclaimed one of the Hardcore Uproar T-shirts, while another declared 'I lived the dream'.

A BMW salesman from Maidenhead, Rob Tissera had been to many of the M25 raves, and when he was invited to one of the early Blackburn parties he expected more of the same. 'I thought it would be like a big Colston-Hayter production with scaffolding and Adamski playing keyboards, but it was 300 people jacking to acid house in this dirty warehouse with no windows in it, one set of speakers and one strobe light. It was just raw energy, everybody tripping out of their box, and this guy playing Jim Morrison poetry over mad acid house music. I drove up from Maidenhead every single week after that, and became totally absorbed in it. I can't explain how different it was, how friendly, and what it meant to people up here. One Friday night, I put all my stuff in the car, called work to tell them I'd left, and moved up north.'

The safety precautions were rudimentary at best, and there were constant rumours about ravers falling through openings in the floor intended for lifting cranes, or from crumbling balconies. Sasha remembers one party in a warehouse that had been storing firelighters a few days before, and was still full of intoxicating fumes. Another was in an old abattoir, with the revellers climbing on to a high shelf and jumping down to get in, then dancing with crushed drink cans tied to the soles of their shoes because the floor was so cold.

'It was basic, but you had your own show in your head,' says Sally Parkinson, another Blackburn regular. 'At the abattoir, it was when Russia had started breaking up and the Berlin Wall had just come down. This man stood there off his face shouting, "The revolution is here! They've done it in Berlin, they've done it in Romania, now its coming to Blackburn!" And everyone was cheering. I was really idealistic and thought we were all going to live together as one big happy family. I really believed that. I even thought they should put E in the water.'

Mobile phones were used, and Tommy Smith had a friend who was a CB radio enthusiast and would scan the airwaves for police transmissions. But this was far from the high-tech games down south – here they relied on the power of numbers and sheer brute force. The police would be physically prevented from confiscating equipment, and even if they succeeded, they rarely stopped the music for long. When officers took a generator, a shop was ram-raided by supporters to steal a new one. When they got the decks, a nearby house was burgled and a tape deck snatched until another set of decks could be found. After the DJ's record box was taken one night and put in the police van, the result was a stand-off between police and ravers during which the box was retaken. There were frequent fights, one culminating in squad cars being set alight.

'They didn't really give a shit about the police up here,' says Jane Winterbottom, whose fanzine *Ear to the Ground* monitored both the press and the police's responses to the raves. 'There were loads of riots in Blackburn. We *wanted* a revolution, that's what we were aiming at. We wanted hardcore uproar. That's why we got more clamped down on than anywhere. Because the police knew what was going on by then. It was a serious thing. It wasn't just some kids doing a party. And they were going to stop it by any means they could.'

The peak of the parties was Christmas and New Year's Eve, with two huge parties in a mill just by Blackburn football ground. By the start of 1990, the local papers were running campaigns, and questions were being asked by local MPs. (East Lancashire MP Ken Hargreaves gave enthusiastic support to Graham Bright's bill when it was debated in Parliament, expressing dismay at the number of local parents who seemed pleased that the parties offered their children something to do.)

Meanwhile, as the authorities closed in, the usual problems were beginning to surface within the culture itself. 'These people were working-class, they've got to graft for a living, and selling drugs was an easy way of making money,' says Sally Parkinson. 'You soon had drug gangs. The first time I ever saw crack was in Blackburn. They were making it themselves, washing their own coke.'

The promoters had already been visited by various hard men from Blackburn and Liverpool when a Salford gang moved in and took over, paying the Hardcore Uproar team £5,000 for putting on the parties and then pocketing the door money themselves. 'After that it was a race against the gangsters and the police as to who was going to ruin it first,' says Jane Winterbottom.

The showdown came at 7.30 a.m. on 24 February, at a party in a brand-new warehouse in Nelson, near Burnley, attended by some 10,000 people. Sasha was due to play that night: 'There were always police outside, but it seemed like there was a lot more than usual as we were driving up to the venue, so I left my tunes in the car. The sun had come up and everyone was dancing to Candyflip's 'Strawberry Fields Forever'. Suddenly the shutters opened and the police just steamed in with full riot gear, dogs, shields and those flash-guns photographers used to have in the fifties. They were flashing them in people's faces and completely disorientating them.

'It was horrendous, this whole surge of people pushed over to one side of the warehouse. A girl next to me got knocked out of her wheelchair. There was no need. But they really wanted to put a stop to it, and they did. After that, a lot of people didn't want to go back to Blackburn.'

There were a few more parties in the area, but by then Salford had taken over. 'I can remember going out for a wee and the Salford people wouldn't let me back in, saying I was a policewoman,' says Jane Winterbottom. 'There were people in the party robbing people, it was rough as anything. It went literally from being heaven one week to the following Saturday being a living hell.'

Later, the Salford crew were to apologise, to admit that they spoiled something special. But meanwhile the parties moved north, over the county line into west Yorkshire. Brave New World was held in an indoor equestrian centre near Bradford in June: Manchester duo Together made their live début with their tune 'Hardcore Uproar', and Blackburn's Steve Kirrane was handing out flyers for a party he was fronting in the same area on 19 July, Love Decade. 'I can remember watching him, the look on his face,' says Jane Winterbottom. 'He was going to fund the next party, it was his little baby.'

But like Ken Tappenden in Kent, the West Yorkshire police were experienced in mass conflict after the miners' strike, and they quickly moved against the parties. At an unconnected event held under a motorway bridge at Horbury Lagoon near Wakefield, they arrested 236 people – including an off-duty police constable from Bradford – and took the names of 700 more, charging promoter Andy Link with 'conspiracy to cause a public nuisance'.

This proved to be a mere dress rehearsal for Love Decade, which happened a week after the Bright bill became law. Hundreds of police in riot gear stormed the warehouse in Gildersome near Leeds at 5 a.m. Rob Tissera had become a DJ by then, and was behind the decks when they arrived.

'I got the mic on and said, "Listen, if you want to keep this party going, we need to barricade the doors and keep the bastards out!" And everyone cheered. There was a van inside the venue selling drinks and fresh fruit, and we got it up against the main doors and put it in first gear. The police were on the other side with a fork-lift truck, but we held them off for three hours. It got nasty, a lot of people started picking up broken bits of wood and fighting the police. Which was a bit stupid. But everybody got caught up in it. We wanted not just for this party to go on, but *every* party to go on, and in order to do that, we had to stop the police coming in. That's how it felt. The movement had got to that stage where we thought we were a law unto ourselves.'

In the biggest mass arrest in British history, 836 clubbers were taken to twenty-six stations across the county in hired coaches. One policeman was badly injured after being hit with a plank; from the slings and bandages on display when the ravers trickled back to the site to collect their cars the next day, accusations of heavy-handedness by the police were not unfounded.

'That party was the most violent thing I've ever witnessed in my life,' says Jane Winterbottom. 'I can remember standing on my own so as not to confuse the police, making myself cry so they wouldn't hit me. They were beating people in their faces. There were women on the floor and they were kicking them. Afterwards, we all got taken outside in a line and then carted off like we were going to Auschwitz. They kept me for sixteen hours in Morley police station, till the evening. I was one of the last to be let out of the cells.'

She later sued the police for false imprisonment, and won £600 in compensation. Friends who were badly beaten got more. 'Which proved how wrong they were. Everyone should have done it really.'

Only seventeen people were finally charged, including Rob Tissera, whose outburst on the mic had been captured on video. At twenty-four he was the oldest of the defendants, and the only one in a suit. Perhaps believing the tabloid stories about a scene controlled by yuppie 'Mr Big' figures, the court decided that he was the ringleader. His lawyer had told him to expect a £300 fine or a suspended sentence; despite having no previous convictions, he got three months in prison. He says it gave him the motivation to make a living from club culture, as well as a certain notoriety to capitalise on, and he has since become a successful DJ, remixer and producer.

After the Love Decade, Tommy Smith and Jane Winterbottom went to America for a few weeks to clear their heads. Soon after they came back, Winterbottom was in Manchester visiting the Donnelly brothers' clothing business Gio Goi when she heard the news. Tommy Smith and Steve Kirrane had been arrested, apparently in possession of 68,000 trips. In the following weeks, all of the original collective were arrested on various drugs charges, with the exception of DJ Shack. When they came up for trial a year later, Smith was acquitted; the others received sentences from two-and-a-half years upwards. Steve Kirrane got the most: twelve years.

Smith went to India for a while, and in 1995 became an eco-protester camping out on the site of an M65 extension. Winterbottom is now a DJ and sound engineer, and still promotes underground parties. Sally Parkinson has also made a life within the scene, running a successful company in London promoting small dance labels. But she is under no illusions about the long-term effects of this revolution, about the opportunities it opened up for many of those involved.

'In the north, people just ended up going back to their lives. Or to prison. I used to look back and think, "Oh, those were the days!" But lately I've been reassessing it. In the end, perhaps it *was* just us dancing about in the dark.'

The Comedown

Claire Leighton was sixteen when she travelled up from Cannock in Staffordshire to visit the Haçienda on 14 July 1989, but her mum had borrowed another girl's birth certificate so that she'd be able to get in. Once there, she took an E, and soon after began sweating profusely, vomiting and losing her balance before collapsing. She was already haemorrhaging internally, and three days later she was dead. Her boyfriend, nineteen-year-old Tim Charlesworth, was later given six weeks' detention for supplying the drug to her. At the inquest, the coroner noted that hers was a highly unusual reaction to the drug, but that this was no reason for complacency amongst other users.

'That's when it stopped being a joke,' says Paul Cons of the tragedy. 'Before, it was all a bit of a laugh, with everyone out of their heads. But then we realised that there was a large degree of medical experimentation taking place. No one really knew what they were doing. We were incredibly naive. I still think that really. The same people who check for additives when they go to a supermarket will stuff anything down their neck and they don't know where it's from, what's in it.'

For a while the Haçienda had been, like so many other places at the start of this explosion, a fantasy world where it felt as if nothing bad could ever happen. The E generation took over so quickly that by the time most managers knew about it, their clubs were already overrun with enterprising youths serving up to their friends from a plastic bag. And for a while, it didn't seem so wrong. There were no fights. No raised voices. Spill someone's pint and they'd usually laugh.

As the licensee for the Haçienda, Paul Mason admits that his first worry was that Leighton had been under-age. 'It sounds selfish, but my reaction initially was to clamp down on age control on the door rather than people buying or selling drugs.'

But sad as it was, the death of a young girl wasn't the only sign that the honeymoon was over. As the quantities of drugs consumed grew, so the supply began to fall into the hands of gangs from areas such as Cheetham Hill, Moss Side and Salford – loose alliances sometimes based around criminal families, more often based around growing up in the same area. The younger gangs who began hanging out in the city centre clubs were often as concerned with face, with looking harder than the rest, as they were with profit. For a while, such concerns were forgotten in an Ecstatic daze. But when the E buzz wore off, as it inevitably does, more of them got into cocaine – an addictive drug with a tendency to bring out aggression and paranoia. In Manchester, as elsewhere, it was a recipe for violence.

Even as Madchester broke big at the end of 1989, Shaun Ryder was already hinting in *The Face* at the cancer eating at its insides. 'E was great two years ago. It made everything peaceful. But now the violence is coming back in the Manchester clubs. There's too much freebasing going on. It's taking over in Manchester. Everyone had a binge on E, only the people who had a binge on E from the start are now having a freebase binge on cocaine. All the lads we know in London, it's the same.'

At first, the shift in mood and the growing presence of the gangs in the clubs was barely noticeable away from the door. Everyone had their comedown, their realisation that something was seriously wrong, at different times. 'The first violence that I saw, I tried to put it out of my mind,' admits Mike Pickering. 'One of the Cheetham Hill gangs started on the security men down the side of the DJ box by the bar. It was really heavy, they had weapons. I went to America the next day to do the Haçienda tour with Paul Oakenfold, I mentioned what I'd seen and he said it was creeping into London too.'

But in London, many of the problems were tucked away out of sight, or in areas like the East End where club-associated violence was hardly new. The very village atmosphere that had helped the Manchester scene to thrive now worked against it; happening in the heart of the city centre, in a place close-knit enough for stories to spread quickly, the gang problem was more visible than it was in the capital. The fact that the world's media was focused on the city at the time made it even more noticeable.

For Ian Brown, the realisation came at the Moss Side festival in 1990. 'There was a big show-out of one of the big gangs in the area and kids with guns just walked from one side of the park to the other, with everybody running backwards: police, security, the local people. Suddenly these sixteen-year-old kids were running it. They used to go in the downstairs bar at the Haçienda with a holster under their armpit, showing off. It was within weeks, really, at the end of '89. A lot of the kids I knew that were dealing Ecstasy by then were forced to deal it – they were given fifty pills, then maybe a fiver for selling it.'

Youths who had been enterprising enough to find their own sources for the drug had got rich quick at the Haçienda in 1988. But now they began to find the hidden cost. This is one dealer's story, chosen because it echoes many experiences not just in Manchester but in clubs nationwide as the control of the drug trade moved from informal networks of friends to more organised crime:

'I started out as a hod carrier. I started going to the Haçienda, and I'm sure you've heard this story time and time again – you get fifteen for your mates, you dish them out, then you get some more and some more. And all of a sudden, I was making an absolute fortune. And it didn't seem wrong. Because it was all people who were friends. I did so well because I was involved in the scene and I cared about the product being right.

'This is how naive I was: it was 1990, and I didn't know who the Cheetham Hill lot were. Everyone I knew was there for the same thing as me. The music, the atmosphere. One night I came out of the club, pockets full of money, and the tyres were slashed on my car. I drove it round the corner, got out to change the wheels and there were four guys. They had me, my girlfriend and two other people, with guns in our mouths. "Right, we've been waiting to speak to you."

'I did a deal with them where I could go back in the club. I was sort of working with them, they were protecting me. It was horrible. Thinking back now, I don't know how I got messed up in it. Finally, my supplies dried up and I didn't go back for a few weeks. When I did, I was standing in the DJ box chatting and they just dragged me out. They thought I'd been doing business elsewhere, and they beat me up in the club, smashing my nose with knuckle-dusters, blood everywhere. I didn't ever go back after that.'

In May 1990, after a long period of undercover observations at the club following the death of Claire Leighton, the police told Paul Mason that they would oppose the renewal of his licence at the Haçienda, claiming that he had lost control of his premises. As a result there was an immediate clampdown on the door, which explained the muted atmosphere before Spike Island. Many of the club's most enthusiastic regulars were turned away, including some of the team behind *Freaky Dancing*, and the club imposed a dress code for the first time in an attempts to keep both the drugs and the gangs out.

Angry that the police seemed more intent on closing clubs than closing in on the gangs, the Haçienda team were determined to fight the ban. Tony Wilson used his PR skills to enlist the support of the media and hired the expensive and brilliant QC George Carman, known for defending high-profile cases, while Paul Mason went to the council for help. To their credit, the council listened.

By then, people were travelling from all over the world to see Madchester. Applications to the city's universities had soared. In a poll at the end of 1990, forty per cent of New Yorkers questioned said that Manchester was the British city they most wanted to visit.[9] Like Manchester United and *Coronation Street*, the club had become a part of the city's cultural identity.

'We turned the whole thing around from it being about drugs to it being about the Manchester economy and the Haçienda's importance to it,' recalls Paul Cons. 'The social implications of what was happening with the whole Madchester thing were phenomenal.'

At the same time, however, he could see why the police may not have shared this enthusiasm. 'We were treading a very thin line because there *was* major illegal activity going on. Everyone acts with outrage when the police target clubs, but they are there to uphold the law and a major part of what's happened in clubland is totally illegal. It's a very delicate balance. When the Haçienda was at its peak almost everyone in there was on class-A drugs, and it was being fêted around the world and by the council. It was being co-opted as the Eiffel Tower of Manchester when there was an utterly illegal base to it all.'

On 23 July, as *Newsweek*'s cover told America about Madchester and the Mondays prepared to take Glastonbury, George Carman came to court armed with letters of support from council leader Graham Stringer and from the mayor, and with Paul Mason's detailed diary of events at the club. He intended to use this to cross-examine every one of the forty-seven officers due to give evidence. When it became clear that this would take far longer than the few days the magistrates had set aside for the hearing – Carman estimated three months – the parties settled on a compromise: a six-month reprieve to allow the club time to clean up. The months which followed saw the resignation of DJ Dave Haslam, and a lot of bitterness from clubbers who could no longer get into the club they'd once considered their own. The spell was broken, and the atmosphere inside lost its old intensity.

'We wanted to stay open and we wanted to stay within the law, but to do that we had to kill the culture,' says Tony Wilson. 'We had to clamp down very seriously, and that was upsetting.'

It was enough. At its next hearing, on 3 January, the club was given a further reprieve. Others weren't so lucky. Konspiracy had become a favoured hangout for some of the gangs within months of opening, a seething mass of energy that had proved impossible to control. The police claimed that guns had been fired there and that it was only a matter of time before someone got hurt. Unable to afford an expensive lawyer and also exhausted by the pressures they had faced on a weekly basis, licensee Chris Nelson and owner Marino Morgan had been unable to put up a similar fight for their club. But still, the majority of Konspiracy's crowd mourned its passing at the end of 1990.

Justin Robertson had been a DJ there, establishing a popular Balearic room with Greg Fenton in the graffiti-covered caves at the back of the venue. 'It was a good crowd, but more rough round the edges than the Haçienda, so when they were displeased with you they would often show it. I had a few ducks under the decks as bottles came flying towards me. Once or twice a month, it would be sorry, we can't pay you tonight, we've had the wages robbed. It was a shame that it shut, but it was also inevitable.'

But the closure of Konspiracy only served to move the gang problem more fully on to the Haçienda. This was not just about drugs. Few serious gangsters want to come to clubs to actually *sell* drugs – others can be coerced into such menial tasks. 'It was all about being able to walk in without queuing or paying,' says Paul Mason. 'People wanted to be known as someone who could walk in free.' And when they were refused entry or free drinks at the bar, they showed guns.

Within weeks of the reprieve in court, the Haçienda closed. Voluntarily, after one of its doormen was once more threatened with a gun. It was an old-fashioned withdrawal of labour, a strike, intended to draw attention to the club's plight. At a dramatic press conference inside the club on 30 January, Tony Wilson announced: 'We are forced into taking this drastic action in order to protect our employees, our members, and all our clients. We are quite simply sick and tired of dealing with instances of personal violence.'

'Tony had had enough, I had had enough,' adds Paul Mason. 'I knew someone was going to get shot. The police didn't like it at all. It was us playing the game, very successfully. But we were shut too long. We farted about. That was the start of the financial death.'

'In the DJ booth, me and Mike were oblivious to what was going on on the door,' says Graeme Park. 'We were wondering what on earth was going on. It wasn't *gradually* getting quieter, it was plummeting by the week and the atmosphere had gone. When we found out there was all this shit going on, I remember Mike being suitably dramatic and going, "Well thanks for telling us! Me and Graeme were sitting targets up there, anyone could take a pot shot at us!" '

While the Haçienda was closed, there were negotiations with both the police and the gangs. (No one will go into details here: 'I was potty to get involved in it all,' was the most one would say.) One particular incident offered some hope that the club might re-open peacefully, however. At the end of February, a feud between factions in Salford and Cheetham Hill led to a shooting outside the Penny Black pub in Cheetham. The notorious gang leader Tony Johnson, known locally as White Tony and well-known at the Haçienda for threatening staff, was shot once in the mouth and twice through the body and was killed. His friend 'Black Tony' McKie was badly injured. White Tony was twenty-two, the father of a three-month-old child. He had been raised by his grandmother, Winnie, who had already lost one child in tragic circumstances – her son, Keith Bennett, was a victim of Moors murderers Ian Brady and Myra Hindley.[10] He was also the suspect in one murder, and several shooting and robberies.

The club reopened on 10 May with an optimistic one-off party called the Healing. There was a vibrant new colour scheme inside, a metal detector on the door, £10,000-worth of hi-tech surveillance equipment and a new, London-based security team, Top Guard, who had also been looking after the Happy Mondays. Soon after, on 21 June, the club's licence was extended until 4 a.m. for a special Midsummer Night celebration, but after an incident on the door, a group of Salford lads slipped in through an emergency exit and stabbed six bouncers in a well-planned revenge attack. As ever with such incidents, few of the clubbers inside were aware of this. What they *did* know was that the music stopped at around 3 a.m., and they were held for some time before being allowed out of the club.

'We were off our heads coming out, we didn't know what was happening,' says Mike Pickering. 'It was just like a total police state. There were hundreds of police with riot shields surrounding the club, vans all down the street, and helicopters overhead.

'From then on, I don't think there was ever a night where there wasn't a gang element. It started getting really bad on the Friday night; the numbers were going down because people were getting mugged in the toilets.'

Pickering's last night at the club was the tenth birthday party, on 21 May 1992, a spectacular event involving guest DJs David Morales and Frankie Knuckles. Pickering was threatened with a knife by a youth who wanted the beer he was drinking. David Morales was hit by a beer bottle thrown by someone else downstairs. It was a sad end to a decade at the club, but the extraordinary success of Pickering's group M-People's *Northern Soul* album that year would probably have forced him to give up his residency there anyway.

By then, the Haçienda was no longer the clubbing centre of the north. There were excellent club nights all over Manchester, as well as in Stoke, Liverpool, Leeds and many other towns within driving distance. There would be some fine nights in the following years, some spectacular parties, but the club never quite recovered financially from the events of 1991, and it finally closed on 4 April 1997.

The bankruptcy was not unexpected, but the club probably would have reopened with new finance organised by some of the existing Haçienda team had the police not moved in to revoke its licence again. Magistrates touring the city's licensed premises witnessed a violent incident outside the club between a Salford crew and some lads from St Helen's near Liverpool who had unwittingly wandered into the area that had once been known as 'E corner' but was now Salford's domain.

The gang problem didn't end when the Haçienda closed, of course, and with shops and restaurants as well as clubs and bars now being threatened by little Jimmy Cagneys with guns, it is no longer confined to the dancefloor or to the night-time. But Manchester's city centre is lively nonetheless, boasting some of the best small clubs and designer bars in the UK. The dialogue that began between the council, the police, the magistrates and the city's clubs and youth culture in 1991 has continued.

Manchester Council's Safer Dancing guidelines force clubs to offer free water on demand and chill-out areas, and nine years on, there have been no further deaths attributed to Ecstasy in the city's clubs. In 1995, the council chambers even played host to a Safer Dancing conference organised by the influential Manchester drug counselling service Lifeline, in which club promoters, drugs workers, police and other interested parties sat down to discuss the way forward.

The twenty-four hour city policy Manchester evolved to recognise the importance of the night-time economy and to encourage life into the city centre at night has since been adopted with notable success by cities such as Leeds and Liverpool, and councils controlling most big cities now at least pay lip-service to the idea. As for the Haçienda, it was always a pioneer, marking out the territory for others to follow. Many were inspired by its successes. Many also learned from its mistakes.

PART III
AFTER

10 SEX AND TRAVEL

'Do you trust us?' My partner Mark and I bump into Jimmy and Cressida Cauty from the KLF at a party at Pinewood Studios in the summer of 1991. It seems an odd question to ask, but yes, we trust them. We've been to parties at each other's houses, danced together at clubs and raves. They tell us to buy one-way tickets to Glasgow airport the following weekend and to wait at a designated gate at an assigned time – and so we do. And we find ourselves waiting with about fifty others, most of them from the labels which distribute the KLF's records in various countries, most of them alone, all of them as bemused as us.

Eventually we are shepherded on to a chartered jet by a man in KLF robes, flown to the island of Islay off the west coast of Scotland, then taken by coach then ferry to the even smaller island of Jura, where the KLF's Bill Drummond, DJ Tony Thorpe and others are dressed in military uniforms and insist on checking everyone's passports and stamping them with the group's logo. Everyone is taken to the island's only hotel and told to wait – except for Mark and I, who are taken to the KLF's base nearby because our laughter is spoiling the vaguely menacing mood.

Late on midsummer's eve, everyone is dressed in yellow robes and we walk, in procession, across the brooding Jura landscape down towards a boathouse by the sea. By the stony beach stands a huge wicker man sculpture which some of those assembled recognise as part of a pagan ritual that once involved human sacrifice. You can see a flicker of panic in some eyes, a slow realisation that, *hey, I don't know these people and no one back home knows where I am*. Wearing white robes and tusks, the KLF perform strange theatrical rites in the water, the sound system booming out poetry in some unknown tongue. Then the wicker man explodes into flames, the sound system kicks in with the 4/4 rhythms of house, and we all start dancing round the fire. Under a sky that scarcely darkens on this, the longest day of the year, we celebrate the summer solstice, including local people who came along to watch but soon find themselves becoming part of it all.

At the end of the weekend, we get back on a jet and fly down to Liverpool. We put the yellow robes back on, and in the basement of the Playhouse Theatre, Cressida teaches us the words to the KLF's 'Justified And Ancient' and some simple choreography. Then we troop on stage to perform it to a packed house, Jimmy and Bill serving cones to the audience from an ice-cream van oozing green smoke.

In many ways the greatest pop group acid house produced, the KLF inflated the sound until it was stadium sized, remixing and reworking the same set of songs gloriously again and again before disbanding on 16 May 1992 and deleting their entire back catalogue. On 22 August 1994, they returned to Jura carrying a suitcase containing a million pounds in £50 notes. They went to the boathouse, and in the early hours of 23 August quietly burned the money, with their friend Gimpo videoing the act for posterity. It was a puzzling act, a distressing act, which is why so many of us chose not to believe them at first. But it was also quite beautiful in its purity: of all the people who postured and talked of 'no sell out' in the years after acid house, only they can genuinely claim to have destroyed much of what they gained from it financially.

In retrospect, their midsummer celebration seems increasingly audacious: to get people to fly into Glasgow from all over the world, kidnap them, convert many of them to E culture, then put them on stage as the KLF. But these were years when nothing seemed impossible: doing the dead ant in the middle of a chic club in Rimini, dancing in the Black Mountains in Northern Ireland, taking over the space museum in Moscow for a rave, turning a public school in a building that was once home to Oliver Cromwell into a venue for a wild English summer ball, bringing DJs and clubbers from all over Europe together for a weekend of parties in a big top outside EuroDisney, making the garden of a pub just outside Slough into something so exciting that people would travel across the country just to be there on Sunday afternoon.

There were parties on boats, trains, planes, everywhere and anywhere. Nothing seemed impossible, we could all be kings and queens for a day. And everyone joined in the chant started by DJ Brandon Block wherever he played: 'We don't want to go home! We want more!'

By 1990, the unlicensed outdoor raves had become increasingly dodgy and desperate. Driving between the Garage in Nottingham on Saturdays and his new home in London, Graeme Park would often divert off the M1 to play a rave in the fields around the Midlands. 'By then it was everywhere, but a lot of these outdoor, rave-in-a-tent things were nonsense. It would take ages to find who was going to pay you. Often there'd be some big Mercedes Benz with blacked-out windows, the window would wind down a bit and all this smoke would come out, and either a black hand covered in jewellery or a white hand covered in tattoos would come out with some money. You'd take it, the window would close, and if the money was wrong, there wasn't a lot you could do.

'That wasn't the case all the time, but it did happen more and more as time went on. I did one that didn't have any lights. It was just a big tent with a sound system. It was frightening, because it was pitch black and all you could see was cigarettes glowing on and off and the odd lighter.'

Even at the growing number of legal events, the crowd was mostly young, sweaty, into big anthems and music with a raw, relentless energy. These kids waving fluorescent light sticks, wearing white gloves and surgical masks to intensify the buzz seemed threatening and alien, and the old illusion of openness was lost as clubbers who saw themselves as more sophisticated began to distance themselves from these 'cheesy quavers'.

Most of those who had started the acid house boom had either ignored the big outdoor rave scene or withdrawn from it as it began to grow, dismissing it as too commercial, too impersonal, too far away from the music's roots. Positioning themselves as the cooler alternative, they emphasised that their nights played garage, deep house or Balearic.

By 1990, however, they were starting to feel restless. Nicky Holloway's Sin nights at the Astoria in London were still packed. 'I was

241

doing really well. I had a big black BMW, I'd settled down in this house with this girl . . . and I got bored of it all.' When the opportunity came to take over a small, 250-capacity venue next to the Astoria, he jumped at it. In contrast to the garish visuals and over-the-top production elsewhere, he painted the club white – 'this decade's primary colour' – and called it the Milk Bar. Opening on 20 April 1990, it was, said its first flyer, 'intimate so you know you belong, and stylish so you know you've been', marking a deliberate return to smaller club nights which were necessarily more choosy about who was admitted.

Danny and Jenni Rampling also felt it was time to move on. The last Shoom was on 8 November 1989 at the Park in Kensington. 'Everything began to get a bit sordid, seedy and frightening,' says Danny Rampling. 'People had started to let themselves go, and we were not into that at all. Have a good time, yes, but still keep your life together. Unfortunately people were starting to lose it a bit. We knew that things had to change.'

They held a one-off party at the Diorama near Regent's Park, draping the venue in white and putting white feathers on the floor. To signal their new intent, they called it Pure. It didn't quite go off as planned – a few people turned out to have allergies to the feathers – but when they opened up on Wednesdays at the Milk Bar, the name stayed and with it came a new, dressier door policy.

'It wasn't a real authoritarian policy of no fashionable clothes, no entry. It was more just, *let's smarten things up a bit*. The whole nation had become baggy. Everyone was conforming to this look that had been a non-conformist thing in the beginning. We wanted to go somewhere else. A lot of people were feeling that they needed the change. They felt like they were part of a uniform, an extended tribe that didn't have the right feeling.'

At Land of Oz, Ian St Paul was also starting to feel uncomfortable. 'Most of my friends, the people who had been the innovators, were all travelling elsewhere or losing it. The clubs were full of people I didn't know. It became like a business. I'd walk in sometimes and be surrounded by young, sweating kids, and I felt like a rat in the sewer. I wasn't enjoying it any more, I wanted to go back underground.'

Towards the end of 1989, he was attacked during an after-hours party at his home. Some of the northern lads who had been part of the scene since the beginning threw ammonia in his eyes. 'That was one of the breaking points, what broke the family up. They tried to rip me off, steal money from my apartment. I was in hospital for two months, and couldn't see at all for two weeks. Afterwards, I moved down to the countryside. Getting hurt by people who I thought were friends made me wonder what I was doing. Because I was *doing it* for my friends. These were people who I'd always let in, for three years. Sorted them out for free drinks, whatever. Partied with them.'

Paul Oakenfold, meanwhile, had slowed down. Literally. He made a record under the name Movement 98 and tried to slow the music he was playing in clubs from the 121 bpm of house to a more mellow, funky 98 bpm. 'We'd come through E, and what we were into was smoking joints and chilling,' he says. 'For me, at the raves it was all sheep. Everyone would look the same, dress the same, expect to hear the same big tunes. The music kicked up a gear in the rave scene, it was full of younger people, so I went more funky and down-tempo.'

Upstairs in the VIP room at Land of Oz, Jimmy Cauty from the KLF, Youth from Cauty's old band Brilliant and his one-time roadie Alex Paterson were running a 'no-bpm chill out room' playing hypno-therapy tapes and sound effects over Pink Floyd and Steve Hillage tracks or the washes of ambient, synthesised sound that Brian Eno produced in the seventies.

At the start of 1990 the KLF released *Chill Out*, forty-five minutes of soft, dreamy electronica with sounds and samples from middle-of-the-road clarinet player Acker Bilk to Fleetwood Mac and steam trains drifting in and out of the mix. They jokingly christened this music 'ambient house' – a contradiction in terms which nonetheless stuck, and soon became a new genre. Alex Paterson expanded on the idea imaginatively with his group the Orb – initially a collaboration with Cauty – creating hypnotic, meandering, beat-free soundscapes that effectively reinvented progressive rock for the E generation.

The Orb's first single, 'A Huge Ever-Growing Pulsating Brain That Rules From The Ultraworld', was an epic twenty-minute production that sampled Pink Floyd. Some friends of mine in the Midlands swore that, on the right drugs, they could levitate while listening to it. Before long, other 'intelligent techno' acts like the Aphex Twin were talking of concept albums.

But not everyone was ready to take the style-setters' lead and chill out. In 1990 Land of Oz went on the road, taking a good sound system, their production and their DJs on a tour of twenty-one towns and cities across the UK. Commonplace now, this was then an adventurous, ground-breaking move – a club acting like a rock band, taking its unique atmosphere from venue to venue.

'We got to Plymouth, which was completely out of the way then,' remembers Oakenfold. 'We started playing the music that we were playing: still fast, but more soulful. But the manager of the club went, "What are you doing? I booked a rave!" He wanted strobes, the room full of smoke, and I'm saying, "No, we've moved on now." The crowd had obviously read the newspapers and magazines and they wanted a 1988 rave. It ended up kicking off between us and the owner, with him saying he wasn't going to pay us. I realised that we'd missed the point, that we were too far ahead of the game for the rest of the country.'

After Land of Oz closed, Ian St Paul went travelling again, forever searching for that perfect beat, that serotonin leap. He ended up in Goa, in India, in 1992 and became involved in the trance scene there, one of the few truly international party scenes to have evolved since Ibiza. With cows wandering through the dancefloor, *chai* ladies camped around the parties offering drinks and snacks, and palm trees decorated with fluorescent paint (hence Oakenfold's Fluoro label), the full-moon parties on beaches there have managed to retain much of their underground feel, and similar word-of-mouth events are now quietly held everywhere from Ibiza and the English countryside to the Japanese mountains – often with St Paul's involvement.

Oakenfold meanwhile concentrated on production and began playing in stadiums, touring with Happy Mondays and later U2. In the summer of 1990, he played the Glastonbury Festival for the first time, alongside the Mondays. With Graham Bright's bill clamping down on the illegal raves, other refugees from the summers of '88 and '89 found themselves drawn to the site where farmer Michael Eavis has held rock concerts-cum-hippie-gatherings over the summer solstice since 1970.

Fiona Cartlege, known in London for her Sign of the Times parties and across the country for her influential clubwear shop of the same name, was one of the many clubbers who went searching for a third summer of love at Glastonbury: 'I'd heard of it for years, but I thought it was all long hair and rock bands. Then I was told there was going to be lots of dance down there and the Happy Mondays were playing, so we went to see what was going on. Because of the problems in London, we were looking for somewhere we'd be able to party the whole weekend. And that's exactly what we found.'[1]

The music came along uninvited at first, through renegade sound systems who set up in the fields or drove their vans around the site, blasting out house. Eavis had turned down the idea of a dance stage in 1990, worried about the negative coverage of the rave scene in the press. His fears were confirmed when a battle broke out between some of the sound systems and the security in the travellers' field, and the festival was cancelled the following year as a result. But after Orbital's live set stole the show in 1994, a dance stage and dance tents were finally introduced the following year, and Glastonbury has become an annual event on the club calendar, a gathering of the clans that ranks alongside outdoor festival/raves such as Tribal Gathering and Creamfields.

But in 1990, clubbers felt they had to protect their culture against the influx of ravers rather than find common ground. At one Sunday-afternoon session at Queens, the music was stopped because a lad had taken his top off, the DJ making clear his disapproval of such 'ted' behaviour. Justin Robertson, who refused to go to the Blackburn raves and played an emphatically Balearic mix in the caves at the back of Konspiracy and later at his own night Spice in Manchester, says his crowd dressed in white Levis, Palladium shoes and Italia '90 football tops and saw themselves as cooler than the sweaty youths waving light-sticks in the main room of Konspiracy. 'We were very influenced by *Boy's Own*, and we had it in our heads that we were trying to be more sophisticated. And it *was* exciting – we were a gang, we didn't want to be part of the mass commercialisation of the rave scene.'

In a *Mixmag* review later, however, he admitted it went too far:

The end of 1989 saw the once-fun world of acid house degener-
ate into a media circus with money-grabbers and charlatans
thieving off a gullible public desperate for spectacle and the
all-night party. Naturally the Shoom/*Boy's Own*/Spice world
tried to distance themselves from the lilac-clad rave people ...
The beginning of 1990 saw this once-happy world become what
it most despised: elitist, closed, fashion-conscious and distant.
The great slow-down was coupled with a new attitude of snob-
bishness and charlie [cocaine] tooting ...

But towards the end of the year, things got silly again. Very silly.
Charlie Chester had been one of the promoters of a two-week holiday
in Ibiza that summer, taking over venues for the night and bringing in
their own DJs, bands and clubbers for a mellow event recorded in
Channel 4's aptly named documentary, *A Short Film About Chilling*.
'At Ibiza '90 it was acts like the Grid and Bocca Juniors, and the beats
slowed down,' he remembers. 'Then in 1991 it just exploded again. We
all rebelled against it. We didn't want the white gloves, but we dressed
up too much and started standing round being cool. So we all went
back.'

In London, Chester opened Flying at the Soho Theatre Club, a
small, low-ceilinged dive behind the Astoria Theatre that recaptured
some of the madness that venue had seen during the height of the
acid boom. In Manchester, Justin Robertson and Greg Fenton began
to DJ at Most Excellent, a night which stressed its return to the old
hedonism by reclaiming the smiley logo on its flyer. In Colnbrook
near Slough, Phil Perry and Fiona Crawford opened Full Circle, a
Sunday-afternoon session at a pub with a large garden conveniently
near the M40, that people would drive miles to attend.

Joyous Italian house with its thumping piano riffs and shameless
pop hooks filled the floor, along with a new generation of US disco
divas: Ce Ce Peniston, Alison Limerick, Crystal Waters, Rozalla, Kym
Sims. And fun was definitely back on the agenda. People danced on
tables, on the bar. They carried tambourines and horns, and for a
while, at Venus, everyone inexplicably began turning up with egg
whisks to twirl. Far from being distressed by such behaviour now, the
promoters were usually in the middle of it.

'We weren't in the office counting money,' says Charlie Chester. 'We were enjoying ourselves in there more than anyone else. If the punters see the person who was working the door going barmy on the dancefloor, they're going to go for it too.'

There were no illusions about changing the world any more, no talk of peace and love. This was about *friendship*, about big, boisterous gangs of clubbers having fun together, about hedonism and polydrug excess. It was also about business built out of these friendships: making records, setting up labels and specialist dance record shops together, DJing, promoting, distributing flyers, selling clubwear, tickets or pills. Like many clubs, Flying quickly became a mini-empire, its logo on T-shirts and record bags. There was a record shop, a DJ agency, a dance label, and organised clubbing holidays in the Italian club capital of Rimini as well as in Ibiza.

Opening in Nottingham in June 1990, Venus provided a central meeting place for these new club gangs. James Baillie was the promoter, a large, affable Scot who had promoted acid house parties in the East Midlands in 1988, then managed a bar which had been the meeting place for the coaches going to raves in 1989. Baillie's idea was simple but effective: rather than travel to visit the best club nights in other cities, he wanted them to come to him.

Flying were the first to agree, although they didn't promote the event too heavily. They simply booked a coach and spread the word amongst the regulars. 'We didn't even do a flyer,' recalls Charlie Chester. 'We expected to take one coach, but in the end we took nine, with 450 people. And it was just bananas. We hadn't even got to Luton and everyone was off their knackers. People just wanted to find something different.'

The trip to Nottingham became a monthly event, and Baillie also arranged regular visits from Most Excellent in Manchester, the popular Love Ranch in London, and later Chuff Chuff, a Birmingham organisation that was starting to gain a following with small boat parties on the Worcestershire canals. As with the raves, the journey became as much a part of the night as the dancing. 'We used to travel a lot, to Venus in Nottingham and then later to Up Yer Ronson in Leeds,' remembers Flying regular Kate Harper. 'The coach was the best part. You'd all meet in some pub out by the motorway, all getting excited, then it was like being in a cocoon with your best mates having a real good laugh.'

In 1987, *Boy's Own* had written about a trip to see New Order play at Manchester's G-Mex as if it was an incursion to a foreign, possibly hostile, country. Clubbers rarely travelled then, and in London in the early eighties there were frequently fights in the West End between groups from different areas of London, let alone from outside. But now the country seemed to shrink in size under the influence of Ecstasy. Tentatively at first, but then with increasing enthusiasm, clubs began forging links, exchanging DJs and then arranging joint parties and coach trips for their crowds. A 'Balearic network' began to emerge as clubs with a similar attitude began to open across the country: Slam in Glasgow, Back to Basics in Leeds, Golden in Stoke, Wobble in Birmingham. Nights sprang up everywhere with the same DJs hopping between them to play guest spots.

James Baillie says he often got phone calls after a night at Venus from worried girlfriends and boyfriends trying to track down partners who hadn't come home. Increasingly they would turn up having been to after-hours sessions in houses not just in Nottingham, but all over the country. 'If you wanted to find anybody, you'd probably find them at Full Circle on Sunday,' he laughs. 'I used to go down and see half the people who had been at the club on Saturday night there.'

In contrast to the big, impersonal and increasingly dangerous raves, these clubs stressed the idea of *family*, a close-knit community that was about more than just dancing. 'Our thing was brotherhood, everyone looking after each other,' says Dermott Ryan from Chuff Chuff, while Lisa Loud, who quickly became part of the Flying family, says she found a closeness she hadn't felt since the early days of Future. 'It went beyond work. I was going out with them, getting a plane to Glasgow for a night out when I wasn't even DJing. That was the birth of the travelling DJ. After that, I could have worked in any town, anywhere in Britain.'

The weekend began to stretch ever longer, with people piling back to someone's house after the clubs closed on Saturday night, then carrying on until it was time for the Sunday-lunchtime session at Full Circle. For a few weeks there were wild scenes in Hammersmith tube station on Sunday night as a tiny bar inside, El Metro's, got taken over by the Flying crew. Later the same team opened Volonte in a pub in Slough, where DJ Dave Dorrell once entertained 400 lost souls by playing the Bay City Rollers at the end of one particularly excessive night. Sunday night clubs became more common across the UK, and many of those attending them hadn't been near a bed since Friday.

For many, these were the years of excess. Of losing the plot, getting messy, peaking for England and gurning like fuck. Where 'Let's have it!' was the rallying cry and the best compliment anyone could be paid was that they were 'up for it'. Where losing the plot was something to be proud of, proving you were no lightweight. They were the years of surfing down the stairs of grand hotels on a tea-tray, of week-long parties in Ibizan villas, of staying for hours, sometimes days, round someone's house, watching daft videos and cartoons, laughing at stupid jokes, saying 'wouldn't it be great if . . .' and then later actually putting these ideas into action.

The antics of party animals such as Dave Beer from Back to Basics, his southern soul-mate Charlie Chester and DJs like Brandon Block became the stuff of club legend, and everyone had their own favourite story about the DJ who had to stop his set because he thought he was melting, the club promoter caught standing naked in a hotel corridor, convinced he was waiting for a bus.

'We were all just mentalists,' says Justin Robertson. 'Those were the lost years for me. Complete debauchery. *Let's have it!* was the phrase of the time, and we certainly did. I trapped Mike Pickering in my house once, because I just couldn't bear the thought of everyone going. I remember saying, "You can't go, I've still got loads more records to play!" It was ludicrously self-destructive, and eventually it just got on top of you. I couldn't keep up the pace. It's hard because I remember all those seventies rockers saying, "Kids, don't do it." *After* they'd had their fun. I wouldn't recommend it to people because it wasn't very good for you – but in all honesty, it *was* good fun.'

The names of the clubs reflected the mood: Ask Yer Dad in Nottingham, Shave Yer Tongue in Bracknell, Up Yer Ronson in Leeds, and London nights such as Fubar (an acronym for Fucked Up Beyond All Recognition), the Betty Ford Clinic and Bob's Full House with its joke flyers featuring game show hosts.

In the mean time, Britain was plunging deep into recession. The euphoria, the sense that the world was changing for the better which underpinned the dance boom of 1988 and 1989 had crumbled away. After the Berlin Wall came down and Communism ended, there were no new freedoms after all. All East Europeans seemed to have won was the right to buy burgers from McDonald's if they could afford it, and the racism and nationalism that had been repressed during the years of socialist rule came oozing out of the cracks like an ugly, primal slime. Neo-Nazis marched in Germany, the civil war in Yugoslavia led to the horror of 'ethnic cleansing' and the Soviet Union collapsed into a mess of in-fighting.

At home, the ousting of Margaret Thatcher as Tory leader at the end of 1990 should have been a cause for celebration, but instead it was mean and dispiriting, an act of panic by a party desperate to retain power at any cost. Her replacement, John Major, was a grey, uninspiring figure who talked of traffic cones, citizens' charters and nostalgia for a drab, fifties England of warm beer, cricket and church.

Torn apart by in-fighting, the Government seemed incompetent, directionless, beset by corruption, sleaze and scandal. There were riots in Cardiff, Birmingham, Oxford and Tyneside. There was the Gulf War. Yet in April 1992, the Conservatives were unexpectedly elected for a fourth term. But the old certainty of the Thatcher years was gone, with Major struggling to appease a deeply divided party and hold on to a slim majority.

Faced with this lack of hope, it's little wonder that clubbers took a pill to make them better and escaped into a world where the weekend and your friends were all that seemed to matter. Illustrated with a still from the seventies sitcom *The Good Life*, a flyer for a Sitcotheque party in London on 18 July 1992 underlined the point:

In Russia Communism has collapsed and the evil of capitalism has spread to the East, leaving in its wake a country in ruin. In Britain, the Tories are in office for a fourth term and two generations of voters have never known a socialist government. In Yugoslavia, fighting still rages in a war that no one can win and only people are the losers ... But that's all right because Sitcotheque is back and we've got the good life!

Musically, *Boy's Own* caught the flavour of the time: paraphrasing the punk fanzine *Sniffin' Glue*, they urged their readers to take one sampler, two decks and form a band. The Boy's Own record label was just one of a whole host of new independents springing up to release this deluge of material. Happy Mondays PR Jeff Barrett formed Heavenly to release records by St Etienne and Flowered Up, a group of lads from the Cumberland Park Estate in King's Cross who briefly looked like a southern answer to Madchester. The northern independent Deconstruction was charting regularly with the kind of dance singles Factory had been ideally placed to access via the Haçienda, but never did. The major labels were recruiting DJs to run small boutique labels: Paul Oakenfold with Perfecto, Gilles Peterson with Talking Loud. Meanwhile, clubs that had called themselves Balearic in 1990 now had a new way of distinguishing themselves from the herd: the harder, more instrumental mix played at clubs like Full Circle, Slam and Love Ranch was now called progressive house.

No longer dependent on radio play or the attentions of London-based A&R staff, people would press up a few white labels to distribute to influential DJs and sell through the growing number of specialist dance music shops springing up all over the country. If club play followed, a record deal was rarely far behind: in fact, increasingly, record shops began setting up their own labels simply to release some of the great tunes that were walking through their doors or being created by the DJs working behind the counter. Whereas up-and-coming acts once boasted of support slots to major stars, now there was a new form of endorsement to strive for – every other piece on a new band ended with news of a possible Paul Oakenfold or Andrew Weatherall remix. No one knew nor cared what the people actually making this music looked like: the DJs were the stars now, but accessible stars you could meet and chat to with relative ease.

Clubbers meanwhile turned deliberately back to clothes that were as far from baggy as possible: men wore leather trousers and military-style waistcoats from Michiko Koshino, and from the start of 1991 the ponytails gradually began to be replaced by short crops. For women, these were the Wonderbra years, in which androgynous comfort was exchanged for a revealing top, a choker tied round the neck, a split skirt and clumpy shoes.

Names like Love Ranch, Kinky Disco, Pure Sexy and Come made it clear that sex was back on the agenda for a generation who had grown up with the fear of AIDS, and by 1992 the clothes had become more sexual still: tight child-size T-shirts, baby-doll nighties. While Madonna bared her fantasies in her book *Sex* and Michelle Pfeiffer played Catwoman as an S&M dominatrix in the second *Batman* movie, female promoters like the Pussy Posse and Ultravixens set out to bring an assertive, woman-centred sexuality to the clubs. At one Pussy Posse event in a warehouse in King's Cross, the entrance tunnel was draped in pink, the shape unmistakable: clubbers entered the central party womb via a giant, gaping vagina.

Not everyone welcomed this return to fashion and flirting. Articulating a feeling shared by many women at the time, Sally Parkinson, a veteran of the M25 and the Blackburn raves, remembers it as a betrayal. 'I stopped going to the clubs when the emphasis moved to leather trousers and looking nice. I've never looked neat. I was never a pretty girl, so when acid house and the raves came along, I felt like I'd come home. To me it was about going out in jeans, T-shirts, baseball boots and no make-up, and feeling that I belonged, that I didn't look like a scruffy kid in the corner.'

But this new emphasis on sex could also be liberating. A new breed of gay nights emerged, taking the production values of the house boom back to the gay scene along with a defiant confidence again shown by the names chosen: Spunk, Trade, Dick, Queer Nation. Opened in December 1990 after his garage night High on Hope had runs its course, Patrick Lilley says his Sunday-night Queer Nation 'was like the provisional wing of High on Hope, the gay wing. The people for whom this music was originally designed were feeling excluded.'

'They were very crude names, very much in the face,' adds Trade's Laurence Malice. 'We were saying we're here and we're queer, basically. The AIDS epidemic hit clubs really badly. I remember in 1986 going to Heaven on a straight night and people were saying they wouldn't drink out of the glasses. Sheer ignorance! Venues didn't want to be seen as gay because it affected them every night of the week.'

Trade opened in 1990 in Turnmills, a basement venue in Clerkenwell, just outside the West End. It was the first club in London to open with a twenty-four hour music and dancing licence, and Trade opened at the unheard-of hour of three o'clock on Sunday morning, just as the Saturday-night clubs were closing, and went on until well after Sunday lunch. Eight years on, it is still packed. 'One of the reasons we wanted Trade to be mixed is to show that not every person is contaminated. It broke down a lot of barriers.'

When Paul Cons opened his monthly Flesh night at the Haçienda in 1991, it gained notoriety by asking straight-looking people in the queue to snog a friend of the same sex before allowing them in. Coaches came from all over the north, and the city nicknamed Gunchester began to blossom into Gaychester.

'People in Manchester had got so dull, unglamorous, unsexual and straight. House music came out of the gay scene, and Flesh took the whole thing full circle from clubs like the Saint and the Paradise Garage in New York. It was amazing. The first night of Hot again. It got rid of the gang problem because at that stage, they wouldn't go to gay clubs.'

Other clubs quickly caught on to this idea, in Manchester and elsewhere. Men didn't *have* to wear a dress to get in to Vague in Leeds, but it certainly helped ensure admission. This dressing up helped the atmosphere inside, and deterred beer boys and homophobes from even trying to approach the notoriously picky Claudia on the door outside.

In London, the Ramplings had always gone out of their way to attract a gay following and so discourage the 'ruffian' elements of the scene. They were regulars at Kinky Gerlinky, a series of lavish drag balls that managed to preserve the kind of gay abandon of pre-AIDS club life in the late eighties/early nineties in London, and one night met three lads there dressed in identical frocks who called themselves the Pleased Wimmin. The Ramplings had renamed their own club night Glam, and the Pleased Wimmin became regulars there, paid £30 a night to dance and play havoc, plus all the alcohol they could drink – 'Which was quite a lot,' says Jon Pleased Wimmin, who eventually graduated to playing records as warm-up for Danny, in full drag.

'I never thought I'd make a living out of going to clubs,' he laughs. 'For us, dressing up was like a licence to be really cheeky and loud. And the crowd at Glam would spur us on to go even further – we just loved it, we went every week for two years. And we brought in a younger gay crowd who would see us and realise it was OK to go in.'

Having a drag queen on the door was such an effective way of putting off undesirables and diffusing potential trouble that it quickly became a club cliché – London promoters Puscha even opened an agency hiring out pet trannies to spice up everything from clubs and one-off parties to car shows and sales conventions.

As the number of house nights across the country grew, they all clamoured to book the same DJs. 'I didn't expect it to explode in the way it did,' says Jeremy Healy. 'I never thought DJing would become a full-time job for me. But that whole scene just took off and it was like, "Where are you going this week?" I was thrilled that people wanted me to play, but it got to the point where I would spend two or three hours every day on the phone and it was driving me mad.'

Like many DJs, he eventually got a friend in to organise his bookings. Like many DJs, he began to realise that, by plotting his route carefully, it was becoming increasingly easy to play two or more clubs in one night. (There were persistent rumours at one point that Healy was flying between gigs in a helicopter, but he dismisses them as hype: he tried it, but it's actually faster by road.)

DJ agencies began to proliferate, and a new professionalism emerged alongside them. DJs began to threaten legal action against promoters using their names on flyers without permission, to demand contracts confirming bookings and fees. People who had previously promoted clubs for a laugh and some cash in hand suddenly had to see themselves as employers in charge of small companies, with tax returns and VAT to calculate. The scene was coming out of the black economy, and becoming a legitimate business.

Like many clubbers, Mark Radcliff began to look for ways to integrate what he'd learned on the dancefloor into his working life. He worked at the advertising agency HK McCann, and in 1992 he put on a conference to explain the huge shift in attitude amongst the young to his colleagues in the advertising industry. Dave Dorrell was the main speaker. Comparing this explosion to what happened to the Woodstock generation, the DJ told them, was like comparing video pingpong to *SuperMario Brothers*. Radcliff began to tell clients that this new generation were setting up their own business structures, that they were media-literate enough to know when they were being sold to, and were *discerning* in their choices rather than blindly loyal to a certain brand. A new respect was needed for these empowered young consumers, and he began taking selected clients out to the clubs to see for themselves.

'We took them to the Drum Club, Betty Ford Clinic, and we used to do parties of our own. They couldn't believe it. Back in '92, '93, people like Coca-Cola, their mouths were hitting the floor when they saw it. They'd grown up with the Beatles, the Rolling Stones, a view of popular culture that had the pop star up here, and us down there looking up. Here the focus wasn't on the pop star, it was on the consumers.

'One of the funniest things was sitting with somebody in their forties and watching them realise why their seventeen-year-old daughter was coming in at six on a Sunday evening looking like she'd been dragged through a hedge backwards. It opened their eyes to what was happening in their own lives. They suddenly realised that this was really big, that they had to acknowledge and respond to it.'

At the end of 1991, Radcliff and his team were called in to the UK's biggest-selling newspaper, the *Sun*, to do some research into rave culture. 'They'd done those fantastic, funny articles about people biting the heads off pigeons. But some people there realised that this thing was here to stay, that a large part of their audience was young, so they were having a dig at their readers' own culture. They started doing a two-page weekend pullout about clubbing, and Pete Tong had a column for a while.

'The beginning of '92 was an interesting time. Newspapers and the brewers were starting to reassess it, and ad agencies started to pay a bit more than lip service to it. In 1990–91 when the Bob's Full House parties started and the flyers were really silly, a lot of creatives in ad agencies were going along, seeing that kind of communication and thinking, "We can do that." Outsiders who thought it was all about peace and love missed the subversive humour that was a really big part of it right from *Boy's Own*. That irreverence and silliness without having to justify yourself was a big influence. Things like the original Tango campaign, Drum cider, came out of that culture. '

Radio 1 too began a period of reassessment that would eventually lead to the vibrant programming they have now, in which dance music dominates the weekends. The national pop station which had banned all records mentioning the word 'acid', and which had always been suspicious of music made for the clubs, began a gradual change. Afraid, perhaps, of misjudging the mood again and appearing uncool, when the Shamen released their absurd 'Ebeneezer Goode' single in September 1992, the station accepted the group's story that it was about a club character and kept it on their playlist. The song, with its catchy chorus of '*Eezer Goode, Eezer Goode*', went to number one.

'We wrote this rap in which every single line was ambiguous,' laughs Mr C, who by then had become a full-time member of the group he first met at the Clink Street parties. 'It could mean he or it could mean E. And we pulled it off, lying through our teeth saying it wasn't about Ecstasy. It was so funny. When we did it on *Top of the Pops* and I'm shouting, "*E's are good, E's are good*", the producer was getting the right needle. They made us take it again and again, looking for the drug references all the time. At one point in the song, I said, "*Has anyone got any underlay?*" This was on the last and final take. It was a drug reference – speed, from Speedy Gonzales, "Riba riba, undalay underlay!" – but I denied it all.

'A week later, I'm on Radio 1 talking to Mark Goodier. He's asking if it's about Ecstasy, and I'm saying it's this Dickensian character called Ebeneezer derived from different people we know from the party scene, and giving him the whole spiel. Then he asked about the underlay, and I said, "Oh, it was a rug reference."

'So the whole thing was a complete piss-take. But it wasn't about promoting Ecstasy. On the contrary, it was taking the piss out of dodgy dealers selling dodgy pills that weren't very good: *E's the kind of geezer that shouldn't be abused*. That was when the poison started coming through, the crap pills.'

THE BREAKS

'It's like a jungle / Sometimes I really wonder / How I keep from
going under.'
    Grandmaster Flash and the Furious Five, 'The Message', 1982

'I was there when rave just went too fast. So fast that unless you
were taking elephant-size wraps you weren't going to dance to shit,
and my friends would take me to rave after rave after rave and I'd
stand up and screw my face until they played two little tunes with a
ragga influence and I'd jump up with the sound until it disappeared. Then hardcore went underground and I went with it – went
underground and evolved into jungle – and all the ravers that were
into hardcore slid into happy house or back to their garage roots.
Back to that false high, that false hope. That false love when you're
EEEEing off your face and then tripping off your nut and the music
goes: DUFF! DUFF! DUFF! DUFF! . . . House is a false sound, a
false consciousness, a false sense of reality . . . Jungle is truer to
humanity's real roots. It cuts away the falseness, gives you the ups
and the downs, the dark and the light.'
    from *Junglist*, a novel by Two Fingers and James T. Kirk, 1995[1]

The spread of E culture across Britain was astonishingly fast. At the
end of 1987, only a select few in London knew how to get their hands
on MDMA, usually buying it from a dealer they all knew. A year later,
it was widely available in every small town across the country, and a

club scene that had involved only a few thousand people in London and Manchester seemed to have enveloped the whole country.

'There was a period in the late eighties when it seemed we had everybody,' says Pete Tong. 'It was almost like the Pied Piper, as if we'd cast some magic spell over sixteen and seventeen-year-olds. It seemed that everybody left school, got their first spending power, went for their first night out, took an E and were into dance music. It just exploded.'

One nation under a groove, the youth tribes of the eighties seemed to dissolve away: everyone wore the same trainers and T-shirts, and it was no longer easy to tell the DJ from the guitarist, the student from the clubber. At a time when the political ideology was all about the individual, E culture offered a glorious communal experience, an illusion of unity that was exhilarating. But by 1990, the separate strands meshed together by this great rush of energy had already begun to unravel.

'It fragmented quite quickly,' observes DJ Dave Haslam, who left the Haçienda in 1990 to run his own nights at Manchester's Boardwalk. 'All the influences that went into house music – New York disco, Hi-NRG, Chicago, Detroit techno – were seen as being one thing, acid house. But then it all separated again. In Manchester you had people who stopped going to the Haçienda in 1989 because Mike Pickering was playing too many vocals and went off to the Thunderdome, where the Spinmasters would play Belgian instrumentals. When Graeme Park started at the Haç, he was playing hip hop, disco and house, but by 1991 he was a garage DJ.

'Instead of there being 1,500 people off their heads on a Saturday night in the Haç, by then there were probably 15,000 people in clubs dotted around Manchester, plus clubs like Quadrant Park in Liverpool, Back to Basics in Leeds. In March 1988 the whole scene was undiscovered, and within three years it was massive.'

By 1990, it was no longer possible to talk of one single 'scene', but far from weakening the growing club culture, this fragmentation only served to make it stronger. As everyone took the basic ingredients and adapted them to their own needs, backgrounds, tastes and drugs of choice, the music began to mutate endlessly, splitting off into inter-linked scenes and sub-cultures that continue to influence and feed back into each other in the most unexpected ways.

By its very nature, club culture cannot stay still. There is always a new crop of seventeen-year-olds for whom all this is fresh and new. There is always a group of more mature clubbers who resent their intrusion and so reposition themselves as more intelligent, progressive, sophisticated or mellow. The conflicts between beauty and darkness, soul and raw energy, élitism and popularism, structure and pure noise are repeated in cycles again and again. Examine any new scene closely, and inside it is already splintering and regrouping, pulling itself apart and pushing forward in the process.

The first offshoot came before acid house had even really begun. At Nicky Holloway's weekly Special Branch soul sessions in a south London pub in 1987, Gilles Peterson and Chris Bangs played jazz in the smaller room upstairs. They had always been the bad boys, the rebels, constantly threatened with the sack for smoking weed. But then came the fateful trip to Ibiza, and everything changed.

Just after his return from Ibiza that year, Nicky Holloway held a soul weekender at Rockley Sands, taking along some strobes and dry ice to go for the Balearic vibe. Johnny Walker climbed inside a speaker, beckoning to the soul boys on the dancefloor, 'Come on in! It's lovely in here!' Gilles Peterson remembers looking on in horror. 'Seeing them all flying high was quite a shock to me. *We'd* always been the druggies, and suddenly we were the lightweights.'

A little later, at a one-off party at Waterman's Arts Centre in Brentford, the two jazz DJs were booked to play after Nicky Holloway, who again played an acid house set. Although they had played comfortably alongside rare groove and rap, this was something entirely different. 'Chris and I were looking at each other going, "What are we going to do?" Because this was a different vibe to what we were used to. So Chris took the mic and said, "If that was acid house, *this* is acid jazz." We played "Iron Leg" by Mickey and the Soul Generation, which has this mad twenty-second grunge noise intro, and we whisked the varispeed from minus eight to plus eight to make it sound twisted. The crowd went bonkers!'

Acid jazz started out as a joke – the first real coverage of it was an April Fool in *i-D* in 1988, in which a few friends from the jazz dance scene crowded together in the Wag club for a photo shoot of the spoof movement. But it proved a useful marketing tool for a music that might otherwise have been left behind. 'The energy was incredible, and we wanted to be part of it, not to be the boring jazzheads,' says Peterson. 'It was about modernising what we were doing.'

Later, he was to become a convert to E culture, and his Sunday-afternoon jazz sessions at Dingwalls in north London became a curious mix of loved-up jazzers, goateed trainspotters and ravers negotiating their comedown from the night before. But despite the smiley perked up with a goatee and a beret, despite Rob Galliano's jazz raps, despite some fine records on the Talkin' Loud label, it would be a while before the kind of modern, relevant sound they were striving for would be created. In the mean time, the innovations in rave culture came from the reggae sound systems, and the hip hop breakbeat.

The two are inter-linked. Clive Campbell arrived in New York from his native Jamaica in 1967, bringing a passion for the funk records of James Brown, a knowledge of the reggae sound system tradition, and an athletic prowess that soon earned him the nickname Hercules. When he set up his own sound system in the mid-seventies, he called himself DJ Kool Herc and adapted the booming bass bins of the sound system and the funk music he loved to suit the tough South Bronx crowd. He would cut between two copies of the same record on two turntables to prolong the short drum breaks for as long as the dancefloor wished – creating the breakbeat.

As he refined the technique, Herc would search out obscure records for good percussion breaks to drive his crowd wild, covering up the labels to keep them secret. One of his most famous was the 'Apache' break, a drum section taken from a cover of the Shadows number by the Incredible Bongo Band that is still widely used twenty years later. He would also chat over records on the mic like Jamaican MCs, sending out requests for the crowd and boasting of his prowess on the decks. Soon others joined in, rapping over his beats, and an acrobatic style of break-dancing emerged, with B-boys spinning on the ground at breathtaking pace. Other DJs came along too, amongst them Joseph Saddler, aka Grandmaster Flash, a turntable virtuoso whose quick-cutting style on his 'Adventures On The Wheels Of Steel' single in 1981 influenced a generation of scratch mix DJs.

In the UK, hip hop was sold not just as a new sound but as a complete lifestyle package. The early live shows included graffitti artists, DJs, rappers, dancers and the Double Dutch girls with their extraordinary gymnastic skipping skills, but it was the movies that really captivated British youth. Many current club stars recall going to the cinema to see *Wildstyle*, *Breakdance* and *Beat Street* again and again in their early teens, checking out the trainers, the hats and the casual sportswear, the aerosol art, but most of all the dance moves. In the mid-eighties, every town shopping centre had a small group of lads gathered around a tape recorder and a square of lino, practising their spins.

'Hip hop was the first music that really brought the races together, especially in this country, because it didn't really belong to any of us, we were all borrowing it,' says Mushroom (Andrew Vowles), who in 1983 joined a new Bristol sound system called the Wild Bunch with Nellee Hooper, Grant Marshall (Daddy Gee) and graffitti artist Robert '3-D' Del Naja.[2] Hooper would later move to London, work on the ground-breaking album that would take the sound system Soul II Soul into the pop mainstream, and produce records for the likes of Bjork and Madonna. The remaining Wild Bunch members formed the equally influential Massive Attack, and from 1989 began fusing together the hip hop, sweet lover's rock reggae, booming dub basslines and quirky indie pop they'd all grown up with into a new, distinctively British sound.

When house came along, few lost their passion for breakbeats. Although the house and hip hop scenes were completely separate in the US, here they were viewed as equally fresh, futuristic electronic sounds from across the Atlantic. When British youths were inspired by acid house and the raves to begin making their own dance records at home on cheap synths and home computers, they naturally turned to the hip hop records in their collections and began using more complex breakbeats as well as the regular, programmed four-on-the-floor rhythms of house.

Liam Howlett was typical of this new breed, a hip hop fan from Braintree in Essex who was introduced to house via raves such as Sunrise and Energy. 'I liked it because everyone was on the vibe – not like the dark hip hop and ragga jams I was used to. On the hip hop scene it was about being a moody cunt and keeping to your corner. So this was a big culture shock.'[3]

In 1989 he became a regular at the Barn in Braintree, where Mr C had a weekly residency. 'I remember Liam giving me a cassette of some music he'd made,' laughs the DJ now. 'It was very cheesy sort of breakbeat stuff, and I was like, "Get rid of the breakbeats, get into the programmed rhythms, and you might get somewhere." Thank God he didn't listen to me!'

Instead, Howlett asked Keith Flint and Leeroy Thornhill, two of the Barn's most extravagant dancers, to join a band he'd already named after a Moog synthesiser. The Prodigy's first live PA was for a hundred clubbers at the Labyrinth in east London, but within weeks they were playing to a crowd of 10,000 at a Raindance rave. At the raves, new British dance acts such as N-Joi, K-Klass, Shades of Rhythm and Altern-8 could reach the kind of numbers a struggling new rock band could only dream of.

The raves didn't end when Graham Bright's bill became law. Far from it; they flourished. In 1990, a new generation of promoters came through to run legal, licensed open-air events and big parties in indoor sports halls and concert arenas, exhibition centres and leisure complexes: Raindance, Amnesia House, Storm, Rezerection, Fantazia, Living Dream, Perception and the Pure Organisation's Dance '90 and Dance '91 events all attracted young, predominantly working-class ravers in their thousands.

But despite the numbers, this scene became virtually invisible. The raves were no longer big news for the tabloids. The youth press too turned their attentions elsewhere: the style magazines were immersed in the emerging Balearic/progressive house network, while the music press focused on Madchester, and the increasingly interesting attempts of former indie groups like the Shamen to incorporate what they'd experienced in the clubs into their live shows. In 1990–91, there were the first classic albums by bands inspired by acid house: the Beloved's *Happiness*, Primal Scream's *Screamadelica*, the KLF's *The White Room*, St Etienne's *Fox Base Alpha*, and a new breed of thought-ful, dance-based electronic bands such as Orbital, the Orb, Trans-global Underground and Future Sound of London which intrigued the music papers far more than 'faceless' DJs.

A new breed of techno rebels continued the outlaw tradition of the 1989 raves, motivated not by profit but by passion, by the idea that there really was a revolution in progress. Circumventing the new law by not charging admission, new techno sound systems like Spiral Tribe began organising free parties, plugging into the old hippie free festival circuit and the nomadic, travellers' lifestyle. Their growth went largely unnoticed until a convoy of 400 vehicles rolled on to Castlemorton Common in Worcestershire on 21 May 1992, including the Spiral Tribe, Bedlam, DiY, Adrenalin and Circus Warp systems. When the TV news covered the start of the spontaneous festival, cars began rushing to the area and a riotous hundred-hour rave resulted.

The spectacle gave a desperate Tory government a moral crusade to cling to, and clauses further restricting free parties and outdoor raves were inserted into 1994's Criminal Justice Act.[4] The word 'rave' was enshrined in the British statute book, and house music defined for m'learned friends as 'Music [which] includes sounds wholly or predominantly characterised by the emission of a succession of repetitive beats.'

Yet although the implications for civil liberties were depressing and the persecution of travellers unfair, the Act had little effect on the clubs and licensed raves. The tabloids portrayed the Castlemorton flare-up as a problem caused by dirty, dole-scrounging travellers rather than clubbers up for a party – in the summer of 1992, the *Sun* in its new incarnation as the ravers' best friend covered a Fantazia rave for well over 25,000 people in glowingly positive terms.

The *business* of rave got gradually easier between 1990 and 1992, says Fantazia's James Perkins. 'In 1990 you'd have to go to court with eight experts to testify before the magistrates on everything from traffic to noise control, plus an aggressive lawyer to counter whatever stories the local police came up with – people injecting drugs with needles, possible riots, and all the other things they'd say might go on at such an event. But slowly, the authorities began to realise that organisations like Fantazia knew what they were doing.'

The music of rave also shifted radically during this time, with the emphasis moving from records made in the USA to Europe and then the UK. By 1990, techno was no longer made exclusively in Detroit. It came from Belgium, where the New Beat scene's slowed-down mixes of industrial electronica like Throbbing Gristle and Cabaret Voltaire had prepared them well to create hard-edged instrumental dance, and where the R&S label picked up on both home-grown talent and emerging new US stars such as the precocious young New Yorker Joey Beltram. Released via R&S in Europe, Beltram's rumbling instrumental 'Energy Flash' and 'Mentasm' singles were hugely influential in the UK, shamelessly sampled, reworked and used as a template for the emerging British rave sound.

Sheffield was the first British city to produce its own form of the music, with a record made by Cabaret Voltaire's Richard Kirk and Parrot, one of the DJs at the city's original house night Jive Turkey. Together they made a playful, minimal techno track to play in the club in 1989, kicking off the northern techno strain that became known as 'bleep'. Local dance specialist shop WARP released it as a single in mid-1990, and the success of Sweet Exorcist's 'Test One' led to similarly sparse, industrial-sounding dance successes from LFO, Tricky Disco, Unique 3 and Nightmares on Wax.

But DJs who played this harder mix quickly found themselves ostracised by the Balearic/deep house fraternity. 'To his credit he always booked us for his events, but I remember Nicky Holloway saying, "Listen, guys, you've got to play stuff with vocals, these rhythm tracks are boring people to tears!" ' says Fabio, who by 1990 was playing at Energy's West End club night Fun City, mixing the emerging Sheffield sound with deep US house.

'In those days you could mix everything, you could play LFO alongside a David Morales mix and it worked fine, because everything was at the same speed, basically. But gradually the bleep stuff we were playing got totally outlawed. A split happened then which led into the hardcore techno thing, and we were outlawed for many, many years.'

Meanwhile, new fusions were forming between ravers and Funki Dreds from the more progressive London sound systems. When east London duo Shut Up and Dance made '5, 6, 7, 8' in 1989, it was aimed at the jump-up reggae crowd, but became an unexpected rave hit. Their next record '£10 To Get In' (with its remix '£20 To Get In') made fun of a culture they saw as a rip-off, but the breakbeats they used also continued to find common musical ground. East London rave clubs like the Dungeons and Labyrinth increasingly began to attract an edgy but exciting mix of dope-smoking dreads and pill-popping ravers, dancing to sub-sonic dub basslines and frenetic breaks.

'A lot of different people began making music, bringing their own backgrounds to it,' says Jumping Jack Frost, a Brixton-based DJ who had played at the Sunrise and Energy raves and continued to headline at raves across the UK in the early nineties. 'There were people from a rock background, others who came out of the funk and reggae scenes, and they were all putting their own stuff into it.

'House music got bland after 1991, and we left it alone. People were going into the studio for themselves and seeing what they could come up with. We stopped playing four-to-the-floor music and started playing the breakbeats. And we got a lot of stick about it, a lot of people smirked.'

But despite sneering from outsiders, the breakbeat sound became the dominant one at the raves. Catering to a younger, more energetic crowd, the music grew harder, faster, the tempo matching the racing hearts of the dancers as the drugs got speedier too. DJs would play techno over speeded-up hip hop breaks, forcing open their Technics 1200 turntables to adjust the variable resistor governing pitch control in order to play records so fast that the vocals sounded like chipmunks on helium. The deep, heavy dub basslines moved at half-speed, vibrating through the ribcage, while the MCs screamed out messages that barely qualified as raps: 'Let's go!' 'Rush!' 'Hold tight!' Everything was designed to intensify the rush, a series of never-ending climaxes, always moving but never reaching any destination, and therefore without an end. *Harder, faster, higher, more.* Ravers had once taken drugs because they enhanced the feeling of the music; now the music seemed made to enhance the feeling of the drugs.

And the feeling was changing. Many younger ravers preferred the cheaper speed and acid to Ecstasy, but taken in quantity, the empathetic qualities of even pure MDMA fade away to be replaced by a twitchy, amphetamine rush. The user's face will often distort involuntarily as they grind teeth or chew on the inner cheek ('gurning'). Not that many of the pills being sold as Ecstasy by then contained MDMA.

At the big raves, where the sheer size of the crowd made it easier for dealers to rip off their customers without being caught, many pills contained nothing at all: £10 for an aspirin. Everywhere, the heavier MDA and speedier MDEA compounds became more common, offering a similar experience to MDMA, but without the same warmth and sociability. As one of Alexander Shulgin's original testers remarked, words can be difficult to form on a high dose of MDEA, and users tend to lapse into long periods of introverted silence.[5]

As Britain sank into the worst recession since the War, the old positivity began in any case to look false, lightweight to these new young ravers. The class of '88 and '89 had made it clear that they didn't want these sweaty, unsophisticated kids spoiling their clubs; for their part, the new generation wanted less and less to do with the fluffy escapism of house. They took their cue instead from the bleak, gritty realism of gangsta rap and the fast, coded mix of sexual innuendo, bragging and social comment then favoured by Jamaican ragga MCs.

Raving became a *mission*, a determination to push the rush, to become submerged in the music, to be consumed by it, to escape into oblivion. Ravers saw their music as 'digital terrorism'; they viewed themselves as 'nutters', enjoying the same excessive chemical intake and irreverent humour as the Balearic/progressive house clubbers, but without any of the pretentions. 'Hardcore!' the MCs would shout at rave clubs like the Eclipse in Coventry or Kinetix in Stoke-on-Trent. 'You know the score!'

Many of the early British hardcore records were crude, made on cheap synths and home computers by sampling original techno and house over breakbeats and adding dub-style breakdowns and nutty oscillating riffs. Few of the MCs at the raves and on London pirate stations such as Rush, Pulse, Destiny and Touchdown did more than bellow clichés over the beats, and there was no longer any attempt to disguise the chemicals inspiring their banter: requests would be sent out to 'all you nutters rushing out of your heads, speedfreaks out there, you know the score', or they would admit to be 'absolutely flying in the studio, 100 mph'.[6] To outsiders, this 'nosebleed techno' was a hideous, clattering cacophony of noise, but this only confirmed the music's outlaw status to its fans. They were the rejects, the ruffnecks, the real hardcore.

Virtually ignored by the media and the established record companies, the scene instead developed its own, fiercely independent infrastructure. At first many producers would press up one single copy of their track on record – an acetate, or dub-plate in the language of the reggae sound systems who had long used this as a way of keeping the music they played exclusive. As the music grew in popularity, record labels began to spring up based in provincial towns such as Romford, High Wycombe, Coventry, Northampton. Inevitably, a small scene started to grow from the Bristol sound systems, and A Guy Called Gerald also began experimenting with the sound in Manchester – much to the disappointment of his new label Sony, who had expected him to keep churning out facsimiles of 'Voodoo Ray' rather than continue to explore new territories.

In the end, this period of isolation became the scene's biggest strength. 'It put us in the position to create our own record labels and become businessmen ourselves,' shrugs Jumping Jack Frost. 'If we'd had that early exposure, maybe we wouldn't be in the position we all are now, when we can sit down and negotiate deals, we've all got offices, proper businesses.'

Detroit techno innovator Derrick May was also scathing about the hardcore sound, unable to accept that a music he had helped create, which had come from black America and had its roots in gay disco clubs, had mutated into something made by European teenagers who saw its roots in British acid clubs and raves. 'The first time we came to Britain people were wearing suits in clubs and weren't digging the music at all,' he later told *Muzik* magazine. 'Then we came back eight months later and it was total hands-in-the-air mayhem. Guys in England had started making their own music and it sort of seemed like we weren't invited to the party any more.'[7]

In response to his hostility, Shut Up and Dance showed their usual irreverent humour, taking a sample from a record by May's protégé Carl Craig, running it over the popular Amen break and releasing it as 'Derek Went Mad'. (The Amen break was originally taken from 'Amen Brother' by the Winstons, an obscure sixties soul band. In the nineties it has been used as the basis for literally thousands of hardcore and jungle records.)

This sense of fun is often forgotten now: Stafford's Altern-8 pulled off a whole series of daft publicity scams during this time, planting increasingly preposterous stories in the tabloids and culminating with the duo's Chris Peat standing for Parliament in the 1992 election. His Altern-8-ive (Hardcore) Party promised free raves funded by the poll tax, police uniforms that would include smiley badges and bandannas as part of an 1988 acid revival, Radio 3 to be changed to a national rave station 303, and a number 303 bus connecting Stafford with the Stoke rave club Shelly's on Friday and Saturday nights. With only 178 votes he failed to topple the sitting Tory MP Bill Cash, but their single 'E-Vapor-8' went top ten during election week.

Fabio points out that few of those involved in making the music had access to sophisticated studios at first. Few of them even had any musical or programming skills. 'They were young, working-class, black and white kids from council estates making these amazing, raw tunes on really basic equipment. And that's why a lot of the early stuff was really crude, two-note keyboard bashings.'

But the music quickly began to evolve as these youths began to learn their craft and push the equipment they had to the limits and beyond. Rob Playford was typical of this new breed of producer. A hip hop DJ in the mid-eighties, entering scratch mix contests in towns around his native Hertfordshire, he eventually joined a sound system and in 1988 was drawn into the acid house scene, breaking into warehouses and setting up the sound for promoters such as Ibiza and 2000AD.

When the police became more active and the raves went legal, Ibiza became a record label and Playford retreated to his home studio in Stevenage and began creating the music instead. He was one-third of the trio 2 Bad Mice, whose 'Waremouse' single helped reshape the sound towards the end of 1991. Before, hardcore records had tended to use one breakbeat looped so that it is endlessly repeated throughout, as it is on rap tracks. Acts like 2 Bad Mice began cutting up the breaks, restarting them or introducing new ones so that the rhythms constantly changed.

Soon, few breakbeats were played whole. Producers began chopping up the original beats by feeding them through samplers, dividing hi-hats from kick drums, cymbals and hand-claps, cutting them up into four, five or more pieces and then reconstructing them into complex, polyrhythmic patterns. It was still a brutal, relentless sound, enlivened by grainy, lo-fi samples of Jamaican ragga MCs or roots reggae chants, snippets of film dialogue, the killer bee/Hoover drone of Beltram's 'Mentasm'.

Once it had been used on one record, a sample would often be stolen by others and used again and again: the point was not originality, not single records, but a messy, raging collage of noise made not just from the records but from the DJs' manipulation of the sound in the mix, the MCs' raps, the sirens and horns on the dancefloor. No one claimed ownership of ideas: they were simply thrown into the pot for the pleasure of seeing what shape they took when they came out again.

By the middle of 1992, the music was getting darker, bleaker, reflecting the mood of uncertainty in the country as a whole in the post-Thatcher years. There had always been a darker flipside side to rave, a side which capitalised on those speedy jitters that verge on the edge of panic, on the alienation, the disconnected nature of the drug experience. As early as the autumn of 1989, there were events with names like Holocaust, Freakout, Schizophrenia, their flyers using horror comic graphics such as demons, skulls, metal robots and masks in a reaction to the sunny optimism elsewhere.

In 1991, 4 Hero's 'Mr Kirk's Nightmare' featured a spoken-word section in which a father is informed by the police that his seventeen-year-old son has died from a drug overdose; DJ Rap, one of the few women on the hardcore scene, nearly destroyed her career by unwittingly playing it at a Telepathy rave, just after a youth in the crowd had been stabbed.

Some found this kind of dark, urban realism preferable to the mindless optimism of the big rave anthems. Records like 'Bring On The Drumz' by Coventry's Doc Scott were like a call to arms, a relentless battering of cyber-rhythm. But many ravers complained about this growing 'moodiness' in both the music and the attitude, longing for a return to uplifting, happy 1991 anthems like Bizarre Inc's 'Playing With Knives' or K-Klass's 'Rhythm Is A Mystery'. As the scene was peaking in the summer of 1992 with the biggest raves the country had yet seen, it was fracturing from within.

The commercial success of the Prodigy's single 'Charly' in the summer of 1991 – a tune which sampled the cartoon cat from a seventies road-safety film over clattering breakbeats – led to a host of imitators covering children's TV theme tunes or using cartoon samples. This 'playground techno' only served to confirm outsiders' belief that rave was juvenile, catering to the lowest common denominator.

It was a time of reassessment for many. Altern-8 faded away as the duo concentrated on their more serious techno project, Nexus 21. After flirting briefly with ragga techno, the Prodigy moved towards a more aggressive, experimental electro-punk showcased on the 1994 album *Songs For A Jilted Generation*. Stars like Sasha and Carl Cox turned away from the rave scene and repositioned themselves as house or techno DJs.

'It became so dark that people weren't raving any more and the music was scaring you into oblivion,' says Cox, who admits the music was also running away from him. 'Grooverider would turn up with about 200 dub plates, and I'd have one. The rest of my records were white labels or released. I thought, "This has gone way past me here." '

Despite the licences, some raves were badly run: tickets were forged or promoters sold far more than the agreed numbers, leading to chronic overcrowding. Flyers often promised outrageous line-ups of big-name DJs, few of whom had actually been booked to appear. Muggings and violence were becoming commonplace at bigger events, and the drugs were getting worse.

In 1992 the smaller clubs and the raves alike were flooded with fat white pills nicknamed snowballs which administered a punch so heavy that they often rendered the user 'cabbaged' or 'monged' at the side of the dancefloor. Containing a large dose of MDA, they came from cash-strapped pharmaceutical labs in the former Communist countries of Eastern Europe. There were persistent rumours that these pills were cut with smack (they never were). But people took them anyway – even if they didn't make you feel that good, at least they made you feel *different*. As the culture accelerated ever further into chemical excess in search of that elusive top buzz, the paramedics at big events were increasingly busy, and the number of deaths attributed to Ecstasy began to rise.

The summer's biggest party was a huge Vision rave at Popham

Airfield in Hampshire for an extraordinary 38,000 people. Two hours after it ended, seventeen-year-old soldier Robert Jeffrey was found alone by the side of the A303, miles from the party, dying of dehydration after taking Ecstasy. The dreams of unity, love and universal togetherness that had fuelled that first rush in '88 and '89 had never seemed more distant.

In the next few years, the various strands of this collapsing rave scene developed into genres of their own. In the Netherlands, the music speeded up to the manic 180–250 bpm of gabber, a sound which also gained favour in Scotland. The self-explanatory happy hardcore scene began to evolve in England, and the first purist techno nights began to appear in the clubs, with DJs like Andrew Weatherall starting to specialise in the sound. Most of these scenes became overwhelmingly male, as women began to find them increasingly unappealing: rendered temporarily incapable of sex by their chemical intake, few of the lads sweating it out on the dancefloor actually seemed to notice they'd gone.

The breakbeat scene meanwhile went underground, with a London club night providing a focus for its seething energies. Rage had started at Heaven on Thursdays at the end of 1988 as another acid house night (the choice of name in a time of hippie optimism was, says promoter Kevin Millins, 'sheer perversity'). 'Rage was a little more cutting edge than Land of Oz,' says Fabio, who went there often to dance. 'The music was a lot darker. Colin Faver and Trevor Fung used to play some amazing sets in there.'

Fabio and Grooverider eventually began playing in the small upstairs bar, and one night when Fung and Faver were away, they took their mix into the main arena. 'We tore the arse off the club,' laughs Fabio. 'I've never seen a promoter look so shell-shocked about what was happening on his dancefloor.' They took over as the main DJs at the end of 1991, and made the night a laboratory for the new breakbeat science. They would play entire records at the wrong speed, play techno tracks over speeded-up hip hop breakbeats, fast-cut and mix sections of records together, forever searching for a sound they said they could *feel* but never quite reach.

Kemistry and Storm, later to become two of the scene's leading DJs, were regulars at the club. 'The first time we went to Rage, we queued three and a half hours to get in and we didn't give a damn,' Storm told Martin James in *State Of Bass*, a history of the breakbeat sound. 'We just wanted to get in that club so much. When we finally got in, we only had about an hour and a half left but it didn't matter because we knew this was something totally different. A really cutting-edge thing. We all felt the music was special even then. It had never been heard before.'[8]

Later, Kemistry brought along Goldie, a charismatic mixed-race youth from Wolverhampton in the West Midlands who had chatted her up while she was at work in the Red or Dead shoe shop. Born in 1965, Goldie's mother was Scottish, his (absent) father Jamaican. Soon his mother was gone too, leaving him in care, although she chose to keep his younger brother. In his teens, the troubled youth found a home of sorts in the emerging UK hip hop scene: a talented graffitti artist, he created paintings with Bristol's 3-D, and later had his work exhibited in New York.

He lived in New York for a while, and later Miami – setting up a business making the customised gold teeth which gave him his nickname. For a two-year period he became a Rastafarian. But the scene he found at Rage was the first to give a real focus to his restless energies. 'Everyone was just going for it. The adrenaline that was pumping around the place! Obviously we were taking Es and all that, and it was pretty hardcore. But hearing them play this hybrid of music was completely freaky. You still had the late rave stuff – Beltram's "Mentasm" – then this hybrid stuff, like an urban jungle. It was very ethnic, but it wasn't a black thing. It was an *urbanite* thing.

'It was just a mad fusion, it was very punky. I've always been the kind of kid who wanted to belong to a unit of some sort, who'd dreamed of making music. And being an outsider . . . A lot of the kids making this music were from outside of London. It was always guys who were outside of it, trying to get in to play, to make the music.'

He started creating artwork for the Reinforced label, and made his first record – sampling vocals by Phil Collins and laying them over the Amen break. Along with Reinforced's Mark and Dego (who record together as 4 Hero), Goldie would sit in the studio for days on end, taking drugs, experimenting with sounds, forcing the technology beyond what it was designed to do in search of the ghosts in the machine.

Goldie tells a story about Doc Scott and the Reinforced crew playing sonic ping-pong with sounds taken from 'Mentasm' and early tracks by Detroit's Underground Resistance, re-sampling them from each other's records again and again until someone had the idea of hiring in a Juno 2 synthesiser and simply re-creating the original riffs. But what they heard disappointed them: it was too clean, too sterile.

'We needed the white noise and the dirty crustiness within the sample that made it the sound it was. It had become its own sound, nothing like the original. We'd ripped it apart, played table tennis with it, and it became something completely different in the process. That clean sound in the Juno 2 wasn't what I was looking for. We wanted something else, the ghost in the machine that had given it its distortion.'

This music first began to be called jungle early in 1992, although Jumping Jack Frost says the word was used by some DJs to describe the bass-heavy house records made by young Britons such as Kid Bachelor as early as 1989: 'Bang Your Mind' by Bachelor's group Bang the Party is the first he recalls being called tribal house or jungle. The origins of the term are disputed (and indeed many, including the influential Shut Up and Dance, feel it is racist), but Fabio says it came from the dancefloor. At Rage, the cries of 'Jungle!' were led by a proud black dread called Danny Jungle, who would dance on the podiums and lead the crowd in the chant, just as Gary Haisman had screamed 'Acieed!' there four years before.

It was a blaggers' music, made up of debris gathered by youths for whom ducking and diving was a way of life after growing up through four terms of Conservative rule. One of the aliases Goldie used to release records in 1992 was Rufige Kru, and 'rufige' is what he says the music was built from: 'The shit left over from the surface, that's all it ever was. I just scraped the top of a stagnant pool and put it all together.' Even the name Metalheadz is taken, from a phrase Grooverider used on his radio show. 'We were bouncing off each other. It was the young bouncing against each other rather than off the older generation. We thought, "Fuck them, let's do our own thing." And it created something different altogether.'

The DJs were also part of this process, their mixes in the club often turning the music into something different again: on the dancefloor at Rage, the breakbeat scientists heard new ghosts on records they had made, some coming out of the speakers, some from their heads due to the drugs.

'I remember one particular moment hearing Doc Scott in the mix with one of my tunes, and me and Scotty looking at each other completely E'd out of our brains and hearing something completely deranged,' says Goldie. 'At that point neither tune was our own. It belonged to them, to Fabio and Groove, in the mix. That fusion, the chemical reaction that happened, was what made us want to make more music. For everyone, they were the makers. It was like worker bees, you wanted to keep taking it back to the hive.'

You didn't have to have a record released to have it played at Rage. It cost £30 to cut a dub plate, and the point was not to get rich, but to have your music played, to be somebody in this small, tight world. Like the graffitti tags that cover the walls of many inner-city housing estates, it was about being *recognised*, making your mark. Goldie would lovingly customise his acetates with a scalpel, cutting through the plastic to the metal in the centre to carve his Metalheadz logo, then cutting a message into the run-out groove, or a simple dedication to the DJs. If the track was played, and got a good response from the crowd, he would get the cash together to have a few records pressed, taking them round the shops himself in the battered Ford Sierra he'd bought from his friend Doc Scott.

Later, through the music he made, Goldie would form a close friendship with Fabio and Grooverider. But at first he would climb the stairs on to Heaven's narrow balcony to stand by the DJ booth above the dancefloor and just watch, his face pressed against the wire mesh that separated DJs from clubbers. 'At first I was this deranged kid with gold teeth shining, this nutter talking at a million miles an hour. I remember clutching the cage, watching Fabio or Groove take the record I'd made out of the box and put it on the deck and thinking, "Fuck, fuck!" And you'd just run downstairs [on to the dancefloor] with sweaty palms, you'd close your eyes and be coming up on an E and that'd be it, game over.'

'Terminator' was the record Goldie made in homage to Groove-rider, the forty-foot graffitti art masterpiece he'd dreamed of creating to make his mark on the scene. A journey into the heart of darkness, it was an evil terrordome of sound, a bad trip into the future. Many DJs contributed to the evolution of the breakbeat sound, many raves and clubs, many backroom/bedroom producers. But if you had to pin-point the exact moment hardcore morphed into something new, if you had to locate the birth of drum'n'bass, it would probably be the night 'Terminator' was first played in Rage, and those robotic-sounding rhythms coiled out of Heaven's huge system.

The breaks on the track had been fed through an expensive piece of studio equipment designed to be used for live guitars and vocals rather than digital samples. Goldie and engineer Mark Rutherford used it to make the drums sound faster without changing speed. 'We were joy-riding the technology, like a twelve-year-old driving a Ferrari or a graffiti kid pushing the aerosol can to make the nozzle spray wide or thin. I put analogue and digital together to create an abyss.'

Others took the ball and ran with it immediately, mixing it with samples snatched from horror movies and deliberately ugly sounds in a movement some called darkcore. 'For us it was like rebelling with the music, we wanted to just rip into people's souls,' explains Goldie. 'We were angry, we were rejects, we were fucked off, and we wanted to release our demons, all that stress of that time, into the music. And there were little frictions within the dance, people falling out. That dark era happened because it was winter and it was time for that, but also because Rage was closing. It was always under threat, and we were like Greenpeace – we wanted to tie ourselves to the decks and fight to keep it open.'

There are all kinds of conspiracy theories as to why Rage closed in March 1993. The word was that the gay clubbers didn't like it in their venue. Or that it was too black. Or that the house scene was running scared. Fabio says the truth is more pedestrian: the future shock of the sound was too much for many of the regulars. 'We totally alienated the Rage faithful. It got so ghettoised. A lot of people stopped coming down, and it got a reputation as a druggy, ragga place where the craziest music was being played. But the vibe in Rage then was absolutely amazing.'

After the night closed, Fabio and Grooverider began to spend much of their time in the Midlands, where the hardcore sound was as strong as ever and clubs like Shelly's and the Eclipse provided an eager audience for their evolving sound. 'The Eclipse was the northern version of Rage, it was absolutely seething in there, hardcore heaven. It was totally the opposite of the house crowd, no girls in stilettos. It was hands in the air with gloves, tops off, little hardcore ravers with whistles and horns. And they were so up for the music.'

As ever, the birth of a new music coincides with the arrival of new technology, and drum'n'bass came about partly due to the Akai S1000 sampler. Launched in 1989, it gave breakbeat pioneers access to techniques that were previously only available in the most hi-tech, expensive recording studios, allowing them to manipulate their sampled beats as never before.

One of its features was the ability to time-stretch, to make a sample longer or shorter without changing the quality of the sound. (Normally, if we play a record faster, the pitch goes up so the sound is higher; if we slow it down, it sounds deeper.) This had clear professional applications: the voice-over on an advertisement, say, or a TV news clip, could be made to fit the visuals exactly. But as ever, the equipment was misused in ways the makers never intended to produce the metallic, staccato rhythms that we now call drum'n'bass.

Rob Playford, who was later to collaborate with Goldie on his classic album *Timeless*, explains the technique. 'We didn't want to change things without affecting the sound quality. We actually used it to *affect* the sound quality. We did exactly the opposite of what they made it for.

'If you don't go with Akai's suggested pre-sets, you get what in their eyes is a very bad side-effect. Time-stretching works by cutting up the sound into thousands, millions of little pieces, and then puts a gap between each one to make it longer. It's like cutting film up. If you put a blank frame between each frame you'd shot, it would create a strobing effect, which is what we do. We strobe the sound and make it last for twice as long.

'Then we double the pitch of it, increase it by a whole octave. So it plays for the same length of time it originally did, but it's effectively an octave higher so it sounds like it has a lot more energy to it, and it has this metallic, broken-up sound. That was the unique thing – this very metallic, robotic-sounding breakbeat which no one had ever done before.'

In London, AWOL (A Way of Life) became the main focus for the scene after Rage closed. Promoted by the team behind the World Dance raves, it opened from 10 p.m. to 10 a.m. at the Paradise Club in Islington every Saturday from March 1992, with a monthly extension till 1 p.m. It was initially conceived as a hardcore *and* house club, with DJs like Ritchie Fingers, Jeremy Healy and Trevor Fung playing in the club's garage room early on. But it soon became a forum for the emerging sound, an intense, serious club where the crowd loved the music with a passion but the emphasis was on a self-contained *control* on the dancefloor rather than hands-in-the-air abandon and sweaty hugs.

The resident DJs Randall, Mickey Finn, Darren Jay, Kenny Ken and Dr S Gachet played every week without fail unless they were working overseas, and people travelled from all over the country to hear music that it was impossible to hear elsewhere. Nearly everything played at the club was on dub plate, with special mixes being created by producers exclusively for specific DJs. As with the reggae sound systems, if the crowd approved of a track they would shout for it to be played again and again, the MCs on the mic taking up their chants of 'rewind, rewind' until the DJ cued it up once more.

'What used to motivate the DJs so much is that they were playing to their peers,' says AWOL's Chris Leonard. 'You'd look round the crowd at the Paradise Club later on in the morning, after they'd done their work elsewhere, and there would be Grooverider, Fabio, the Suburban Base lot, Reinforced – the people who have become the very basis of the drum'n'bass scene. If they'd made a new record, they'd come down with it on dub plate.

'It was such a tight, gelling thing. Anybody who was making music wanted it tested at AWOL, and the only way you could do that was by giving it to one of those five DJs. So everyone did an AWOL mix, a VIP mix or a dub plate, and you'd hear that there on an exclusive basis. And if the crowd liked it, there'd be horns, whistles, shouting, scream-ing, banging on the floor, jogging on the record desk, getting it rewound and played again and again and again.'

'That was definitely a landmark in the scene, no doubt about it,' adds Jay, an AWOL regular from Maidstone whose magazine *Atmosphere* has charted the journey from hardcore to drum'n'bass. 'It was a school of music, a testing ground, and the crowd knew that. There was an atmosphere of unity, but not cheesy. Everyone was on the same wavelength, everyone was there for the same reason: to hear new music played by the scene's finest.'

The following for the ragga strain of jungle had been growing steadily during this period. In April 1992, SL2's 'On A Ragga Tip' took the sound into the singles charts, eventually selling over 200,000 copies. The overlap of reggae bass, breakbeats and ragga chants drew black clubbers to the rave scene in significant numbers for the first time, and Jumping Jack Frost says that his mix finally began to gain approval from his home crowd.

'Living in Brixton, where there's a heavy black, West Indian vibe, I'd get a lot of people saying I was playing gay music. "What are you doing, man?" It was only OK when the drum'n'bass, jungle came in. Up till that point it was never OK, never. Then I'd get people saying they checked some of the tunes I was playing.'

The first pure jungle raves came in the summer of 1993, when Ibiza Records put together a Jungle Fever tour of venues in London and the south-east in conjunction with Kool FM, an east London-based pirate which had made the sound its own. In keeping with the dark mood, Gothic statues, gravestones and coffins formed part of the décor. That summer saw the start too of the popular Jungle Splash nights at the Roller Express in Edmonton, north London, where DJs would hold sound clash-style contests, competing for the crowd's loud approval from a boxing ring in the middle of the arena.

At jungle raves, the dancefloor moved not to the impossibly fast 160 bpm clatter of the breakbeats but to the slow, sensuous 85 bpm bassline. Dressed in skimpy 'batty rider' shorts, thigh-high boots, ornate plaited hairstyles and tight, skimpy clothes, the women would dance in groups, celebrating their sexuality in a similar way to girls in the house clubs at that time. The men favoured bright, loud designer gear (Versace and Moschino were big favourites) and plenty of gold: flash in the face of recession, consumerism as defiance.

This emerging scene was viewed with suspicion from the house scene, where it was seen as dangerous, alien and frankly scary. There were frequent shootings at jungle events, the rumour mill insisted, and the sweet, sickly smell of crack was unavoidable. There *was* violence at some events, and the muggings that had become common-place at house/techno raves continued at jungle events. Crack cocaine was starting to get a grip in Britain's inner cities, and its presence in the rave was acknowledged by records such as DJ Ron's 1993 single 'Crackman On The Line' – although when it came to class-A sub-stances, a raid on any big house night would have paid off far more handsomely than a raid on a jungle club.

What these rumours expressed was an unvoiced fear: of the new, of the black, of the underclass, of anything that might disturb the fluffy Cloud-cuckoo-land of the E generation. For outsiders, the scene was also difficult to access: it was hard to know who were the stars, which records to buy, and after their years in exile the scene's inner circle were distrustful of the media, often unwilling to co-operate even when coverage was offered.

The music finally broke into the mainstream in the summer of 1994, with two ragga-style hits: Shy FX and UK Apache's 'Original Nuttah' and 'Incredible' by M Beat with General Levy. The take-up was instant: within weeks, Zig and Zag, the puppets on Channel 4's *The Big Breakfast*, had taken up Levy's chant of '*Booyaka, booyaka*'. Breakbeats were featured in advertising, and the big house nights were quick to offer a taste of the music in their 'alternative' back rooms.

But the music was already moving on, with producers switching from dark to light with a more mellow sound that was inevitably labelled 'ambient' or 'intelligent' jungle. The percussion breaks were now so fast that they bypassed the body completely, their shifting, ever-changing patterns swirling around at hyperspeed to form a backdrop for sweeping strings, soul diva vocals, jazz improvisations, dreamy synth sounds and a calm, deep bassline that anchored the listener into the eye of a quiet storm.

In October 1994, LTJ Bukem cemented this transition from jungle to drum'n'bass at Speed, a small West End night at the former Milk Bar, which had been repainted and renamed Mars. Bukem's lush, mellow soundscapes had marginalised him in bigger venues, and he and Fabio had opened Speed simply to give themselves a place to play: 'There was a much mellower underground vibe coming through, I was collecting this stuff, and Speed was somewhere to just play a couple of tunes on a Thursday night,' says Fabio. 'And it all went mad, it started again.'

Goldie had become the first jungle artist to sign to a major label, and his first single via Pete Tong's Ffrr subsidiary of London Records was 'Inner City Life', a breakbeat symphony in which the soul vocals of Diane Charlemagne floated like the song of an urban siren. It became one of Speed's signature tunes, and soon the club was attracting a capacity crowd. Female clubbers bored of the mainstream house clubs but alienated by the maleness of the specialist techno nights embraced the music, finding it not just fresh but sexy. Followers of jazz, soul, reggae and all kinds of other club strands found echoes of the music they loved in the mix. For many, this new sound felt like the home they'd been searching for.

'Drum'n'bass is like meditation,' says Louise Rhodes, a Manchester-based singer who formed her group Lamb after finally finding the framework she'd been seeking for her ethereal songs. 'It's got that calmness. It never gets repetitive, it's always changing and it's always fluid, and that's what's brilliant about it. People don't realise how much intelligence it takes to make those records, to programme those drums, because they're always changing.'

'If we could have had a music to go with acid jazz when we first came up with the idea, that would have been it,' says Gilles Peterson of the music he heard at Speed. 'I loved the attitude, that it was really open, honest and *passionate* about the music. The house scene had become corporate and a lot of people weren't really into it any more, it was just a business. And also drum'n'bass was multi-cultural, and to see clubs mixed again like that was really fresh. I hadn't experienced that kind of atmosphere for a long, long time, and it really excited me again.'

'It was a breath of fresh air, because for years and years everyone had gone for this high-impact stuff,' adds Fabio. 'But when it got out that there was something fresh happening at Speed, all the A&R men descended on the place. There were nights there'd be twenty of them propping up the bar, picking who they wanted to sign.

'It got so famous that it dissolved, crumbled under the pressure. Suddenly everyone wanted to get in: Bjork, Tricky, Arthur Baker and Carl Craig were in there, Oasis got turned away. It was cool, but it was only a little club and everyone thought it was a place where the stars went, that was really hard to get in, so all the real street people stopped coming. It was really sad, because there were nights there that were as good as anywhere I've ever played, when the atmosphere was unbelievable.'

This was the first new dance sound ever to emerge from Britain, the first that our club culture can truly claim to have invented. It closes the circle between Jamaica, America and Britain, bringing together all the different strands of black music that have shaped our club culture over the past twenty years and remaking them into something new. In retrospect, the frantic scene-hopping of eighties clubland, the jumping from jazz to rap to ska and funk, can all be seen to be leading up to this: the creation of identities that are British, that reflect our experiences growing up in multi-cultural cities.

A prodigiously talented vocalist, Cleveland Watkiss grew up in east London listening to reggae sound systems like Jah Shaka and Fatman before becoming involved in the eighties jazz scene, forming his own quartet and singing with the Jazz Warriors, a big band set up to nurture black British talent. When he first heard jungle at a rave, it was the deep, rumbling dub bass that instantly grabbed him. Then, at Speed, he found a sound that could finally pull together all of the disconnected parts of his musical life.

'Where I live in Hackney, you'll encounter every culture from Hasidic Jews to Hindus. Walk that stretch from Bethnal Green to Camden, and you'll meet just about every nationality. I pick all those elements up, it's in the air. I knew there was something that was going to come from all that was going on, a music that reflects the diversity of cultures in Britain.'

He began to work with Goldie's Metalheadz collective, MCing over the music live at their Sunday-night sessions at the Blue Note club in east London in 1985, rapping, singing and scatting. 'It was a great platform for me to really explore my voice, and gave me a confidence I'd never felt before. That music opened up a lot of melodic ideas to me, because it's very abstract, harmonically and rhythmically. It opened up so many ways to go with your voice. I feel comfortable, settled now. It's all fused together.

'It was an amazing experience. A friend of mine in her sixties came, and she described it as a real tribal gathering, she felt it almost had a church-like feel to it. Devotional. It wasn't aggressive – it was a small space, but everyone found their space, everyone knew their space. It was hot, intense. For a lot of people it felt like, "Wow, this is it! This is the *British* sound we've been looking for." '

Drum'n'bass may be the first music where we can meet, create, dance, fight and fall out (the latter two are important too, for this is not utopia, just a club scene) on something approaching equal terms. Which is why, from ragga rapper UK Apache to Anokha, the club/musical project initiated by classically trained tabla player Talvin Singh, British Asians have for the first time played a major, conspicuous role in the evolution of a new movement.

The breakbeat tradition drum'n'bass helped preserve has paved the way for big beat, a genre named after the Brighton club night Big Beat Boutique but which is now used to describe any kind of eclectic, breakbeat-led dance music. The time-stretching techniques drum'n'bass pioneered were later adapted to great effect by the speed garage movement, in which DJs who kept the faith with the original garage sound adapted it to the urban, dressy, mainly black crowd at clubs like Twice As Nice at the Coliseum in south London. Big beat was a sound spread by the music press, by a young, mainly white audience into boozy fun nights on the dancefloor. It has few pretensions, and is all the more enjoyable for it. The rise of underground garage came once more through the London pirates, and may well revitalise mainstream house nights across the country. More turns of the wheel, more revolutions, cycles, reinventions.

Goldie has a range of Metalheadz clothing and trainers now. He is writing soundtracks to Hollywood movies. He is taking *roles* in Hollywood movies. Few of the pioneers are now without major record deals. Fabio and Grooverider are on Radio 1. Jumping Jack Frost fronts one of Kiss FM's most popular shows. Bristol's Roni Size and Reprazent won the prestigious Mercury Music Prize for best British album in 1997, giving the music a new veneer of critical respectability, and also helping it reach a new audience outside the clubs. Drum'n'bass is now another flavour for pop acts to appropriate, another background noise for ads and trailers, but it also remains elusive, restless and moving.

'Drum'n'bass will always change its cloak, but underneath it will always be one dark wolf,' says Goldie. 'The code this music makes is the weirdest thing. I can hear twenty bars of any tune and tell you whose record it is. It's no different to looking at graffiti. The transit authorities thought it was a bunch of kids making a mess, but each of those writers knew all of those fonts, they knew whose wildstyle it was.

'With drum'n'bass, everyone contributed, made the whole thing fuse and happen, and it's just kicked into another level. The music became the Betty Ford Clinic for a lot of us. Making the music *was* the drug. Audible drugs. I don't have to take Es any more because I can hear that music and still get a kick from it.

'And look at us all now, this little dirty breakbeat scene from sweaty clubs that they said would never get anywhere. It's a beauty, and I'm proud to be part of it.'

SUPERCLUBS

London, September 1991

London clubber Justin Berkmann arrived in New York in 1986, at the start of a world tour he was undertaking to learn his father's wine business, sampling and buying. But then he went to the Paradise Garage, and everything changed. 'As soon as I heard the system and heard Larry Levan playing, I knew what I wanted to do, and I've never really questioned it since. I called my dad and said, "Forget the wine, I'm going to become a DJ." '

Berkmann stayed in Manhattan and went to the club regularly until it closed, then promoted a few nights of his own before returning to London just as acid house broke big. Slotting comfortably into the growing scene, he played at MFI, Spectrum, Apocalypse Now and Back to the Future, and held down a residency at Heaven's Garage night. And to anyone who would listen, he talked about how London needed a club like the Paradise Garage.

One night, Humphrey Waterhouse listened closer than most. He took the idea to James Palumbo, his best friend from Eton and Oxford. The son of the former Arts Council chairman and multi-millionaire Lord Palumbo, James had gone into the City after reading history at Oxford, starting at Merrill Lynch as a bond dealer, becoming managing director of Morgan Grenfell's property division at the age of twenty-seven, then working as a protégé of the charismatic banker George McGann, whose company specialised in hostile takeovers.

After paying tax on his City earnings, Palumbo had about £500,000 in the bank by 1990. Berkmann persuaded him to invest half of it in his club. 'I'd never been to a nightclub,' admits Palumbo. 'But Justin was so passionate. In the eighties there were a lot of arseholes like me who made big bonuses who would put up a couple of hundred thousand into a restaurant or a wine bar or somebody else's business. And normally they all go disastrously wrong.'

It took a while to find a suitable site. Berkmann and Waterhouse systematically searched non-residential areas around the capital until they found a disused warehouse in the run-down, largely unloved area around the Elephant and Castle roundabout just south of the Thames. 'It had dead pigeons in it, the roof was falling down,' says Palumbo. 'It was shocking. You couldn't even access it then because there was a garage in front of it – you had to go through a little door. But Justin knew that this was the right site.'

To choose a name for the venue, the three men each wrote down their ideas and read them out loud: Quatermass and the Pit, Outland, Lucifer's, Get Off My Foot, the Ghost and Mister Chicken, Biscuit Eater, and the Mad Axeman on Acid were some of the more surreal suggestions. Rejecting these, they divided a page in half, wrote words describing organisations on one side, and then words describing music on the other. Combining them, they got ideas like Organisation of Beat, Association of Rhythm . . . then Ministry of Sound.

All they needed now was an all-night licence. No London club had ever been granted a twenty-four hour music and dance licence before, but they went to endless meetings with their solicitor, working out what the objections would be and finding solutions. They would have a metal detector on the door to search for weapons, an elaborate membership system, entry for over-twenty-ones only, no alcohol after 3 a.m. They would get clubbers to testify that there was a demand for all-night clubbing, and to explain that the places they danced in now were unsafe, unregulated and illegal.

On the night of their hearing, a team from the Clink Street warehouse that had housed RIP in 1988 were applying too, and the men from the Ministry listened while the police representative poured out his tales of acid house and drugs.

'When he was asked to describe the difference between ravers and normal people he said, "Well, they wear really bright clothes", recalls Berkmann. 'There was an African woman on the panel wearing really bright African clothes with a head-dress. And she said, "What, like me?" Clink Street didn't stand a hope in hell – there's no parking there, and lots of residents – but it was good because they made us look really professional.

'Our hearing didn't start till two in the morning. They were going to adjourn it, but decided to get it over with. We had five professionals, then twenty more witnesses who were ravers, just friends of mine, to prove there was a demand. But I think we only called two professionals and two friends. I guess the mood was ready. We got out of there at five in the morning with the licence.'

One of the rumours afterwards was that Palumbo had swung the licence through his father's government contacts. But Southwark was a Labour council, Palumbo didn't speak at the hearing, and he has been estranged from his father since leaving home at the age of eighteen. (He has since sued Lord Palumbo over his management of the family trust fund, a matter which has now been settled out of court.) And with the pay party units finding the battle against the illegal raves increasingly expensive, the mood *was* ready – Turnmills in Clerkenwell was also granted a twenty-four hour licence around this time. Since it was already open, it became the first venue in London to be legally open all hours.

It took twelve weeks to convert the Ministry's warehouse into a club. The sound system came from New York, of course, built by the company established by Richard Long, creator of the Paradise Garage's mighty system. The opening on 21 September 1991 was deliberately low-key, with very little press to promote it, but the club's reputation spread rapidly by word of mouth. Every Friday and Saturday in the following months it played host to some of the best DJs in the world, the originators of the New York and Chicago undergrounds, at prices that would make today's promoters weep.

Justin Berkmann kept a list of names and fees: Bobby Konders, DJ Camacho (£200); Claudio Cocolutto, Benji Candelario (£300); Mike 'Hitman' Wilson (£350); Pal Joey, Victor Rosardo, Roger Sanchez, Kenny Carpenter (£400); Danny Tenaglia (£450); Todd Terry (£550); François Kervorkian, DJ Pierre (£650); David Morales, Masters at

Work, Frankie Knuckles, Tony Humphries (£750).

Most important of all, of course, was Larry Levan (£400). Prior to the opening, Berkmann flew over to New York, and eventually met his hero at the Shelter club, where 'he was asleep out of his mind on the sofa'. After agreeing to play, the DJ arrived in London eight days late, with no records. He had to borrow music from other DJs, but none of that mattered.

'His first record was Gwen Guthrie's "It Should Have Been Me" and the system just came to life,' says Berkmann, his face shining at the memory. 'It was like going from black-and-white to colour. He just had this ability to make it sparkle. He stayed for three months, we spent a lot of time down there tweaking the system, talking. He taught me about the *texture* of sound, and the ability to add colours or a third dimension to it by continually changing the frequencies.'

Little more than a bare warehouse when it opened, the Ministry nonetheless set new standards in Britain: ravers were ready to go back into clubs, but not to go back to the old zig-zag carpets, fake glitz and plastic palm trees. At the Ministry, it was the mighty sound system which drew the crowds, and the music played on it. But despite its growing reputation, by the end of 1992, the club was struggling financially. Palumbo moved in full time, persuading Mark Rodol to join him. A chartered surveyor making a more than comfortable living specialising in restaurant properties in the West End, Rodol was also a regular at the Ministry and had promoted a small club night of his own.

It was, he admits, an odd career move. 'I went from working 9.30 to 5 in a nice office overlooking Green Park and driving a company BMW, to standing in the Elephant and Castle at three in the morning having my life threatened by a bouncer I'd caught with a bag of Ecstasy, and then driving home in my brother's Mini Metro.'

They began to install more rigorous stock-taking, straighten out the books, bring in more commercially minded promoters to pack out the nights and set up merchandising and record deals. But slowly, they also began to realise that there was a more serious problem that had to be confronted if they wanted to run a legitimate business: the organised drug dealing.

Since the club explosion of the late eighties, the drugs trade in

British clubs has been increasingly lucrative. A big club represents a potential drug market worth far more than the bar take or the door money combined, and the best way for criminal firms to control the dealing inside a club is to control the security. Bouncers can then let in the dealers under their protection without searches, while barring any competition. These dealers will often have their own regular pitches inside, areas that tend to be mysteriously free of security staff.

This is still commonplace. Promoters who try to interfere with such operations are frequently threatened, and although it is hard to get anyone to discuss it on the record, privately many admit that they are controlled by their security rather than the other way round. 'I have no choice,' one club owner told me in 1997. 'I pay these people to stand on the door and keep trouble out, or I have them outside waving guns, threatening staff and being a big part of that trouble.'

Since it is difficult to admit to the authorities that your venue is rife with drugs, it can also be hard to report to the police what is happening without risking closure. Even if they are sympathetic, they rarely intervene: the policing of a nightclub is effectively the job of the individual named on the licence.

There is, of course, another worry for promoters. 'We did wonder whether people would stop coming if we stopped organised drug-dealing,' admits Rodol. 'But we wanted to take a long-term view of what we were doing, not for six months' time but six *years*' time, and we needed to be in control of the club, particularly as we were getting involved in other things: records, merchandise.'

It was a massive culture shock for Palumbo, who has never taken illegal drugs, never experienced the euphoria of a club scene unfolding to its peak. He experienced the side of E culture that is hidden from those on the dancefloor, or from clubbers buying ten pills to share with their mates who see the trade as largely benign. And what he saw was frankly terrifying: 'I was shocked when I worked out what was going on. I was sitting here in fear of my life as we were going through this thing, and you are disabled. Mentally, physically, emotionally. There's no point in doing anything, because you could get stabbed.'

'I used to live in the caretaker's flat at the top of this huge office building in Savile Row,' adds Rodol. 'I'd start walking up these stairs when I came home from the Ministry at five in the morning, and at the top of each flight I'd turn and wonder if there was going to be someone standing there with a shotgun ready to blow my head off. Then, after a while, you resign yourself to the fact that you've gone over the edge, and if you're going to get shot, you will. This immune system kicks in – you cannot go on living your life being nervous about every corner that you turn.'

It should be made clear that no charges were ever brought against any employees of the club at that time. It should also be stressed that nothing was happening at the Ministry in the early nineties that wasn't happening in other clubs, many of whom have yet to fight the same battles. A story in the *News of the World* in September 1993 claimed that Chris Raal, one of the bouncers working on the Ministry's door at that time, was wanted in connection with a murder in South Africa, while another, Mark Rothermel, had been sentenced to six years for hacking the head and hands off the body of a murdered youth to help conceal the crime.[1] With no central registration scheme for security staff, despite the best efforts of managers people like this continue to work the doors not just of the independent dance clubs but of establishments owned by the leisure chains and big breweries.

But no longer at the Ministry. It now has a highly paid professional door team, all of whom are checked for criminal records. The team who work on the door outside come down from Birmingham every weekend, making it harder for London-based villains to intimidate them. Although smaller venues could not afford the sums the Ministry spends to keep its door clean, the systems and checks it has developed serve as a model for other large clubs.

It is, of course, impossible to prevent people carrying pills or wraps into a club in their underwear, and obviously promoters cannot control what their customers choose to swallow before they come in. There are still inevitably some illegal drugs in the Ministry, as there are in any club in Britain. Drugs are rife in Britain's *prisons*, let alone our nightclubs. But there is no organised crime. No fear. Some would say there is less excitement too, but everything has a price.

The Ministry, like all well-run clubs, has agreed a code of practice with the local police. Clubbers caught with one or two pills for personal use will have their drugs confiscated and put in an amnesty box for collection by the police. Anyone caught with more is handed over to the authorities. Like the promoters of Cream, who have a similar agreement with their local force, Mark Rodol says this can cause discomfort at times. 'We all know from when we used to go out that there's one guy who buys everyone's Es for them, or who can't afford to go out and so he buys five pills and sells three. And it's just sad. But most people know now not to do it here, that the Ministry of Sound is so high profile that if you *do* get caught, the police get called.'

Meanwhile, the Ministry has grown. It owns a thriving record label, has a radio show that is broadcast in over a dozen countries, a magazine, an Internet site, a shop, a DJ agency, a tour team that will stage 150 events around the world in 1998, a clothing/merchandising business, and a sponsorship team talking to brands who want to be involved in club culture. They employ eighty-five people full time and a further thirty or so part time, many of them in their early twenties.

The Ministry was the first club to seek sponsorship from a major brand, organising a tour of colleges and a rave for 8,000 people at Wembley under the banner of Pepsi. 'I remember walking into Pepsi's office with James in 1993, and they didn't know who we were,' says Rodol. 'They were incredibly nervous. Now you have people controlling brands and marketing and media spend who were down here on a Saturday night five years ago completely losing their mind and understand it all.

'When we did that Pepsi tour in 1994, we got absolutely slated. Now you only have to go through *Mixmag* and see who isn't sponsored in one shape or form. Brands now realise that clubs are the places to hit eighteen- to twenty-four-year-olds.'

James Palumbo has done much to make nightclubs a legitimate, respectable business, and other clubs have profited by following his lead. But he is not well liked in his industry. He is not One of Us. He has never met Boy George or Pete Tong, the DJs who mix his best-selling CDs. He has never been to a club and danced purely for fun. His passion is for opera, his huge CD collection all classical. The life-sized cardboard cut-out of his *Star Trek* hero Captain Jean-Luc Picard which stands in his glass office at the Ministry is an uncharacteristic show of frivolity: Palumbo is fond of saying that his team stay ahead by working harder.

The company's mission statement is prominently displayed around the walls of its bustling offices: 'We are building a global entertainment business, based on a strong aspirational brand, respected for its creativity and quality. The Ministry of Sound team will be more professional, hard-working and innovative than any other on the planet.'

The Ministry of Sound's turnover in 1996/7 was £20 million: £3.5 million from the club, £12.5 million from the label, a further £4 million from the tours, merchandising, media and sponsorship. For James Palumbo, this is nowhere near enough.

Mansfield, March 1992

Geoff Oakes was first taken to the Wigan Casino when he was fifteen. It was a scary experience: changing trains at Crewe, walking through Wigan town centre at night being jeered by the drunks as the pubs closed, the crush in the queue. But then he walked on to the balcony, looked down at the seething mass on the dancefloor below, and that was it. 'I went through four or five crazy years there, then when it finished in 1981, I was condemned to years of going to Ritzy-type clubs with my mates, who weren't really my mates. Their idea of a good night out was standing at the bar until half an hour before closing time, then venturing on to the dancefloor and asking a girl to dance so they could go home with her.

'Then one night in 1988 some guys asked me to go to the Haçienda. It was a Friday, I walked in and it was exactly the same feeling I got when I first went to Wigan ten years earlier. I was just blown away by it. For two or three years, it was phenomenal there.'

When the Haçienda began to turn sour, Manchester-based club photographer Gary McClarnan took over Shelly's Lazerdome in Stoke-on-Trent on Friday nights, installing Sasha as the resident. One of the first nights to take the atmosphere of the rave indoors into a club, Delight was a genuine phenomenon: long queues outside at opening time, full-on tops-off, airhorns and whistles abandon inside. Having built his reputation at Blackburn and the illegal raves in the Midlands, Sasha frequently shared a bill with hardcore DJs at the raves, but he usually played at the end of the night, the crowd hanging on to hear his energetic mix of banging Italia house piano riffs, techno and house.

He was revered like no other DJ, bootlegged tapes of his set changing hands for £10 or more a time. Such mix tapes were common in the early nineties, sold by specialist record or clubwear shops who did a brisk under-the-counter trade despite the often poor sound quality. (DJs rarely got paid for them; few of the artists whose records were played on them rarely knew that such tapes existed, let alone got a royalty cheque.)

When *Mixmag* put Sasha on their cover in 1991, they called him the 'son of God' – a fair assessment of his standing with many of his fans, although it wasn't a title he relished. 'It was weird. I didn't really handle it very well. I wasn't prepared for travelling round the country and complete strangers giving me shit for the article. I had panic attacks and I couldn't handle all the attention.'

After Shelly's every week, about forty people would travel in a convoy to Geoff Oakes' two-bedroomed cottage near Stoke, which they turned into their own private club. It even had a name, the Broken Table, in homage to the original Northern Soul club the Twisted Wheel. There was chill-out music in the kitchen, reggae in the lounge, Sasha playing in the second bedroom – the Tunes Room – for days on end without sleep. 'I had no record company contacts then, no remixes or business to do, and I didn't really have any responsibility from Monday to Friday. It was like a family, the same faces there every week.'

But the scene at Shelly's soured just as Manchester had, and after being booked to play Venus in Nottingham, Sasha asked promoter James Baillie to help him manage the transition to the cooler club scene. Baillie decided the DJ should no longer play at the raves (he claims he received death threats from angry promoters as a result), and after Sasha left Shelly's in May 1991, he played his first club dates in the capital.

'It was extremely daunting. Compared to the tops-off and whistles up north, walking into a London club night like Kinky Disco where it was all leather trousers was strange. I felt like this little boy from up north coming to the grown-ups' town, like I really had something to prove. I remember doing a *Boy's Own* party out in Windsor some-where. I'd played a really good set and I was really pleased with myself, then I went into the VIP room and there were these London gangster types who just gave me so much shit. "Where did you get a name like Sasha then? It's a girl's name, innit!"

'I just left. I didn't even get my money. "DJ Big Oop North", they called me in *Boy's Own*. It's quite amusing now. They were even doing a drug called cocaine. I'd never ever heard of anyone doing that up north in 1991, '92. If people took that, it meant they were real drug addicts.'

Success in the south followed, but Sasha and Geoff Oakes still talked about recreating the excitement they'd experienced at the Haçienda and at Shelly's, the rapport between DJ and crowd that grows out of playing the same club every week. They found a new venue in the small east Midlands mining town of Mansfield, and Oakes opened up a Saturday night called Renaissance – a rebirth of the good times. Venue 44 was perfect: it was new territory, exciting for clubbers and also far enough away from a big city to avoid the problems that had plagued the Haçienda and then Delight.

Renaissance opened there on 12 March 1992 with a night grandly billed as 'the restoration of Sasha to the north'. The décor was heavily influenced by Ibizan clubs like Pacha and Ku, and after the raw, sweat-soaked energy of the indoor raves, the white drapes, the opulent surroundings and above all the strict door policy felt like a breath of fresh air. Mansfield was too out-of-the-way to rely on word of mouth, and Oakes went overboard on the promotion. There were full-colour flyers featuring details from paintings by Botticelli, da Vinci and Rap-hael. There were lavish full-page colour ads in the dance magazines.

The mood was ready for something more spectacular, more luxuri-ous. In London, Pushca were revitalising the London party scene with spectacular themed balls in one-off venues. From their base in Bir-mingham, Chuff Chuff were more ambitious still, taking clubbers on magical mystery tours to grand old houses in the countryside across Britain, where there would be marquees, a cinema, a swimming pool, a casino, a trad jazz band, circus acts or Indian classical musicians – whatever details were needed to make the day special. 'Our idea was that everyone could be king or queen for a day.'

Renaissance also sold itself as special, a select gathering for clubbers who appreciated the finer things and who were willing to travel to get it. On the opening night, Geoff Oakes remembers driving to the club, worrying that the venue was a little too far off the beaten track, then pulling round the corner in his car to see 3,000 people outside. 'It just exploded. That was a mad time. I don't think there were any clubs in the north of England apart from Back to Basics who were doing anything like that. The focus was more on the rave scene and the Eclipse [in Coventry] in those days. We were just lucky to hit the market at the right time.'

Sasha would come on between four and five in the morning every week, playing until the club closed. 'He used to come out of the studio and play the music he'd made that day on DAT tape. The last two and a half hours when he went on were just incredible. You could *feel* the electricity in the club.'

Eventually Sasha was joined by John Digweed, a DJ from Hastings on the south coast who had spent years on the outer fringes of the club scene before finally getting his big break. In the autumn of 1994, Oakes captured that electricity on the club's first mix CD, featuring the partnership of Sasha and Digweed. *Renaissance Mix Collection* was, says Oakes, 'a total labour of love', preserving an era perfectly. At the time, the Ministry's most popular mix CDs were selling around 30,000. The Renaissance CD topped 100,000 in its first six weeks. 'As a result, the marketplace transformed overnight,' he observes. 'When we released the second one, there were about six club compilations released within the same two weeks.' A trade that had once been illicit, under the counter, had suddenly become big business.

Renaissance moved from Mansfield to Derby in late 1993, and then a year later left to go on the road while Oakes acquired a venue of his own. His club should finally open towards the end of 1998, but despite being homeless now for three years, Renaissance was established enough as a brand name to continue to be a player on the club scene. Oakes has continued to organise big one-off parties and regular nights at venues like the Cross in London. There is still a market for Renaissance CDs, and the club also tours overseas: 'We go to places like Singapore, Russia, Italy, Australia and there's just this massive response to us because of all the marketing we've done in the UK.'

In the mean time, Oakes has slowly made the transition from

up-for-it clubber to more serious businessman. In 1995, an ambitious series of parties in some of Britain's grandest stately homes went horribly wrong, and he found himself on the verge of bankruptcy. 'I didn't even cost it out. I just thought, "I'm going to blow everybody away with this!" That was the biggest lesson of all for me. I nearly lost everything.'

Now, he says, he finds himself reading books on management and having meetings with brands who want to sponsor his clubs. He worries sometimes that this is selling out, that he is no longer part of the underground club scene he came from. 'But with the experience we've gained over the years, we are able to create the best possible environment for people to enjoy themselves. My mission is to make it as incredible as possible. To make the lighting, the décor and the music so mind-blowing that they have the ultimate experience.'

Liverpool, October 1992

As the rave scene became big tabloid news in 1989, the Mersey police came down hard on Liverpool's house scene, closing down first the State and then the Underground, the small basement club run by James Barton and John Kelly. 'It was closed because of drug dealing,' says Barton. 'They tried to pin the whole thing on the licensee, saying that he knowingly allowed it. The charges were subsequently dropped, but they achieved what they wanted to do, which was shut down another nightclub which was playing dance music. The Underground wasn't particularly heavy – it was more to do with the fact that they didn't understand it.'

Afterwards, Barton and Kelly moved to Quadrant Park, a huge 3,000-capacity disco in nearby Bootle which former State DJs Mike Nolan and Andy Carroll had already established as a rave venue, pulling in coachloads of clubbers from other areas as well as a strong local crowd. 'Dropping a big record at Quadrant Park was like scoring a goal in the Kop,' recalls Barton. 'I mean, the cheer . . . the euphoria was incredible.'

When the owner discovered a loophole that enabled the club to stay open all night, the DJs were thrilled. But within months, the atmosphere inside changed as a new clientele began to come in attracted not by the music but by the fact that it was open after hours. There were muggings, fights, and the news soon spread across the UK that the Quad was unsafe.

Barton left to concentrate on the promotions company he had set up with Andy Carroll. They booked bands into clubs, and hired the Royal Court Theatre in Liverpool to put on shows with rising dance acts such as N-Joi, Sub-Sub, K-Klass, Adamski and the Prodigy to sell-out crowds. They began managing K-Klass, who signed to Deconstruction and immediately began producing top ten singles.

When Barton was asked to promote the 051 club, it seemed like his time had finally come. In a cellar underneath the 051 media centre, it was to be a European-style nightclub in Liverpool. 'It was my Haçienda. And we went major league on it. Everything was perfect. A purpose-built dance venue. Me and Andy went ballistic in terms of promotion and media. We designed top-class posters and flyers. We booked people Oakenfold and Danny Rampling. And we opened up and it was a smash.'

But again, things quickly went wrong. Door prices went up, parts of the club were left unfinished. The wrong people were getting in. The right people were being turned away. Barton was making money because the club was packed, but it wasn't what he'd intended. Darren Hughes, a friend of K-Klass, had started working for him at the promotions company. A psychology student from Chester, he got involved in the club scene rather later via the Haçienda, and decided to re-create a sense of fun in Liverpool with a one-off Monday-night party called A Right Rum Do. It was at Nation, a small venue on the quieter, student side of the city centre away from the other clubs, restaurants and pubs. 'It was an adult crowd, our old faces. We all got pissed and danced around to disco.'

Hughes was offered the venue for a regular Saturday-night event, and he eventually badgered Barton to give up the 051 and do it with him. After the embarrassment of the 051, they aimed to build it quietly, from the bottom up, getting details like the sound system and the music right and bringing the old faces out again. As a statement of intent, they called it Cream, and opened up in October 1992.

Cream hardly made a national impact at first. Its biggest night that year was a party on 26 December which attracted 650 people. Indeed, when a Birmingham crew who had been running illegal all-nighters under the same name first contacted them, they considered changing the name to Taste, then dismissed the idea. 'There was no way at that time we thought that there would be anyone who would confuse a night in Liverpool called Cream with a night in Birmingham called Cream,' says Barton. 'Our club only held a few hundred people. Why would anyone in Birmingham get lost and end up in Liverpool?'

But with Manchester's club scene in decline because of the gang problem, Cream continued to grow. By its first birthday, there were well over a thousand people outside queuing for a venue that held half that number. Stuart Davenport, one of the two owners of Nation, took them to the huge empty warehouse space at the back of what is now Cream's annexe. His point was simple: 'We *have* to go in there.' The next day, they sat down and cut a new deal. Cream became a company, with the four of them as directors. They spent £50,000 on refurbishing the main room, then a further £15,000 on the launch party with Frankie Knuckles and David Morales. And suddenly Cream was one of the biggest clubs in the country.

'We never had a plan,' says Barton. 'We made it up as we went along. Cream was built out of pure energy and jealousy, anger that we never had anything of quality in Liverpool. Throughout my teenage years Liverpool suffered a lot. Whenever there was a great band touring, they always went right through the middle of the country and left us out. We felt we had to do things twice as well as everybody else because we had to overcome the old stereotypes of you come to Liverpool, you get your car nicked. The stories about Quadrant Park had swept the country, so we always felt we had to give that extra twenty-five per cent, just to make sure.

'People ask if being in Liverpool was important. It was *crucial*. There were a lot of people in Liverpool who felt the same as me, that we didn't want to go to Manchester, London, Leeds or Glasgow on a Saturday night. Club after club after club in one shape or form had been closed down or hadn't delivered.'

The now-famous logo came about at the end of 1992, when they placed their first ad in *The Face*. The most expensive of the monthly youth magazines for advertisers, it also had the most overseas sales. 'We just thought it would be so cool for some German kid to buy *The*

Face in Frankfurt and see that we were there in Liverpool.'

Mark Farrow, the award-winning designer behind Deconstruction's packaging, styled it on Japanese car logos, the yin and yang symbol and the word 'cream', leading to an idea based around three droplets. The night before the ad was due, Barton and Hughes were on their knees in the office, looking at the different variations spewing out of the fax machine. 'We chose the one that seemed to look best with the word "Cream" under it. Everyone thinks it was part of some master plan, but actually it was a last-minute, eleventh-hour thing because Farrow was down in London behind his computer going, "I need to send this off in the morning. *Choose your logo!*" '

Everything else grew organically. They opened a bar – Mello Mello, managed by James Barton's dad Dave – to cater for the crowds gathering around Cream at night. The shop seemed logical, the merchandising came out of wanting T-shirts as good as the Haçienda, the mix CDs from wanting to emulate Renaissance's success.

'Back in 1988, it was just, "*Let's go!*" ' says Barton. 'We didn't know we were part of a cultural revolution. I didn't think that there'd be adverts and movies, that record companies would build on this, and that M-People would go on to sell five million albums. We grew up with it. And then we were so busy building up our business that we didn't really stop to think.

'But when Cream took off we started acquiring staff like you couldn't imagine, and we woke up one morning and we had major responsibilities. And that's when we made the step of going, "Right, if we're going to be in this business for a long time, there's a few things that need to be ironed out." '

Jayne Casey had been at the centre of Liverpool's cultural life since punk, when she had fronted the bands Pink Military and Big in Japan (with Holly Johnson of Frankie Goes to Hollywood). By working on community issues and organising big licensed events in the city, she had built up a good relationship with the police. When she went to work at Cream to help with the ironing out of those problems in 1995, one senior officer tried to warn her off. But she was determined that this wouldn't be yet another Liverpool club closed due to lack of communication or understanding.

At her instigation, Cream joined the chamber of commerce, and began talking about the number of hotel beds they were filling on a Saturday night, the visitors they were bringing into the city, the positive publicity they were generating. They began discussions with the police that were marked at first by distrust on both sides. But the chief superintendent in charge of the city centre understood their arguments about economic regeneration, and they began long philosophical discussions on the issue of drugs.

'There was a lot of ground to be made up,' says Casey, who led the discussions. 'The first stage was for them to accept that Cream and the night-time economy had a role to play, and for them to agree that it couldn't all be down to the club owners and licensees to deal with organised drug-dealing.

'Clubs are easy targets. The drugs could be stopped by Customs when they come in. They could be stopped at a hundred other points before they arrive at the club, and closing clubs won't really solve something which in the end is society's problem. They eventually wrote "glasnost" all over the Cream files. That is what they called the period. Perestroika.'

The police set up a safer clubbing scheme, agreeing to put on extra officers in the streets outside to ensure the safe passage of clubbers who were coming from out of town. Unbeknown to Cream, they were also observing what went on inside. By the time the club first approached them, the police were already a few months into a ten-month undercover investigation into the club, code-named Operation Top.

In a series of dawn raids on 28 February 1996, they arrested more than twenty people on charges relating to drug-dealing inside the club. The head doorman was also arrested, along with one other member of the security team and two associates. Had they not opened discussions when they did, the club would inevitably have had its licence revoked. Instead, the police offered Cream support while they set up a new door team.

After long discussions, it was decided that this meant using trained stewards to do some of the work previously done by an organised door crew. At the time, city regulations specified one bouncer per seventy-five clubbers. But like most independent dance clubs, Cream never has fights or violence inside its premises, making such a show of muscle redundant. 'It took away a lot of the power from doormen,' notes Casey.

But none of this was easy. When word got around that Cream's door was up for grabs, it seemed like every firm in the country, let alone the city, began to express interest. All were turned down. But as they worked to resolve the problem of keeping their door clean, there was a period in which they felt their lives were in danger.

This was complicated by the situation in Liverpool as a whole. In 1995, as attendances at Cream hit their peak, a turf dispute broke out between two south Liverpool gangs. It began with a dispute between the Ungi family and a rival group over the right to drink at Cheers, a wine bar in Aigburth. A fight was arranged to settle the dispute, but although David Ungi won, he was accused of unfairly using knuckledusters. On 1 May, the thirty-five-year-old father of three was shot dead in a street in Toxteth. Cheers was immediately burned out in an arson attack, and in the following weeks there were shootings all over the city – some related to the gang war, others simply by would-be hard cases swept up by the atmosphere.

In the summer of 1996, the war kicked off again with the murder of Johnny Phillips, whose name had often been mentioned in connection with the Ungi shooting. Although these incidents happened in the Toxteth/Aigburth area, the police were worried about the problems spilling over into the city centre. Determined not to let gun culture take hold here as it had in Manchester, Chief Constable Jim Sharples put on an impressive show of strength.

'It got so bad that the police resorted to putting armed policemen in cars, driving around the city openly displaying sub-machine guns,' says Barton. 'It was a very scary year, because we had record attendances in 1995. The company itself rocketed. But we still had this massive market in our club for drugs, and people wanted that market.'

They set out to discourage clubbers from buying their drugs inside Cream, putting out literature from the Manchester-based drugs advisory service Lifeline, sending out letters to their members, trying to convey that the cycle that had been played out again and again in the story of British E culture could be broken. If no one bought their drugs inside clubs, then there would be no market to control.

'A doorman was hacked to death in a pub, and the city had gone mad,' says Jayne Casey. 'There was a war going on about territories and it was being backed up by doormen. It made the company more determined not to go with an organised door crew, and we started bringing in new doormen, a lot of doorwomen, and the new stewarding system. And as we were doing this the city was going apeshit around us, there were guns, and we felt seriously under threat.'

For six months it was agreed that a car would sit outside Cream, with two armed officers. Everyone had learned the lessons of the Haçienda, and by then Cream was seen as a resource worth protecting, rather than part of the problem. A 1996 survey carried out by John Moores University indicated that 70 per cent of all new students chose to study in Liverpool because of the club, which now forms part of the tour given to prospective students. Few of those travelling from all over the country to visit the club that year were aware of the problems, and the customers inside were in less danger of violence than in most mainstream discos.[2] But behind the scenes, James Barton says there was a lot of tension.

'It was a very scary time. They were sitting there with guns on their laps. And we had to have nerves of steel to get through it, because we didn't know how far the whole thing would go. The great thing was that we had the support right down the line from the police, the council and everyone else in Liverpool.'

Which, he points out, is exactly how it should be. 'What's the difference between Cream and Everton Football Club, Aintree racecourse or the Royal Court Theatre? We deserve the same sort of support which is given to all these other companies.'

Disco's Revenge

In March 1995, journalist Andy Pemberton coined the term 'super-clubs' in a small piece in *Mixmag* noting how organisations such as Cream, the Ministry, Renaissance, Back to Basics and Hard Times were more than just clubs. They ran DJ agencies, record labels and tours. Their distinctive logos appeared on clothing, merchandise and mix CDs. They were emerging new youth brands.

The music at these clubs was often dismissed by the white boys on the pure techno scene as cheesy, fluffy, lightweight. It was 'handbag' – music for Sharon and Tracy to dance to. But the girls and gay men the term treated with such contempt were dancing in clubs when the kind of lads using it were propping up the bar honing their chat-up lines and downing enough lager to have the courage to use them. And in 1994, handbag became disco's revenge as the scene exploded.

By 1995, there were house nights in every city and town in Britain, and almost all of them had queues round the block. A culture which had once catered to obsessive dance fans or freaks who failed to fit anywhere else was now a mainstream leisure activity, and the odd kids now were the ones who hadn't ever been to a such a club, not those who went.

The fashions on this scene quickly became codified. Girls wore fluffy bra tops, high heels, short skirts and shorts or stretchy full-length dresses; the boys sported short hair and designer labels. People dressed to be noticed, but also to fit in. These were not places for clubbers to experiment, to try out new sexual and cultural identities. They were places where the joy came from a sense of belonging, of being part of a crowd. Less participants *creating* the spectacle, more consumers now expecting to have it created for them, tellingly more and more clubbers began to dance facing the DJ, watching the show.

After the Ministry's sponsorship deal with Pepsi, corporate sponsors began flooding into these clubs, anxious to buy their own chunk of credibility and to communicate with a generation who seemed curiously immune to their previous advertising techniques. Very few club flyers are now without a few brand logos. Very few clubs are free of some kind of advertising: toilets refurbished by a fragrance company, a corner full of computer game consoles, banners associating a product with the club name, free samples of cigarettes, alcohol or hairspray, side-shows set up to draw attention to a new camera, credit card or mobile phone.

'The Ministry without a doubt did help bring companies into clubland,' says Paul Van Bergen, a former brand manager for the soft drink Tango who now sets up club sponsorship deals via his company Encompass Marketing. 'Companies who were a bit nervous but wanted to dip their toes in the water went with them because it was the safest bet on the market. When it was a case of selling it internally, with the Ministry it was easy to say that a big company like Pepsi had already done it.'

By the middle of 1996, the scene had reached saturation point. The clubs in Ibiza were overrun with British promoters, all of them desperately battling each other to attract the same crowds, most of them losing money. At home, the big house nights were still packed, guests DJs were still collecting huge pay-packets from playing three or more clubs a night, but many felt that there was something missing behind the eyes of the clubbers dancing on the podiums, a sense of people going through the motions, acting out the rituals of release and abandon without actually *experiencing* them.

'People have danced to those drum rolls and breakdowns for so long now that they're just going through the motions of what they should be feeling,' Felix Burton of Basement Jaxx told *i-D* in August 1996. 'And I don't know if a lot of people are feeling it any more. Because I know I'm not.'[3]

Some turned to smaller club nights in an attempt to find a more 'real' or authentic experience, or to clubs opening in the middle of the night or Sunday afternoons to avoid the Saturday night herd. The Heavenly Sunday Social started in a small pub basement in central London in 1994, providing a chance for the staff at Jeff Barratt's Heavenly label and resident DJs the Chemical Brothers to play all of the records they collected, not just house and techno. Old-school hip hop, Northern Soul, indie rock and funk were amongst the musics in the mix at this and a handful of similar nights around the country, where drinking beer and sniffing amyl nitrate almost seemed like an act of rebellion in the face of the all-pervasive E culture. By 1995 it had become an institution, its cheerful, boozy eclecticism spreading to other clubs, pubs and bars and eventually giving birth to big beat.

But 'corporate clubbing' continued to thrive too, with the lines between mainstream and underground increasingly blurred. The big clubs are no longer places where DJs are likely to forge new musical styles by building up a rapport with a regular crowd. But when something new does appear, these clubs are quick to pick up on it, and DJs are playing to a dancefloor educated in cutting-edge dance sounds by the radio, club magazines, and compilations. As for the 'underground', even small, specialist club nights now have commercial sponsors, and with so many publications chasing so few stories, nothing stays secret for long.

Cream began 1997 by announcing that it was no longer using many of its old guest DJs, that it was sticking to a more select roster in the main room and installing residents in the two smaller rooms. As part of its 'Blueprint 97', the club also spent some $500,000 (£375,000) installing a new, state-of-the-art sound system built by the team behind the Sound Factory's system in New York.

'We'd helped create this monster,' explains James Barton. 'The thing that made Cream special was the fact it was exclusive, and we lost that towards the end of 1995 because the DJs we were booking were playing thirty miles up the road before they got to us. They were turning up late, playing shite, and then walking home with a bagful of money. We got really pissed off with it. If they want professional wages and superstar status, they should turn up at the club and say hello to kids who want to talk to them, and not turn up with the same box of records every week and disappear.'

Playing at Cream forty-two weeks a year, Paul Oakenfold says he finally began to recapture the old rapport he had felt with the crowd at Spectrum. Witness the hushed anticipation before he takes to the decks there at midnight, and you can believe the often-repeated cliché that clubs are the churches of the new millennium.

But despite the sponsorship deals, few clubs are making the same profits they were in the peak year of 1995. Admission prices have hardly risen since then, yet clubbers now expect a far higher level of service, from the quality of the décor and sound system to the speed with which they are served at cloakroom or bar. And if they don't like what they see at a club, then they'll go elsewhere.

'Compared to what else we're doing, the club takes up a disproportionate amount of time,' says Mark Rodol. 'But it's a manifestation of the brand. The girls who run the clothing company can see what people are wearing, the people who run the label can hear what people are listening to. There aren't many businesses where all your customers arrive in one place on a Saturday night and you can see them and know what they're thinking.'

Changes are coming in clubland once more. Quietly, many of the big promoters admit that their numbers are down. Some long-running nights have already closed their back rooms and annexes, moved to smaller venues, or closed completely while they are still on a high. Many DJs who were playing three gigs a night in 1995 are now struggling to find dates in British clubs, although the demand overseas has never been higher. Clubbers are going back to bars, to mid-week nights, to pubs with pumped-up sound systems. This doesn't mean that clubbing is over. It just means it is mutating once more.

The bigger clubs now talk about venues that would be more like leisure complexes, Ibizan-style venues that could appeal to all age groups, to all interests with bars, restaurants and chill rooms as well as dancefloors. Promoters who came up through acid house now talk about applying what they have learned to hotels, restaurants, drinking clubs and bars, often catering to an older crowd who grew up in the clubs but no longer want to dance all night.

'Much as we want to expand aggressively, we're also aware of the Pierre Cardin belt scenario,' says Rodol. 'There is only so far you can take it. We get lots of offers to do men's aftershave and things like that, and even with chunky advances on offer, it's obvious we shouldn't be doing them. There are only so many people you can get into a club, there are only twelve or fifteen records we can release in a year, so you do get to a point in the UK where you can't do any more without diluting the brand. We've got to look to other parts of the world. It is a shrinking place, and people are aware of the Ministry name.'

Meanwhile, the business of clubbing continues. Gatecrasher in Sheffield spent £1.5 million buying its own premises in spring 1998, and many other successful promoters are going through the tortuous process of bidding for property and arranging licences. As Dermott Ryan from Miss Moneypenny's points out, 'No one has built the ultimate club in Britain yet. No one has come anywhere near it.'

On New Year's Eve 1997, an ISDN line linked the Ministry's parties in London, Manchester and New York. Pete Tong played the Ministry in London from midnight to 3 a.m., with the sound being broadcast at Manchester's Nynex Arena. Todd Terry played the following two hours in Manchester, with his set fed back to London. Then Danny

Tenaglia's set in New York went live to London and Manchester. It was a clever gimmick, intended as a one-off, but Mark Rodol was surprised at the number of clubs who called to see if they could buy in a feed. The era of the virtual DJ playing in one club but heard in hundreds more cannot be far away, and if that happens then the big name on a flyer will become the modern equivalent of the half-price drinks offer – unable to respond to the mood of the crowd, the DJ becomes just a soundtrack, a marketing ploy.

Mr C, meanwhile, is more optimistic about the possibilites technology has to offer. By installing sequencers and drum machines into the DJ booth at his London club the End, he is increasingly able to create a mix in which records are only a part of the overall sound coming out of the speakers and clubbers can enjoy spontaneously produced music that will never be repeated again.

'The experience will evolve and change,' says Mark Rodol. 'In ten years' time, people might not be happy hearing a DJ and just seeing some flashing lights. But the idea of going somewhere on a Friday and Saturday night where 2,000 other young people are all going to get together won't go away.'

'It's like being the wizard in *The Wizard of Oz*,' adds Cream's Darren Hughes, a man who takes the business of pleasure very seriously and who still gets passionate about clubbing all these years on. 'We're creating an illusion, and we want it to be the best. So there we are, behind the scenes, cranking away to make it all work.'

13 SMILEY'S PEOPLE

Leah Betts didn't take the Ecstasy tablet that led to her death in a nightclub. She collapsed on 11 November 1995 at a remote farmhouse in Latchingdon, near Basildon in Essex, where she was holding her eighteenth birthday party.[1] Her father, Paul Betts, a retired policeman, and his wife Janet, a school nurse, were in the house at the time, watching *The Bodyguard* on TV in the kitchen while they kept an eye on the small gathering. They were called upstairs to the bathroom as soon as it was clear there was something wrong with Leah, and did everything possible to save her as she went into a fit, including mouth-to-mouth resuscitation. She was, however, probably brain-dead before she even got to the hospital. Five days later, the machines that were keeping her body functioning were switched off.

By then, the nation was following the story avidly. In an attempt to make something positive of the tragedy, her parents had co-operated with the media to an unusual degree, permitting the publication of a distressing, close-up picture of Leah in her hospital bed, tubes running from her nose and open mouth, which was quickly turned into an anti-drug poster by the *Sun*. It was her very ordinariness which made it all so shocking: this was no club freak or juvenile delinquent, but a nice, *normal,* white college student from the suburbs. As Detective Constable Ian Shead, one of the Essex policemen dealing with her case, stated while she lay in her coma, 'This girl comes from a good home and a nice respectable family.'[2]

Such stories tend to follow a familiar pattern once they become public property: the hospital vigil, the tearful press conference, the search for a scapegoat. At first, Paul Betts followed the script to the letter, calling for the death penalty for the evil pusher who had peddled the pill to his daughter. But day by day as the story unfolded, the layers were peeled away and the secret life of the E generation was exposed.

Leah Betts didn't take her pill in a club. But her death was a defining moment in British club culture. Afterwards, clubbers could no longer cling to the illusion that the wonder drug that laid the foundations of their hedonism was harmless or benign. And for those who had been unaware of the huge shift in attitude that had happened since 1988, it changed the image of the drug-user for ever.

In the following few weeks, the Betts family – and through them, the nation – learned that drugs were available everywhere. That they were taken not by losers tricked into a spiral of addiction by cunning pushers, but by bright, ordinary kids who did so because it was fun, an acceptable leisure option. They learned of pills stamped with apples and doves, of bouncers turning a blind eye to organised dealing in clubs, of a level of everyday, illegal activity amongst the young few had ever dreamed of.

In an effort to stem this tide, a video of Leah's funeral was made available to schools. By Christmas, her picture was smiling down from huge, black-and-white billboards on 1,500 donated sites across the country, accompanied by a single, stark word: 'Sorted'. Underneath, a smaller line of text warned, 'Just one pill took Leah Betts'. But it soon emerged that Leah and her best friend Sarah Cargill had taken E on four previous occasions, and had also tried LSD, amphetamines and cannabis together. (None of which makes them anything but ordinary: a number of surveys confirm that more than half of Britain's eighteen-year-olds have tried at least one of these substances.)

Nor was there any demonic pusher – just a network of grieving friends who had supplied the drug at Leah's request. After she and Leah had decided to take Ecstasy at the party, Sarah had asked a college friend, Louise Yexley, to help them get it. She in turn had pressured her boyfriend, Stephen Smith, who paid £45 for four pills during the course of a night out with three other friends at Raquel's nightclub in Basildon. No one made any profit as the pills were passed back down the line. Like thousands of young people around Britain every week, they saw it as simply doing a favour for a friend rather than drug dealing. There was no hard sell, no drinks spiked or innocents corrupted. As one of the lawyers involved was later to remark, 'It is a network repeated up and down the country, day in and day out.'[3]

Cargill and Yexley were formally cautioned. Smith was given a two-year conditional discharge. Steven Packman, who went to Raquel's with Smith, endured two trials in which the juries failed to reach a verdict before being cleared of buying the pills in the club. There was no anger expressed at these outcomes, least of all from Paul Betts. By then he admitted that his views on drugs had changed, and that he now realised that to most teenagers passing on a pill to a friend was no different from offering a cigarette. These too were nice, normal kids. Parents who had looked at Leah and felt that she could have easily been their child, now looked at these teenagers and felt the same.

Tony Tucker was named in the press as the man most likely to have supplied the drugs to Raquel's, but soon he too was dead. His body was one of three found by a local farmer in a blood-splattered Range Rover in a country lane in Essex on 7 December, 1995. Two men were later found guilty of the shootings, which were apparently provoked by a dispute over a cannabis shipment. 'The manner of the killing and the double-crossing involved signalled a new ruthlessness in the increasingly competitive drugs business,' noted the *Guardian*'s crime correspondent Duncan Campbell.[4]

Another layer had been peeled back, another set of unpalatable truths revealed. Afterwards, former Raquel's head doorman Bernard O'Mahoney (also known as Bernie King and Patrick Mahoney) published a frank, terrifying memoir, *So This Is Ecstasy?*, which details a violent world of bouncers, dealers and organised crime. He claims that Tucker was a murderer whose firm controlled the door and the drug trade in clubs across the south (including the now-defunct Club UK in South London), with dealers paying him 'rent' in exchange for support from the doormen while unauthorised dealers were beaten and had their drugs taken for recycling by the firm.

Drugs were becoming more prevalent, bringing in huge rewards for villains. The more money there was, the more violence there was. The more violence there was, the more guns were being used. The stakes were being upped all the time.[5]

Meanwhile, few clubbers saw any of this as a reason to modify their behaviour. Statistically, the argument went, you were more likely to die from swallowing a peanut than a pill. Reports of the inquest into Leah's death were examined and a theory that she died due to a swelling of the brain after drinking excessive amounts of water was seized upon by many as 'proof' that E wasn't to blame at all. But this couldn't mask the fact that an eighteen-year-old was dead. And, had she chosen not to take a pill that night, she would most likely be alive.

Mark Gilman, Director of Research at the Manchester-based drugs organisation Lifeline, said that users he had spoken to around the time of Leah's death saw it as sad, 'but a tragedy like any other – like a friend being killed in a car crash'. There has been little evidence since to indicate that recreational drug use is in decline, although there are signs that, as the culture matures, it has also become self-regulating. 'Losing it' is no longer a badge of pride: younger clubbers tend to see people who get messy on the dancefloor as objects of pity or scorn, the clubland equivalent of the sad old drunk in the corner of a pub.

The official answer to this widespread normalisation of illegal drugs – the answer Leah's parents still support – is to tell us to just say no. Quietly, however, Government-funded organisations like the Health Education Authority have accepted that such a strategy doesn't work. They now support harm reduction, accepting that people will continue to take drugs despite the warnings, and therefore giving advice on how to do so as safely as possible.

The debate on drugs is clouded by hypocrisy, fear and lies, with people who say one thing in public but do or believe quite the opposite in private. The division between legal and illegal drugs is arbitrary, largely due to politics, class, race and accidents of history, and little to do with health. Alcohol, our favourite drug, kills some 33,000 people a year in the UK, and is a major factor in violent crime. Eight out of ten admissions to Casualty departments involve drink in some way. A report that happened to be released by the Royal College of Physicians in the week that Leah Betts died stated that alcohol was *ten times* more likely to cause death amongst teenagers than all of the illegal drugs combined. There was no outcry, no posters, no campaign. Three years on, there appear to be no plans to include alcohol in the Government's proposed education programme against drugs.

'There is undeniably a chasm opening up between youth culture and the establishment,' Dr Christopher Luke of the Royal Liverpool Hospital's busy casualty department said at a conference on club health in 1997. 'The well-intentioned messages about health and care are disregarded because young people simply do not trust the establishment who demonise them and put out a lot of silly, contradictory messages about cannabis, alcohol and so forth. The consequences are that drug taking is now firmly embedded within the club culture. But drugs are by no means the issue overall. The main problem we have as doctors, nurses and health care workers is of course the old one of drink and drink-associated violence.'

But asked by a clubber at this conference whether he would rather people use cannabis and Ecstasy than cigarettes and alcohol, Luke was exasperated. Few people take any new drug *instead* of an old one, he pointed out. They simply add them to the list of indulgences. The cigarette machines and busy bars in clubs, the sponsorship from tobacco and drinks companies, show that the old killers are still thriving in clubland.

Although the majority of people use the drug with no short-term effect other than a mid-week mood swing, a small number of those taking Ecstasy *do* die – and some of them die horribly, bleeding from every orifice. As to the long-term consequences, it has been proved that MDMA causes damage to nerve endings in the brain, although experts disagree on whether this damage is permanent, or even harmful. Evidence regarding other problems is meanwhile largely anecdotal, but everyone who has been part of the culture for long does have a story to tell: a breakdown witnessed, a friend unable to cope, severe depression or epilepsy that may or may not have been caused by chemical intake.

'I'd spent so many years on drugs that when I stopped, it went all wrong,' says one of the more idealistic early Shoomers about her own crisis. 'I was left with the sediment and I had to sift it and purify it until I was really clear who I was again. Because drugs are really a blanket, they protect you from you. And when it's gone, you're left just with you. That clubbing experience was a short-cut, a window into the possibility of being that free, of being able to connect to your neighbour with no problems. But then you have to backtrack and work very hard to attain what you saw.'

Ten years on, she feels she may be getting close. Like many of those overpowered by the optimism and euphoria of the early Balearic scene, she has since begun to explore various New Age ideas and options. Others from the class of '88 and '89 can be found propping up the bars in Ibiza, Tenerife, Goa or Thailand, regaling club tourists with tales of the good old days. Some are simply travelling, still searching for that seratonin leap. Others are refugees from drug deals gone wrong.

'Those people turn up all over the world,' says Heavenly's Jeff Barrett. 'I went to Tokyo to see Primal Scream a while ago, and I was in the dressing room when the tour manager was getting the guest list together before the gig. He asked [guitarist] Andrew Innes if he'd got any names for the guest list, and he said, "Just put down every ex-pat drug dealer who got chased out of their home town, so they can come backstage and drink my rider." And sure enough, later on, in walks some kid who used to hang with Flowered Up: "All right Jeff, are you sorted?" '

Ecstasy is a drug which offers diminishing returns, even in its pure form. It can't change your life every time. The buzz gets weaker, the insights it offers more banal. As one raver said mournfully, 'I didn't give up on the E. The E gave up on me.'[6] There is no doubt that it has served as a gateway to other substances, that it is now just one flavour in the pick-and-mix selection many will dip into in the course of a weekend: speed, acid and cocaine are also commonplace now. A small minority of clubbers also graduate to substances that are still considered 'bad' and taboo by the majority (although it should be pointed out that cocaine can actually be as addictive as heroin).

'I started seeing people go to prison, seeing people using really hard drugs and then using them myself as well, all of which came directly from taking Ecstasy,' says one veteran of the 1989 raves. 'I then started meeting a different type of drug user, people who used drugs because they were *addicted* to them. I started meeting people who were HIV positive, who would die, commit suicide, or OD. And I saw people getting shot on the news and I realised that I *knew* these people. And I remember thinking, "*I shouldn't know about these things. I'm a nice girl. I shouldn't be here.*" '

Attitudes towards recreational drugs are now in a period of transition. The Government still talks of fighting a war against drugs even though this war has long since been lost. The figures are mind-boggling. In Britain, it is estimated that the Ecstasy trade is worth £1 billion a year – as much as we spend on tea and coffee combined. A Home Office study, *Tackling Local Drug Markets*, estimated that there are 30 million drug deals every year in London alone. The United Nations Drug Control Programme estimates the annual global turnover in illegal drugs to be $400 billion, or eight per cent of the total international trade. Such huge profits mean that corruption and violence inevitably follow the trade wherever it goes.[7]

Edward Ellison, who headed the Metropolitan Police's drugs squad from 1987–92, has been a vocal supporter of legalisation. Not because he thinks we all have the right to harm our health, but because he'd like to take the money it generates out of the hands of the criminals he spent years observing and chasing. Other officers see the law as unenforceable when so many simply choose to ignore it. It is, in the words of a Manchester policeman who spoke out at Lifeline's conference, 'the policing of illness and choice'.

Meanwhile, a decriminalisation of sorts is already taking place with an increase in cautioning for those caught with drugs for personal use. The Government's current 'drugs tsar' Keith Hellawell once suggested that this cautioning rate would continue to increase, and has pointed out that the war on drugs is a war on ourselves, having a go at our own people.

For a while, after the Labour victory in 1997, the new Home Secretary Jack Straw repeated his mantra that parents had to take responsibility for the actions of their children. But then another ordinary, seventeen-year-old college student was unlucky. Chatted up by an attractive woman in a pub, at her request he went and acquired some cannabis resin. When this youth was revealed to be the Home Secretary's son William, the response was largely sympathetic. Few believed that he should be classed as a criminal, few believed his family were to blame.

What it proved, more than anything, is that legislating against recreational drug use now is not just shutting the stable door after the horse has bolted. It is shutting it after the car has been invented and made horses obsolete. What the last decade had been about is the democratisation of recreational drugs, a pleasure that was once accessible only to the wealthy and the bohemian becoming available to all.

The current government thinking seems to be that the answer is more education, given at an ever-younger age. This costs relatively little, and makes it look as if something is being done. It may even lead a few more people to just say no, but not many. The fact is that most people experimenting with drugs *know* the risks, but they continue to do it anyway. They do it because they enjoy it. They do it because their friends do. They do it because they are young and they think they are immortal. And most of them come out the other end unscathed.

Supported by Leah Betts' parents, towards the end of the last Parliament Barry Legg, then the Conservative MP for Milton Keynes South West, sponsored a private member's bill amending the 1963 London Government Act and the 1982 Local Government (Miscellaneous Provisions) Act, to allow dance clubs to be shut down immediately if there is proof of a serious drug problem on the premises. The Public Entertainments Licences (Drug Misuse) Act 1997 is supposedly aimed at 'rogue clubs' where the dealing is condoned or even controlled by the licensee, and aims to prevent such clubs remaining open for months, even years, as they go through the appeals process.

Applied literally, however, it could close every club in the country, since promoters who claim their premises are drug-free are being either extraordinarily naive or economical with the truth. But closing them all overnight would not stop recreational drug use, any more than it would stop people dancing. If everyone who used Ecstasy was arrested this weekend and locked up for the full period the law allows, no one truly believes that Britain would be a better place.

At the moment, the law is largely a lottery. Some are cautioned, some are jailed. Twenty-two-year-old Joanne Maplethorpe was one of the losers, convicted in 1997 for giving her friend Alexandria Thomas an Ecstasy tablet. Thomas, who had also drunk heavily that night and taken amphetamines, ended up in hospital and Maplethorpe ended up in prison after being completely open with the police. She tried to kill herself twice in Holloway before being released on appeal after serving half of her nine-month sentence. Had she succeeded, she would have been just as much a victim as Leah Betts.

Meanwhile, back in the Casualty department, the NHS is left mopping up the mess. 'We're surrounded by people enjoying themselves, drinking themselves stupid, taking every drug and sniffing, snorting and injecting themselves into oblivion, but nobody has questioned the bill that has to be paid,' says Christopher Luke. 'And as far as we're concerned, the tab for social self-indulgence is being picked up by health care staff. We are under enormous pressure.'

At the end of 1996, just before he started his residency at Cream, I spent a Saturday with Paul Oakenfold. We went to see his beloved Chelsea beat Manchester United at Old Trafford, and Mike Pickering came along for the afternoon. A Man City fan, Pickering wasn't a frequent visitor to United's vast stadium. The last time he'd been, he said with studied casualness, was when his band M-People had played a huge concert there.

After a few drinks, we went to the airport and got into a small private jet that had once belonged to Hollywood stars Meg Ryan and Dennis Quaid but which was now on loan from Ron McCullough, owner of Glasgow's Tunnel Club. We were going to the Music Factory. In Lerwick, Shetland. (Population: 7,500; nearest town: Bergen in Norway.)

It wasn't the plushest place Oakenfold had ever played. It smelled of stale beer and rotten carpet, the lighting was basic and the sound constantly distorted. But the smiles on the dancefloor were just as wide here as anywhere else. The Music Factory may not be able to compete with the £1 million-plus pleasure domes being opened across the mainland, but the point is that it exists at all: that even this small, isolated island which forms the northernmost part of Britain has its own banging house night.

Radio 1 is a dance station at weekends now, with Pete Tong heading a team that also includes Shoom promoter Danny Rampling, illegal warehouse party organiser Judge Jules, and former pirate DJs such as Tim Westwood, Trevor Nelson, Fabio and Grooverider. The requests and messages read out on air every weekend show just how far clubbers are now willing to travel for that big night out: people travelling to Cream in Liverpool from Scotland, Wales, Cornwall. Carloads of youths driving hundreds of miles up and down motorways to get to the Ministry in London, to Gatecrasher in Sheffield, the Lakota in Bristol.

Clubs are open all night now, legally. Huge open-air, rave-style events are now listed and reviewed in national newspapers. When the Prodigy released their *Fat of the Land* album in 1997, it went straight to number one in twenty-two countries, including the USA – where this music is sold as British electronica, its roots in black American gay clubs long since forgotten.

Everyone wants to be a DJ now: pop stars, artists, boxers, footballers, authors all jump behind the turntables. Once a guitar was the standard prop for a teenage bedroom; now it is two decks and a mixer. The DJ remix is a standard music marketing tool, dance compilations are advertised on TV. Stadium rockers like U2 have incorporated ideas from dance music into their sound. Other groups, such as the Verve and Primal Scream, are now making music about negotiating the comedown from the old blissed-out euphoria: '*If you play with fire/You're gonna get burned/Some of my friends are gonna die young*' a computerised voice intones, expressionlessly, on the Primals' 1997 album *Vanishing Point.*

Articles about drugs are now as much a part of the youth magazine formula as music or film reviews. Trippy imagery, breakbeats and four-on-the-floor rhythms are used to sell everything from cars to snack foods, while some clubs are so heavily sponsored that you may be forgiven for thinking that you've paid to step inside another advertisement. With the success of Irvine Welsh and short story collections such as Sarah Champion's *Disco Biscuits*, the combination of drugs and clubs has even become a niche publishing genre.

This culture has left us all accepting that there is no such thing as an original, finished version, that everything is up for remixing, rearranging, sampling and reinvention. Recorded sound is now viewed not as a finished product, sacrosanct, but as raw material to be plundered. It has inspired boutique hotels and huge, theatrical bar/restaurants, a renaissance in British fashion, and city centres which now buzz with bars, shops and businesses that wouldn't have existed without it.

We now live in Cool Britannia, where the Labour Party fought the last election with D:Ream's hands-in-the-air Ecstasy anthem 'Things Can Only Get Better' as their theme tune and celebrated their victory on election night with an all-nighter at the Albert Hall which looked like a rave for the middle-aged. Where the Prime Minister holds soirées at Downing Street to celebrate a creativity largely built on illegal drugs, illegal dancing, and poses for pictures with Noel Gallagher (who said, after Leah Betts' death, that for most young people taking drugs was as normal as drinking tea). Where the tourist board markets our clubs as a vibrant attraction even as laws are being passed to close them.

So what did it all mean? It is easier, first of all, to say what it did not. One of the most pervasive myths repeated by those seeking to extract a meaning from the acid house explosion is that it brought an end to football hooliganism. But attractive though the idea is, it isn't particularly true. Violence in the top clubs was all but over by 1988. After the Heysel Stadium disaster in 1985 and then Hillsborough in 1989, football changed. The terraces came down, the money poured in from satellite TV, the game became gentrified.

'After Heysel, the people who connected with dressing up and fighting in football decided that it wasn't cool to fight any more and that a) they'd prefer to go and listen to Norman Jay and smoke puff, and also that b) fighting was no longer viable,' says Chelsea fan/*Boy's Own* founder Terry Farley. 'People decided that if they wanted to be involved in criminal activity, they were far better off selling drugs. They all invaded the house clubs when acid started, but the cooler ones were already going to rare groove clubs. It's a myth that acid house and Ecstasy stopped violence. The violence had already stopped, unless you were a right div.'[8]

Some people did take an E and were transformed on the dancefloor. Some simply grew up, got kids and stopped caring about their old firms. But for others the intimidation went on; it just found new, more profitable targets within the growing scene: many former terrace faces began dealing drugs, promoting raves and setting up security firms.

The second myth is that alcohol was, overnight, replaced by soft drinks and mineral water. Comforting as the notion may be to those who wish to continue thinking of Ecstasy as benign, the E generation never really stopped drinking altogether. At most venues, outside promoters have to guarantee a minimum bar take, as well as pay for hire of the club for the night. If this minimum isn't reached, then they have to make it up out of their door money. Neither Nicky Holloway at the Astoria or Ian St Paul at Heaven ever had to do this; sales of alcohol may have dipped for a while, the weekend blow-out may have replaced nights in the pub, but according to the market research company Mintel, pub attendances were in decline across *all* age groups in the late eighties/early nineties.

The amount spent in pubs dropped fourteen per cent between 1990 and 1992. People were drinking at home, staying in to watch videos, refusing to drink and drive. Employers no longer tolerated lunch-time drinking.[9] The pub trade was also shaken up in 1989 by the Monopolies & Mergers Commission, which reported that seventy per cent of all pubs were 'tied houses', owned by the big breweries and obliged to stock their beer lines. In 1992, a law was passed to correct this, leading the big names to sell around 11,000 pubs.

Bob Cartwright, communications director for Bass Taverns, reckons this was a time when the big brewers 'had their eye off the ball'. There was clear panic in the drinks industry in the early nineties as they realised that new young consumers simply weren't learning to drink in the volumes they had before. But like the music industry, the brewers quickly adapted with designer lagers, bottled cocktail mixes, alcoholic soft drinks and new pubs themed to attract women, pre-club crowds and hip bar crowds. Surveys now suggest that young people are drinking more alcohol than ever.

Clubs are often misunderstood by social commentators, seen as hedonistic and therefore reactionary. Rock is rebellion, whereas dancing is mere escapism. (There is another assumption underlying this: that rock is predominantly male, and therefore virile and valid, while club culture is girly and gay, and therefore trivial.) But it is club culture that the authorities seem to perceive as the real threat. Three laws have been passed in the UK in an attempt to sanitise and contain it since the explosion of 1988, but it has shown a remarkable capacity to mutate and survive.

At their best, clubs are places where the marginalised can feel at home, where we can experiment with new identities, new ways of being. They are places where cultures collide, where people dance alongside each other and then, when they meet again in the real world outside, understand each other a little better. (One of the anxieties most often expressed about nightclubs this century is that they are places where men and women of different races can meet and mix freely.)

Music that is more overtly radical, about protest, inevitably comes round when times are more affluent: hippies in the late sixties, punks in the late seventies. When times get tougher, people tend to escape down the rabbit hole, through the K-hole, past the doorman, down the corridor and into wonderland. And survival, taking pleasure at a time when misery is all that's on offer, can surely be a political act in itself. Overwhelmingly, the acid house and rave scenes were about a generation denied a place in society as a whole creating a space in which they could express themselves. It was also about the survival of the teenager: they were, in the nineties, a threatened demographic, overwhelmed by the far larger numbers born in the sixties.

But as clubs enter the mainstream, they inevitably become more conservative. If the acid boom seemed like it had, as I wrote in *The Face* in 1988, put an end to Lycra-clad disco dollies, the old sexism soon returned. Clubs now promote nights with flyers that would have been condemned as tacky if Peter Stringfellow had used them a decade ago. Dancing on a podium in your underwear may once have felt liberating, but many women now feel it is exploitative: part of the floorshow.

Promoters now position themselves as entrepreneurs. DJs who were happy to earn £50 a night a decade ago now earn £15,000 a remix and £1,000 an hour behind the decks. With clubbers treated as consumers rather than participants, DJ wages are discussed in the same way as footballers' transfer fees.

But there is always something new developing around the edges of all this. Mid-week nights. Parties in pubs rather than clubs. Avoiding the Saturday night fever altogether in favour of full-on Sunday afternoon abandon. As the mix spreads across the developed world and beyond, it adapts to local conditions and comes back as something new.

And the future? It is already here, somewhere. A piece of technology that has yet to come of age, a few friends in a back room enjoying that first rush of discovery, a breakaway faction which will soon be huge. If the cocaine, big cars, consumerism and bloated excess found in some parts of the current club scene resemble the last days of disco, then soon there will be something equivalent to the Loft or the Paradise Garage rising out of the decay. Maybe there already is: such clubs have never advertised. You have to seek them out. And when you find them, there's no feeling like it.

On the phone with Goldie one night, we're talking about my experiences in 1988 and 1989, about the intensity he felt at Rage, about the intensity he later created for others at his Metalheadz night. About how hard it is to describe to those who have never experienced it.

'Do you know what it smells like when everyone leaves a club, when the lights go on, and they sweep the floor?' he asks. 'Have you ever stood there? It's a funny atmosphere. It's so different, so surreal, after that vibe when the atmosphere is there, the floor is full and it's really kicking off. No drug can replace that feeling.

'You can't stop rebellion. You can't stop youth culture chasing what it believes in. You can't stop people having faith in one, tiny club.'

And this is the thing. All of the theory in the world can't explain what it's like to be there, in the middle of the floor, when a night takes off. To dance so hard you forget yourself, you lose track of time, you feel that the music, the crowd, the building itself is all one living organism, of which you are just a tiny part.

Perhaps, in the end, all it really comes down to is that feeling. We did it because it was fun. And many of us had the time of our lives.

NOTES

Put the Needle on the Record

1. Albert Goldman, *Disco* (Hawthorne, US, 1978).
2. Sarah Thornton, *Club Cultures – Music, Media and Subcultural Capital* (Polity Press, Cambridge, 1995).
3. Robert Amsel, *Back To Our Future – A Walk on the Wild Side of Stonewall*, from *The Advocate*, 15 September 1987.

The Road to Paradise

1. Stephen Harvey, 'Behind The Groove – New York City's Disco Underground', from *Collusion* magazine, date unknown.
2. Frank Owen, 'Paradise Lost', from *Vibe* magazine, 1993.
3. Goldman, op. cit.
4. Frank Rich, 'The Gay Decades', from US *Esquire*, November 1987.
5. Harvey, op. cit.
6. Owen, op. cit.
7. Ann and Alexander Shulgin, *Pihkal – A Chemical Love Story* (Transform, Berkeley, 1991).
8. Kevin Lewis, 'Was This Man The Best DJ In The World?', from *Jockey Slut* magazine, December/January 1997.
9. Harvey, op. cit.
10. John McCready, from transcript of a Bruce Forest interview originally published in *Mixmag*.
11. Boy George with Spencer Bright, *Take It Like A Man* (Pan Books, 1995).
12. Lewis, op.cit.
13. US Centre For Disease Control figures, quoted by Randy Shilts, *And The Band Played On* (Penguin, London, 1987).

14.   Lewis, op.cit.

House Music All Night Long

1.   Jonathan Fleming, *What Kind Of House Party Is This?* (MIY Publishing, Slough, 1995).

Machine Soul

1.   Steve Taylor, 'The Werk Ethic', from *The Face*, March 1982.
2.   Stuart Cosgrove, 'Seventh City Techno', from *The Face*, May 1988.
3.   Ze'ev Chafets, *Devil's Night*, quoted by Jon Savage, 'Machine Soul – A History Of Techno', from *The Village Voice*, Summer 1993.
4.   David Toop, *Rap Attack* (Serpent's Tail, London, 1984).
5.   Fleming, op. cit.
6.   From transcripts of interviews by John McCready for a feature originally published in *NME*, 1988.
7.   Cosgrove, op. cit.

Keeping the Faith

1.   Pete McKenna, *Nightshift* (ST Publishing, Scotland, 1996).
2.   From *The Axe Falls*, a paper on the war against the Manchester beat clubs delivered by C.P. Lee at the first Critical Musicology Conference in Salford, October 1994.
3.   Robert Elms, 'The Cult With No Name', from *The Face*, November 1980.
4.   Mark Heley and Matthew Collin, 'Summer Of Love 89', *i-D*, September 1989.
5.   Ibid.
6.   John Godfrey, 'Where Have All The Soulboys Gone?', *City Limits*, 22–29 May 1986.
7.   Matthew Collin, *Altered State* (Serpent's Tail, London, 1997).
8.   *London Evening Standard*, 18 July 1986.

Fantasy Island

1.   Paul Richardson, *Not Part Of The Package: A Year In Ibiza* (Pan, London, 1993).
2.   Quoted in Richardson, op. cit.
3.   Don MacPherson, 'Holiday Babylon', from *The Face*, September 1985.
4.   Collin, op. cit. One of the major faces on the acid house scene, Adam Heath died in 1996. Many of those interviewed for this chapter asked for it to be dedicated to him.

Mad For It

1. Collin, op. cit.
2. John Godfrey, 'Clubs', from *i-D*, September 1988.

Fields of Dreams

1. Paul Staines, *Acid House Parties Against The Lifestyle Police And The Safety Nazis* (Libertarian Alliance, 1991).
2. Wayne Anthony, *Class Of 88* (Virgin, London, 1998).
3. For more details on the east London scene and the alleged involvement of the ICF, see Collin, op. cit.
4. Seumas Milne, *The Enemy Within* (Pan, London, 1994).

Northern Exposure

1. Nick Kent, 'The Manchunian Candidates', *The Face*, January 1990.
2. Ibid.
3. This paragraph shamelessly stolen from notes by John McCready.
4. From John McCready's sleevenotes to the highly recommended *Viva Haçienda* compilation (Deconstruction).
5. Mick Middles, *Shaun Ryder* (Independent Music Press, London, 1997).
6. Ibid.
7. *Manchester Evening News*, June 1988.
8. Quoted in Dave Simpson's *Stone Roses* (Hamlyn, London, 1996).
9. *Guardian*, 29 December 1990.
10. *Manchester Evening News*, 25 February 1991.

Sex and Travel

1. Danny Scott, 'A Survivor's Guide to Festivals', from *The Face*, May 1993.

The Breaks

1. Two Fingers and James T. Kirk, *Junglist* (Boxtree, London, 1995).
2. From a Massive Attack interview by Andrew Smith, *Sunday Times*, 19 April 1998.
3. Alexis Petridis, 'Everything Started With An E', from *Q* magazine, June 1998.
4. For a far more detailed account of the travelling techno sound systems and the fight against the Criminal Justice Bill, see Collin, op. cit.
5. Shulgin and Shulgin, op. cit.

6.   Descriptions of pirate radio MCs and other references in this chapter taken from features orginally published in *Melody Maker* and *The Wire* and written by Simon Reynolds, one of the few journalists to cover the hardcore scene, let alone do so intelligently.

7.   Andy Crysell, 'Nothing To Prove', *Muzik*, June 1998.

8.   Martin James, *State Of Bass* (Boxtree, London, 1997).

Superclubs

1.   *News of the World*, 19 September 1993.

2.   Dr Christopher Luke of the Liverpool Royal Hospital's busy casualty department says that of all the people who pass through his department after going out clubbing, the majority have injuries from fights, often inflicted by bouncers. Of those intoxicated, the vast majority are drunk, although increasing numbers of those patients who cause violence in the department have taken cocaine. Cream is the biggest club in Liverpool, but it is rare for one of its customers to end up in Casualty.

3.   Bethan Cole, 'High in the Basement', *i-D*, August 1996.

Smiley's People

1.   Leah didn't live at the Betts' remote farmhouse full-time. She stayed with her family at weekends, but in the week lived with the family of her best friend Sarah Cargill, in order to be closer to college. This account of her death from *The Party's Over – Living Without Leah* by Janet and Paul Betts (Robson, London, 1997).

2.   *Daily Express*, 13 November 1995.

3.   *Guardian*, 6 February 1997.

4.   *Guardian*, 21 January 1998.

5.   Bernard O'Mahoney, *So This Is Ecstasy?* (Mainstream, Edinburgh, 1997).

6.   Jerry Ross, 'All E'd Out', from *M8*, January 1998.

7.   All figures from Phillip Knightley, 'The Drugs World War', *Independent*, 25 January 1998.

8.   Andy Crysell, '88 State', from *NME*, 25 April 1998.

9.   *Pub Retailing*, Mintel International, 1996.

INDEX

If you enjoyed this book here is a selection of other bestselling non-fiction titles from Headline